Praise for *Meaning and Argument*

"*Meaning and Argument* is especially strong on the subtleties of translating natural language into formal language, as a necessary step in the clarification of expression and the evaluation of arguments. The range of natural language constructions surveyed is broader and richer than in any competing intro logic text that I am aware of. As such, the book provides a solid and attractive introduction to logic not only for philosophy students, but for linguists as well."

Richard Larson, *Stony Brook University*

"I can thoroughly recommend Ernest Lepore's *Meaning and Argument*, particularly for those seeking to teach or learn how to paraphrase into formal symbolism, a much neglected aspect of logic. It contains a wealth of examples and is informed throughout by a deep theoretical knowledge of contemporary linguistics and philosophy of language."

Alan Weir, *Queen's University Belfast*

"Lepore's book is unusual for a beginning logic text in that it contains no natural deduction proof system but rather concentrates on finding models and countermodels by means of a semantic tableaux method. It is also unusual in containing many translation examples that exemplify constructions that linguists have found interesting in the last decades. In both of these ways the book is well-suited for use in educating philosophy students in the importance of logic even when these students do not intend to go further in the study of formal logic as a discipline."

Francis Jeffry Pelletier, *University of Alberta*

"*Meaning and Argument* is a beautiful display of both the power of first-order logic and the complexity of natural language. The book focuses on the use of logic to expose and remedy many difficulties with understanding a sentence's exact meaning. Lepore's user-friendly style makes the book enjoyable for beginning logic students, and his coverage of the details makes it useful for advanced students and professionals. There is no logic textbook that comes even remotely close to accomplishing what *Meaning and Argument* does."

Kent Johnson, *University of California at Irvine*

Meaning and Argument

An Introduction to Logic Through Language

Revised Edition

Ernest Lepore

Blackwell
Publishing

350 Main Street, Malden, MA 02148-5018, USA
108 Cowley Road, Oxford OX4 1JF, UK
550 Swanston Street, Carlton South, Melbourne, Victoria 3053, Australia
Kurfürstendamm 57, 10707 Berlin, Germany

First edition published 2000
This revised edition published 2003 by Blackwell Publishing Ltd

Library of Congress Cataloging-in-Publication Data

Lepore, Ernest, 1950–
Meaning and argument : an introduction to logic through language / Ernest
Lepore. – Rev. ed.
p. cm.
Includes bibliographical references and index.
ISBN 1-4051-0783-9 (pbk. : alk. paper)
1. Logic.   2. Language and logic.   I. Title.

BC108.L44 2003
160 – dc21
2002038482

A catalogue record for this title is available from the British Library.

Set in 10 on 12.5pt Sabon
by Graphicraft Limited, Hong Kong
Printed and bound in the United Kingdom
by MPG Books, Bodmin, Cornwall

For further information on
Blackwell Publishing, visit our website:
http://www.blackwellpublishing.com

Contents

Preface to Revised Edition

Some typographical errors and other infelicities were found in the first edition of this book. I want to thank Blackwell Publishing and in particular Jeff Dean for encouraging me to put together a new revised edition. Most of the corrections I have already put up on the home page for the book: http://www.MeaningArgument.com. It also seemed to me (and my students) that some of the exercises were less helpful than they should be. So I have revised many of the exercises – cutting here, adding there, re-ordering – throughout. In addition, I've elaborated on issues I thought should be elaborated upon – e.g., anaphora, predicative adjectives, 'exactly', negation of existentials, and numerical quantifiers.

I had wanted to add new chapters on natural deduction – in addition to the tableaux ('truth tree') method already in the book – but discovered that this addition would require too many chapters for merely a revised edition. So I have put up a natural deduction system with strategies and exercises on the book's home page.

A number of people have sent me useful comments on this book since its publication. I'd like to thank them here. Herman Cappelen, Walter Dean, Tobyn DeMarco, Georg Dorn, Ray Elugardo, Edmund Gettier, Kent Johnson, Matt Philips, T. W. C. Stoneham, and Alan Weir.

A very special thanks goes to Sarah-Jane Leslie. Sarah-Jane has been a participant in every single aspect of this book and its uses since its publication. She was in the first class I taught using the book after it was published. She found several errors and has made numerous recommendations for how to improve this new edition, including writing up some of the new sections. She put together the home page for the book and continues to maintain it. I cannot thank her enough. I dedicate this new revised edition to her.

Acknowledgments

I (and others) have taught various drafts of this book; so first I thank the literally dozens of classes that have had to put up with my working out these materials in front of them. I enjoyed it immensely (I still do), but I also realize how frustrating it must have been for many students. Many other logic books have influenced me in one way or another, so many that I cannot even recall them all. In addition, so many discussions with colleagues and students have caused me to rethink much of what I had said that it's impossible for me to thank each and every person who has contributed to the final product. I don't even like the sound of that – the final product. The only way I was able to convince myself to let this book go into print was by thinking of it as but one more draft, to be revised as soon as I distribute the first published copy and begin a new semester.

Logic is not the sort of subject that jumps to mind in pondering friendship, but in reminiscing about who among my colleagues contributed to the development of this book I was struck with a rather strong (but not perfect) link between colleagues and long-term, recent, past, or current friends.

I began thinking about reasoning in high school. My then and still close friend, my first friend, is Brian McLaughlin. We spent years trying to solve various logical *conundra* like how on earth the Virgin Mary could have been a virgin and still have given birth to Jesus. In college I had the good fortune to find myself in the classroom of several terrific teachers, but three that stand out vis-à-vis logic are Ed – the Jet – Gettier, Terry Parsons, and Steve Herman. From Steve I learned about the joy of philosophy, and I'll say more about him below. Ed Gettier continues to make me wonder what went wrong with my generation. I was under 20, barely articulate, a terrible Jersey public high school education holding me back, yet Ed never failed to figure out and answer what I was trying to ask. Like many others who went through UMass, I still treasure my collection of napkins chock full of Ed's ideas and notes and passion for logic and philosophy. Terry Parsons was the first philosopher I got to know who knew a lot of logic, and, boy, could he teach it. I don't have napkins from Terry, but I have precious notes. I continue to learn from him. It's rare to hook up with someone as smart as Terry who also takes joy in teaching esoteric subjects and does it so well.

When I got to graduate school I thought I knew a fair amount of logic. I suppose I did, but not as much as I thought. John Wallace spotted that right away. He was the first philosopher who taught me how powerful a tool logic can be without having to ram it down everyone's throat. Michael Root, the other chief influence on me in graduate school, taught me how to teach logic. I assisted him in several introductory logic courses. Lots of the examples in this book are cribbed from his excellent notes.

Sometime toward the end of my graduate education I came into personal contact with Donald Davidson. Under his influence I came to see that logic was an important device for thinking about natural language. I'm not sure why it took so long for me to figure that out. This book has ultimately been shaped by Davidson's wisdom about the importance of semantics for thinking about natural language. Just one more debt I owe Donald.

In 1979, I spent a summer living with Barry Loewer while we were both attending a National Endowment of Humanities seminar run by Dick Grandy. I got a lot out of that seminar, but most memorable from that summer is the beginning of a long and continuing intellectual and loving friendship. Anyone who knows Barry knows that he knows his way around hard philosophy as well as anyone in the profession. After having been set straight by him, we merrily proceeded over the next decade to collaborate on well over a dozen articles, some of which we both still believe.

When I took a job at Rutgers University, I hooked up with Bas van Frassen – the Bas. We were both single and new to New Jersey. I still smile thinking about our hopping back and forth between my place on St Mark's Place in the East Village and his home in Princeton. Bas did a lot for my self-confidence. If anyone as smart as he is didn't think what I was saying was stupid, I figured I had to be on to something. More importantly, Bas, even when critical, knew how to dish it out gently and affectionately – we can all learn a lot from his example.

Around that same time I joined a trio, Dr E. Saarinen and Colin – the Ace – McGinn being the other two members. Esa, Colin, and I bounced around Helsinki, London, and New York City. Although we were all intensely interested in philosophical logic, I'm not sure how much influence we exerted over each other on that front. What I do recall quite fondly about the two of them, though, is how they pressed me to work things out for myself, and to rely less on others. I hope some of that comes through in this book. To the extent that it does, it's intentional.

As the years passed, I came to know Willard Van Orman Quine. It took me about five years not to be intimidated just by being in his presence. Once I got over that initial star shock, I began to talk with him about logical form. It's no accident that he has come to be known as the father of American philosophy. No introductory logic book can replace his *Methods of Logic*, and it would be folly to try to do so. My route was to try to amplify on his superior lead.

More recently I came under the spell of Jerry Fodor. We wrote a book together and a number of critical essays. No matter how strange one finds what Jerry sometimes says in and out of print, there is no denying how damn good he is at philosophy. No one else I know sees the dialectic as quickly and as well as he. I'm more than appreciative for the good number of times he's challenged me on a piece of faulty reasoning before I put it into print.

Three years ago I decided I should try to publish my logic notes. That decision brought me back full circle to Steve Herman, my first philosophy teacher. I had a draft of the book ready to hand to Steve Smith, my friend and editor at Blackwell Publishing. I visited Steve Herman in Maryland one weekend and showed him that 'final' draft. After a few hours he told me he thought it could be turned into a good book with another year's hard work. He also agreed to help. It never occurred to me to move any faster. Steve was off by at least two years; but it's been great fun helping him finish my book.

There are many others. I've been blessed to have so many clear-headed, smart friends, young and old. During the past year or so a number of graduate students have become involved in helping me re-write: in particular, Jeff Buechner, Kent Johnson, Jonathan Cohen, and Phillip Robbins. In the final stages of putting together this book, Herman Cappelen graciously taught it at Vassar College. He and his students offered keen criticism. Stephen Neale has taught us all much about descriptions, from which chapter 16 has benefited. On the penultimate draft, Bernie Linsky, Barry Schein, and especially Bob Hale showered me with criticism, all of which was very helpful. There are others I'm sure I've neglected to thank. Next time. I would also like to thank Philip Aslett for providing an index; Jean van Altena, Mary Dortch, and Simon Eckley for copy-editing; Lisa Eaton for the lay-out; and Beth Remmes for helping to bring this project to completion.

The book is dedicated to two old friends, for whom it would be nothing close to exaggeration to say that this book is as much theirs as mine in ways only they know.

For Steve Herman and Dick Foley.
I'm a lucky person to be their friend.

Introduction

Often misunderstanding or conflict results from people not getting clear with each other. We take for granted that our language is an adequate vehicle of expression, but it isn't. Although formal logic texts typically take on the task of helping students clarify ambiguous language, they tend to focus more on proof making, determining when a conclusion follows from its premises. Students should be taught to test the validity of formalized arguments, but a reasonable expectation is that they express themselves clearly before drawing conclusions. A primary task of logical skill development should be to give students tools for capturing adequately in a notation arguments they express in a natural language. To this end, language should play about one half of the project in a logic course, though it rarely does, at least not explicitly. Whether logic teachers are aware of it or not, it's impossible to teach how to evaluate arguments from natural language without dabbling a bit in philosophy of language. (Of course, introductory logic can be taught exclusively on formal proofs in formal languages. Many try to do so. Why such courses should be taught in philosophy programs and not in mathematics or computer science programs is a mystery to me; indeed, why they should be taught at all eludes me as well.) *Meaning and Argument* shifts away from traditional emphasis on proofs (manipulation of a formal system) to symbolization of arguments of English in a formal system. It does so while still introducing students to what they ordinarily learn in an introductory logic course: truth tables, validity, propositional logic, predicate logic without and with identity, formal proofs, consistency, and so on. *Meaning and Argument* is not so bold as to claim that symbolization techniques are mechanical, but nor is it so cavalier as to suggest that manipulating natural language arguments into formal languages is an unteachable skill that one either has or doesn't have.

Another distinctive feature of *Meaning and Argument* is that it shows how the need for expressive power and for drawing distinctions forces formal language development. In this sense the book is Quinean in spirit: symbolization (or, to use Quine's term, regimentation) should be ruled by the maxim of 'shallow analysis'. As Quine counsels us, 'expose no more logical structure than seems useful for deduction or other inquiry at hand' (*Word and Object*, p. 160). Symbolization is a tool useful for sorting out those linguistic constructions which can be rendered within the framework of a given logic from those that cannot be so regimented.

Some logic teachers might be tempted to dismiss rudimentary systems like the Propositional Calculus because they lack the complexity of logical apparatus needed to prove the validity of arguments we know intuitively to be valid. *Meaning and Argument* starts with these more elemental systems, however, using them to guide students through an idealized journey of thought. The purpose is to retrace what one might imagine was the paths which great logicians traveled as they elaborated simpler formal systems. In this way the book tries to get at why things might have happened as they did. The process is not necessary. Given modern tools and diagnostic devices, a mechanic can be trained to identify a malfunction and correctly replace the malfunctioning part without ever having torn apart an engine and rebuilt it. Intuitively there is something to be said on behalf of the latter approach, at least insofar as getting back on the road is one's primary objective. But in the case of formal logic, we should want more than mechanical translation and testing of validity. Understanding formal systems and how they work and develop can be a valuable part of a curriculum that has as one of its goals to train systematic and scientific thinkers.

At the introductory level much that has passed as logic teaching is how-to, feel-good education, which has as its main purpose to help students get the right answers. Often this endeavor leads to well-intentioned efforts to give students recipes, step-by-step techniques, that render the processes of symbolization and proof making mechanical. Teaching students to treat conjunctions, conditionals, universal statements, or any other sort of logically complex expression as a purely grammatical matter is too facile, giving a temporary illusion of success at the early stages. This book stresses understanding; it sensitizes students to the contextual nature of language, and thus to the importance of not being lulled into automatic symbolizations based on grammatical structures alone. At each stage of system elaboration and development, the book seeks to answer the meta-logical questions:

Why is a particular formalism needed?
What form should it take?

These questions engage students in an inquiry, which allows them to see logical studies as a human enterprise aimed at achieving well-understood goals – clarity and good reasoning. When students realize that systems are elaborated and developed so that increasingly complex and ambiguous statements can be clearly stated and so that valid arguments can and invalid arguments cannot be proved, the entire subject matter begins to make sense. Instead of symbolizing statements and devising proofs without knowing why, students come to see the forest for the trees.

This book answers its main questions by proceeding from a simple formal language to increasingly more complex formal languages and by explaining the reason for each complication. The moves from propositional to property predicate logic, to relational predicate logic, and finally to relational predicate logic with identity are made clear to the student at each step. In this sense the book is progressive; yet, from the first chapter to the last, the book should be accessible to a novice.

In addition, this book introduces the student to the differences between logical and conversational implications. Throughout, the case is made that many logical fallacies may best be understood as failures to distinguish reasonable conversational inferences from strict logical deductions.

Instructional method: *Meaning and Argument* proceeds inductively in a pedagogical sense. An example either of a statement or an argument is given. The student's intuitions are tested: What does the statement mean? Is the argument intuitively valid? Does the logical system presented, at its current level of development, enable us to capture this sense, clear up ambiguities, and prove validity? If not, how might the system be elaborated?

In the case of symbolization, *Meaning and Argument* contributes to the literature of logic pedagogy. It provides the student with procedures for symbolizing complicated locutions from English into the appropriate formal notation, a systematic and manageable process that leads almost invariably to correct symbolizations.

Relation of book to current linguistic theory: In the last 40 years linguists, logicians, philosophers, and computer scientists have assembled a substantial and highly sophisticated body of work on the structure of natural language. Inasmuch as *Meaning and Argument* aspires to be an introduction to the tools and techniques for studying natural language, one might expect the book to incorporate some of this burgeoning literature. However, anything less than a comprehensive, even if not a critical, review of that literature would be superficial and, I expect, confusing for most introductory students. Furthermore, an introductory book of this nature is better kept independent of current technical trends. For example, some very important recent contributions by formal semanticists are not acknowledged here. The bibliographies at the end of most chapters, however, list this burgeoning literature.

1

A Brief Introduction to Key Terms

1.1 Arguments

Arguments crop up in conversations, political debates, lectures, editorials, comic strips, novels, television programs, scriptures, films, graffiti, posters, on the net, and so on. Ordinarily when we argue with others, we try to persuade them of some point. The forms of persuasion are many. We can persuade others by hitting them, by screaming at them, by drugging them, and so on. These kinds of persuasion are, unfortunately, prevalent. However, in this book we will use the term 'argument' exclusively to pick out sets of statements of the following sort:

Provided the fetus is a person, a fetus has a right to life. Should a fetus have a right to life, it is false that someone has the right to take its life. However, if abortions are moral, someone does have the right to take the life of a fetus. Consequently, if a fetus is a person, abortions are not moral.

Lung cancer is not caused by smoking, and this is so for the following reasons. Lung cancer is more common among male smokers than among female smokers. If smoking were the cause of lung cancer, this would not be true. The fact that lung cancer is more common among male smokers implies that it is caused by something in the male makeup. But if caused by this, it is not caused by smoking.

Anyone who deliberates about alternative courses of action believes he is free. Since everybody deliberates about alternative courses of action, it follows that we all believe ourselves to be free.

What do these passages have in common in virtue of which each is an argument in our sense? In this book an argument is any set of *statements* – explicit or implicit – one of which is the *conclusion* (the statement allegedly being defended) and the others are the *premises* (statements allegedly providing the defense).[1] The relationship between the conclusion and the premises is such that the conclusion purportedly *follows from* the premises. This description of an argument leads us to ask what statements are, and what it means to say that one statement follows from others.

1.1.1   *What is a Statement?*

A statement is any indicative sentence that is either true or false.[2] The following are statements:

> Galileo was an astronomer.
> Provided the fetus is a person, a fetus has a right to life.
> No one but Nixon knew the truth.
> Lung cancer is not caused by smoking.
> Everybody deliberates about alternative courses of action.
> Martin Van Buren was not the ninth president of the United States.

Interrogatives, imperatives, and exclamations are sentences that are not statements; for example:

> Is George Washington president?
> Shave yourself!
> Wow!

1.1.2   *Premises and Conclusion*

A main aim in learning logic is to enhance skills in assessing arguments as we find them. But arguments cannot be assessed unless they are first identified as arguments. Although there are no sure signs of whether an argument is present, fairly reliable indicators exist.

Premise indicators: Premise indicators are terms that indicate that a premise will immediately follow. In the second argument in §1.1 above, the first sentence ends with 'this is so for the following reasons'. This clause indicates that the statements which follow are the premises of this argument. The third argument has a second sentence that begins with the word 'Since', indicating that a premise is about to be introduced. Other such expressions include 'because', 'for', 'after all', 'given', 'whereas', 'although', 'suppose', 'assume', 'let us presume', 'granted', 'here are the facts'. When a premise indicator starts a clause, then what follows the premise indicator is usually a premise.

Conclusion indicators: Likewise, when a conclusion indicator starts a clause, then what follows is usually a conclusion. In the first argument in §1.1 above, the last sentence begins with the word 'Consequently', indicating that it is the conclusion. Other conclusion indicators include 'therefore', 'so', 'hence', 'it follows', '. . . proves', '. . . shows', 'we can now infer', 'it cannot fail to be', 'let us conclude', 'this implies', 'these facts indicate', 'this supports the view or claim', 'let us infer', 'as a consequence we can deduce'.

Many passages contain arguments but none of these indicators, and some passages contain one or more of them without stating a premise or a conclusion. Indeed, the indicators seen most frequently are often used as neither conclusion nor premise indicators, as in the following sentences.

How long has it been **since** you last saw him?
He is **so** good at what he does.
For two years he has been away.
After all these days, you come home.
Let us go **hence**.

None of these sentences is being offered as a premise for some conclusion or as a conclusion from some premises. Even though each contains familiar indicator terms, obviously the terms are not being used as indicators in these sentences.

Alternatively, one may simply announce that an argument is forthcoming, and then go on to affirm several statements. In this case, the context makes clear that the last statement is the conclusion and the others are premises. Still, some terms are almost always used as conclusion or premise indicators. It's hard to imagine a context in which 'on the assumption that' is not a premise indicator or 'as a consequence it follows' is not a conclusion indicator.

1.2 Putting Arguments into a Standard Format

Having determined that some piece of discourse contains an argument, the next task is to put it into a standard format. This task may involve all of the following:

i.   Identifying the premises and the conclusion.
ii. Placing the premises first. (Order does not matter.)
iii. Placing the conclusion last.
iv. Making explicit any premise or even the conclusion, which may be only implicit in the original but essential to the argument.

So standard forms for the above three arguments are:

Provided the fetus is a person, a fetus has a right to life.
Should a fetus have a right to life, it is false that someone has the right to take its life.
If abortions are moral, someone does have the right to take the life of a fetus.
If a fetus is a person, abortions are not moral.

The first three statements are premises, and the fourth is the conclusion.

Lung cancer is more common among male smokers than among female smokers.
If smoking were the cause of lung cancer, this would not be true.
The fact that lung cancer is more common among male smokers implies that it is caused by something in the male makeup.
If it is caused by this, it is not caused by smoking.
Lung cancer is not caused by smoking.

The first four statements are premises, and the fifth is the conclusion.

Anyone who deliberates about alternative courses of action believes he is free.
Everybody deliberates about alternative courses of action.
We all believe ourselves to be free.

The first two statements are the premises, and the third is the conclusion.

In none of the arguments is a premise or a conclusion missing. Nothing said so far explains exactly how we were able to devise these standard forms based on what we were presented with. So far our process has been rather loose, and it cannot be tightened until we say something substantive about when one statement follows from some others.

1.3 Multiple Conclusions

As we have characterized arguments, no argument can have more than one conclusion. Of course, sometimes we do find passages with more than one conclusion. There are two types of cases. The first occurs when more than one conclusion is drawn from the same set of premises. For such a case we adopt the convention that distinct arguments can have the same premises, but different conclusions. So, for example, (1)–(4) below include two distinct arguments. (1)–(2) are premises, and (3)–(4) are conclusions. So (1)–(3) constitute one argument; and (1)–(2) and (4) constitute another distinct argument.

1. All women are mortal and rational.
2. Andrea is a woman.
3. So, Andrea is rational.
4. So, Andrea is mortal.

The second case occurs when we chain arguments together so that a single statement serves as both a premise and a conclusion. In this case the conclusion of one argument functions as a premise of another. (5)–(9) include two arguments.

5. Killing children is evil.
6. Children were being killed in Bosnia.
7. Therefore, someone was doing something evil in Bosnia.
8. When someone does something evil, he should be punished.
9. So, whoever killed children in Bosnia should be punished.

(5)–(6) are premises of an argument with (7) as its conclusion. However, (7) is also the premise of an argument, which along with (5), (6), and (8), has (9) as its conclusion.

Exercise 1.1   **Standard form**

- Put arguments (1)–(4) into a standard form.

1. If we are going to avoid a nuclear war in the next few years, we will have to adopt strong punitive measures now. But if we adopt such measures, many nations will be very unhappy. Thus, we are going to avoid a nuclear war in the next few years only if many nations are going to be unhappy.

2. The state will increase its financial support of our university only if the priorities of the legislature shift in favor of higher education. But if such a shift were to occur, the people who benefit from other state projects would complain bitterly. If the state does not increase financial support for the university, tuition will have to be raised. So, tuition will be raised.

3. If a man is to play some role in society, that role must be determined by nature or by society. However, if his role is determined by nature, that role will be the role of the selfish hunter on the make. Hence, either society determines a role for man, or man will play the role of the selfish hunter always on the make.

4. If it is true that 30 out of every 50 college coeds have sexual intercourse outside marriage, then it is very important to have birth control information available from the Student Health Service. It is very important to have birth control information available from the Student Health Service. Thus, we know that 30 out of every 50 college coeds have sexual intercourse outside marriage.

1.4 Deductive Validity

What is it for one statement to follow from others? The principal sense of 'follows from' in this book derives from the notion of a deductively valid argument.

> **A deductively valid argument is an argument such that it is not possible both for its premises to be true and its conclusion to be false.**

So, consider argument (10)–(12).

10. The current Vice-President will win the next election.
11. If the current Vice-President wins the next election, then the country will prosper.
12. So, the country will prosper.

This is an argument in which the conclusion follows intuitively from its premises. But what is it about (10)–(12) that makes us think that (12) can be concluded on the basis of (10)–(11)? We know it's not the truth of the premises, because we are in no position to know whether they are true. The relevant events haven't even occurred yet. So what is it? One salient feature is that, were the premises true, the conclusion would have to be true as well. These considerations should help the reader to appreciate the difference between the deductive validity of an argument and the truth of its premises.

Another argument will make this point even more evident.

13. All fish fly.
14. Anything which flies talks.
15. So, all fish talk.

Even though each statement in (13)–(15) is obviously false, the argument is deductively valid, because it is not possible for its premises to be true and its conclusion to be false. If it so happened (even though we know otherwise) that the premises were true, would the conclusion have to be true as well? Say that, due to some strange release of radiation, all fish flew and anything which flew talked, it would then be, and have to be, true that all fish talk. In this sense the conclusion (15) follows from its premises (13)–(14), and the argument is deductively valid.

What about an invalid argument? Consider argument (16)–(18).

16. If God exists, then the creation is perfect.
17. God doesn't exist.
18. So, the creation is imperfect.

Argument (16)–(18) is invalid. (16) merely tells us what the state of the creation would be if God exists. It doesn't assert anything about the state of the creation if God does not exist. The creation could be perfect whether or not God exists. Consider an analogous argument. If you prepare for a chess game, you win. But suppose you don't prepare for it. It doesn't follow that you lose. Plainly you might win even if you don't prepare. Your opponent might forfeit, for example.

In ordinary English the terms 'valid' and 'true', on the one hand, and 'invalid' and 'false', on the other, are often used interchangeably. People will say that statements are valid or invalid, and that arguments are true or false. But logicians use these terms in a much more restricted way, such that 'valid' and 'invalid' apply only to arguments, and 'true' and 'false' only to statements. We will adopt this restrictive practice in this book.

Exercise 1.2   **Deductive validity**

- With this characterization of deductive validity, it is already possible to evaluate many arguments. Which of (1)–(8) is deductively valid?

1. Mary either plays basketball or baseball.
   She does not play basketball.
   So, she plays baseball.
2. Al will play tennis or he will play baseball.
   Al will play tennis.
   So, Al will not play baseball.
3. You play in the National Basketball Association only if you are over three feet tall.
   Bill Clinton is over three feet tall.
   So, Clinton plays in the National Basketball Association.
4. Any creature with a kidney has a heart.
   Not every creature has a heart.
   So, not every creature has a kidney.
5. Bill ate steak for dinner this evening.
   So, Bill ate dinner this evening.
6. Everybody loves someone.
   So, someone is loved by everyone.
7. Some birds do not fly.
   Therefore, not every bird flies.
8. There is evil in the world.
   If there were a God, there would be no evil.
   Therefore, there is no God.

Truth, falsity, and deductive validity　　　　Exercise 1.3

- Give an example, if possible, for each box in the following diagram.
- If it's not possible, explain why.

Devising a deductively valid argument for box 7 demonstrates that there is no connection between actual truth and validity. Someone may assert only false sentences, and yet his argument may be deductively valid.

　Devising an argument for box 2, on the other hand, demonstrates that someone may assert only truths, and yet his argument may be deductively invalid.

　Together these show that we might criticize in two distinct ways those who offer an argument in order to persuade us of some point: they might go wrong because they are ignorant (box 7), in which case what they say is false; or they might go wrong because they are illogical (box 2), in which case what they conclude does not follow from what they believe or assert as premises.

Premises	Conclusion	Valid	Invalid
True	True	1	2
At least one false	True	3	4
True	False	5	6
At least one false	False	7	8

1.5　Soundness

A good argument is not simply deductively valid; (13)–(15) is deductively valid but unlikely to persuade anyone.

13.　All fish fly.
14.　Anything which flies talks.
15.　So, all fish talk.

Though it is not possible for both (13) and (14) to be true and (15) false, the argument is unlikely to persuade any knowledgeable person, because (13)–(14) are patently false. Normally, good arguments are not only deductively valid. They also have true premises. Such arguments are called *sound*.[3]

Suppose an argument is valid, yet its conclusion is false. Then at least one of its premises must be false, and the argument, though valid, is unsound. Once we decide that an argument is deductively valid, we may direct attention to the question of its soundness.

1.6   Missing Premises and Conclusions

Intuitively, argument (19)–(20) is deductively valid, because an obviously true premise (21) is missing from it.

19.   New York City is in New York State.
20.   So, Manhattan is in New York State.

21.   Manhattan is in New York City.

Almost anyone familiar with the facts about New York City, when presented with (19)–(20) as an argument, would effortlessly add (21) as a premise. But we must be careful about adding premises to arguments, since any argument can be turned into a deductively valid argument if the right 'missing' premise(s) are added. On its face, argument (22)–(23) appears to be invalid; but if we treat this argument like we did argument (19)–(20) by adding the 'missing' premise (24), we too easily turn a bad argument into a deductively valid argument.

22.   The Yankees are losing.
23.   So, we should elect a new president.

24.   If the Yankees are losing, we should elect a new president.

Clearly, until some independent reason is provided, why should we add (24)? Why should we suppose a connection between the Yankees losing, on the one hand, and electing a new president, on the other?

The question we need to take a stab at is why many people would refrain from postulating (24) as a missing premise from (22)–(23), even though they intuit that (21) is implicit in argument (19)–(20)? According to one hypothesis, the difference has something to do with successful communication. When we communicate, we normally share a background of beliefs or assumptions and recognize that we share them. When I discuss politics with a colleague, we each take elementary facts about our government for granted, and we each assume that the other does too. We assume that Washington DC is the capital of the United States, that the White House is located there, that the President lives there, and so forth. The more we share, the easier it is to communicate. If we did not share any beliefs, we probably could not communicate at all.

Typically, a conversation depends in part on what we want to convey and in part on what we assume about the listener's beliefs. We do not usually say what is already common knowledge, since that would be banal. Nor do we ordinarily say what we believe is inconsistent with our shared beliefs, since that would sabotage our conversation.

Although many facts and opinions are assumed in conversation, we frequently need to bring them to the fore, in order to evaluate properly the validity of an argument. Which premises to make explicit is not always easy to decide. The interpreter of an argument has a choice: to declare an explicitly invalid argument invalid or to make that argument valid by adding premises he thinks implicit but unstated. No matter how unpromising an argument may seem, you can always conjure up premises sufficient to make the conclusion follow. When should you add premises thought to be implicit, and when not? If, to save an argument, you would need to put into the mouth of its author beliefs he probably does not or would not hold, then the best course of action is to declare the argument invalid.

Though much of the above explanation may seem abstract, you will find that you already have strong intuitions concerning which premise(s), or even which conclusion, is missing. On its face, for example, argument (25) is deductively invalid.

25. Only children are admitted free. So none of our executives is admitted free.

However, were someone to propose (25), we would probably realize that he was assuming an unstated connection between the premise and the conclusion. No formula exists for finding such connections; but in this example we readily see that some connection must be made between children and executives: namely, 'Our executives are not children.' If we add this statement as a missing premise, the argument is deductively valid.

Exercise 1.4   Missing premises and conclusion

- Figure out which premise(s) or conclusion could be supplied to make arguments (1)–(2) valid.
- But try to choose premises in accordance with the restrictions stated above.

1. Either the key is in my pocket or it is on the hall table; and if it is on the hall table, we are locked out. ((1) is interesting because it is not at all clear which conclusion is missing, and therefore we can readily see that there is no such thing as *the* conclusion of a set of premises. There will often be more than one reasonable conclusion to draw, and it may be arbitrary which one.[4])
2. Either I pay Jerry off, or he publishes those photos; but if I pay him off, I'll be broke. So either I will be broke or I will lose my job.

Notes

1 Sometimes spelled 'premisses'.
2 Many philosophers argue that not every indicative sentence is a statement. While avoiding detail at this stage, our definition can accommodate such sentences, should there be any.
3 Sometimes offering a deductively valid argument with known false premises is worthwhile. *Reductio ad absurdum* arguments are examples. See ch. 8 for more on these.
4 I state without proof that for any set of premises there are infinitely many conclusions that we can deductively validly draw from these premises. Of course, some are more appropriate than others.

2

Argument Forms and Propositional Logic

In this chapter I will describe and explicate two different ways in which an argument can be deductively valid. It can be formally valid: that is, valid in virtue of its form. Or, it can be non-formally valid: that is, valid not in virtue of its form but in virtue of what some of its 'non-logical' words mean.

2.1   Formal Validity

In order to determine whether an argument is deductively valid, we must determine whether it is possible both for its premises to be true and its conclusion to be false. But unless we know something about the subject matter of the argument, it may not be possible for us to make this sort of assessment. So, for example, consider an argument indicating how Boyle's law may be derived from the kinetic theory of gases.

The pressure exerted by a gas in a container results from the impacts of the molecules upon the containing walls and is quantitatively equal to the average value of the total momentum that the molecules deliver per second to a unit square of the wall area. If this is so, then the pressure of a gas is inversely proportional to its volume and is directly proportional to the mean kinetic energy of its molecules. The mean kinetic energy of the molecules of a fixed mass of gas remains constant as long as the temperature remains constant. If the pressure of a gas is inversely proportional to its volume and directly proportional to the mean kinetic energy of its molecules, and the mean kinetic energy of the molecules of a fixed mass of gas remains constant as long as the temperature is held constant, then the pressure of a fixed mass of gas at a constant temperature will be inversely proportional to its volume. It follows from all of the above that the pressure of a fixed mass of gas at constant temperature is inversely proportional to the volume of the gas.

Unless you know something about the kinetic theory of gases or about Boyle's law, you are not in a position to determine whether it is possible both for all the premises of this argument to be true and for its conclusion to be false. Nevertheless, we need not throw up our hands in despair. More often than not, we do not need to understand an argument in its entirety in order to evaluate its deductive validity.

Consider the following three sets of arguments.

SET I

War is cruel, and world leaders know this to be so.
So, war is cruel.

Bill went home, and so did Joe.
So, Bill went home.

Frank is polite, and Mary should be.
So, Frank is polite.

SET II

If Rutgers wins, then Duke loses.
Rutgers won.
So, Duke lost.

If Rome is south of Paris, then Rome is south of Oslo.
Rome is south of Paris.
So, it is also south of Oslo.

If Lassie is dead, then the children are sad.
Lassie is dead.
So, the children are sad.

SET III

Either Martha is paid by check, or she is paid in cash.
Martha is not paid by check.
So, she is paid in cash.

Either today is Tuesday, or it is Thursday.
It's not Tuesday.
So, it's Thursday.

Either Ken can stay, or he can leave.
He cannot stay.
So, he can leave.

The three arguments in each set have something in common. Each is deductively valid. But, more important, they share a certain form or structure. In order to say what structure or form they share, I will introduce two sorts of notation, familiar *quotation marks*, which will allow us to talk about specific linguistic expressions, and *metalinguistic variables*, which will allow us to talk about linguistic expressions in general.

2.2 Quotation Marks

There is a difference between *using* an expression and *mentioning* it. When we say that Bob Dylan is not Frank Sinatra, we *mention* the entertainers Frank Sinatra and Bob Dylan. In order to do so, we *use* their names, 'Bob Dylan' and 'Frank Sinatra', placing the two words 'is not' between them and *not* between two people. When the objects mentioned are people, as they are here, use and mention are unlikely to be confused. But consider statement (1).

1. Robert Zimmerman is the name given to a famous American entertainer by his parents.

In (1), the name 'Robert Zimmerman' is used to refer to a person. So the subject of (1) is the person, but what is said about him is that he is a name, which, needless to say, is blatantly false.[1] One way to turn (1) into a true statement is to flank his name with single quotation marks so as to make clear that it is his name, not his person, that is being referred to.[2] Properly rewritten, (1) would read as (2):

2. 'Robert Zimmerman' is the name given to a famous American entertainer by his parents.

Now consider (3). Not only is it untrue; it is also ungrammatical and meaningless.

3. The second word of the Gettysburg address is score.

In order to convert (3) into a grammatical, meaningful, true statement, single quotation marks can be used to mention the linguistic expression 'score'.

Failure to understand the differences between using and mentioning an expression can easily lead to confusion. Both (4) and (5) are false. Were anyone to assert either, she would display what we might call a *use/mention confusion*.

4. The *Iliad* is written in English.
5. 'The *Iliad*' is an epic poem.

(4) is false because 'Iliad' is the English title of a Greek epic poem, whereas (5) is false because 'The Iliad' has but two words, and no epic poem has only two words.

(6) is ungrammatical because '2 + 2 = 4' is a (mathematical) sentence, and no sentence can be the grammatical subject of a sentence; only a noun (phrase) can be the grammatical subject of a sentence.

6. $2 + 2 = 4$ is a mathematical truth.

So, in order to convert nonsense into truth, quotation marks must be placed around '2 + 2 = 4', as in (7).

7. '$2 + 2 = 4$' is a mathematical truth.

At first blush, quotation seems a simple linguistic practice, but the above examples show that ascertaining the truth about statements with quotation marks can get thorny. The following two exercises are designed to test your grasp on the practice of quotation in English.

Use/mention   Exercise 2.1

- Use single quote marks to punctuate (1)–(4) in a way that renders them true.

1. Archie Leech is a name of Cary Grant.
2. Italo Svevo is a pseudonym of Ettore Schmitz.
3. Even if x is the twenty-fourth letter of the alphabet, some writers have said x is the unknown.
4. Oswerk is not a word in English.

Use/mention   Exercise 2.2

- Assuming that single quotes are used in accordance with our convention, which of (1)–(4) are true?

1. 'New York City' and 'the largest city in New York state' mention the same city.
2. '7 + 5' = '12'.
3. 'The 42nd president of the United States' is 'the husband of Hillary Clinton'.
4. (3) does not mention the president of the United States.

2.3 Metalinguistic Variables

The arguments in set I (and the arguments from sets II and III as well) in §2.1 have something in common. How might we display what they have in common? As we saw in §2.2, we can use quotation marks to mention specific linguistic expressions, as in (8).

8. 'If Mary is tall, then Bill is happy' is a longer string of words than 'It is not the case that Mary is tall'.

But in order to discuss what the arguments in set I have in common, we want to talk not about specific linguistic expressions, but about linguistic expressions in general. It will be our practice in this book to use Greek letters – for example, 'α' and 'β' – to talk about linguistic expressions in general. Greek letters are in effect placeholders for unspecified linguistic expressions.[3] Metalinguistic variables allow us to say that each argument in set I in §2.1 – for example, 'War is cruel, and world leaders know this is so. So, war is cruel' – begins with a statement of the form

α and β

where α and β are statements themselves, and concludes with a statement of the form

α

In this context, the use of 'and' all by itself determines each argument in set I to be deductively valid. The word 'and' plays many roles in English, but one important role is to conjoin elements grammatically. It can link statements together. By and large, whenever 'and' conjoins two or more statements to form a complex statement, the resulting complex is true just in case its conjoined simpler parts are true, as with the first statement in each argument in set I. This feature of 'and' accounts for why any argument which shares the form of the arguments in set I must be deductively valid.[4]

Analogous points apply to the arguments in sets II and III. Each argument in set II is deductively valid, partly because of how 'if, then' statements function in our language. If an 'if, then' statement is assumed to be true, and if, in addition, its antecedent (i.e., the part which follows 'if' and precedes 'then') is true, then the consequent (i.e., the part which follows the 'then') would also have to be true. Put schematically, if any statement of the form

If α, then β

is assumed to be true, and if, in addition, its antecedent statement

α

is assumed true; then its consequent statement

β

follows deductively. All such arguments are valid.

Lastly, consider the arguments in set III. Each begins with a statement of the form

Either α or β

followed by a negation of a statement of the form

Not α

(i.e., the denial of α) and then concludes with a statement of the form

β

The validity of each argument in this set is determined by how the expressions 'not' and 'either, or' (to put it rather vaguely at this stage), interact with each other. It is not possible for the premises to be true and the conclusion false.

This discussion of the three sets of arguments shows that at least for some deductively valid arguments, you don't need to understand all the terms used in an argument in order to recognize its validity. If you understand 'and', you should recognize that the three arguments in set I are valid; analogous points hold for the arguments in sets II and III. Consider this example, which we could add to set I:

Many philosophers embrace holism, and some are atomists.
So, many philosophers embrace holism.

Though many readers will be unfamiliar with the doctrines of holism and atomism, it's a safe bet that all will recognize that it's not possible for the premise in this argument to be true and its conclusion false.

2.4   Non-formal Validity

Still, not every deductively valid argument is valid in virtue of form alone. Consider the following arguments:

John is a **bachelor**.
So, John is **unmarried**.

Something is **red**.
So, something is **colored**.

John **knows** that it is raining.
So, it is raining.

Each of these arguments is deductively valid. It is not possible for any of them to have true premises and a false conclusion. Yet these arguments are not deductively valid in virtue of form. The standard intuition is that they are valid by virtue of the meanings of some 'non-logical' vocabulary. The first argument is purported to be valid in virtue of what 'bachelor' means, the second in virtue of what 'red' means, and the third in virtue of what 'know' means. To see that these arguments are not valid in virtue of their form, consider the following three grammatically analogous, but deductively invalid, arguments:

John is a **policeman**.
So, John is **unmarried**.

Something is **square**.
So, something is **colored**.

John **hopes** that it is raining.
So, it is raining.

Each seems to *share a form* with an above argument. The first is obtained by replacing 'bachelor' with 'policeman', the second by replacing 'red' with 'square', and the last by replacing 'knows' with 'hopes'. Yet none of these three latter arguments is deductively valid. Policemen need not be unmarried or squares colored, and hopes may be dashed. Examples like these have convinced many logicians to draw a line between arguments valid due to the meanings of their non-logical expressions and those valid due to their logic (or logical form). Although where one should draw that line is controversial,[5] this does not undermine the significance or utility of the distinction between arguments deductively valid in virtue of form and those deductively valid but not in virtue of form.

2.5 The Need for Propositional Logic

Chapters 3–7 comprise a detailed study of the logic of the four types of complex statements discussed in §2.3: what are commonly called 'conjunctions', 'negations', 'disjunctions', and 'conditionals'. The logic which governs these types of complex statements is called Propositional Logic.[6] In learning this logic, students learn ways of representing arguments correctly and ways of testing the validity of those arguments.

We can express logical conjunctions in English by grammatically conjoining two statements with the word 'and'; we can represent logical conditionals by grammatically conjoining two statements with the words 'if, then'; we can represent logical disjunctions by grammatically conjoining two statements with the words 'either, or'; and we can represent logical negations by inserting the expression 'not' in a statement to form its denial. But sometimes such grammatical constructions do not issue in logical conjunctions, conditionals, disjunctions, or negations. More interestingly, there are constructions quite different from these which often do express logical conjunctions, conditionals, disjunctions, and negations. A major part of our task will be to determine what these constructions are. Once we know how to recognize and use them, we can learn various techniques for determining whether arguments containing these types of statements are deductively valid in virtue of their form as represented in Propositional Logic (PL).

One of our primary aims is to devise methods for deciding correctly whether a given argument is deductively valid. As indicated, the methods we develop for this purpose are formal. So we must devise adequate means for representing arguments. To accomplish this task, we symbolize the statements of the argument in PL. For this, we need symbols. In PL we utilize three types of symbols.

2.5.1 Symbolic Notation

The first type of symbol comprises capital block letters of the alphabet: 'A', 'B', 'C', 'D' . . . 'Z'. If we need to use more than 26 letters of the alphabet, we can use subscripts like, 'A_1', 'A_2', 'A_3', . . . ,'A_n', 'B_1', 'B_2', . . . , 'B_n', and so on. Use of subscripts like '1', '2', and '3' makes available an endless (indicated here and throughout by the ellipsis '. . .') supply of statement letters. Thus, we guarantee that there is no arbitrary, finite limit placed on the number of simple statements that an argument may include. These symbols are what we will call *statement letters*. With this notation we can introduce our first symbolization rule:

Rule 1:   A simple statement is symbolized by a single statement letter.

Which statements are simple? As noted earlier, PL has four types of complex statements. Simple statements are statements which do not fall into any of these four classes. This answer is not very illuminating until we can identify the members of all four classes. For the moment we will identify simple statements as statements which lack proper parts which are themselves statements. So the following are all simple statements:

George Washington crossed the Delaware River.
Ronald Reagan was the fortieth president of the USA.
All men are mortal.
Some dogs have paws.
Many sentences come from novels.[7]

Consider set I in §2.1 above. According to rule 1, if we let 'A' and 'B' represent the simple statements 'War is cruel' and 'World leaders know this to be so' in the premise, and 'C' to represent the simple statement 'War is cruel' in the conclusion, then the argument expressed in set I can be symbolized as follows:

A and B
So, C

However, this symbolization fails to recognize that in set I 'A' and 'C' refer to the same statement. In a sense, the same simple statement occurs more than once. This sense is easier to grasp with the distinction between types and tokens in hand.

2.6   The Type/Token Distinction

How many words occur in (9)?

9.   Kennedy was the president of the United States.

Some might answer seven, others eight. Since both answers are correct, the question must be ambiguous. If the question had been how many *types* of words are there in (9), the correct answer would be seven.[8] If the question were how many *tokens* of words are there in (9), then the correct answer would be eight. There are seven types and eight tokens, because the word 'the' has two occurrences in (9).

The type/token distinction obviously extends to formal languages. How many simple statement letters are there in (10)?

10.   If P and Q, then P.

The question is ambiguous. If the question means how many types of simple statement letters are there in (10), the correct answer is two: namely, 'P' and 'Q'. If the question means how many tokens (or occurrences) of simple statement letters are there in (10), the correct answer is three, since there are two tokens of the expression type 'P' and one token of the expression type 'Q'.

Type/token distinction   Exercise 2.3

1.   How many types of letters are there in 'Read my lips'? How many tokens?
2.   How many (tokens) occurrences of the word 'the' occur in 'The masked bandit asked the people to remove their hats'?
3.   How many (tokens) occurrences of the sequence of letters 'the' are there in 'The masked bandit asked the people to remove their hats'?

Returning to symbolization in general, the virtue of symbolic notation depends on our not assigning one and the same simple statement type to different statement letter types in the course of reasoning. So, we introduce a second rule.

> **Rule 2:   If a simple statement type occurs more than once in an argument, then each token of that type must be symbolized by the same statement letter type everywhere it occurs.**

Using this rule and letting 'A' and 'B' stand for the distinct simple statement types occurring in the three arguments in set I, the correct symbolization of each of these arguments is the same:

A and B
So, A

There is a good reason for amending rule 2, however. Consider the argument

If John goes to the store, then he can buy what he wants.
John went to the store.
So, John can buy what he wants.

Strictly speaking, given the first two rules alone, the following correctly symbolizes this argument:

If A, then B
C
So, D

No simple statement type occurs more than once in this argument. The statement type 'John went to the store' does not literally occur as the antecedent of the first premise. The present tense of the statement occurs instead; and the conclusion 'John can buy what he wants' is not identical with the consequent of the first premise. The subject of the consequent is the pronoun 'he'. The subject of the conclusion is 'John'.

So, rule 2 must be understood with some charity. The spirit of the requirement should allow that, though not of grammatically identical types, the pairs 'A' and 'C' and 'B' and 'D' express the same idea, at least in the context of the argument in which they occur. We augment the rule accordingly.

> **Rule 2′:   If two distinct simple statement types can be properly treated as paraphrases of each other, relative to the context of an argument in which they occur, then each should be symbolized by the same statement letter type.**

This addition raises the difficult question of how we are to identify distinct statement types in a given context as paraphrases (at least for the purposes of evaluating an argument). We will not try to answer this extremely difficult question here. Rather, we will take for granted that because we all understand English, we can, at least for the purposes of evaluating an argument's validity, rely on our own good sense of everyday idiom in deciding whether two statement types, relative to their context, express the same idea or content.

Argument forms   Exercise 2.4

- Abiding by the first and the augmented second rules, symbolize arguments (1)–(3). This requires you to replace simple statement types by statement letter types.
- Indicate which statement letters go with which simple statements.

1. If Lee Harvey Oswald assassinated John F. Kennedy, then he didn't act alone. Lee Harvey Oswald did act alone. So, he did not assassinate Kennedy.
2. Either Nixon was impeached, or he resigned the presidency of the United States. Nixon wasn't impeached. So, Nixon must have resigned.
3. Spiro Agnew was Vice-President under Richard Nixon, and Hubert H. Humphrey was Vice-President under Lyndon Baines Johnson. Neither Spiro Agnew nor Hubert Humphrey was ever President. So, it follows that not every Vice-President becomes President.

Notes

1   The expression 'subject' (of a sentence) may be used to mean the thing or things the sentence is about, and may also be used to mean the part of the sentence (hence expression or phrase) which tells us what thing or things the sentence is about (or, what may be equivalent, near enough, it may mean the expression with which the main verb should agree). The subject in the first sense is usually (but not always) non-linguistic; in the second, the grammatical sense, it is always a linguistic entity. Context should make clear what sense is in use.

2   In American English there is a tendency to use double quotes, whereas in British English the rule is to use single quotes. The British practice is adopted

in this book because it is simpler, especially inasmuch as we will often have reason to iterate quotation marks.

3   More accurately, they are metalinguistic variables that we will use to range over statements and other types of linguistic expressions: i.e., variables that take any type of linguistic expression as values. For more on the values of variables see ch. 12.

4   This claim requires qualification, which will be provided in ch. 3 and in §A1.

5   Which expressions are the logical ones? A traditional view is that logical expressions are topic-neutral; they introduce no particular subject matter. Something seems right about this view: 'and', 'or', 'not', and 'if, then' seem topic-neutral in a way that 'Rome', 'Rutgers', and 'check' are not. This approach seems promising, since logic pertains to reasoning in general. However, many expressions not usually treated as logical expressions seem equally topic-neutral. For example, 'as', 'because', 'by', and 'so' seem no less topic-neutral than 'and'; yet logicians don't assign any special logical status to these expressions.

6   Sometimes referred to as the 'Propositional Calculus', 'Sentential Logic (Calculus)', or 'Statement Logic (Calculus)'.

7   This rough characterization of simple statements does not actually even identify each of these statements as simple. 'Men are mortal' is part of 'All men are mortal', which is nevertheless a simple statement. Similar points may be made about other listed 'simple statements'. For this reason the characterization is intended merely as a rough guide. Simple statements will not really be identifiable until we can identify the four types of complex statements. Then any statement which is not a complex statement will be a simple statement.

8   Readers may see the expression 'types of words', and opine that there are four types of words in (1): nouns, verbs, articles, and prepositions. As will become apparent, that's not how we will be using 'type' here.

Bibliography

Cappelen, H. and Lepore, E., 'Varieties of Quotation', *Mind* 106 (1997), 429–50.

Kneale, W. and Kneale, M., *The Development of Logic* (Oxford: Oxford University Press, 1962).

Quine, W. V. O., *Philosophy of Logic*, 2nd edn (Cambridge, MA: Harvard University Press, 1986), ch. 1.

—— *Methods of Logic*, 4th edn (Cambridge, MA: Harvard University Press, 1982), ch. 4.

Sainsbury, Mark, *Logical Forms* (Oxford: Basil Blackwell, 1991), chs 1, 2, and 6.

Tarski, Alfred, 'On the Concept of Logical Consequence' (1936), in *Logic, Semantics and Metamathematics*, trans. J. H. Woodger, 2nd edn, ed. John Corcoran (Indianapolis: Hackett Publishing Co., 1983), 409–20.

—— 'What are Logical Notions?', *History and Philosophy of Logic* 7 (1986), 143–54.

3

Conjunction

3.1 Logical Conjunction

We begin the study of Propositional Logic (PL) by investigating logical conjunctions. We know that logical conjunctions can take the form

α and β

where α and β themselves can both be replaced by statements – simple or complex. But there are other common articulations of logical conjunctions in English. (1)–(8) exhibit the same logical conjunctions.

1. John went to the store, **but** Bill stayed home.
2. John went to the store, **while** Bill stayed home.
3. John went to the store, **even though** Bill stayed home.
4. John went to the store, **though** Bill stayed home.
5. John went to the store, **yet** Bill stayed home.
6. John went to the store; **however**, Bill stayed home.
7. John went to the store; Bill stayed home.
8. John went to the store; **nevertheless**, Bill stayed home.

Why are (1)–(8) all logical conjunctions? It is not simply because each consists of two statements grammatically coordinated by some coordinating term or a coordinating punctuation mark, such as 'but' or 'while'. (9) and (10) each consist of two statements grammatically co-ordinated by a coordinating term, 'because' in (9) and 'or' in (10), yet neither is a logical conjunction.

9. John went to the store **because** Bill stayed home.
10. John went to the store **or** Bill stayed home.

So why are (1)–(8) logical conjunctions, but (9) and (10) not? Each of (1)–(8) is true just in case both of its component statements (a left and a right conjunct) are true: if both components are true, the complex statement must be true as well, and if the complex statement is true, both components must be true. (9) and (10), however, do not stand in this relationship to their components. On the one hand, suppose it is true that John went to the store and it is true that Bill stayed home. It still needn't be true that John went to the store *because* Bill stayed home. So the truth of the components in (9) is insufficient to establish the truth of (9). On the other hand, if (10) is true, it doesn't follow that it is true that John went to the store and it is true that Bill stayed home. So the truth of (10) is insufficient in this case to establish the truth of its components.

We seem to have isolated what's essential to logical conjunctions:

> **A statement θ is a logical conjunction just in case from the truth of its component statements α and β the truth of θ follows; and from the truth of θ, the truth of α and β follows.**

The accompanying table codifies this information:

α	β	α conjoined β
T	T	T
F	T	F
T	F	F
F	F	F

Each horizontal row represents a possible circumstance. The first row represents the circumstance under which statement α is true and statement β is true. Under this circumstance, the logical conjunction is also true. So the logical conjunction 'The Yankees won the pennant in 1981, and the Mets did not win the pennant in 1981' is true, because its two components, 'The Yankees won the pennant in 1981' and 'The Mets did not win the pennant in 1981', are both true. The second row represents the circumstance under which α is false and β is true. Under this circumstance the conjunction is false. So the conjunction 'The Yankees won the World Series in 1981, and the Mets did not win the pennant in 1981' is false, because one component 'The Yankees won the World Series in 1981' is false, even though the other is true. And so on for the remaining two cases.

3.2   Distinguishing Deductive from Conversational Aspects of Conjunction

(1)–(8) make clear that logical conjunctions can be expressed in various ways, not only by 'and' but also by 'but', 'though', and 'yet', and even by unspoken punctuation. Reflection on 'but' and 'yet' is instructive, for it elicits a distinction between deductive and what we might call, by way of contrast, conversationally implicative aspects of language.

We are likely to say (11) instead of (12) or (13) owing to the contrast between being part of and not being part of.

11.   Sicily is part of Italy, but San Marino is not.
12.   Sicily is part of Italy, and San Marino is not.
13.   Sicily is part of Italy, yet San Marino is not.

But the sort of circumstances under which (1)–(8) are true are the same as those under which (11)–(13) are true. All are true just in case the two component statements are true, regardless of whether 'and', 'but', 'yet', or any of the other conjunctive expressions is used. All are logical conjunctions. The difference in meaning between 'and' and 'but' and 'yet' is conversational, not logical; 'but' and 'yet' are typically used to express a contrasting relationship. In the second conjunct of (11) and (13), the term 'not' establishes the contrast; 'but' and 'yet' prepare the reader for it, but 'not' does the work. For this reason, 'but' and 'yet' are eliminable; a semicolon would do. Therefore, if someone infers (14) on the basis of hearing a speaker utter (13), the inference is conversational and not deductive.

14.   It is surprising that Sicily is part of Italy and San Marino is not.

In order to see that the presumed deductive inference from (13) to (14) is not deductively valid, notice that the inference is *cancelable* in this sense: what's being inferred can be explicitly denied without contradiction. That is to say, there is nothing contradictory in asserting (15).

15. Sicily is part of Italy, yet San Marino is not, and there is nothing surprising about this.

This means that (13) can be true and (14) false; that is, the inference is deductively invalid.

This distinction between conversational and deductive implicative features will crop up again and again throughout this book as we encounter further examples of the assimilation of diverse expressions of ordinary language to our uniform logical notation.

3.3   Phrasal Logical Conjunctions

The characterization of logical conjunction in §3.1, as stated, excludes certain statements that many logicians would want to classify as logical conjunctions, for example:

16. John **cut and raked** the lawn.   (conjoined main verbs)
17. John **was and will** be here.   (conjoined auxiliary verbs)
18. John speaks **quickly and quietly**.   (conjoined adverbs)
19. John cut **the grass and the hedge**.   (conjoined objects)
20. **John and Bill** are tall.   (conjoined subjects)

Much of grammar consists of devices for shortening and compacting locutions. In (16) two verbs are coordinated to make one complex main verb; in (17), two auxiliary verbs; in (18), two adverbs; in (19), two objects; and in (20), two subjects. Why should we treat (16)–(20) as logical conjunctions? Suppose (16) were true, then (21) and (22) would be true too.

21. John cut the lawn.
22. John raked the lawn.

Conversely, if (21) and (22) were both true, (16) would be as well. Similar arguments can be constructed for (17)–(20). Even though (16)–(20) are not logical conjunctions by our characterization of logical conjunction (since (16)–(20) do not consist of two component statements conjoined by another expression), each has this same special feature: that each can be taken to express independent statements such that if these were true, the original statement would be true also, and vice versa.

3.4   Series Decompounding

It is generally assumed that conjuncts need not be restricted to two component statements. (23) is a logical conjunction, but it conjoins five statements.

23.   Joy, Bill, Frank, Harry, and George went to the store.

It can be decompounded into (24).

24.   Joy went to the store, **and** Bill went to the store, **and** Frank went to the store, **and** Harry went to the store, **and** George went to the store.

   In general, statements containing multiply conjoined verbs, auxiliaries, subjects, objects, and adverbs can be decompounded into logical conjunctions.

3.5   Using 'Respectively'

Statement (25) is a logical conjunction, and it should be analyzed into components (26) and (27).

25.   Philip and Bill passed and failed respectively.
26.   Philip passed.
27.   Bill failed.

   In general, a statement of form (28) is decomposable into conjuncts (29) and (30) (where 'α' and 'β' are metalinguistic variables (see §2.3) ranging in this case over noun phrases and 'Γ' and 'Δ' are metalinguistic variables ranging in this case over verbs).

28.   α and β Γ-ed and Δ-ed respectively.
29.   α Γ-ed
30.   β Δ-ed

3.6   Symbolizing Logical Conjunctions

So far we have introduced one type of symbol: capital letters for simple statements. With this type of symbol we could symbolize (31) as (32),

31.   John went to the store, and Bill left for school.
32.   W and L

where 'W' and 'L' represent the simple statements 'John went to the store' and 'Bill left for school' respectively.[1]

We now introduce a symbol of another type for logical conjunction. The conjunction symbol is '&' (the ampersand).[2] Accordingly, we symbolize (31) as (33),

33.   W & L

(34) is symbolized as (35)

34.   John, Bill, and Mary left.
35.   J & B & M

where 'J', 'B', and 'M' represent 'John left', 'Bill left', and 'Mary left' respectively.

Logical conjunctions   Exercise 3.1

- Symbolize (1)–(16). This exercise involves the following steps:

  - First, decide whether a statement is ambiguous.
  - If it is, symbolize its alternative readings.
  - Secondly, decide whether each statement is a logical conjunction or a simple statement. Determining which statements in ordinary language are logical conjunctions is not purely mechanical. Each statement must be considered in its own right, and careful attention must be paid to its context.
  - If you deem a statement to be a logical conjunction, state its conjuncts, introducing a dictionary whereby I mean associating a distinct simple statement letter with each simple statement type.

1. Hercules will arrive tomorrow, and he is quite strong.
2. John and Bill ate meat and fish respectively.
3. Michael Jordan is first in scoring, the Pistons are first in defense, and the Lakers are first in offense.
4. A 55 mile per hour speed limit could save more lives, but getting drunk drivers off the road could save even more.
5. He aims for the naked truth and hits the nation's jugular.
6. Simon is very happily, and Bill miserably, married.
7. John judged him to be awkward but acceptable.
8. John and Bill like to tease their respective wives.
9. He saw an old and an orange house.
10. Mary is beautiful but strong.
11. Enjoy your achievements as well as your plans.
12. Nick trimmed, and Bill weeded, the garden.
13. John liked it, while others panned it.
14. Pro- and anti- forces were at work.
15. Some are born great, some achieve greatness, and some have greatness thrust upon them.
16. Fred Astaire both sang and danced.

Now that you have completed exercise 3.1, let's test your skill for symbolizing logical conjunctions on (36)–(41).

36. Romeo loves Juliet, and Juliet loves Romeo.
37. Romeo and Juliet are lovers.

38. Tom moved the piano, and William moved the piano.
39. Tom and William moved the piano.

40. The red flag is on the pole, and the blue flag is on the pole.
41. The red and blue flag is on the pole.

Did you automatically try to symbolize (36)–(41) as (36′)–(41′) respectively?

36′. R & J   R: Romeo loves Juliet; J: Juliet loves Romeo.
37′. R & J

38'. T & W
> T: Tom moved the piano; W: William moved the piano.

39'. T & W

40'. R & B
> R: The red flag is on the pole; B: The blue flag is on the pole.

41'. R & B

If you mechanically symbolized (36)–(41) in this way, thinking that (37), (39), and (41) are straightforward logical conjunctions like (36), (38), and (40), you were too hasty. Although our purpose is to provide a mechanical way of detecting whether arguments are deductively valid or invalid, the process of symbolizing statements into the notation of PL does not lend itself to purely mechanical transformation. You need to think about the meaning of the statement you are symbolizing. The mere appearance of 'and' or some other coordinating conjunction or similar expression does not guarantee that the elements which are joined together are explicit or tacit conjuncts of a logical conjunction.

> **A chief aim of this book is to establish convincingly that language resists simple formula symbolization.**

Let's now give brief consideration to the problems related to symbolizing (37), (39), and (41). Despite the superficial appearance of (37), some logicians believe that the statement is not a logical conjunction, because the truth of (42) and (43) follows from the truth of (37), but the truth of (37) does *not* follow from the truth of (42) and (43).

42. Romeo is a lover.
43. Juliet is a lover.

From (42) and (43) it does not follow that Romeo and Juliet love *each other*. The main idea behind this criticism is that whatever parts (37) divides into do not 'add up' to the whole. The contents of (42) and (43) combined do not yield the content of (37). If this is a sound criticism, it means that 'and' is ambiguous in English. (For further discussion, see §A1.1.)

Like (37), (39) has a compound subject. Many writers contend that (39) is ambiguous between distributive and collective readings.

39. Tom and William moved the piano.

On one reading, its collective reading, (39) is alleged to mean that Tom and William did something *together*, and on another reading, the distributive reading, that they did something *separately*. If (39) means the same as (44), then (39) is not a logical conjunction.

44.   Tom and William moved the piano **together**.

From the truth of (44), the truth of (45) and (46) may follow, but from the combined truth of (45) and (46), the truth of (44) does not follow.

45.   Tom moved the piano.
46.   William moved the piano.

Therefore, (39) is not a logical conjunction on interpretation (44).

What about on the second reading? Suppose (39) paraphrases (any of) (47)–(49).

47.   Tom and William moved the piano **separately**.
48.   Tom and William **each** moved the piano.
49.   Both Tom and William moved the piano **alone**.

Is (39) then a logical conjunction? Can we in general say that if a compound subject, or more generally any phrasal conjunction, takes the reading with 'each', 'separately', or 'alone', then it is a logical conjunction? It seems not. From the truth of any of (47)–(49), the truth of (50) and (51) follows, but (47)–(49) cannot correctly interpret (39), since from the truth of (39), the truth of (50) and (51) does not follow.

50.   Tom moved the piano alone.
51.   William moved the piano alone.

The problem is that (39) all by itself is neutral between whether Tom and William worked as a team or solo. (For more discussion, see §A1.2.)

Next, consider (41), in which prenominal adjectives are conjoined by 'and'.

41.   The red and blue flag is on the pole.

On the basis of (41), we have no reason to believe (52) or (53).

52. The red flag is on the pole.
53. The blue flag is on the pole.

On the basis of (41), we do not even have reason to believe that there is a red or a blue flag. Similarly, on the basis of (52) and (53) together, we have no reason to believe that there is a red and blue flag on the pole. (For more discussion, see §A1.3.)

These examples should suffice to show you that you need to think before you symbolize. Here are some tips. Be especially careful when you encounter the following kinds of constructions:

Compounds: Coordinating conjunctions like 'and' are often used to economize on the number of sentences used to express thoughts. This compression or integration of two or more sentences into one sentence can be achieved by conjoining parts of sentences like nouns, verbs, adjectives, adverbs, and phrases into compounds. (37), (39), and (41) are examples. As elegant and mature as such compression might be stylistically, meaning can be changed in the process. Attempts to decompound joined parts into an explicit conjunction comprised of two or more simple statements sometimes fail.

Idioms: By general agreement, idioms are expressions that have generally accepted meanings which do not correspond to the literal meaning of the terms used to form them. Since idioms take on meanings that are not standard, you should be cautious when symbolizing them in PL. The idiom 'John wined and dined Bill' is not a logical conjunction. But the problem is not merely that the statement includes a compound verb. This idiomatic expression does not in any sense mean that John wined Bill or that John committed an act of cannibalism with respect to Bill. The idiomatic expression as used in this statement means: 'John treated Bill lavishly', a simple statement.

Quantifiers: Quantifier expressions contain quantity terms like 'all' and 'some'. There does not seem to be any obvious way of decompounding (54) into (55) and (56), which together encompass its meaning.

54. Some planes stop in Chicago and Detroit.
55. Some planes stop in Chicago.
56. Some planes stop in Detroit.

(55) and (56) could be true even though no plane stops in both Chicago and Detroit. So the truth of (54) does not logically follow from the truth of (55) and (56), if (54) is taken to mean, as it usually is, that some planes stop in *both* Chicago and Detroit. The problem here has to do with what is called the 'scope' of the quantifier 'some'. Scope is discussed in detail in chapters 5, 10, and 14.

An attempt to give an exhaustive list of language constructions that can frustrate straightforward symbolization in PL would probably be futile, and none is offered here. In addition, no attempt is made here to help students determine how to symbolize such problem locutions correctly. Such questions have been, or still are, matters of debate among professional logicians and are beyond the scope of an introductory course. But if you are motivated to learn more about these discussions and about logicians' proposals for treating problematic constructions related to conjunction, see §A1 and the bibliography at the end of this chapter.

Although you may not know how to symbolize statements correctly in all cases, you are expected to think about what you are trying to symbolize. If you practice asking yourself what a sentence means before you attempt to symbolize it, you will form a good habit of thought. Once you have ventured a symbolization, ask yourself whether it adequately captures the meaning of the statement. The habit of checking your symbolic notation against the English version will likewise avert many errors. However, on occasion you will discover that you are unable to find a way of symbolizing an English statement in PL without compromising its meaning. Your recognizing that a statement resists a straightforward rendering in PL is as important as finding a correct symbolization, especially if you can explain why different symbolizations that you might naturally attempt nevertheless fail to do justice to the English statement. Keep in mind that some English statements resist even the best efforts of professional logicians.

Exercise 3.2   Logical conjunctions

- Which of (1)–(30) are logical conjunctions?
- If a statement is a logical conjunction, state its conjuncts.
- If a statement is ambiguous, cite its different readings.
- If a statement is a logical conjunction under a certain reading, determine what its conjuncts are under that reading.

(Consulting §A1 will help with this exercise.)

1. Danny went into a lengthy psychological analysis of Willy Loman's delusions and talked about how crucial it was to be able to distinguish between reality and fantasy.
2. Oedipus and Jocasta are a small team.
3. Jan and Mary are married. (Suppose Jan is married to Mary. Then we know that Mary must be married to Jan. So there is an interesting question about whether there is any reason to treat statements with symmetric predicates in them, like 'married', as logical conjunctions. See §A1.6 for further discussion.)
4. No barber gives any customer both a shave and a haircut.
5. Dale and Roy debated.
6. John and Bill left together.
7. John and Bill are brothers.
8. A man and a woman married yesterday.
9. John and Bill got in on one ticket.
10. Lines A and B are parallel.
11. John and Bill are cousins.
12. Red and blue flags are on the pole.
13. No one but you can come to my party.
14. I like no one but Bill.
15. I like no one except Bill.
16. Mary and Jane jointly bought a dress.
17. I believe that Bill and Mary will be there.
18. John and Mary sang, and they danced too.
19. Post- and pre-modern art is always interesting.
20. A few cities were mentioned, and I wanted to give the name of one, but it escaped me, although I know I spent two very pleasant days there.
21. He saw not John but Bill.
22. Bacon and eggs is a popular American breakfast.
23. Omar does nothing but smoke hashish and play the flute.
24. I live between 10th and 11th.
25. Of Frank and Bill, Bill is faster.
26. Mary's dress is black and white.
27. Bill and Frank are twins.
28. Dana and David were tied for second place.
29. Both boys didn't leave.
30. The members of congress are Republicans and Democrats.

Notes

1   It does not matter what statement letter is used in symbolizing statements, but for the purposes of easy identification the general practice is to choose the initial letter of a prominent expression – e.g., the first letter of the main verb or the subject.
2   In other books, you may find other symbols being used for logical conjunction – e.g., '∧', '+', and '·'.

Bibliography

Lakoff, George and Peters, Stanley, 'Phrasal Conjunction and Symmetric Predicates', in D. Reibel and S. Schane (eds), *Modern Studies in English* (Englewood Cliffs, NJ: Prentice-Hall, 1969), 113–42.

Massey, Gerald J., 'Tom, Dick and Harry, and All the King's Men', *American Philosophical Quarterly* 13 (1976), 89–107.

Schmerling, Susan F., 'Asymmetric Conjunction and Rules of Conversation', in P. Cole and J. Morgan (eds), *Syntax and Semantics 3: Speech Acts* (New York: Academic Press, 1975), 211–32.

4

Negation

4.1 Logical Negation

Another type of complex statement is logical negation. Negations are sometimes formed in English by prefacing a statement with the expression 'It is not the case that'.

1. It is not the case that Lorenzo Medici is Richard Nixon.

But comparatively few negations in English begin with this expression. More commonly, negations have the word 'not' inserted somewhere in the statement one or more times, as in (2)–(4).

2. Lorenzo Medici is **not** Richard Nixon.
3. Dishonesty is **not** morally acceptable.
4. The British will **not** leave Northern Ireland.

A negation may also involve a contraction, as in (5)–(6).

5. Lorenzo Medici is**n't** Richard Nixon.
6. The British wo**n't** leave Northern Ireland.

Negative words other than 'not' may also express negation, as in (7)–(10).

7. **It is false that** dishonesty is morally acceptable.
8. Notre Dame is **un**beatable.
9. It's **im**possible to buy a cheap car.
10. Clinton is **un**convinced.

Why are (1)–(10) all logical negations? In each, some statement is denied. For example, each of (1), (2), and (5) denies (11).

11.   Lorenzo Medici is Richard Nixon.

From the truth of (11), the falsity of (1), (2), and (5) follow; and from the falsity of (1), (2), or (5), the truth of (11) follows. More generally:

> **A statement θ is a logical negation just in case it is analyzable into a component statement α such that θ is true if and only if α is false.**

So, for example, (1), (2), and (5) are all logical negations because each can be analyzed into a component statement (11), such that each of the former is true if and only if (11) is false. (3) is also a logical negation because its component statement 'Dishonesty is morally acceptable' is false if and only if (3) is true. (8) is also a logical negation, since, if we remove the prefix 'un-' from 'unbeatable', the resultant statement 'Notre Dame is beatable' is false if and only if (8) is true.

The following table codifies this information:

α	θ
T	F
F	T

(where θ is the negation of α). Since each negation denies a single statement, this table requires only two rows: one represents the circumstance under which the negated statement is true, and the other represents the circumstance under which it is false.

4.2   Some Other Negative Expressions

Each of (12)–(17) contains a negative expression: 'no one', 'nothing', 'none', 'nowhere', 'nobody', and 'never'.

12.   No one has three arms.
13.   Nothing matters.
14.   None of his friends came.

15. John was nowhere to be found.
16. Nobody loves me.
17. The IRS never leaves me alone.

What, if anything, is each of (12)–(17) denying? In order to find out, we might try adopting a convention. Suppose we try to adopt for 'none' a convention that replaces it with 'not everyone'. This convention deems (14) the negation of (18).

18. Every one of his friends came.

But (14) does not deny (18); they are not *contradictories*. Two statements contradict each other just in case if one of the statements is true, the other is false, and if one of the statements is false, the other is true. 'John died' and 'John did not die' are contradictories. Statements (14) and (18) are, instead, *contraries*. Two statements are contraries just in case they cannot both be true (even though both may be false). 'Most people left' and 'Few people left' are contraries. They can't both be true, but they might both be false. Maybe exactly half the people left.

Suppose only some, but not all, of his friends came? Then both (14) and (18) are false. What you should recognize is that (14) denies (19), not (18).

19. Some of his friends came.

Since (19) is what (14) negates, let's adopt the convention that an adequate replacement for 'none' is 'not some'. Similar arguments would justify the following conventions:

Replace 'no one' with 'not someone'.
Replace 'nothing' with 'not something'.
Replace 'nowhere' with 'not somewhere'.
Replace 'nobody' with 'not somebody'.
Replace 'never' with 'not ever' (or just 'not').

Accordingly, (12)–(17) are the negations of (20)–(25) respectively.

20. Someone has three arms.
21. Something matters.
22. Some (one) of his friends came.

23. John was somewhere to be found.
24. Somebody loves me.
25. The IRS (sometimes) leaves me alone.

The key idea is that expressions like 'nobody' and 'somebody' are, speaking loosely, contradictories. They deny each other. But 'nobody' and 'everybody' are only contraries. They can't be true together, but they don't deny each other. Other negative expressions can be similarly treated.

4.3 A Point about Methodology

One of our goals is to devise a set of practices for correctly representing English statements in PL. Different conventions might be adequate because they too satisfy that goal. However, in order to standardize procedures, we will adopt the conventions recommended here, not only because they work adequately, but because they are natural and customary. In doing so, we are adopting the customary decision from within the class of acceptable choices.

4.4 A Point on Ambiguity

Ordinarily, prefacing (20)–(25) with 'It is not the case that' will issue in a paraphrase of (12)–(17) respectively. However, in certain contexts, a change in inflection or emphasis can also change meaning. When focal stress is placed on 'one', (22) prefaced by 'It is not the case that' means (26).

26. Many of his friends came.

Similarly, focal stress on 'somebody' in (24) prefaced by 'It is not the case that' produces a reading which means (27).

27. Many people love me.

Such focal stress has the effect of denying that just one of his friends came.

4.5 Symbolizing Logical Negations

We now introduce a symbol for logical negation. The negation symbol is '~' (the tilde).[1] Accordingly, we symbolize (28) as (29),

28. It is not true that the Yankees stink.
29. ~Y

where 'Y' represents the simple statement 'The Yankees stink'.
   (30) is symbolized as the double negation (31),

30. Notre Dame is not unbeatable.
31. ~ ~B

where 'B' represents 'Notre Dame is beatable'.

4.6 Ambiguity and the Need for Groupers

One thing we must avoid in symbolizing statements in PL is ambiguity. One source of ambiguity is punctuation. The failure to punctuate sentences correctly can produce unclarity as to the meaning of a sentence. For example, (32) is ambiguous.

32. It is not true that Bill is tall and Frank is tall.

(32) might mean that Bill is not tall and Frank is tall, or it might mean that it is not the case that both Bill and Frank are tall. We want to *disambiguate* (32) in PL. To avoid ambiguity, each statement of a logical system should have one and only one meaning. To this end, we introduce groupers – the left and the right parentheses – '(' and ')'. This strategy will be familiar from mathematics. '2 + 5 × 7' is ambiguous. To disambiguate such formulas, mathematicians use parentheses to group expressions together. Depending on the placement of the parentheses, '2 + 5 × 7' means '(2 + 5) × 7', which equals '49', or it means '2 + (5 × 7)', which equals '37'. Punctuation makes a difference.
   Using parentheses, logicians can disambiguate too. (32) can be disambiguated to read either as (33) or as (34).

33.   ~(B & F)   B: Bill is tall; F: Frank is tall
34.   ~B & F

(33) is a negation of a conjunction of two simple statements. It means that at least one of the two men is not tall, perhaps both. (34), however, is a conjunction of a negation of a simple statement and another simple statement. It means that Bill is not tall, but Frank is. As you can see, in logical notation punctuation also makes a difference.

4.7   Review of Symbols

A, B, C, D, . . . , Z   Simple statements
&, ~   Logical connectives: conjunction, negation
(,)   Groupers

Exercise 4.1   **Logical negation and conjunction**

- Using (1) and (2) as paradigms, symbolize (3)–(18) in the language of PL. This involves the following steps:
- First, decide whether the statement is ambiguous.
- If it is, symbolize its distinct readings.
- Secondly, decide whether a statement is a negation, a conjunction, or a simple statement.
- This exercise requires introducing a dictionary, which in turn involves introducing a simple statement letter for each simple statement.
- Use groupers, when necessary, for complex statements.

   1. Today is the 394th day of captivity, and the hostages are not to be released in the near future.
       Symbolization: T & ~R
       T: Today is the 394th day of captivity; R: The hostages are to be released in the near future.
   2. It is not true that John got an 'A' in logic.
       Symbolization: ~J
       J: John got an 'A' in logic.
   3. John stayed at home all day, and so did Mary.

4. John could not solve the problem, and none of his friends could either.
5. John could not go, and neither could Mary.
6. He has never been on time to a meeting.
7. He did not see anyone he knew.
8. He has not ever been on time to a meeting.
9. No one read the book.
10. The book was not read by anyone.
11. None of his students understands.
12. That Jack ever slept here is impossible.
13. He doesn't go to church at the university.
14. This struck me as unintelligible, and I did not need to know further particulars.
15. I was unaware at the time.
16. My story is not unknown.
17. Paranoid people are not rare and are more dangerous than useful.
18. This is not all Frank offers.

4.8 Using 'Without'

The word 'without' carries with it a negative connotation. When we use it, we seem to be denying something. For example, (36) paraphrases (35).

35. I will do logic without taking the tests.
36. I will do logic, but I will **not** take the tests.

This paraphrase recommends treating (35) as a conjunction with the right conjunct being a negation. So letting 'L' symbolize 'I will do logic' and 'T' symbolize 'I will take the tests', we symbolize both (35) and (36) as (37).

37. L & ~T

However, this strategy does not work for the statement 'Without going to the store, John can't eat dinner tonight'. This statement is best understood as an 'if, then' statement, rather than a conjunction. (More on this in chapter 7.) So we cannot introduce a simple uniform convention to the effect that 'without' means 'and not'.

4.9   Argument Forms Continued

In chapters 3 and 4, we have been distinguishing two types of complex statements, logical conjunctions and negations, and we have learned how to symbolize statements having one or other of these types in the notation of PL. Since arguments are sets of statements with one of the statements being the conclusion and the others being premises, we now have some tools for symbolizing arguments in the language of PL.

Some additional conventions need to be adopted, however. For every statement, there should be one and only one symbolization. In this way every statement in an argument represented in the language of PL will be uniquely identified, so no confusions should occur. To accomplish this task, each simple statement type in an argument must be labeled with one and only one simple statement letter type, which will be used to represent that simple statement throughout the symbolized argument in the language of PL. In this way, each simple statement type is symbolized by a simple statement letter type that is unique to it.

There is what might appear to be an exception to the rule that every statement should be represented by a single symbolization. Sometimes we find two statements, both a premise and the conclusion, expressed in the same English sentence. Consider (38) and (39).

38.   I hit him, **since** he asked for it.
39.   We will win the game, **because** our team is better conditioned.

The expressions 'since' and 'because' both can indicate (recall from §1.1.2) a premise. But within the same sentence there is also a conclusion. So, since premises and conclusion need to be separated in argument form, we will treat these English sentences as making two statements (and more, since it also asserts a logical connection between them). In (38), 'He asked for it' is the premise, indicated by the fact that it is introduced by 'since', and 'I hit him' is the conclusion. This argument is as follows:

He asked for it.
So, I hit him.

In (39), 'Our team is better conditioned' is the premise, and 'We will win the game' is the conclusion, with the argument being:

Our team is better conditioned.
So, we will win the game.

(Note that both these arguments are deductively invalid. Neither conclusion follows from its premise.)

We turn now to a more complicated argument. Consider argument (40).

40. Diego was not in both Italy and Switzerland. He was in Switzerland, so he was not in Italy.

Before symbolizing a passage, you must first decide whether the passage is trying to persuade you of something. Is there a conclusion being inferred on the basis of some reasons presented in the passage? In (40), we are led to conclude that Diego was not in Italy. Why? The conclusion indicator 'so' tips us off. The passage tells us that he was not in both Italy and Switzerland and that he was in Switzerland. On this basis the conclusion that Diego was not in Italy follows deductively.

How should we symbolize (40)? Letting 'I' stand for 'Diego was in Italy' and 'S' for 'Diego was in Switzerland', it is correct to represent (40) in PL as (41).[2]

41.   ~(I & S), S ∴ ~I

Is (41) deductively valid? Its first premise is a negation of a conjunction, so we know from the truth table for the negation that this premise can be true only if what it negates is false. Since what it negates is a conjunction, we know from the truth table for the conjunction that what's negated is false just in case at least one (maybe both) of its conjuncts is false. However, the second premise asserts that one of the conjuncts, 'S', is true, so we can infer that the second conjunct, 'I', must be false; hence its negation '~I' must be true, which is the conclusion. So the argument is deductively valid.

In the next chapter we will go through this again, more slowly and precisely. At this stage I merely want to give you a taste for how one might proceed in evaluating an argument with respect to its deductive validity.

Exercise 4.2   **Arguments**

- Symbolize arguments (1)–(3) in PL, following all the above instructions.
- Be sure to include a dictionary for simple statements.

1. Kennedy, Johnson, and Nixon were all presidents. It is not true that Kennedy and Mondale were both presidents. So, it is also not the case that Nixon and Mondale were both presidents.
2. Notre Dame is clearly not unbeatable, since they are clearly beatable.
3. I will do logic without taking tests. So, I am not taking tests.

4.10 Symbolizing Logical Negations Continued

Now that you have been taught how to symbolize logical negations, try symbolizing each of (42)–(47).

42. It's false that some dogs are fuzzy.
43. Some dogs are not fuzzy.
44. John didn't see Mary leave.
45. John saw Mary not leave.
46. It's not true that John is particularly competent at fixing cars.
47. John is particularly incompetent at fixing cars.

If you automatically came up with answers like (42′)–(47′), thinking that (43), (45), and (47) are straightforward negations like (42), (44), and (46), you were mistaken.

42′.	~D	D: Some dogs are fuzzy.
43′.	~D	
44′.	~M	M: John saw Mary leave.
45′.	~M	
46′.	~C	C: John is particularly competent at fixing cars.
47′.	~C	

What are the problems raised by trying to symbolize (43), (45), and (47) in PL? Suppose we try to analyze (43) as the logical negation (42). (42) is the denial of (48).

48. Some dogs are fuzzy.

But (43) is *not* the denial of (48), since both statements can be true together. In general, if we try to analyze a statement with a quantifier expression (like 'some', 'all', 'every', 'many', 'most', and 'few') that precedes a negative expression (as in (43)), we change the meaning of the statement if we treat it as a logical negation. (For a more thorough discussion of this topic, it is first necessary to learn about quantifiers (chapters 9–15) and also about scope (chapters 5, 10, and 13); for still further elaboration, see §A2 as well.) So, from the point of view of PL, (43) is a simple statement.

(45) presents us with a different sort of problem. (45) seems to say that John saw Mary *refrain* from leaving, or stay; but from the fact that John did not see Mary leave, it does not follow that he saw her stay. He might not have seen her leave because he wasn't there. But, in order to see her refrain from leaving, his eyes must have been on her.

The difference between the logical negation (44) and (45) is an instance of a general phenomenon concerning negative words and phrases within the scope of various psychological and perceptual verbs like 'saw'. (49)–(51) are also not logical negations.

49. Harry wants Bill not to leave.
50. Harry believes that Mary didn't hurt Bill.
51. Harry promises not to come.

Each statement ascribes to Harry a psychological state with a negative content: in (49) a desire for Bill not to leave, in (50) a belief that Mary did not hurt Bill, and in (51) a promise not to come. These claims are different from those that Harry would make if he were merely to deny that he had a want or a belief or had made a promise. From 'It is not the case that Harry wants Bill to leave', you cannot deductively infer that Harry wants Bill not to leave. Harry could be merely neutral about whether Bill leaves or stays. By disconnecting the negative expression 'not' from the object of the verb in which it is embedded ('Bill not to leave') and then expressing negation up front at the start of (49), you are changing the meaning of the statement. So, from the point of view of PL, (45) and (49)–(51) are all simple statements.

Turning now to (47), why is it not a logical negation like (46)? We first note that some negative particles, mostly prefixes, fuse with the expressions to which they attach themselves. Excising them can change the meaning of the statement. John may not be particularly competent at fixing cars, but from this it does not follow that he is particularly *in*competent at doing so. He may be somewhere in between. The point is that 'incompetent' means not merely 'not competent', but in fact 'particularly deficient'. Other negative particles can have the same effect, as with 'ir-' in '**ir**rational' and 'un-' in '**un**lucky' and '**un**happy'. But if (47) is not a logical negation, how then should we represent it in PL? In PL (47) is treated as a simple statement.[3]

These examples suffice to establish a general point: You cannot simply remove or extract a negated word, phrase, or particle and expect that what remains is a statement which the original statement denied. To repeat what I emphasized at the end of chapter 3:

> **A chief aim of this book is to establish convincingly that language resists simple formula symbolizations.**

You need to be careful in symbolizing English in PL, particularly when you spot negative terms embedded in a sentence. You cannot automatically negate statements by pulling out the negative expressions in them and substituting for these expressions 'It is not the case' as an introduction to the sentence you are symbolizing. Sometimes putting a negative expression up front will work; sometimes not. When you fall back on the natural inclination to express negation by repositioning a negative expression embedded in a sentence, you need to ask yourself whether you are retaining the meaning of the original. Continue to follow the tips in §3.6.[4]

Exercise 4.3   **Complex statements**

- Symbolize (1)–(31) in PL.
- Include a dictionary.

1. Some of his students did not understand.
2. That Jack ever slept here is unlikely.
3. The solution must not be obvious.
4. John is unhappy about something.
5. He saw nothing of interest in it.

6. John dislikes having to tell anyone what to do.
7. I will force you to marry no one (ambiguous).
8. No one had nothing to eat.
9. It isn't often that he really *doesn't* understand.
10. Half the country doesn't like Clinton.
11. On the whole, I am not *dissatisfied* with myself.
12. John doesn't leave school at 3 o'clock.
13. Until Bill leaves, Frank cannot pay.
14. You cannot stay up until midnight.
15. John is *disabled*.
16. This is not all Frank offers.
17. It was *unknown* to me.
18. It was an *uncommon* experience.
19. *Unhappy* inmates escape.
20. Many of the boys didn't leave.
21. Not many of the boys left.
22. Happy boys didn't leave.

(In (23)–(26) the position of the negative particle with respect to the adverb influences meaning.)

23. He really doesn't understand.
    (He doesn't really understand.)
24. He doesn't really like her.
    (It is not the case that he really likes her.)
25. He hasn't often paid taxes.
26. He often hasn't paid taxes.

((27) is ambiguous. What are its different interpretations?)

27. John doesn't beat his wife because he loves her.
28. I don't think John will arrive until Tuesday.
29. John doesn't leave school until 3 o'clock.

(The logical properties of (29) are not easy to discern. If it's a negation, which statement is it denying?)

30. Both John and Bill didn't go.
31. John and Bill didn't go.

Notes

1   In other books, you may find other symbols being used for logical negation
    – e.g., '−', and '¬'.
2   The symbol '∴' represents 'therefore' or 'so' or 'hence' or any other manner
    of indicating that here comes the conclusion.
3   This point doesn't mean that prefixes like 'in-' in 'incompetent' play no
    negative role. English is compositional. Idioms aside, the meaning of its
    grammatically complex expressions is a function of their grammatical struc-
    tures together with the meanings of their grammatical constituents. There-
    fore, unless we intend to treat 'incompetent' as idiomatic, we will at some
    point need to assign some logical role to 'in-' (if we maintain that this
    negative prefix makes a difference to which logical relations statements par-
    ticipate in). (Further discussion is deferred until chs 9 and 14.)
4   A slightly more detailed discussion of quantification and negation (and mo-
    dality and negation) are presented in §A2. That discussion is far short of
    exhaustive. It may be more useful to read it only after being introduced to
    the notions of scope and quantification in later chapters. See bibliography
    below as well.

Bibliography

Atlas, J., 'Negation, Ambiguity, and Presupposition', *Linguistics and Philosophy*
    1 (1977), 321–36.
Baker, C. L., 'Double Negatives', *Linguistic Inquiry* 1 (1970), 169–86.
Frege, G., 'Negation' (1919), in P. T. Geach and M. Black (eds). *Translations
    from the Philosophical Writings of Gottlob Frege* (Oxford: Basil Blackwell,
    1952), 117–35.
Gale, R. M., 'Negative Statements', *American Philosophical Quarterly* 7 (1970),
    206–17.
Horn, L. R., *A Natural History of Negation* (Chicago: University of Chicago
    Press, 1989).
Klima, E., 'Negation in English', in J. Fodor and J. Katz (eds), *The Structure of
    Language* (Englewood Cliffs, NJ: Prentice-Hall, 1964), 246–323.
Langendoen, D. T. and Bever, T. G., 'Can a Not Unhappy Person be Called a
    Not Sad One?', in S. Anderson and P. Kiparsky (eds), *A Festschrift for Morris
    Halle* (New York: Holt, 1973), 392–409.

5

Truth Tables

In chapters 3 and 4 you have begun to learn how to put arguments in English into the symbolic language of PL. You are now almost ready to take up the important task of evaluating these arguments for deductive validity; but before you can do this, you need to be introduced to some further preliminaries.

5.1   Well-formed Formulas

How many tokens of simple expressions are there in the PL statement (1)?

1.   (P & Q) & ~P

So far, you have been introduced to only three types (or kinds) of grammatical statements, or what we shall call *well-formed formulas* in PL: simple statements, logical conjunctions, and logical negations.[1] So, the question of how many occurrences (or tokens) of well-formed formulas of PL there are in (1) becomes that of how many occurrences of simple statements, logical conjunctions, and logical negations there are in (1). The correct answer is six: 'P' (twice), 'Q', '(P & Q)', '~P', and '(P & Q) & ~P'.

Bear in mind that '& ~P' is not a token of a well-formed formula of PL in (1), though it is a token of a formula. Rather, it is a token of an *ill-formed* formula. It is neither a logical conjunction, nor a logical negation, nor a simple statement letter.

Exercise 5.1   **Well-formed formulas**

- Which of (1)–(4) is a well-formed formula in PL?
- What kind of statements are they?
- For those that are well formed in PL, make up English statements which they might symbolize.

1. P & ~(T & (R & S))
2. ~T & ~R
3. ~(T & Q
4. ~& P Q

5.2 Scope

Now we can introduce the important notion of *scope*. The scope of a token of an expression is the shortest well-formed formula in which this expression occurs. For example, the scope of the sole token of '&' in (2) below is '(P & R)', since this is the shortest well-formed formula of PL in which this token of '&' occurs.

2.   ~(P & R)

'&' does occur in '& R', but '& R' is not a well-formed formula of PL, because it is not a simple statement letter; it is not a logical conjunction; and it is not a logical negation. '&' also occurs in the well-formed formula '~(P & R)', but this formula is not the shortest well-formed formula in PL in which '&' occurs, where the shortest is determined simply by counting tokens of symbols in the expression.

Given this characterization of the scope of a token of an expression in a well-formed formula, we can move on to the useful notion of *relative scope*. In (2) the sole token of '~' has **wider** scope than the sole token of '&'. The scope of the sole ampersand in (2) is a part of the scope of the tilde in (2). One formula is a proper part of another formula just in case it is fully contained in it.[2] Put more generally, the scope of a token of an expression α is *wider* than the scope of a token of an expression β

within some well-formed formula Γ just in case the scope of the said token of β is a proper part of the scope of the said token of α within the well-formed formula Γ.[3]

Since the scope of '&' in (2) is '(P & R)' (the shortest well-formed formula in which '&' occurs) and since the scope of '~' in (2) is all of (2), which includes '(P & R)', it follows by definition that the scope of '~' in (2) is wider than the scope of '&'. Put the other way around, we can also say that the scope of '&' is *narrower* than the scope of '~' in (2).

Scope   Exercise 5.2

1. What is the scope of the second token of '&' in '(P & Q) & (~R & T)'?
2. What is the scope of the first token of '~' in '~P & (Q & ~R)'?
3. What is the scope of the third token of '&' in '~(P & Q) & (R & ~S)'?

Relative scope   Exercise 5.3

•   Answer questions (1)–(4).

1. Does the first token of '&' have wider scope than the first token of '~' in '(~P & Q) & R'?
2. Does the second token of '&' have wider scope than the first token of '&' in '~(P & Q) & (R & ~S)'?
3. Which has wider scope, the first or third token of '&' in '(P & Q) & ~(R & S)'?
4. Does '~' have a narrower scope than the first token of '&' in '(P & ~R) & T'?

5.3 Main Connective

The **main connective** in a well-formed formula in PL is the connective with the widest scope. For example, the main connective in (2) is '~'.

2.   ~(P & R)

The main connective in (1) is the second token of '&'.

1.   (P & Q) & ~P

The main connective determines a statement's logical status. (2) is a logical negation, since its main connective is '~', and (1) is a logical conjunction, since its main connective is '&'.

Exercise 5.4   **Main connective**

- What is the main connective in each of (1)–(4)?

1.   (P & Q) & ~(R & ~R)
2.   ~ ~P
3.   ~(P & Q & R)
4.   P & ~(R & ~S)

5.4   Truth Tables

One of the chief concerns of this book is to devise methods for establishing whether a given statement does or does not follow deductively from some other statement(s). We are now ready to turn to this important task. Methods that issue in reliable verdicts about whether inferences are deductively valid vary. The method we shall develop here is the truth table method.[4] Before introducing this method, let us first review briefly some basic details about deductive validity and also explain why we need to move beyond merely relying on our intuitions about deductive validity to the more rigorous formal approach of the truth table method.

As we saw in chapter 1, some deductively valid arguments have true premises and a true conclusion; some have one or more false premises and a true conclusion; and some have one or more false premises and a false conclusion. The only scenario ruled out by our definition of deductive validity is an argument with true premises and a false conclusion. It is impossible for an argument to have both true premises *and* a false conclusion and be deductively valid. The following argument, though obviously uninteresting, is still deductively valid, because it is impossible both for its premises to be true and for its conclusion to be false.

All men are mortal.
Socrates is a man.
So, Socrates is mortal.

In other words, this argument is valid because it is impossible for both 'All men are mortal' and 'Socrates is a man' to be true, yet 'Socrates is mortal' to be false.

Often we can tell at a glance whether it is possible for both the premises of an argument to be true and its conclusion to be false. Consider argument (3)–(5).

3. Jimmy Carter has blue eyes.
4. Jimmy Carter weighs 200 pounds.
5. So, Jimmy Carter weighs 200 pounds.

As a matter of fact, Jimmy Carter does have blue eyes, and even though he is not a 200 pounder, it is surely possible that he continue to have blue eyes and weigh 200 pounds. He might, for example, go on an uncontrollable eating binge. But that's not our concern. Our concern is whether it is possible *both* for (3) and (4) to be true and yet (5) be false. It is not possible, because if (4) were true, obviously (5) would be too. They are tokens of the same type. So this argument is deductively valid.

Could premises (6) and (7) be true, yet the conclusion (8) be false?

6. If Ronald Reagan is 20 feet tall, his stride is 10 feet.
7. Ronald Reagan is 20 feet tall.
8. Therefore, he has a 10-foot stride.

What we need to know in order to establish the deductive validity of (6)–(8) is not whether the premises are possibly true, but only whether it is possible for (6) and (7) to be true and yet (8) be false. Could it be true that Reagan is 20 feet tall *and* also true that if he is 20 feet tall, that he has a 10-foot stride, *yet* it be false that he has a 10-foot stride? Obviously not. So (6)–(8) is deductively valid.

Since we have determined that the argument (6)–(8) is deductively valid, perhaps it is already becoming clear to you where we are going.

Consider next the argument (9)–(12). Is it possible for its premises (9)–(11) to be true, but its conclusion (12) to be false?

9. If the sun is not made of cheddar, then the moon is made of green cheese.
10. If the moon is made of green cheese, then the sun is made of cheddar.
11. Either the moon is or is not made of green cheese.
12. Hence, the sun is made of cheddar.

This is not so easy to figure out. The issue is not whether the premises could be true, but whether their truth would be compatible with the falsity of (12). If the answer is not intuitive for you, truth tables can help. We will begin by first discussing the notion of a truth table for a statement (§5.4.1), and then extend the notion to arguments (§5.4.2).

5.4.1   Truth Table Analyses of Statements

The operative principle in employing truth tables is that for every statement in which a connective ('~' or '&') occurs, we can decide whether that statement is true using a truth table alone, provided that we know the truth-values of its constituent simple statements alone. A logical conjunction is true just in case both conjuncts are true; and a negation is true just in case its unnegated counterpart is false. Combining the truth tables for conjunction and negation, we have:

α β	α & β	α ~α
T T	T	T F
F T	F	F T
T F	F	
F F	F	

According to these truth tables, (13) is false.

13. Lorenzo Medici died in 1492, but he did not know Sandro Botticelli.

Lorenzo Medici did as a matter of fact die in 1492, but he did know Sandro Botticelli. If 'M' symbolizes 'Lorenzo Medici died in 1492' and 'B' symbolizes 'Lorenzo Medici did know Sandro Botticelli', we correctly symbolize (13) in PL as 'M & ~B'. The truth-value for (13) is determined by the truth tables for negation and conjunction as follows:

14. M & ~ B
    T F F T

At this stage, rather than memorizing truth tables, concentrate on trying to understand how they are used to build more complicated truth tables for actual statements. If truth tables seem mysterious, don't panic! Understanding comes with practice. Let's try another. Consider statement (15).

15. Berlin is in Germany, but it's not the case both that Berlin is the capital of Germany and that London is the capital of England.

If 'G' symbolizes 'Berlin is in Germany', 'C' symbolizes 'Berlin is the capital of Germany', and 'E' symbolizes 'London is the capital of England', (15) is then correctly symbolized as (16).

16. G & ~(C & E)

What, then, are the logically possible truth-values for (16)? First, in order to exhaust every possible combination of truth and falsity for the simple statements that comprise (16), we need eight rows. The completed truth table for (16) is:

G C E	G &	~(C	& E)
T T T	F	F	T
F T T	F	F	T
T F T	T	T	F
F F T	F	T	F
T T F	T	T	F
F T F	F	T	F
T F F	T	T	F
F F F	F	T	F

The T's and F's in the first three columns are arranged systematically so that every possible combination of truth-values gets represented once, but no more than once. The first row in this table represents the possible circumstance under which all three simple statements tokened in (16) are true (the circumstance under which Berlin is in Germany, Berlin is the capital of Germany, and London is the capital of England). The second row represents the possible circumstance under which 'G' is false and both 'C' and 'E' are true; and so on until the last row, which represents the possible circumstance that Berlin is not in Germany and is not the capital of Germany, and London is not the capital of England.

Four points need to be made about this truth table and about truth tables for statements in general.

First, there is a combinatorial point: A truth table for n simple statements (where n is any natural number) requires 2^n rows. So, a statement which contains a single simple statement requires a truth table with only two rows; a statement which contains two simple statements requires a truth table with four rows, and a statement like that in (15) which contains three simple statements requires a truth table with eight rows. For four simple statements, sixteen rows are required; for five simple statements, 2^5, or 32 rows; six simple statements require 2^6, or 64 rows, and so on.

A second essential point concerns the order in which we should place simple statements, from left to right, when constructing a truth table for a complex statement. For (16) we placed to the far left of the table the simple statements 'G', 'C', and 'E' in precisely that order. Suppose we had instead reversed the order as 'E', 'C', and 'G'. How would this have altered the truth table, and would the alterations have mattered for determining the actual and possible verdicts of (16)? Had we ordered the simple statement constituents of (16) as 'E', 'C', and 'G', although we would have arrived at a distinctively different-looking truth table, the verdict would have been exactly the same; only it would have been presented in a different order. There are in fact exactly eight possibilities for any three simple statements, and any well-devised truth table for (16) must represent each possibility. The order in which it examines them will vary depending on the order in which we place the simple statement constituents at the top left of the truth table, but that order is irrelevant to the final verdict of the truth table; it is only the order of examination that we change when we shuffle simple statements.

A third point concerns a method for guaranteeing that you neither repeat yourself nor miss any possibility in devising a truth table for a statement. As truth tables become more and more complex, you will be able to rely less and less on your intuition and memory for deciding whether every possibility has indeed been exhausted. The following recipe for constructing rows in a truth table guarantees that you exhaust every possibility. Let the leftmost column consist of nothing but alternations of single T's and single F's, for however many T's and F's are required. Since three simple statements require eight rows, they require four alternations of single T's and single F's. Four simple statements require eight alternations of single T's and single F's. Let the second column, if needed, consist of nothing but alternations of pairs of T's and pairs of F's. So two simple statements would require one pair of T's followed by one pair of F's; and four simple statements would require four alternations of pairs of T's and pairs of F's. Let the third column, if needed, consist of nothing but alternations of quadruplets of T's and quadruplets of F's, and so on. The main idea is this:

> **Each time a column needs to be added to a truth table, the number of T's and F's doubles.**

A fourth point concerns the column which determines the possible truth-values for the statement. The relevant column is the column under the *main connective* of the statement. Recall from §5.3 that the main connective of a complex statement in PL is that connective with widest scope in the statement. So in (16) the main connective is the first occurrence of '&', which is just to say that (15) (and (16)) is a logical conjunction. The final verdicts about the possible truth-values of (15) are those listed under the main connective in (16).

5.4.2 Truth Table Analyses of Arguments

How can we utilize truth tables to determine deductive validity and invalidity? Consider PL argument (17).

17. ~(A & S), A ∴ ~S

A truth table for (17) will consist of nothing more than truth tables for each and every statement in (17), lined up next to each other in a row, with the premises listed first and the conclusion last (with a plus symbol under the column for the main connective in each statement). A truth table for (17) looks like this:

```
A S   ~(A & S),   A  ∴  ~S

T T   F   T        T      F
F T   T   F        F      F
T F   T   F        T      T
F F   T   F        F      T
        +              +      +
```

The table for this argument has four rows, since it consists of only two statement types, 'A' and 'S'.

Once we have devised a truth table for an argument, we need to look to see whether there is *any* horizontal row in it in which every one of its premises is true. Why must we? Because an argument is valid just in case it is not possible for its premises to be true and its conclusion false. In the truth table above there is only one row, the third, in which both its premises are true. In complex statements like the first premise, the truth-values under the main connective are the relevant ones. As a way to avert paying attention to the wrong columns, you could draw a line through irrelevant columns of truth-value assignments. In the first premise, for example, you could cross out the column under the ampersand (after having constructed the column under the negation) because the main connective is '~', not '&'.

Now look back at the third row. Its premises are assigned the value T. The conclusion in that row is likewise assigned T. Since this is the only row in which both premises are true, this truth table demonstrates that whenever the premises of argument (17) are all true, its conclusion must be true as well. Because this truth table represents every possible combination of truth and falsity for every simple statement letter constituent ('A' and 'S') of argument (17), it establishes that it is impossible for the premises of (17) to be true yet its conclusion false. (17) is therefore a deductively valid argument in PL. Put more generally:

> **If in a truth table for an argument there is no one row in which every premise has a T under its main connective, yet the conclusion has an F under its main connective, then the argument is deductively valid; otherwise, it is invalid.**

Consider argument (18).

18. ~(P & Q), ~P ∴ ~Q

A truth table for (18) looks like this:

P Q	~(P & Q),	~P ∴	~Q
T T	F T	F	F
F T	T F	T	F
T F	T F	F	T
F F	T F	T	T
	+	+	+

The truth table for this argument also has four rows, since it consists of only two statement types, 'P' and 'Q'. First we look to see whether there is *any* horizontal row in it in which every one of its premises is true. In this truth table there are two rows, the second and the fourth, in which both its premises are true.

Now look back at the fourth row. Its premises are assigned the value T. The conclusion in that row is likewise assigned T. If this were the only row in which the premises were both true, we would judge the argument to be valid. But there is another row in which both premises are true: namely, the second. And in this row, since the conclusion is assigned F, the truth table demonstrates that it is not true that whenever the premises of argument (18) are all true, its conclusion must be true as well. Therefore, this truth table establishes that (18) is a deductively invalid argument in PL.

Argument truth tables   Exercise 5.5

- Construct truth tables for the PL argument (41) in §4.9 as well as for the correct PL symbolizations of each argument in exercise 2 in chapter 4.
- Explain why the argument is deductively valid, if you conclude that it is.
- Explain why it is invalid, if you conclude that this is so.

Notes

1 A complete grammar for well-formedness for PL formulas is provided in ch. 7.
2 Nothing can be a proper part of itself. In this sense a well-formed formula β is a proper part of a well-formed formula α just in case β is a part of α and not identical to α.
3 Recall from ch. 2 that Greek letters are variables replaceable by any linguistic expression. So, although it's been our practice to use, e.g., 'α' and 'β' as metalinguistic variables replaceable by statements, they in fact are replaceable, unless otherwise noted, by any sort of linguistic expression, including connectives.
4 If you want to become proficient in using what are called *natural deduction* systems and/or *axiomatic* systems, consult the bibliography below. A number of introductory logic books, strong on methods of natural deduction (but unfortunately weak on methods of formalizing English arguments into logical notation) are listed.

Bibliography

Carston, R., 'Explicature, Implicature, and Truth-Theoretic Semantics', in R. Kempson (ed.), *Mental Representations: The Interface between Language and Reality* (Cambridge: Cambridge University Press, 1988), 155–81.
Copi, Irving, *Symbolic Logic*, 5th edn (New York: Macmillan, 1979).
Gazdar, G. and G. Pullum, 'Truth-Functional Connectives in Natural Language', *Chicago Linguistic Society* 12 (1976), 220–34.
Grice, H. P., *Studies in the Ways of Words* (Cambridge, MA: Harvard University Press, 1989).
Harnish, R., 'Logical Form and Implication', in T. B. Bever et al. (eds), *An Integrated Theory of Linguistic Ability* (New York: Thomas Y. Crowell, 1976), 464–79.
Hodges, Wilfred, *Logic* (London: Penguin, 1977).
Lemmon, Edward J., *Beginning Logic* (London: Nelson, 1965).
Martinich, A. P., 'Conversational Maxims and Some Philosophical Problems', *Philosophical Quarterly* 30 (1980), 215–28.
Sperber, D. and Wilson, D., *Relevance* (Oxford: Basil Blackwell, 1986).
Strawson, P., *Introduction to Logical Theory* (London: Methuen, 1952).
Suppes, Patrick, *Introduction to Logic* (Princeton, NJ: Van Nostrand, 1957).
Tennant, Neil, *Natural Logic* (Edinburgh: Edinburgh University Press, 1978).

6

Disjunction

6.1 Logical Disjunction

Logical disjunction is another type of complex statement. We ordinarily articulate disjunctions in English by grammatically conjoining statements with the expressions 'Either, or' or with 'or' alone. (1)–(3) are logical disjunctions.

1. Tom cut the lawn, or Bill cut it.
2. Either Bill left for school, or he left for the movies.
3. Either Tom cut the lawn, or he cut the hedge.

Another way to articulate logical disjunction in English is to disjoin phrases. (4)–(9) are all logical disjunctions.

4. Tom cut or raked the lawn.   (disjoined main verbs)
5. Tom was or will be singing.   (disjoined auxiliary verbs)
6. Tom speaks quickly or quietly.   (disjoined adverbs)
7. Tom cut the lawn or the hedge.   (disjoined objects)
8. Either Tom or Bill won.   (disjoined subjects)
9. Either the red or blue flag is gone. (disjoined adjectives)

Unlike logical conjunctions (in §3.3), (9) shows that we can create logical disjunctions by grammatically disjoining subject modifiers.

Why are all of (1)–(9) logical disjunctions? Each can be analyzed into two components (a left and a right disjunct) such that the complex statement itself is true just in case at least one of its disjuncts is true. Put more generally:

> A statement θ is a logical disjunction just in case it can be analyzed
> into components α and β, and from the truth of either α or β the
> truth of θ follows, and vice versa.

The following truth table codifies this information:

α	β	α disjoined β
T	T	T
F	T	T
T	F	T
F	F	F

The only circumstance under which a logical disjunction is false is when
both its disjuncts are false.

We will use the symbol '∨' (the wedge) to symbolize logical disjunctions. If 'T' represents 'Tom cut the lawn' and 'B' represents 'Bill cut the
lawn', the correct symbolization for (1) in PL is (10).

10.   T ∨ B

6.2   Disjunction and Negation

It is tempting to think of (11) as a disjunction.

11.   Neither the Uffizi nor the Accademia was open.

Anyone who thought this would mistakenly believe that (11) is asserting only that either the Uffizi was not open or the Accademia was not
open. But (11) is a much stronger statement than that. (11) is denying
both disjuncts. So, we will treat (11) as a logical negation – in particular, as equivalent to (12).

12.   It is not the case that either the Uffizi was open or the Accademia
      was open.

Because (12) paraphrases (11), and (12) denies (13), (11) denies (13) as
well.

13. Either the Uffizi was open, or the Accademia was open.

If 'U' represents 'The Uffizi was open' and 'A' represents 'The Accademia was open', then (11) (and (12)) should be symbolized as (14).

14. ~(U ∨ A)

In general, we will symbolize statements of form (15) as negations of disjunctions.

15. Neither α nor β
    ~(α ∨ β)

We have set as our goal to establish uniformity in symbolizing statements. To that end we have adopted, and will continue to adopt, certain conventions for symbolizing statements in the various logical notations we study in this book. Once a convention is adopted, using an alternative convention is no longer a matter of choice. Symbolizations that are incompatible with our system are wrong, even if they happen to be right under some other convention.

This point needs to be emphasized over and over again. Unless you understand it, you may completely misunderstand the entire purpose of our enterprise, or you may put the whole undertaking down to arbitrariness or caprice. We are not trying to discover, identify, isolate, uncover, or locate the 'true' logical form of statements in English; rather, we are trying to devise conventions for symbolizing English in PL in a simple and natural way so that we can then determine the deductive validity of indefinitely many English arguments. This task is designed to provide us with a common language governed by common rules. Conversing in such a language allows us to reason together and to evaluate each other's work easily. If we try to converse using different conventions, it becomes much harder, a bit like native French speakers trying to converse with native German speakers. To the extent that our conventions are correct and yield uniformity, we should have no grounds for complaint.

(16) and (17) also negate disjunctions and should be symbolized in accordance with our convention. Letting 'A' represent 'John is an athlete', 'M' represent 'John is a musician', 'S' represent 'Tom is short', and 'T' represent 'Tom is tall', (18) and (19) symbolize (16) and (17) respectively.

16. John isn't an athlete or a musician.
17. That Tom is short or tall is false.

18. ~(A ∨ M)
19. ~(S ∨ T)

Neither (18) nor (19) should be confused with statements of form (20).

20. ~α ∨ ~β

(20) is a disjunction, where each disjunct is a negation. It is not a negation. Both (21) and (22) should be symbolized by means of form (20).

21. Either Tom is not short or he is not tall.
22. It is false that Tom is short or it is false that Tom is tall.

(21) and (22) are compatible with Tom's being short or his being tall, but not both. But (19) denies both that he is short and that he is tall. Once again the value of groupers is apparent; they help to distinguish between *negations of disjunctions* (i.e., statements of form (15)) and *disjunctions of negations* (i.e., statements of form (20)).

6.3 Iterations and Groupers

When compounds combine into a single complex statement, groupers may be needed to disambiguate that statement. (23) is ambiguous; it can mean the same as either (24) or (25).

23. Mary left and Bill stayed or Julie stayed.

24. *Either* Mary left and Bill stayed or Julie stayed.
25. Mary left and *either* Bill stayed or Julie stayed.

Strategic placement of 'either' has the same effect that parentheses have in PL. So, in order to symbolize (23) correctly, we must first interpret it either as (24) or as (25). If we interpret (23) so that, speaking loosely, 'or' has wide scope over the entire statement, as in (24), then (26) correctly symbolizes (23). If we interpret (23) so that 'and' governs the whole, as in (25), then (27) correctly symbolizes (23).

26. (M & B) ∨ J
27. M & (B ∨ J)

(28), however, is ill-formed (or ungrammatical) in PL, because it does not indicate which of '∨' or '&' has wide scope.

28. M & B ∨ J

Every well-formed formula θ in PL can have only one connective with wide scope: namely, the main connective of θ.

Iterating the same connective need not result in ambiguity. (29)–(31) are unambiguous, so groupers aren't required.[1]

29. P ∨ Q ∨ T
30. P & Q & T
31. ~ ~P

For convenience, we will relax grammatical rules to allow (29)–(31) to be acceptable symbolizations of (32)–(34) respectively.

32. Either John, Mary, or Bill left.
33. John, Mary, and Bill left.
34. Notre Dame is not unbeatable.

None of these is ambiguous, even though parentheses are not used to punctuate them.

Complex statements   Exercise 6.1

- Symbolize (1)–(7).
- If ambiguous, symbolize each reading.
- At this stage in our development of PL, every statement is either simple, a negation, a conjunction, or a disjunction.

- Provide a dictionary for simple statements.
- Use groupers when necessary.

1. Give me liberty, or give me death!
2. Either John eats meat, or Henry eats fish.
3. I do not demand liberty, and I do not demand death.
4. Neither coffee nor tea comes with the meal.
5. I'll be with Abby tonight, or I'll be with Sharon, or I'll be with Igor.
6. I did not have a good time in France or in England.
7. It has not been the first or the last experience to reinforce my belief.

Exercise 6.2   Arguments

- Symbolize each of arguments (1)–(4) in PL.
- Include a dictionary for simple statements.

1. I will become either a professor or a rich man. I will not become a rich man. Therefore, I will become a professor.
2. Shane is not an officer, since neither he nor Omar is an officer.
3. Because neither the US nor Japan were in the 1980 Olympics, it is not true that the US and Canada were in the 1980 Olympics.
4. Frank or Bill but not Mary is on the hill. Frank isn't on the hill. So, Bill is on the hill.

Exercise 6.3   Here again is the truth table for disjunction:

α ∨ β

T	T	T
F	T	T
T	T	F
F	F	F

- Extend the truth table method from chapter 5 to evaluate your symbolizations for arguments (1)–(4) in exercise 2.
- Present your work in full.

6.4 Inclusive versus Exclusive 'Or'

According to some logicians, 'or' in English is ambiguous in the same way that 'light' is ambiguous between color and weight. In some of (35)–(41) 'or' indicates 'either . . . or . . . , but not both', while in others it indicates 'either . . . or . . . , and perhaps both'. The former is the exclusive sense of 'or', the latter the inclusive sense.

35. You can get paid by check or by cash.
36. You can have cake or soda or coffee.
37. Jeff will be with either Bill or Suzi today.
38. Today is either Monday or Tuesday.
39. Frank Sinatra was born in either Newark or Hoboken.
40. Arlene bought either a margarita or a grasshopper.
41. Either you eat your vegetables, or I'll spank you.

Is 'or' in (37) exclusive or inclusive? Upon hearing (37) asserted, you would most likely infer that Jeff will be with at most one of the two, Bill or Suzi, not both. But if the exclusive 'or' is part of the meaning of (37), then the following argument would be deductively valid.

37. Jeff will be with either Bill or Suzi today.
42. So, he won't be with both Bill and Suzi.

So what determines whether (42) follows from (37)? For logicians who believe that there are two senses to 'or', if both disjuncts were true, (37) would be false. The following truth table represents the exclusive 'or'.

α	β	α (exclusive) or β
T	T	F
F	T	T
T	F	T
F	F	F

According to this table, there are two conditions under which a disjunction can be false: the standard one, in row four, when both disjuncts are false, but also, in row one, when both disjuncts are true.

Is there any reason to believe that such exclusive disjunctions exist in English? Reconsider (37). Suppose Jeff is out with both Bill and Suzi. If he is out with both, then he is out with Bill *or* Suzi. Is (37) then false? Of course, if Jeff had expected to be out with both, then (37), very likely, would not be used to describe the situation, since it's good conversational etiquette that a speaker try to make as informative a claim as is consistent with his beliefs. But suppose in fact that Jeff went out with Bill, and, by a stroke of good luck, they met Suzi. The three then spent the rest of the day together. Under such circumstances we would be disinclined to say that (37) is false, or that the speaker had lied or misled us when asserting it, or that the speaker is in any way irresponsible in asserting (37) even though both disjuncts are true. It appears that it is not part of the meaning of (37) that it logically implies (42); so it appears that (37) is an inclusive disjunction.

Some proponents of the exclusive 'or' will cite statements like (38) and (39) in support of the claim that not every English disjunction employs an inclusive 'or'. This is a confusion.

> **In order for a statement to provide support for the existence of an exclusive 'or', it has to be possible for both disjuncts in that statement to be true.**

Otherwise, the first row of the truth table is not pertinent, and only that row can be relevant to determining whether there is or is not an exclusive 'or' in English. Since both disjuncts cannot be true together in either (38) or (39), 'or' in both (38) and (39) is not even a candidate for the exclusive 'or'.

(36) clearly employs an inclusive 'or'. Nothing indicates that you cannot choose more than one item. Although you might refrain from choosing all three for reasons of good manners or appearance, logic or meaning should not prevent you from choosing all three. Similarly, for (40).

Next consider (41). Children build up their expectations that when statements like (41) are uttered, they will be spanked only if they do not eat their vegetables. But (41) itself is no guarantee; merely their past experiences are. In order for the 'or' in (41) to be exclusive, there can be no state of affairs where both disjuncts are true yet (41) is false. If a parent asserts (41) to her child, who then eats his dinner and also proceeds to throw his dish on the floor, the mother can perfectly well spank her son without fear of contradicting her earlier warning – that is, (41).

How many 'or's are there in English? Nothing established so far proves that there is only one, the inclusive 'or'. All that's been established is that the alleged examples of exclusive 'or' are at best inconclusive. The burden lies with the logician who contends that there are two 'or's to provide a plausible example of an authentic exclusive 'or'.[2] Nothing examined so far establishes anything this strong. If the logicians who think that there is an exclusive 'or' in English are right, then many inference forms judged invalid would in fact be valid – for example, (43)–(45).

43. α or β
44. α
45. ∴ It is not the case that β.

From the fact that either John ate breakfast or dinner, and he did eat breakfast, we cannot deductively infer that he did not eat dinner. Maybe he ate both.

When we deny that 'or' is ambiguous in the way discussed, we deny the legitimacy of this inference form. We can assume that for (38), only one disjunct can be true, without buying into a change in PL of the radical sort that the above inference would introduce.[3]

6.5 Symbolizing Logical Disjunctions Continued

By this stage, you should recognize as a matter of course that not every statement with an 'or' in it is a logical disjunction. You should have no trouble recognizing that (46)–(47) and (48)–(49) need not be synonymous pairs.

46. Either Tom wants a cat or Tom wants a dog.
47. Tom wants a cat or a dog.

48. Either Carrie weighs less than Arlene, or she weighs less than Suzi.
49. Carrie weighs less than either Arlene or Suzi.

Suppose you were to try to symbolize the pairs identically, as in (46′)–(49′).

46'. C ∨ D   C: Tom wants a cat; D: Tom wants a dog.
47'. C ∨ D
48'. A ∨ S
    A: Carrie weighs less than Arlene; S: Carrie weighs less than Suzi.
49'. A ∨ S

(46) and (48) are clearly logical disjunctions correctly symbolized by (46') and (48') respectively, but (47) and (49) are at best ambiguous, with only one reading being a logical disjunction. The ambiguity in (47) is reflected by the differences between (50) and (51).

50.   Tom wants a dog or a cat, but I don't know which.
51.   Tom wants a dog or a cat, but he doesn't care which.

If embellishing (47) with (50) is correct, then (47) is a logical disjunction, because if Tom wants a dog, then (47) is true. If Tom wants a cat instead, (47) is also true. The truth of (47), under the sense of (51), doesn't guarantee the truth of either (52) or (53).

52.   Tom wants a dog.
53.   Tom wants a cat.

Therefore, on interpretation (51), (47) is not a logical disjunction.
    What we are highlighting here is that ordinary connectives do not behave in familiar ways when they fall within the scope of certain psychological verbs. In (47) 'or' falls within the scope of 'wants', so we can interpret (47) to be ascribing to Tom a disjunctive psychological state. We can construct similar examples using other psychological verbs – for example, 'believe', 'hope', 'desire', 'fear'.

54.   Massimo believes that either Juventus or Milan Inter will win the Italian Cup.
55.   The president fears that either his wife or his daughter will talk to the press.

Consider (49) next. Like (47), it is ambiguous. On one of its readings (49) is a logical disjunction, as in (48). But if focal stress is placed on 'or', we get a reading according to which (49) is not a logical disjunction but, instead, a logical conjunction. On this second reading, from the truth of either (56) or (57) alone, the truth of (49) does not follow.

56. Carrie weighs less than Arlene.
57. Carrie weighs less than Suzi.

Carrie might weigh less than Arlene without weighing less than either Arlene or Suzi.

(58) also is ambiguous between (59) and (60).

58. Vegetables or fruits are good for you.
59. Vegetables are good for you, *or* fruits are good for you.
60. Vegetables are good for you, *and* fruits are good for you.

Once again we see that a familiar word like 'or' can play a radically different role from the one we ordinarily associate with it. On reading (59), (58) is a logical disjunction; but, surprisingly, on reading (60), it is a logical conjunction.[4] The lesson from these examples is clear and familiar: *language resists simple mechanical symbolizations.* You need to think before you symbolize.

Notes

1   Strictly speaking, every well-formed formula in PL must have only one main connective. We relax the convention here because we can repair unambiguous but nevertheless ill-formed formulas simply by inserting parentheses appropriately.
2   Some logicians argue that Latin has distinct words for the two senses of 'or': 'vel' for the inclusive and 'aut' for the exclusive. We will not pursue this line of thought here.
3   Someone, after reading this discussion of exclusive versus inclusive 'or' might wonder why we aren't expressing an exclusive 'or' when we say, 'Either . . . or . . . , but not both'. It is true that statements of this form have the same truth conditions as an exclusive 'or'. So we can express in English something which has the same sense as an exclusive 'or'. But that's not what's at issue. The issue is whether there are any English statements with 'or' *without* the adjoined 'but not both' that are false when both disjoined statements are true. To this question, the appropriate response is that we have, as yet, no reason to believe so.
4   We can express the same idea by employing either the word 'and' or the word 'or', as in (61):

61. Carrie weighs less than Arlene *and* Suzi.

However, we tend to read statements like (61) as saying that Carrie weighs less than whatever Arlene and Suzi weigh together. No such tendency exists for corresponding 'or' statements.

Bibliography

Barrett, Robert B. and Alfred J. Stenner, 'The Myth of the Exclusive "Or"', *Mind* 80 (1971), 116–21.

Browne, A. C., 'Univocal "Or" – Again', *Linguistic Inquiry* 17 (1986), 751–4.

Copi, Irving, *Symbolic Logic*, 7th edn (New York: Macmillan, 1986).

Goddard, L, 'The Exclusive "Or"', *Analysis* 20 (1960), 97–105.

Jennings, R. E., *The Genealogy of Disjunction* (Oxford: Oxford University Press, 1994).

Pellitier, F. J., 'Or', *Theoretical Linguistics* 4 (1977), 61–74.

Quine, W. V. O., *Methods of Logic*, 4th edn (Cambridge, MA: Harvard University Press, 1982), ch. 1.

Suppes, Patrick, *Introduction to Logic* (Princeton, NJ: Van Nostrand, 1957).

7

Conditionals

7.1 Conditionals with Constituent Statements

A paradigm of a logical conditional in English consists of two statements linked by the connective 'if, then', as in (1).

1. If Elvis stays, then Dylan leaves.

The statement following 'if' and preceding 'then' is the *antecedent* of (1), and the statement following 'then' is its *consequent*. Other ways of articulating logical conditionals in English include (2)–(7).

2. **If** Elvis stays, Dylan leaves.
3. **Provided** Elvis stays, Dylan leaves.
4. Dylan leaves **provided that** Elvis stays.
5. **Should** Elvis stay, Dylan leaves.
6. Dylan leaves **should** Elvis stay.
7. **When** Elvis stays, Dylan leaves.

In order to classify (1)–(7) as logical conditionals, we shall say that in each of them their components (8) and (9) are such that if the antecedent component (8) is true and the consequent component (9) is false, then (1)–(7) are false, and vice versa.

8. Elvis stays.
9. ′ Dylan leaves.

7.2 Conditionals without Constituent Statements

Conditional statements can also be indicated in English without using two self-standing statements.

10. Elvis's staying **will result in** Dylan's leaving.
11. Elvis's staying **will bring about** Dylan's leaving.
12. Elvis's staying **will lead to** Dylan's leaving.

None of (10)–(12) includes a component self-standing statement; yet in each, minimally, a condition is being laid down in order for some other state of affairs to obtain. In each, we are being told, at least, that Elvis's staying is a condition for Dylan's leaving. If Elvis stays but Dylan doesn't leave, then (10)–(12) are false. Since this relationship holds between the original statements (10)–(12) and their analyzable components, they are logical conditionals as well.

7.3 Logical Conditionals

(1)–(7), (10)–(12) are all logical conditionals because each is divisible into two components, one component of which provides a condition for the truth of the other. Put more generally:

> **A statement θ is a logical conditional just in case θ can be analyzed into two components, α and β, where α (the antecedent) is a condition for the truth of β (the consequent), and θ as a whole is false just in case α is true and β is false.**

The accompanying truth table codifies this information.

α	β	α conditional β
T	T	T
F	T	T
T	F	F
F	F	T

This truth table defines what we shall call the *material* conditional. The material conditional preserves ordinary usage of English conditionals at least to this extent: a conditional statement is false when its antecedent is true and its consequent is false. Ordinary usage of English conditionals, however, seems uncommitted about the other three rows in the truth table for the material conditional. Suppose Elvis doesn't stay, and Dylan leaves. Is (1) then true? Suppose Elvis doesn't stay and Dylan doesn't leave. Is (1) then true? Suppose all you knew was that Elvis stays and Dylan leaves. Would that suffice all by itself, without knowing anything about the connection between these two states of affairs, to establish that (1) is true? These three possible circumstances correspond respectively to the first, second, and fourth rows in the truth table. According to the table, the English conditional (1) is true in all three cases. This seems odd, although it seems no less odd to say that it would be false in these circumstances. Should we just say that in these circumstances (1) is neither true nor false? The consequences of such a strategy are significant. We will not be able to evaluate arguments containing conditionals without compromising our characterization of a statement if we want to treat sentences like (1) as statements (since statements were defined in chapter 1 as sentences which are either true or false). More significantly, in consequence we will have to sacrifice our characterization of deductive validity: sentences like (1) can obviously be part of an argument; but since our characterization of deductive validity requires that premises and conclusion be assigned all possible truth-values, if sentences like (1) can lack truth-values, we must give up that characterization.

Sacrificing this standard definition of deductive validity is a radical move, but some logicians recommend it. In this book, however, we will take a more conservative route. Without further argument, we will adopt the following three assumptions: (i) that the truth-values of the antecedent and the consequent suffice by themselves to determine the truth-value of the entire English conditional; (ii) that English conditional statements have truth-values *even when* the antecedent is false; and (iii) that an English conditional is in fact true just in case either its antecedent is false or its consequent is true. In short, we will stipulate that the English conditional (at least for conditionals in indicative mood; see §A3.1 for a brief discussion of conditionals in subjunctive mood) is a *material conditional*: that is, that the above truth table provides the correct truth conditions for the English indicative conditional. We will adopt this treatment even though it might not be intuitive for you. (§A3 amplifies the debate about the relationship between conditionals in English and the material conditional.)

7.4   Symbolizing Conditionals in PL

We introduce the symbol '⊃' (the horseshoe) for material conditionals.[1] In symbolizing a conditional, the antecedent flanks the left-hand side of the horseshoe, and the consequent flanks the right-hand side. Thus, (1)–(7) are all symbolized as

E ⊃ D

where 'E' symbolizes 'Elvis stays', and 'D' symbolizes 'Dylan leaves'.

As with statements containing other connectives, you must exercise care when symbolizing statements that contain conditionals. (13) and (14), for example, must not be symbolized identically, since (13) happens to be true, but (14) is false.

13.   If it is false that the Uffizi is open, then the Duomo is open.
14.   It is false that if the Uffizi is open, then so is the Duomo.

(14) is a negation; it is a negation of a conditional. (13), though, is a conditional; its antecedent is a negation. We need some way of distinguishing in PL negations of conditionals from conditionals with negative antecedents.

If 'U' represents 'The Uffizi is open', and 'D' represents 'The Duomo is open', then (13) can be symbolized as

~U ⊃ D

To symbolize (14) we need groupers:

~(U ⊃ D)

The groupers indicate that the '~' is the main connective and therefore that the statement is a negation (and not a conditional).

7.5   Necessary and Sufficient Conditions

Each of (15)–(18) is equivalent to a conditional claim.

15. An 'A' on the final is a sufficient condition for an 'A' in the course.
16. Shooting someone is sufficient for hurting him.

17. Coming to class is a necessary condition for doing well.
18. Oxygen is necessary for a fire.

In general, statements of the following forms support conditional claims:

α is (a) sufficient (condition) for β.
α is (a) necessary (condition) for β.

When someone asserts (15), she is claiming that *if* you get an 'A' on the final, *then* you get an 'A' in the course. Were we to analyze (15) into components (19)–(20),

19. You get an 'A' on the final in this course.
20. You get an 'A' in this course.

the conditional claim that (15) makes is that, if (19), then (20). This rendering has the effect of making sufficient conditions antecedents of conditionals.

If α is a sufficient condition for β, then if α obtains, β obtains as well.

If we let 'F' represent 'You get an "A" on the final in this course' and 'C' represent 'You get an "A" in this course', then the correct symbolization of (15) in PL is:

F ⊃ C

(17) does not claim that if you come to class, you will do well in this course! You might come to class each day and sleep or read the school paper or do something else that is frivolous. So, necessary conditions cannot be represented in the same way as sufficient conditions. Suppose we take the component statements of (17) to be (21) and (22).

21. You come to class.
22. You do well in this course.

In asserting that (21) is (a) necessary (condition) for (22), we claim no more than that should (22) turn out to be true, then (21) must be true as well. Necessary conditions should be treated as consequents.

> **If α is a necessary condition for β, then if β obtains, α obtains as well.**

If we let 'C' represent 'You come to class' and 'W' represent 'You do well in this course', then (17) is symbolized in PL as:

W ⊃ C

If α is a sufficient condition for β, it does not follow that α is necessary for β. In (15) there may be other ways of securing an 'A' in the course. You might have such a high average in the course that you still receive an 'A' despite getting less than an 'A' on the final. Likewise, necessary conditions needn't be sufficient conditions. Oxygen may be necessary for fire, but it certainly isn't sufficient.[2]

Exercise 7.1   **Statements**

- Symbolize (1)–(6) in PL using the dictionary provided.

1. If the book gets published, then Lucy will throw a party. (B: The book gets published; L: Lucy throws a party)
2. If Rachel gets an A, Joan will be pleased. (R: Rachel gets an A; J: Joan is pleased)
3. Mary will feed you if she likes you. (F: Mary feeds you; L: Mary likes you)
4. Wearing clothes is necessary for going outside. (W: you wear clothes; O: you go outside)
5. Bribing the judge is sufficient for going free. (B: you bribe the judge; F: You go free)
6. John's cooking dinner is necessary for Bill's being happy. (J: John cooks dinner; B: Bill is happy)

7.6 Only If

(23) and (24) both seem to be conditionals, but which components are antecedents, and which are consequents?

23. Crina will pass only if she takes the final.
24. Only if Tom is president will Bill be vice-president.

Suppose in (23) we posit that 'Crina (she) takes the final' is the antecedent (because it follows an 'if'), and 'Crina will pass' is the consequent. If this reading is correct, then if the antecedent is true and the consequent is false, the entire conditional will be false. But it is not. Suppose it is true that Crina takes the final, but false that she passes the course. Would (23) be false? Absolutely not! (23) does not guarantee that Crina will pass the course if she takes the final. It only says that Crina must take the final in order to pass the course. There may be other things she must do as well for her to pass. In other words, in (23) 'Crina takes the final' is a necessary, but not a sufficient, condition for passing the course. It is not the antecedent, but rather the consequent, and 'Crina will pass' is not the consequent, but the antecedent. In general, in a statement of form,

α only if β

whatever precedes 'only if' is the antecedent; so each such statement should be symbolized as:

$\alpha \supset \beta$

Be careful not to confuse 'only if' with 'if only'. In (25), 'only' plays an emphatic role, rather than a logical role.

25. If only I had a brain, then I would be happy.

The word 'only' is used in this statement entirely for emphasis. To see that this is so, drop 'only' from (25); it still expresses the same idea. (25) is still a conditional, but its antecedent is 'I (only) had a brain', and its consequent is 'I would be happy'.

To say that statements of form 'α only if β' express a conditional, with α as antecedent and β as consequent, is not to say that such statements are equivalent in every respect – in particular, in every *non-logical* respect – to statements of form

   If α, then β.

All that is being said is that 'only if' statements are conditionals. To see the difference between distinguishing statements on the basis of logical and non-logical respects, consider pairs (26)–(29).

26.   If water is boiled, it evaporates.
27.   Water is boiled only if it evaporates.

28.   My pulse goes up only if I do heavy exercise.
29.   If my pulse goes up, then I do heavy exercise.

The even-numbered statements are grammatical (or acceptable), but the odd ones seem peculiar. (27) affirms straightforwardly that water being evaporated is a necessary condition of water being boiled. Intuitively, (26) in English seems to be less strong. It affirms that water evaporates when boiled, but it seems neutral as to whether it has to. Nevertheless, differences between the odd- and even-numbered statements do *not* establish that the odd statements should not be symbolized as the same material conditional. Consider the truth conditions for each statement. (26)–(29) are all false under exactly the same conditions: their antecedent is true, and their consequents false. So we will adopt the convention of symbolizing the members of each pair identically in PL. Although, given our convention, '⊃' adequately symbolizes both 'if, then' and 'only if' in PL, we should be careful not to presume that these expressions are equivalent in every respect.

7.7   Unless

Sometimes a statement with the word 'unless' can be paraphrased correctly as a conditional. So, for example, consider statement (30).

30.   John will die unless he is operated on.

On the assumption that (30) is making a conditional statement, how should we symbolize it? The 'un-' part seems to make the condition negative. The question is whether the negative condition is a sufficient or a necessary condition. In (30) there is no guarantee that John will live if he is operated on. (30) guarantees only that John will die if he is *not* operated on. So, if we have to choose between (31) and (32), clearly (31) is correct.

31. John will die if he is not operated on.
32. John will not die if he is operated on.

Consider (33), another 'unless' statement.

33. I will stay at home unless you call me.

(33) does not guarantee that I will stay home if you do call me. It does guarantee that I will stay home if you don't call me. So if we have a statement of the form

α unless β

it would seem best to represent it in PL as

~β ⊃ α

Many are tempted to think that, generally, "unless" statements of the form

α unless β

should be symbolized not along the lines of our convention, but rather as

β ⊃ ~α

This approach may seem acceptable in many cases. For example, if (34) is true,

34. Unless fetuses have no right to live, abortion is wrong,

then it's arguable that if abortion is wrong, then fetuses do have a right to life. But even if this were right, it could not be right in general. Surely, if (30) is true, it does not follow that if John is operated on, he will not die. He may die even if he is operated on. He may be hit by a truck and die immediately upon leaving the hospital. But if (30) is true, then surely he will die if he is not operated on. (31) captures this intuition perfectly.

You might test your intuitions here by comparing our convention against the alternative with statements (35)–(37).

35. Tom will demonstrate unless the police lock him up.
36. Abrams is eligible unless he is retired.
37. Al won't be president unless Bill is reelected.

However, you shouldn't take anything we have established so far to mean that it is *never* correct to symbolize 'unless' statements in some other way. Just as we have seen with 'not', 'and', 'or', 'if, then', and other logically interesting English expressions we have encountered, we cannot automatically symbolize statements in logical notation according to some prescribed formula without first thinking about what the statements in question mean. For example, although (38) fits our adopted convention quite well, (39) and (40) do not.

38. John will succeed unless he goofs off.

39. Each student will succeed unless she goofs off.
40. No student will fail unless she goofs off.

The quantifier expressions 'Each student' and 'No student' take wide scope (§5.2) over 'unless'. Further discussion of these statements and an extension of the notion of relative scope to them is deferred until chapters 9 and 11. Until then, we cannot provide an analysis of statements like (39) and (40).

Exercise 7.2   Statements

- Symbolize (1)–(6) in PL using the dictionary provided.

1. Joe will wear his hat only if it rains. (J: Joe wears his hat; R: it rains)
2. Susan will be rich only if her aunt dies. (R: Susan will be rich; A: Susan's aunt dies)
3. I will live to be 100 unless I get hit by a sugar-crazed New York City taxi driver. (L: I will live to be 100; H: I get hit by a sugar-crazed New York City taxi driver)
4. Laura will get an A only if she buys the teacher an apple. (L: Laura gets an A; T: Laura buys the teacher an apple)

5. Jerry will be sad unless his paper gets published. (S: Jerry is sad; P: Jerry's paper gets published)
6. Unless I didn't count correctly, there are three hundred cabbages in this garden. (C: I counted correctly; G: there are three hundred cabbages in this garden)

7.8 Since, Because

In §§1.1.2 and 4.9 the expressions 'since' and 'because' were introduced as premise indicator terms; however, many students symbolize these expressions like 'if'. This can't be right. Note that, intuitively, if either (41) or (42) is true, then both their components must be true. But if (43) is true, neither component need be true.

41. I'll leave the window open **since** it is not raining.
42. I'll leave the window open **because** it is not raining.

43. I'll leave the window open **if** it is not raining.

From the truth of (43), it follows only that if its antecedent is true, then its consequent must be true as well.

It's also the case that if both (41) and (42) are true, (43) must be true as well. But this alone is not sufficient to establish that (41) and (42) should be symbolized as conditionals.

Our practice has been, and will continue to be, to symbolize (41) and (42) as harboring both a premise and the conclusion of an argument, each with the premise 'It is not raining' and the conclusion 'I'll leave the window open'. So if 'R' represents 'It is raining', and 'W' represents 'I'll leave the window open', then (43) should be symbolized as

$$\sim R \supset W$$

But (41) and (42) should be symbolized, assuming there are not other premises surrounding them in the context of an argument, as,

$$\sim R$$
$$\therefore W$$

7.9 Conditionals and Groupers

As we noted in §6.3, we could unambiguously, without using groupers, iterate conjunctions, negations, or disjunctions. (44)–(46) are all unambiguous.

44. ~ ~A
45. A ∨ B ∨ C
46. A & B & C

However, the horseshoe does not have this agreeable feature. (47) is ambiguous. Groupers are required to symbolize such iterated conditionals in PL.

47. A ⊃ B ⊃ C

Consider (48) and (49).

48. **If** oxygen **is sufficient for** a fire, **then** the alarm rings.
49. **If** there is oxygen, **then if** there is a fire, **then** the alarm rings.

Clearly, these statements differ in meaning. If we let 'O' represent 'Oxygen is present' and 'F' represent 'There is a fire' and 'A' represent 'An alarm rings', then the correct symbolization of (48), with groupers, is (50), while the correct symbolization of (49), with groupers, is (51).

50. (O ⊃ F) ⊃ A
51. O ⊃ (F ⊃ A)

Were we to drop the parentheses from (50) and (51), we would have no idea whether they were symbolizing (48) or (49), two statements quite different in meaning.

7.10 If and Only If

Many English statements conjoin two statements by the words 'if and only if', as in (52).

52. You will get an 'A' in this course **if, and only if**, you work hard.

From your knowledge of the symbolization conventions of this book, you might already recognize that statements like (52) should be symbolized as logical conjunctions, where each conjunct is itself a logical conditional. Further, 'just in case' and 'when and only when' behave just like 'if and only if' in this regard. Accordingly, (53) and (54) should also be symbolized in PL as logical conjunctions with logical conditionals as conjuncts.

53. You will get an 'A' in this course **just in case** you work hard.
54. You will get an 'A' in this course **when, and only when,** you work hard.

Letting 'A' represent 'You will get an "A" in this course' and 'W' represent 'You work hard', (52)–(54) are all symbolized alike, as a conjunction of two conditionals:

$(W \supset A) \& (A \supset W)$

Many logic books introduce a new symbol for representing these three expressions in PL: the so-called biconditional '≡'. In this book, however, we will continue to symbolize such locutions using the ampersand and the horseshoe. The rationale for this parsimony is that these types of locutions do not occur often enough, outside mathematics and philosophy, to warrant their own symbol.

Statements   Exercise 7.3

- Symbolize (1)–(5) in PL using the dictionary provided.

1. Nadia relaxes if and only if all her work is done. (R: Nadia relaxes; W: All Nadia's work is done)
2. Since I went to the store, I will not run out of toothpaste. (S: I went to the store; T: I will not run out of toothpaste)
3. If you eat your dinner, then if there's cake in the house, you can eat dessert. (D: you eat your dinner; C: there's cake in the house; E: you can eat dessert)
4. You can go out if, and only if, you clean your room. (O: You can go out; C: you clean your room)
5. Cleaning your room is necessary and sufficient for going out.

7.11 A Revised Grammar for Well-formedness in PL

Let us now collect and systematize the notational innovations that comprise propositional logic.

There are five types of well-formed statements in PL.

a. *Simple statements.* These are capital block letters, A, B, C, D, . . . , Z. There are an indefinite number of such symbols, since we permit the use of subscripts. A_1, A_2, A_3, A_4, . . . , A_n, B_1, B_2, . . . , B_n and so on are all simple statement symbols as well.

b. *Logical conjunctions.* If α and β are statements in PL – complex or simple – then so is (α & β).

c. *Logical negation.* If α is a statement in PL, then so is ~α.

d. *Logical disjunction.* If α and β are statements in PL, then so is ($\alpha \lor \beta$).

e. *Logical conditional.* If α and β are statements in PL, then so is ($\alpha \supset \beta$).[3]

Nothing else is a statement in PL.

Exercise 7.4   **Well-formed formulas**

- Given the characterization of a well-formed formula in §7.11, which of (1)–(12) are well-formed PL statements?
- If well formed, what type of statements are they? That is, what is their main connective?
- For those that are grammatical in PL, make up English statements which they might symbolize:

1. P
2. (P ∨ Q)
3. (R & S)
4. P ⊃ Q ⊃ R
5. (P ⊃ Q) ∨ (R & ~S)
6. ~ (P ∨ Q & R)
7. (R & Q) ⊃ (S ∨ ~F)
8. R ∨ (~ Q ∨ S)

9. $(P \supset Q) \supset V$
10. $P \& Q \& S$
11. $\sim\sim\sim T$
12. $R \vee \sim (R \& V) \supset (T \& F)$

Complex statements Exercise 7.5

- Indicate whether (1)–(42) are conditionals, disjunctions, conjunctions, or negations.
- If a statement is none of these, indicate why not.
- Symbolize each statement in PL.
- Include a dictionary.

1. If you pay for it, you can have it.
2. He will pass the course provided he does the exercise.
3. Feeding the birds results in having to feed more birds.
4. The first two paragraphs are clear and concise.
5. Eating right is necessary for staying healthy.
6. He aimed at, but still missed, the target.
7. You do that, and I'm your slave.
8. Mary has many black and white cats.
9. Since I started early, I'll be done early.
10. I question whether the meal I ate was nutritious.
11. Sue is dissatisfied with her grades.
12. Tax forms are not as complicated as they once were.
13. If Graff defeats Seles, and Fernandez defaults, then Graff and Hingis will go to the finals.
14. Bacon and eggs will be served only if they run out of pancakes and do not serve sweet rolls.
15. While there is freedom, there is equality, and if there is freedom and equality, then all men are happy.

((15) is interesting. We have previously described 'while' as a conjunction-creating expression. But in (15) it does not play this role. What is it doing here? Compare its usage in (15) with its usage in (16).)

16. While you had cake, I had cherries.
17. I cannot tell you any more, but if I am accepted now, then it cannot be enjoyable for me to reflect that some calculation tipped the scale.

18. If New York City is in the USA, then if France is north of India, then South Bend is nowhere.
19. John went east, and if he had only gone west, he would now be here.
20. Getting into law school is a necessary condition for becoming rich.
21. Getting into law school is a sufficient condition for becoming rich.
22. Getting into law school is a necessary and sufficient condition for becoming rich.
23. Getting into law school is a sufficient and necessary condition for becoming rich.
24. Getting into law school is a necessary and sufficient condition for becoming rich and staying bored.
25. Getting into law school is a necessary and sufficient condition for becoming rich and staying bored, respectively.
26. You will graduate if you work hard.
27. You will graduate only if you work hard.
28. You will graduate if only you work hard.
29. You will graduate if and only if you work hard.
30. If you have a specific question, then we will relay it to him if he calls.
31. If the windows are open, we get hot air and outside noise.
32. Having both South Vietnam and Laos go would be sufficient for Cambodia's going.
33. Mary visited the team, but if Bill had been there, she would have left.
34. Should the Yankees win the pennant, then if they play Montreal, I would root for Montreal.
35. Mary left, and either Bill left or Julie stayed.
36. If the news is delayed, and you receive the main selection without having had ten days to notify us, you may return it for credit at our expense.
37. In order that man may usefully cooperate and improve the life of the community, there must be freedom to assess and compare views which seem to have validity.
38. Pour over ice cubes in an old-fashioned glass and serve with short straws.
39. Enjoy your achievements as well as your plans.
40. Being a Jew is worth something if you obey God's laws; but if you don't, then you are no better off than a heathen.
41. You're damned if you do, and you're damned if you don't.
42. 'If it can be proved that dreams possess a value of their own as psychological acts and that wishes are the motive for their construction and that experiences of the preceding day provide the immediate material for their content, then any theory of dreams which neglects

so important a procedure of research and accordingly represents dreams as a useless and puzzling reaction to somatic stimuli, stands condemned without there being any necessity for specific criticism' (Freud, *Freud, Interpretation of Dreams*).

You should now be ready to pull together all that you have learned in chapters 1–7 about symbolizing and evaluating English arguments. The following exercise requires you to draw from information from each of these previous chapters, and provides an opportunity for you to measure your progress.

Arguments   Exercise 7.6

- Symbolize each of (1)–(26) in PL.

We begin with two arguments, (1) and (2), from the first few pages of chapter 1.

1. This is an argument that many people on both sides of the abortion debate would accept:
    Provided the fetus is a person, a fetus has a right to life. Should a fetus have a right to life, it is false that someone has the right to take its life. However, if abortions are moral, someone does have the right to take the life of a fetus. Consequently, if a fetus is a person, abortions are not moral.
    (P: The fetus is a person; R: The fetus has a right to life; S: Someone has a right to take the life of a fetus; A: Abortions are moral)

2. Lung cancer is not caused by smoking, and this is so for the following reasons. Lung cancer is more common among male smokers than among female smokers. If smoking were the cause of lung cancer, this would not be true. The fact that lung cancer is more common among male smokers implies that it is caused by something in the male makeup. But if it is caused by this, it is not caused by smoking.
    (L: Lung cancer is caused by smoking; M: Lung cancer is more common among male smokers than female smokers; U: Lung cancer is caused by something in the male makeup)

3.   Some people do not think that the abortion issue turns solely on the question of whether the fetus is a person. They would offer the following argument:

> Abortion isn't wrong, since it is wrong only if a fetus has the right to use the organs of other persons to stay alive. But (since no one has that right) a fetus doesn't have that right either.

(W: Abortion is wrong; U: A fetus has a right to use the organs of another person to stay alive)

4.   The following argument is adapted from the writings of the father of modern biology, William Harvey:

> If the ventricles transmit two ounces of blood at each beat, then if they beat 60 times a minute, then they will transmit over seven pounds of blood in a minute. Let us suppose that both these conditions are true. They won't transmit seven pounds of blood in a minute unless the veins supply them with that much blood. If the blood doesn't circulate, there is no way the veins can supply that much blood. From this it is clear that the blood circulates.

(V: Ventricles transmit two ounces of blood at each beat; B: The heart beats 60 times per minute; T: The ventricles transmit seven pounds of blood per minute; W: The veins supply the ventricles with seven pounds of blood per minute; C: Blood circulates)

5.   If intelligence is wholly hereditary and identical twins have the same heredity, then being raised in separate households will not reduce the similarity of intelligence between identical twins, but it does reduce the similarity. Identical twins have come from a common sperm and egg. This last is so if, and only if, the twins have identical heredity. Therefore, intelligence is not entirely hereditary. (Ask yourself whether if you were to assert the first premise, you would also be asserting that being raised in separate households does reduce the similarity between identical twins. If your intuition is yes, then the first premise must be a conjunction.) (H: Intelligence is entirely hereditary; I: Being raised in separate households will reduce similarity . . . ; T: Identical twins have the same heredity; P: Identical twins come from a common sperm and egg) (Note: 'and' in 'P' does not indicate logical conjunction.)

6.   If there are an infinite number of points in a finite line L, then if those points have size, L will be infinitely long, and if they do not have size, L won't have length. Line L is neither infinitely long nor without length. This proves that there are not an infinite number of points in L.

(I: There are an infinite number of points in a finite line; H: Points have size; L: Line L is infinitely long; G: Line L has length)

7. The following argument is sometimes called 'Pascal's wager', named after Blaise Pascal, a seventeenth-century French philosopher and mathematician:

> If I believe in God, then if He exists, I gain, and if He doesn't, then I don't lose. If, on the other hand, I don't believe in God, then if He exists, I lose, and if He doesn't, I don't gain. From this it follows that if I believe, I'll either gain or not lose, while if I don't believe, I'll either lose or fail to gain.

(B: I believe in God; E: God exists; G: I gain; L: I lose) (Note: 'lose' is not synonymous with 'not gain'.)

8. If the world is disordered, it cannot be reformed unless a sage appears, but no sage can appear if the world is disordered. It follows that the world cannot be reformed if it is disordered.

(D: The world is disordered; W: The world can be reformed; S: A sage can appear) (Note: 'disordered' is not synonymous with 'not ordered'.)

9. People won't be given bribes if we discourage bribery. But unless people are given bribes, cases of bribery won't come before the public attention, and people won't know that bribery is wrong unless it comes to their attention. Given all this and the moral principle: bribery is wrong provided that people know that it is wrong, we can draw the following startling conclusion: Bribery is wrong only if we don't discourage it.

(B: Bribery is wrong; D: We discourage bribery; G: People will be given bribes; A: Cases of bribery will come before the public attention; K: People know that bribery is wrong)

10. George will leave unless Mary doesn't leave. But unless Phil stays, she will leave, and George won't leave provided that it rains. As a result, if it rains, Mary won't leave.

(G: George will leave; M: Mary does leave; P: Phil stays; R: It rains)

11. All high-ranking officers in our present army are volunteers. Military coups are engineered by high-ranking officers. Provided that both the preceding statements are true, an all-volunteer army would not increase the chances of a military takeover. Consequently, the chances of a military coup would not be increased by the institution of an all-volunteer army.

(H: All high-ranking officers in our present army are volunteers; E: Military coups are engineered by high-ranking officers; I: an all-volunteer army will increase the chances of a military takeover)

12. It is not the case that there will be both a continuation of PLO raids in Israel and peace in the Middle East. The PLO raids on Israel will not continue only if Arabs gain autonomy on the West Bank. So there will

be no peace in the Middle East, since the West Bank Arabs will not gain autonomy.

(C: There will be a continuation of PLO raids in Israel; P: There will be peace in the Middle East; A: Arabs gain autonomy on the West Bank)

13. Hopes for peace in the Middle East are unrealistic unless Clinton makes a secret deal with the Israeli prime minister. Clinton will make a secret deal with the Israeli prime minister if and only if he is not as inexperienced in foreign affairs as we have been led to believe. Since Clinton is as inexperienced in foreign affairs as we have been led to believe, hopes for peace in the Middle East are unrealistic.

(H: Hopes for peace in the Middle East are realistic; C: Clinton makes a secret deal with the Israeli prime minister; E: Clinton is as experienced in foreign affairs as we have been led to believe)

14. We will play tennis and go jogging only if the temperature reaches 45 degrees. It will not reach 45 degrees. So, we will not play tennis, and we will not go jogging.

(T: We play tennis; J: We jog; R: The temperature reached 45 degrees)

15. The Vietnamese ceasefire will lead to a permanent peace only if neither the Communists nor the Saigon regime retain their former tactics. But they are not going to give up their former tactics. So the ceasefire will not lead to a permanent peace.

(P: The Vietnamese ceasefire will lead to permanent peace; C: Communists retain their tactics; S: Saigon retains its tactics) (Note: 'giving up', given this dictionary, must mean 'not retain'.)

The problem in each of the following passages is to determine whether or not it contains an argument, and, if so, to reconstruct it. Reconstruction involves distinguishing between premises and conclusion, and, perhaps, supplying missing premises and/or conclusion. Once you have reconstructed an argument, symbolize it in PL.

16. 'What is not so generally recognized is that there can be no way of proving that the existence of a god, such as the God of Christianity, is even probable. Yet this also is easily shown. For if the existence of such a god were probable, then the proposition that he existed would be an empirical hypothesis. And in that case it would be possible to deduce from it, and other empirical hypotheses, certain experiential propositions which were not deducible from these other hypotheses alone. But in fact this is not possible' (A. J. Ayer, *Language, Truth, and Logic*).

(G: There is a way of proving that the existence of God is probable; E: The proposition that God exists is an empirical hypothesis; C: It is possible to deduce from the proposition that God exists certain experiential propositions)

17. 'As a challenge to theism, the problem of evil has traditionally been posed in the form of a dilemma: if God is perfectly loving, he must wish to abolish evil; and if he is all-powerful, he must be able to abolish evil. But evil exists; therefore, God cannot be both omnipotent and perfectly loving' (missing premise) (John Hick, *Philosophy of Religion*). (W: God wants to abolish evil; A: God is able to abolish evil; E: Evil exists; L: God is all loving; P: God is all-powerful)

18. Background information: suppose you are on the committee which has to plan the release of tickets for a big rock concert; you are faced with a problem. The problem is that some of your helpers will be out of town next week, and the concert is coming up soon; so, if you do not give out the tickets until later, there will not be enough lead time before the concert. You are then presented with the following valid argument by one of your helpers:

    If we have the ticket release next week, we will be short-handed for the release. But if we have the release later, people won't be happy with us. But in fact, people will be happy with us only if we are not short-handed for the release (because they do not want to have to wait too long in line). So, people will not be happy with us.

    (R: The ticket release is next week; S: We are short-handed on ticket-sellers; H: People will be happy)

19. There will be a revolution unless something is done to improve living conditions among the poorer classes. But nothing will be done to improve those conditions. Hence, there will be a revolution.
    (D: Something is done to improve living conditions among the poorer classes; R: There will be a revolution)

20. If Frank and Bill ride bikes, then Mary doesn't ride a bike only if John rides one. Bill doesn't ride a bike unless John rides one. Therefore, Mary rides a bike if, and only if, John rides a bike.
    (F: Frank rides a bike; B: Bill rides a bike; M: Mary rides a bike; J: John rides a bike)

21. If Harry takes drugs, then if he drinks, he is going to get himself into some serious trouble. But Bill drinks without Harry drinking. And Frank doesn't take drugs if Harry takes drugs. Therefore, Bill drinks and Frank takes drugs only if Harry drinks and takes drugs.
    (T: Harry takes drugs; D: Harry drinks; S: Harry is going to get himself into some serious trouble; B: Bill drinks; F: Frank takes drugs)

22. Two people are on the train provided that Bill got off. Bill's getting off is necessary for his getting to work on time. Therefore, if Bill got to work on time, there are two people on the train.
    (B: Bill got off the train; T: Two people are on the train; W: Bill got to work on time)

23. If cars have engines and provided that trains have engines, then boats have engines, but boats don't have engines. Therefore, cars have engines just in case trains have engines.
    (C: Cars have engines; T: Trains have engines; B: Boats have engines)
    (Think about what 'just in case' means.)

24. 'If George were leaving, I think he'd tell me first,' Mr Rogers said. 'He hasn't told me. He hasn't left.'
    (G: George leaves; T: George tells Mr Rogers first)

25. At this very point a disturbing, though obvious, question intrudes. If Harry's thesis is false, then there is no point in his having written the book or our reading it. But if his thesis is true, then there is also no point in his having written the book or our reading it. (This argument has a missing conclusion. Be sure to make it explicit in your symbolization.)
    (T: Harry's thesis is true; W: There is some point in Harry's having written the book; R: There is some point in our having read the book)

26. Some later Greek writer used erosion by water as evidence for the temporal origin of the earth; for, they argued, if the earth has existed from eternity, all mountains and other features would by now have disappeared. (This argument has a missing premise. Be sure to make it explicit in your symbolization.)
    (E: The earth had a beginning; M: The mountains still exist)

7.12   Summarizing Truth Tables

7.12.1   *Validity*

To summarize, validity is a property of arguments. An argument is deductively valid just in case it is impossible for its premises to be true and its conclusion false. Based on this definition, we can use the truth table method to analyze the deductive validity of arguments in PL. An argument is deductively valid in PL just in case there is no row in its completed truth table that has all true premises yet a false conclusion; if there is such a row, the argument is invalid.

Here again is the truth table for the logical conditional:

α   β   α conditional β

T	T	T
F	T	T
T	F	F
F	F	T

Given this table along with the other three truth tables for the logical conjunction, negation, and disjunction, we can construct a truth table for the PL statement

~(E ⊃ (F & G)}

This statement has three simple statement letter types in it, 'E', 'F', and 'G'; so its truth table needs 2^3 rows. We first must write the three simple statement letter types to the left of the statement, as in

E F G   ~(E ⊃ (F & G))

Next we must write three columns of T's and F's, making sure we exhaust all the possible ways in which three distinct simple statements can be true and false together. Recall that in order to be sure that we exhaust all such possibilities, we adopt the technique of writing alternations of T's and F's in the first column and pairs of T's and F's in the second column and quadruplets of T's and F's in the third column and so on, doubling the number of T's and F's for each column we add. Following this advice, we derive the completed truth table for the original statement:

E F G	~(E	⊃	(F & G))
T T T	F	T	T
F T T	F	T	T
T F T	T	F	F
F F T	F	T	F
T T F	T	F	F
F T F	F	T	F
T F F	T	F	F
F F F	F	T	F

Since the statement as a whole is a negation, the column below '~' indicates the resulting truth-values for the different possible combinations of truth-values of its constituents.

Exercise 7.7   **Truth tables and statements**

- Construct truth tables for each of the PL statements (1)–(6).

1. ~V ⊃ ((F & T) & (C & T))
2. ((S ⊃ M) & (M ⊃ S)) & ((~J ⊃ ~S) & ~J)
3. (~R ∨ ~J) & ~((R ∨ J) ⊃ S)
4. ~(H ∨ (M ∨ D))
5. (~I ∨ L) ⊃ W
6. ~(W ∨ S) & (~(T ∨ D) & (~F ⊃ ~L))

Devising truth tables for arguments requires merely that we devise a truth table for each statement in the argument, lined up from left to right, with the conclusion last. We then look to see whether there are any rows in the completed truth tables for each of the statements in the argument in which all the premises are true and the conclusion is false. If there is one such row, then the argument is deductively invalid. If there is no such row, then the argument is deductively valid. So, for example, consider the argument:

  ~A ∨ B, ~(A & B) ∴ B ⊃ A

First we identify the distinct simple statement letter types in this argument. There are only two, 'A' and 'B', so the table needs only four rows. We write them to the far left of the argument and then devise the table, the finished product of which is:

A B	~A ∨ B,	~(A & B)	∴ B ⊃ A
T T	F T	F T	T
F T	T **T**	**T** F	**F**
T F	F F	T F	T
F F	T **T**	**T** F	**T**

Since the first premise is a disjunction and the second is a negation, we first look under the 'v' in the first premise and the '~' in the second to see whether there are any rows in which they are both true. There are two, the second and the fourth. In the fourth, both premises are true, and the conclusion is true as well; but in the second row, both premises are true, and the conclusion is false, so the argument is deductively invalid.

Truth tables and arguments   Exercise 7.8

- Construct truth tables for PL arguments (1)–(6).

1. E ⊃ F ∴ ~F ⊃ ~E
2. D ⊃ (B & C) ∴ B ⊃ (C ⊃ D)
3. (C & D) ∨ E, E ⊃ A, (C ⊃ B) & (D ⊃ B) ∴ A ∨ B
4. (C ∨ D) ⊃ F, ~F, ~(D & E) ∴ ~E & ~C
5. P ∨ Q, Q ∨ R ∴ S ∨ R
6. (P ⊃ Q) ⊃ R ∴ P ⊃ (Q ⊃ R)

7.12.2   *Contradiction, Tautology, Contingency*

We can use the truth table method to distinguish among these three types of statements: contingent statements, tautologies, and contradictions. A *contradiction* is a statement that must be false (and never true). A *tautology* is a statement that must be true (and never false). A *contingent* statement is a statement that can be either true or false.

So consider the following statements:

55. All human beings are happy.
56. Every member of the New York Knicks is over six feet tall.
57. Wan Luck is standing in Tiananmen Square in Peking at this very moment.
58. Either Mary loves John, or Mary does not love John.
59. Mary loves John, but Mary does not love John.

(55)–(57) are contingent. Each might or might not be true. (55) happens to be false, but it doesn't *have* to be false. We can imagine a circumstance in which every human being was happy. Suppose due to a natural disaster that the world population was reduced to two people, who were very happy because they had just discovered each other. Then (55), which happens now to be false, would then be true. So it could be true or false depending on the circumstances. It is contingent. (56) happens to be true, but it could be false if a new player who was shorter than six feet joined the team. (57) is either true or false, but we are not in a position to know which. A person Wan Luck might or might not be standing in Tiananmen Square now. If he is, (57) is true; if there is no Wan Luck, or if he isn't standing there, then (57) is false. Its truth-value likewise depends on circumstances; it too is contingent.

To analyze (58), use the truth table method. Let 'L' be 'Mary loves John'. Since 'L' has only two possible truth-value assignments, T and F, the truth table for (58) is:

L	∨	~L
T	T	F
F	T	T

The truth table analysis reveals that (58) is true for every possible assignment of truth-values. Whether 'L' is true or 'L' is false, 'L ∨ ~L' is true. Any statement which is true for every possible assignment of truth-values to its components is called a 'logical truth'. Other names for logical truths are 'tautologies' (in PL) or 'necessary truths'. The term 'necessary truth' is particularly revealing. 'L ∨ ~L' doesn't just happen to be true; it *must* be true, because it is true no matter what the truth-value of its constituent statements. Its truth is necessary. Its truth does not depend on circumstances. It is a logical truth because it is true by virtue of logic alone. The truth table analysis alone suffices to reveal the statement's truth.

Statement (59) is called a logically or necessarily false statement or a contradiction. It *must* be false regardless of the assignment of truth-values to its constituent parts.

L	&	~L
T	F	F
F	F	T

Contradictions or logical falsehoods are false by virtue of the logical structure of the statements alone.

A statement like (60) is contingent in virtue of form.

60. P ∨ (Q & ~R)

A truth table for it (with its required eight rows) would contain at least one row in which it is false and at least one in which it is true. A statement like (61) is a tautology, since in every row of its truth table, (61) is true.

61. P ∨ ~P

Lastly, a statement like (62) is a contradiction, since, in any correct truth table for it, (62) is false for every assignment of truth-values.

62. (P ⊃ ~P) & P

There cannot be a single row in which (62) is true.

Note that if an argument has a contradiction as one of its premises, this argument must be deductively valid. Because one of the premises is a contradiction, it will be false for every assignment of truth-values. On every line of the truth table, then, one premise at least will be false, so no row can have all the premises true *and* its conclusion false. The argument is deductively valid by definition. For this reason, anything follows from a contradiction. If, however, an argument has a tautology as a conclusion, it must be deductively valid: since its conclusion is always true, there cannot be a row on the truth table in which the premises are true and the conclusion is false.

Statement properties   Exercise 7.9

- Determine for each of (1)–(7) whether it is contingent in virtue of its form, tautological, or contradictory, using the truth table method.

1. P ∨ ~Q
2. (P & Q) & (~P & Q)
3. (P ⊃ Q) & (~P ⊃ Q)
4. P & (P ⊃ (~P & Q))
5. P & (Q ⊃ P)
6. (P & Q) ⊃ (P ∨ Q)
7. (P ∨ Q) ∨ (~P ∨ R)

7.12.3   *Consistency*

Consistency is a property of a set of statements. Often we criticize someone on the grounds of inconsistency. If someone is being inconsistent, then not all of what he is saying can possibly be true. If you tell me that your uncle is a doctor and then later go on to tell me that you have no uncle, then not all of what you told me can be true. To determine whether a set of statements in PL is consistent, we construct a truth table for the statements in the set. If there is at least one row in which each statement of the set is true, then the entire set is consistent. If there is no single row in which each statement is true, then the set is inconsistent.

If you construct a truth table for the following set of statements, you will discover that they comprise an inconsistent set of statements. In the truth table for the set, no single row assigns T to all the statements. They cannot all be true together:

{P ⊃ Q, Q ⊃ (R & ~S), ~S ⊃ ~P, P}

Exercise 7.10   **Consistency**

- Determine whether sets of statements (1) and (2) are consistent. ('{' and '}' indicate set membership)

1.   {(P & Q) ∨ ~R, R ⊃ (~Q ⊃ P)}
2.   {P ⊃ (R ∨ ~T), ~P ⊃ (~R ∨ T), R & ~T}

7.12.4   *Logical Equivalence*

Logical equivalence is also a relation between two statements. Statements can have different forms, yet still be equivalent. (63) and (64) have different forms.

63.   It is not the case that both John and Bill came.
64.   Either John didn't come, or Bill didn't come.

(63) is a negation. It is a negation of a conjunction. (64) is a disjunction, whose disjuncts are both negations. Letting 'J' represent 'John came'

and 'B' represent 'Bill came', (63) and (64), therefore, should be symbolized, given the techniques adopted, as (65) and (66) respectively.

65. ~(J & B)
66. ~J ∨ ~B

Although (65) and (66) have different forms, they are logically equivalent. Intuitively, two statements are logically equivalent just in case they are true under the same conditions. The truth table method enables us to put this point more precisely:

> **Two statements of PL are logically equivalent just in case their truth tables are identical for their main connective.**

The truth tables for (65) and (66) are identical, so these two statements are logically equivalent.

JB	~(J & B)	~J ∨ ~B
TT	F T	F
FT	T F	T
TF	T F	T
FF	T F	T
	+	+

The logical equivalence is established by the resulting *truth-value* assignments to the main connectives of the two statements, the tilde and the wedge respectively. In the first row the truth-values are false for each statement. Although the assignment of truth-values in the first row results in both statements being false, you should not conclude that the first row is inconsequential, or that the two statements are not logically equivalent. Logical equivalence is established just in case the truth-values, whether false or true, of the two statements are identical in all possible cases. If both statements turned out to be contradictions, for example, so that for every assignment of truth-values, the truth-value of each statement was false, then the two statements would be logically equivalent. For each row in the truth table analysis, the truth-values of the statements would be identical.

Logical equivalence requires some special attention, because beginning logic students tend to symbolize statements with logically equivalent forms identically. Usually such symbolizations are mistaken. So, for example, given the symbolizing techniques we have adopted in this book, letting 'W' represent 'Wilson was a president' and 'E' represent 'Wilson was an educator', (67) cannot be symbolized as both (68) and (69).

67. Either Wilson was a president or he was an educator.
68. W ∨ E
69. ~(~W & ~E)

So even though (68) and (69) can be proved to be logically equivalent in PL, we have opted to symbolize statements that look like (67) as disjunctions, not as negations of conjunctions. So, relative to these adopted conventions, (68) rather than (69) correctly symbolizes (67). Although statements having different connectives can be logically equivalent, logical conjunctions are not logical disjunctions; a logical conjunction is not a logical negation, and so on. Keep clearly in mind the difference between statements being logically equivalent and statements having the same logical form (relative to a set of conventions for symbolizing them in logic).

Exercise 7.11   **Logical equivalence**

- Indicate for each of the following pairs of statements whether they are logically equivalent.

1. (A ⊃ B) ⊃ (A ⊃ C), A ⊃ (B ⊃ C)
2. (P ∨ Q) ∨ R, ~(~P ∨ ~Q) & ~R
3. A ⊃ (B ⊃ C), ~C ⊃ ~A
4. (P & Q) ⊃ L, P ⊃ (Q ⊃ L)

Notes

1 In other books, you may find other symbols being used for conditionals, especially, '→' (the arrow).

2 Though we will, as is customary, treat both necessary and sufficient conditions as introducing material conditionals, doing so has its problems. See §A3.1.3 for an elaboration.

3 In general, dropping outside parentheses is permissible if no ambiguity or ungrammaticality results. So $(\alpha \supset \beta)$ can be expressed as $\alpha \supset \beta$.

Bibliography

Adams, E. W., *The Logic of Conditionals* (Dordrecht: Reidel, 1975).

Edgington, D., 'On Conditionals', *Mind* 104, 235–329.

Geis, M., ' "If" and "Unless" ', in B. J. Kachru (ed.), *Issues in Linguistics: Papers in Honor of Heny and Renee Kahane* (Urbana, IL: University of Illinois Press, 1973), 231–53.

Harper, W. L., Stalnaker, R. and Pearce, G. (eds), *Ifs* (Dordrecht: Reidel, 1981).

Jackson, Frank, *Conditionals* (Cambridge: Cambridge University Press, 1987).

—— (ed.), *Conditionals* (Oxford: Oxford University Press, 1991).

Lewis, David, *Counterfactuals* (Oxford: Basil Blackwell, 1973).

McCawley, James, *Everything That Linguists have Always Wanted to Know about Logic but were Ashamed to Ask*, 2nd edn (Chicago: University of Chicago Press, 1993).

Pospesel, H., *Introduction to Logic: Propositional Logic*, 3rd edn (Upper Saddle River, NJ: Prentice-Hall Inc., 1998).

Pospesel, H. and Marans, D., *Arguments*, 2nd edn (Englewood Cliffs, NJ: Prentice-Hall, 1978).

Ryle, G., ' "If", "So", and "Because" ', in Max Black (ed.), *Philosophical Analysis* (Englewood Cliffs, NJ: Prentice-Hall, 1950), 80–6.

Sanford, David H., *If P, then Q: Conditionals and the Foundations of Reasoning* (London: Routledge, 1989).

Strawson, P. F., ' "If" and "⊃" ', in R. E. Grandy and R. Warner (eds), *Philosophical Grounds of Rationality* (Oxford: Clarendon Press, 1986), 228–42.

8

Truth Trees

The truth table method is an effective procedure for determining the validity of arguments in PL. However, this straightforward way can become laborious. For example, if there are ten simple statement constituents in an argument, 1,024 cases must be examined. Is there a less laborious way? In order to answer this question, we will reconsider the truth table method to see whether it suggests any alternative strategies we might adopt.

8.1 Reviewing Validity

How do we determine validity from a completed truth table? We check the column under the conclusion for falsities, and then we check in the corresponding rows to see whether all the premises are true. All the other rows are superfluous, hence disregarded. So in any given truth table we will have entered a lot of material which we end up ignoring.

The question becomes: Is there a way to identify only those truth-value assignments that count for the purpose of determining validity? Put somewhat differently, can we find these assignments without investigating every possibility?

Recall that an argument is valid just in case it's impossible for its premises to be true and its conclusion false all together. Put in the vocabulary of the truth table method, an argument is valid just in case there is no row that assigns true to all the premises and false to the conclusion. With this definition in mind, consider the following argument:

P ⊃ Q, P ∴ Q

Applying the definition of validity to this argument, we infer that it is valid just in case it's not possible for 'P ⊃ Q' to be true, 'P' to be true, yet 'Q' false. But 'Q' is false just in case '~Q' is true. So, the argument is valid just in case it's not possible for 'P ⊃ Q', 'P', and '~Q' all to be true together. Can we find a shorthand way to try to exhaust every possibility for assigning truth-values to see if it's impossible for each premise to be true and the negation of the conclusion ('~Q') to also be true? If so, we will have found a shortcut for determining the validity of arguments.

We will introduce the *truth tree* method for this purpose.[1] First we give a general notion: informally, a truth tree is a chart constructed like an upside-down tree, with the premises listed at the very top of the diagram, forming the beginning of the trunk, and the negation of the conclusion added to the list as an expansion of the tree trunk. Together the premises and the negation of the conclusion form what we can call the main trunk of the tree.

8.2   Tree Trunks and Compound and Atomic Statements

Insofar as a statement in the main trunk is *compound*, we will need rules to analyze or break it down into simpler statements and so on until we are left with nothing other than what we shall call 'atomic statements'. An *atomic* statement is any simple statement or its negation, and a compound statement is any non-atomic statement.

A moment's thought should convince you that there can be but seven types of compound statements in PL: namely, conjunctions, disjunctions, conditionals, negations of conjunctions, negations of disjunctions, negations of conditionals, and negations of negations. Corresponding to these seven types of compound statements there are seven rules.

Having an example of a *completed* truth tree will be helpful as a reference point for our presentation of these rules; so consider the following argument:

A ⊃ B, B ⊃ C ∴ A ⊃ C

A complete truth tree for this argument is as follows:

√1.   A ⊃ B   (premise)
√2.   B ⊃ C   (premise)
√3.   ~(A ⊃ C)   (negation of conclusion)
 4.   A   3, ~ ⊃
 5.   ~C   3, ~ ⊃
                /\
 6.   ~B   C   2, ⊃
          /\   ×
 7.   ~A   B   1, ⊃
        ×   ×

Note first that in this truth tree the conclusion of the original argument does not occur; rather its negation '~(A ⊃ C)' occurs at step (3). Remember that our objective is to see whether it's impossible for the premises and the negation of the conclusion all to be true together. Since a statement is false if, and only if, its negation is true, (1)–(3) represent this circumstance. (For an explanation of √ and ×, see pp. 118–19.)

8.3   Truth Tree Rules

The tree method will allow us to check for validity in a shorthand way. We'll show that the method determines validity correctly later on. For now, we'll just present the method by gathering below all the tree construction rules and showing how to build a tree from them for any given argument of PL.

To begin the process of analysis, we introduce the seven rules that allow us to analyze compound statements like (1)–(3) in the above truth tree into atomic statements. There are two types of rules: *branching* rules and *non-branching* rules. (One and only one of the seven rules applies to each type of compound statement in PL.) The question we must ask about each statement in the main trunk is this: What are the conditions under which this statement is true? After identifying these truth conditions, we can establish rules that allow us to infer simpler statements from compound statements.

8.3.1   *Non-branching Rules*

- Consider the non-branching rule Double Negation (~ ~). A compound double negation statement ~ ~α is true just in case its simpler component α is true. This logical fact is the basis for the non-branching Rule of Double Negation (~ ~), which tells us that when there is a double negation of the form ~ ~α appearing as a line in a truth tree, you are permitted to insert α by itself as an entry lower down on the tree.

- With regard to the non-branching Rule of Conjunction (&), consider the conditions under which a conjunction is true. It is true just in case both its conjuncts are true. The Rule of Conjunction permits us to enter separately as lines lower on the tree (the order is irrelevant) the conjuncts of the conjunction.
- With regard to the non-branching Rule of Negation of a Conditional (~ ⊃), consider the conditions under which a negation of a conditional is true. Take, for example, the negated conditional '~(P ⊃ Q)'. This negation is true just in case 'P ⊃ Q' is false. A conditional is false if, and only if, its antecedent is true and its consequent false – in this case, if, and only if, 'P' is true, and 'Q' is false. The Rule of Negation of a Conditional permits us to enter separately as lines lower on the tree the antecedent and the negation of the consequent.
- With regard to the non-branching Rule of Negation of a Disjunction (~ ∨), consider the conditions under which a negation of a disjunction is true. It is true just in case both its disjuncts are false (i.e., the negations of both its disjuncts are true). The Rule of Negation of a Disjunction permits us to enter separately as lines lower on the tree the negation of its disjuncts.

8.3.2   Branching Rules

Now let's turn to the branching rules.

- For the branching Rule of the Conditional (⊃), we apply the same process. Ask yourself what the conditions are under which α ⊃ β is true. We have already learned in chapter 7 that a conditional α ⊃ β is true just in case *either* α is false *or* β is true. In other words, the truth conditions for a conditional are disjunctive. There is more than one possibility – unlike the statements to which the first four non-branching rules apply. In determining the validity of an argument, we must be sure we are assigning every possible relevant truth-value. For this reason we adopt a *branching* technique, so that each possible assignment of truth-values which would make the conditional true is accommodated in the truth tree. To show that a conditional is true, we list lower in the tree the negation of its antecedent ~ α as a left branch and its consequent β as a right branch.

- With regard to the branching Rule of Negation of a Conjunction (~ &), consider the conditions under which a negation of a conjunction is true. It is true just in case at least one of its conjuncts is false (i.e., in case either of the negations of its conjuncts is true). Take as an example '~(P & Q)'. What it negates, i.e., 'P & Q', is true just in case both 'P' and 'Q' are true. So '~(P & Q)' is true if, and only if, one of these statements is false. The Rule for Negation of a Conjunction permits us to enter lower on the tree the negation of one conjunct as a left branch (i.e., '~P') and the negation of the other conjunct ('~Q') as a right branch.

- Finally, with regard to the branching Rule of Disjunction (∨), consider the conditions under which a disjunction is true. It is true just in case at least one of its disjuncts is true. The Rule of Disjunction permits us to enter lower on the tree one disjunct on a left branch and the other disjunct on a right branch.

The following is a complete list of the seven rules for the truth tree method in abstract form:

Non-branching Rules	Branching Rules
Double Negation (~ ~)	Conditional (⊃)
~ ~α	α ⊃ β
α	/\
	~α β
Conjunction (&)	Negation of Conjunction (~ &)
α & β	~(α & β)
α	/\
β	~α ~β
Negation of Conditional (~ ⊃)	Disjunction (∨)
~(α ⊃ β)	α ∨ β
α	/\
~β	α β
Negation of Disjunction (~ ∨)	
~(α ∨ β)	
~α	
~β	

These rules apply to any statement with the form of the first line of the rule.

8.4 Strategies

To explain further the relevant entries in a truth tree, let us see how the sample truth tree above came about.

1.	A ⊃ B	(premise)
2.	B ⊃ C	(premise)
√3.	~(A ⊃ C)	(negation of conclusion)
4.	A	3, ~ ⊃
5.	~C	3, ~ ⊃

Note that to the right of each line starting with line (4) is an entry that explains from what line the new entry was derived and what rule was used in order to derive it. Lines (4) and (5) are derived from line (3), the negation of the conclusion of the argument, by the Rule of Negation of a Conditional. The value of such entries is that another person (e.g., your grader) can check the process you used in making entries into the truth tree.

Now we are in a position to explain how this sample truth tree works to determine validity. To hold the amount of work involved to a minimum, you will find that *as a general strategy, you are better off applying non-branching rules before applying branching rules.*[2] Following this rule of thumb, we deliberately began the truth tree analysis by analyzing line (3), which allows for the application of a non-branching rule, whereas lines (1) and (2) do not. As you will come to see, branching complicates the tree in a way that non-branching does not.

Notice a check mark to the left of line (3). This check mark is inserted after the analysis of line (3) has been completed. The check mark tells you that you have applied one of the rules. The absence of check marks next to lines (1) and (2) at this stage tells you that two compound statements, lines (1) and (2), remain to be analyzed. When you have put a check mark next to lines (1), (2), and (3), then you will know that you have completed your analysis of all the compound statements in the main trunk. Each statement in the main trunk must be simplified either into a less complex but nevertheless still compound statement (which will need further simplification) or into an atomic statement.

The analyses of lines (1) and (2) both require the application of branching rules, so we arbitrarily choose line (2) first.

1. A ⊃ B   (premise)
√2. B ⊃ C   (premise)
√3. ~(A ⊃ C)   (negation of conclusion)
4. A   3, ~ ⊃
5.   ~C   3, ~ ⊃

6. ~B   C   2, ⊃
        ×

Line (6) puts '~B' and 'C' parallel to each other, as two branches coming off the trunk which terminated at '~C'. Line (6) is justified as derived from line (2) by the Rule of Conditional, since line (2) is a conditional statement. (At this stage it suffices to say that when applying a rule to a line, you place the results of applying that rule at the bottom of the tree. That is why the result of applying the conditional rule to line (2) comes right after line (5), which is the furthest downward point to which the tree has grown so far.)

Notice that an '×' is placed under 'C' in line (6). The '×' indicates that this branch on the tree is *closed*. In order to explain closure of a branch, we need first to develop a vocabulary to describe a truth tree. We have already referred to the premises and the negation of the conclusion of the argument – here lines (1)–(3) – as the main trunk. From the main trunk we can have an extension of the trunk continuing in a downward vertical direction, as in the case of lines (4) and (5). These extensions are the result of applying non-branching rules, rules that keep the tree growing straight downward vertically. We can also have branches extending in a diagonal direction, as in the case of line (6). Such branches are the result of applying branching rules.

At line (6), the truth tree grows two branches, which spring from lines (1)–(5) downward to a token of '~B', and diagonally to the right and downward to a token of 'C'.

After each addition to the main trunk, as in lines (4), (5) and (6), you should pause and, starting with the new entry, progress upward along its branch all the way up to line (1) to see whether the new entry contradicts any previous entry. 'C' in line (6) has on its branch an entry which contradicts it: namely, '~C', its explicit contradictory, on line (5).

When we find a statement and its negation on the same branch, we write an '×' at the end of the branch indicating that that branch is closed. No more work needs to be done on a closed branch. This branch cannot yield the result we are seeking: namely, a condition under which (1)–(3) are all true together.

Although the branch which terminates in 'C' in (6) is closed, the other branch terminating in '~B' remains open. As yet, the compound statement (1) has not been analyzed. So we apply the proper rule, which in this case is the Rule of the Conditional, which is a branching rule. So we form the branches from '~B', terminating in '~A' and 'B' on line (7).

$\sqrt{}$1.   A ⊃ B   (premise)
$\sqrt{}$2.   B ⊃ C   (premise)
$\sqrt{}$3.   ~(A ⊃ C)   (negation of conclusion)
4.   A   3, ~ ⊃
5.   ~C   3, ~ ⊃

6.   ~B   C   2, ⊃
            ×

7.   ~A   B   1, ⊃
    ×   ×

We justify these entries by entering to the right, in the justification column, a '1' to show from which line (7) was derived, and we also include '⊃' to indicate which rule was applied. To complete our application, we write a check mark to the left of line (1), indicating that the premises and the negation of the conclusion have now all been analyzed.

We pause at the terminus point of each branch in line (7) to go upwards through the branches to the main trunk, to see whether any explicit contradiction occurs. You will notice that with regard to 'B' in the rightmost branch in line (7) we find on that same branch in line (6) its explicit contradiction '~B'. Having found its contradiction, we put an '×' below 'B' in line (7), indicating that this rightmost branch terminating in 'B' is closed.

We now proceed to the leftmost branch terminating in '~A' in line (7). We look upward through the branch, which goes through '~B' in line (6) and '~C' in line (5) and 'A' in line (4), where we can stop, because we have discovered in this branch the contradictory of '~A', namely, 'A'. As a result we put an 'x' on the bottom of the branch terminating in '~A' on line (7), indicating that this branch is also closed.

Now we can see that all three branches in this tree are closed. What does this result show us? We started with a main trunk composed of the premises and the negation of the conclusion. We tried to find an assignment of truth-values such that lines (1)–(3) would all be true, given that assignment. Since each of the three branches in this tree exhibited a contradiction, this shows that no such assignment is possible. It is impossible for the premises to be true and the conclusion false (i.e., its negation true) all together. So we have demonstrated that the argument is valid. (Put somewhat differently, had we instead constructed a truth table for this same argument in PL, then for every row in which the premises were true, the conclusion would be true as well.)

8.5   Truth Trees and Invalidity

We proceed now to an invalid argument, to see how to use the truth tree method to demonstrate its invalidity.

Consider the invalid argument:

A ⊃ B, B ⊃ C ∴ C ⊃ A

A complete truth tree for this argument is as follows:

```
√1.   A ⊃ B              (premise)
√2.   B ⊃ C              (premise)
√3.   ~(C ⊃ A)           (negation of conclusion)
 4.   C                  3, ~ ⊃
 5.            ~A        3, ~ ⊃
               /\
 6.    ~B      C         2, ⊃
       /\     /\
 7.  ~A  B  ~A  B        1, ⊃
     ×
```

Lines (4)–(6) are familiar from the previous tree. However, if we look upward from line (6) along the branches, we find no prior lines contradicting either of the two terminating statements, '~B' or 'C'. At this stage in its growth, the truth tree has two *open* branches. Now when we turn to line (1), the last unexamined compound statement in the tree, we must enter whatever the Rule of the Conditional requires to *every* open branch which (1) falls on. Otherwise we are leaving open a possible assignment of truth-values, and we will not have covered every relevant possibility. Put more generally, the constraint guiding us is this:

> **Whenever a rule is applied to a statement α, whatever we derive must be entered lower in the tree on every open branch that α is on.**

Therefore, we must devise two sets of branches, one coming from the branch which '~B' in line (6) is on and one from the branch which 'C' in line (6) is on. The result is line (7).

Line (7) terminates in four distinct branches, only one of which closes: namely, the second leftmost branch. This branch closes because on it we find both a token of 'B' in line (7), and a token of its explicit contradiction '~B' in line (6). We place the customary '×' underneath 'B' in line (7) indicating that this branch is closed. However, there are no contradictions on any of the other three branches. This means that these branches remain open. Each complete open branch indicates conditions under which the original (1)–(3) can all be true together. For example, the leftmost open branch tells us that if 'C' is true, 'A' is false, and 'B' is false: that is, the premises will be true, but the conclusion will be false.

Furthermore, every compound statement in this tree has been checked (i.e., has had the relevant rule applied to it), and no compound statement remains at the lower extremity of any branch of the tree. Each branch has issued in an atomic statement, so no statement remains that could be further analyzed by applying a branching or a non-branching rule. Since every branch is either closed or open after every relevant rule has been applied to every compound statement in it, the resulting tree is said to be complete.

When a complete tree has at least one open branch on it, then it is possible for the statements in its main trunk all to be true together. This result means that it is possible for the premises of the original argument and the negation of its conclusion all to be true together. And this means that it's possible for the premises of the original argument to be true and its conclusion false. In short, a complete truth tree with at least one open branch establishes that the original argument is invalid.

One last truth tree will enable us to answer the most frequently asked questions about the truth tree method. Consider the argument:

~(A & B) ⊃ (C & D) ∴ A ⊃ D

A complete truth tree for this argument is:

√1. ~(A & B) ⊃ (C & D)   (premise)
√2. ~(A ⊃ D)   (negation of conclusion)
3.   A   2, ~ ⊃
4.   ~D   2, ~ ⊃

√5. ~ ~(A & B)   C & D   1, ⊃
√6. A & B   5, ~ ~
7.   A   6, &
8.   B   6, &
9.   C   5, &
10.   D   5, &
                 ×

There is much to learn from this tree. First observe that because there is no contradiction in its left branch the tree is open, so the original argument is invalid. Next notice that the move from line (5) to line (6) is justified by the Double Negation rule. From now on we will relax the rules so that you are not obliged to add a new entry after applying the Double Negation rule. It will suffice simply to cross out the two negation signs. They negate each other, so to speak. So, the following complete open tree is now an acceptable variant on the truth tree (1)–(10) above.

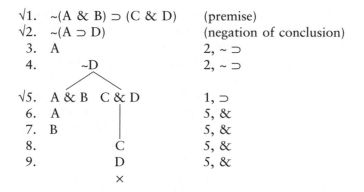

√1. ~(A & B) ⊃ (C & D)   (premise)
√2. ~(A ⊃ D)   (negation of conclusion)
3.   A   2, ~ ⊃
4.   ~D   2, ~ ⊃

√5. A & B   C & D   1, ⊃
6.   A   5, &
7.   B   5, &
8.   C   5, &
9.   D   5, &
                 ×

Another noteworthy feature of this revised tree appears at line (5), which is derived from compound statement (1) by the Conditional Rule.

Although (5) analyzes the conditional in (1) into two conjunctions, these two conjunctions are themselves compound statements that can be further analyzed using the Conjunction Rule. So this tree is incomplete until either both these branches become closed or until the relevant rules have been applied to these compound statements, and they have been broken down into atomic statements.

Lines (6) and (7) result from applying the Conjunction Rule to the statement on the leftmost branch in line (5). Notice that we placed the entries derived from applying this rule to line (5) only on the leftmost branch in (5) because the statement on the rightmost branch in (5) is *not* on the same branch as the statement on the leftmost branch.

> **Only place a token of a statement β derived from applying a rule to a token of a statement α on the branches on which a token of α occurs.**

After deriving lines (6) and (7) by applying the Conjunction Rule to the statement on the leftmost branch of line (5), we wind up with a branch that is both complete and open. It is complete because there are no more unchecked compound statements on this branch, yet it is open because there are no explicit contradictions on the branch. It follows that this complete open branch all by itself suffices to establish that the tree, when completed, will be open as well. Since the discovery of one completed open branch all by itself establishes that the original argument is invalid, the analysis can be truncated here. It need not go on to completion.

However, it is worth our while to examine the rightmost branch as well. When we apply the Conjunction Rule to the statement on the rightmost branch in line (5), we must decide where to place whatever it is that we derive. One might think that it should be placed under both the left and the right branch, since the leftmost branch is open, and its last entry, line (7), is lower on the tree in one obvious sense than both branches in line (5). However, the conjunction on the rightmost branch in line (5) is *not on the same branch* as the entry in line (7). Line (7) is only on the leftmost branch. A relevant constraint is as follows:

> **When a rule is applied to a token of a compound statement, whatever is derived should be placed only on the branches on which the token occurs.**

Had we failed to abide by this essential constraint, we would have erroneously concluded that the argument was deductively valid, as is evidenced by the following badly constructed truth tree.

√1.   ~(A & B) ⊃ (C & D)   (premise)
√2.   ~(A ⊃ D)   (negation of conclusion)
 3.   A   2, ~ ⊃
 4.   ~D   2, ~ ⊃

√5.   (A & B) C & D   1, ⊃
 6.   A   A   5, &
 7.   B   B   5, &
 8.   C   C   5, &
 9.   D   D   5, &
         ×   ×

By misapplying the Conjunction Rule to both conjuncts on line (5), misplacing what is derived on both branches, we would have mistakenly concluded that the original argument is valid, which it is not.

   The obvious lesson to learn from this is that you must be cautious when applying rules to statements. Not only must you make sure that you choose the right rule to apply and that you derive the right statements from it, but you must also be careful where you place whatever it is that you derive.

Exercise 8.1   Arguments and truth trees

- Using the truth tree method, determine whether the solutions to exercises 4.2 and 7.6 are deductively valid.
- Present your work in full.

8.6   Logical Properties and Relations Revisited

8.6.1   Consistency

Recall from §7.12.3 that consistency is a property of a set of statements. There we learned how to employ the truth table method to determine whether a set of statements is consistent. We construct a truth table for each statement in the set. If there is at least one row in which each statement is true, the set is consistent. If there is no row in which each statement is true, the set is inconsistent. Consistency can be determined for PL arguments by the truth tree method as well. In order to determine whether a set of statements is consistent by using truth trees, simply construct a truth tree for the statements. (Do not negate anything, since nothing is a conclusion.) If this tree remains open, then the set is consistent, since there is an assignment of truth-values under which all the statements in the set are true. If there is no such assignment, then the set is inconsistent.

So suppose we want to know whether the following set of statements is consistent:

$$\{(P \,\&\, Q) \vee \sim R, R \supset (\sim Q \supset R)\}$$

We set about devising a truth tree for this set as follows:

√1. $(P \,\&\, Q) \vee \sim R$ (statement 1)
√2. $R \supset (\sim Q \supset R)$ (statement 2)

3. $\sim R$ $\sim Q \supset R$ 2, ⊃

4. $(P \,\&\, Q)$ $\sim R$ $(P \,\&\, Q)$ $\sim R$ 1, ∨
              (open)

There is at least one open completed branch on this tree; so the set consisting of (1) and (2) is consistent.

Consistency   Exercise 8.2

• Determine whether sets (1)–(3) are consistent, using the truth tree method:

1. $\{A \vee B, \sim B \,\&\, \sim A\}$
2. $\{C \vee (B \,\&\, \sim B), \sim K \vee \sim G, (\sim B \vee B) \supset \sim G\}$
3. $\{P \supset (R \vee \sim T), \sim P \supset (\sim R \vee T), R \,\&\, \sim T\}$

8.6.2   *Contradiction, Tautology, Contingency*

Recall our discussion in §7.12.2 of properties of statements: being contradictory, being contingent, and being tautologous. We learned there how to use the truth table method to show whether a statement in PL is contingent, a contradiction, or a tautology. We can also use the truth tree method to prove which of these three categories a statement in PL falls into.

A statement α is contradictory just in case it is false for any possible assignment of truth-values. Any truth tree constructed for α alone satisfies this condition just in case every one of its branches closes: that is, contains a contradiction. For example, consider the statement

(P & (R & Q)) & (~P & (~R ∨ Q))

In order to find out whether this conjunction is a contradiction, we devise a truth tree for it. (1)–(7) is one such tree.

√1.   (P & (R & Q)) & (~P & (~R ∨ Q))
√2.   P & (R & Q)   (2 and 3, from 1, &)
√3.   ~P & (~R ∨ Q)
 4.   P   (4 and 5, from 2, &)
 5.   R & Q
 6.   ~P   (6 and 7, from 3, &)
 7.   ~R ∨ Q
         ×

We close this tree at (7) because lines (4) and (6) contradict each other. Each branch resulting from the application of the Rule of Disjunction (∨) to (7) will contain the same contradiction, and hence close. Since this tree closes, we can infer that statement (1) is a contradiction: there are no circumstances under which it can be true.

A statement α is tautological just in case ~α is a contradiction: that is, just in case any truth tree for ~α closes. So, consider the statement

P ⊃ (Q ⊃ (P ⊃ Q))

In order to find out whether this conditional statement is a tautology, we first negate it and then devise a truth tree for its negation. (1)–(7) is one such tree.

√1. ~(P ⊃ (Q ⊃ (P ⊃ Q)))   (negation of statement)
2. P
√3. ~(Q ⊃ (P ⊃ Q))   (2 and 3, from 1, ~ ⊃)
4. Q
√5. ~(P ⊃ Q)   (4 and 5, from 3, ~ ⊃)
6. P
7. ~Q   (6 and 7, from 5, ~ ⊃)
    ×

Since this tree closes, the original unnegated conditional statement is a tautology. Note also that (1)–(7) establishes that (1), the conditional's negation, is a contradiction. The negation of a tautology (or a logical truth) is a contradiction, and vice versa. Tautologies must be true, so their negations must be false; that is, they are contradictory.

For any statement α, if a completed truth tree for neither it nor its negation closes, then α is contingent, and of course so is ~α. For if ~α were not also contingent, then it would be either a tautology or a contradiction. If ~α were a tautology, then α would be a contradiction; and if ~α were a contradiction, then α would be a tautology. So, if α is by assumption contingent, then so is its negation.

Statement properties   Exercise 8.3

- Determine whether statements (1)–(3) are tautological, contingent, or contradictory, using the truth tree method.

1. (A ⊃ B) ⊃ (~B ⊃ ~(A ∨ C))
2. (P ⊃ Q) & (~P ⊃ (Q & (S ∨ G)))
3. (P ∨ (G & ~D)) & (P ⊃ (~P & (S ∨ ~Q)))

8.6.3 *Logical Equivalence*

Recall from §7.12.4 that two statements α and β are logically equivalent just in case they logically imply each other. So, using the truth tree method, we can determine whether α and β are logically equivalent by devising two truth trees, one for the argument 'α, therefore, β' and one for the argument 'β, therefore, α'. Following our procedure for testing the validity of arguments, we construct a truth table for the premise and the denial of the conclusion. We begin with

α
~β

If that tree closes, then α logically implies β. Only if it does, do we bother to check to see whether the tree for

β
~α

closes. If that tree closes, then β logically implies α. If both trees close, then α and β are logically equivalent; if both trees do not close, then α and β are not logically equivalent.

So, consider the two statements

((A & B) ⊃ B) ⊃ (A ⊃ C), (A & B) ⊃ (B ⊃ C)

These two statements are logically equivalent just in case truth trees for the following two pairs close:

1. ((A & B) ⊃ B) ⊃ (A ⊃ C)　　1′.　(A & B) ⊃ (B ⊃ C)
2. ~((A & B) ⊃ (B ⊃ C))　　　　2′.　~(((A & B) ⊃ B) (A ⊃ C))

You can check for yourself whether these two trees close.

Exercise 8.4　　　　　　　**Deductive implication**

- Determine whether the first statement deductively implies the second in pairs (1) and (2), using the truth tree method.

1. ((A & B) ⊃ B) ⊃ (A ⊃ C), (A & B) ⊃ (B ⊃ C)
2. D ⊃ (B & C), B ⊃ (C ⊃ D)

Logical equivalence   Exercise 8.5

- Determine whether the following pairs of statements (1)–(3) are logically equivalent, using the truth tree method.

1. $P \supset (Q \& R)$, $(P \supset Q) \& (P \supset R)$
2. $(P \& (Q \& K)) \vee \sim R$, $R \supset (\sim Q \supset (P \& \sim(V \vee \sim J)))$
3. $(P \& Q) \supset R$, $P \supset (Q \supset R)$

Notes

1 Also called 'semantic tableau', a method developed by the Dutch logician Evert Beth.
2 It's important to recognize that the truth tree method itself does not dictate that we begin with non-branching rules. From the perspective of the method, it makes no difference which of (1)–(3) we begin with.

Bibliography

Jeffrey, R. C., *Formal Logic: Its Scope and Limits*, 2nd edn (New York: McGraw-Hill, 1981).
Smullyan, R., *First-Order Logic* (Berlin: Springer, 1968).

9

Property Predicate Logic

9.1 Limits of Propositional Logic

There are many obviously deductively valid arguments for which the foregoing methods are ill suited. Both arguments (1)–(3) and (4)–(6) are obviously deductively valid.

1. All dogs are mortal.
2. Fido is a dog.
3. So, Fido is mortal.

4. All philosophers are eccentric.
5. Some philosophers are American.
6. So, some Americans are eccentric.

From the perspective of PL, every premise and conclusion in these two arguments is a simple statement. None is a conditional, a conjunction, a negation, or a disjunction. So the validity of (1)–(3) and (4)–(6) cannot rest on any logical relationship among their premises and conclusion that PL can discern. To clarify this point, try symbolizing these arguments in PL, and then construct a truth table or a truth tree for the resulting symbolizations. For example, letting 'A' represent 'All dogs are mortal', 'D' represent 'Fido is a dog', and 'M' represent 'Fido is mortal', the correct symbolization of (1)–(3) in PL is (7).

7. A, D ∴ M

Any adequate truth table for (7) will have a row, in which its premises are true and its conclusion false. But we know that not every deductively valid argument is valid in virtue of its form. (See chapter 2 for a discussion of the distinction between arguments deductively valid in virtue of their form and arguments deductively valid not in virtue of their form.) Even though no sharp line can be drawn between those arguments that are valid due to the meanings of 'non-logical' expressions and those valid due to the meanings of 'logical' expressions alone, it is noteworthy that arguments (8)–(10) and (11)–(13) are both valid, and each seems to share whatever form (1)–(3) has. (The point obviously extends to (4)–(6) as well.)

8.   All boys are tall.
9.   John is a boy.
10. So, John is tall.

11. All people with jobs are working.
12. The woman next door is a person with a job.
13. So, the woman next door is working.

What the arguments (8)–(10) and (11)–(13) suggest is that, even though there is an intuitive sense in which the subject matter of (1)–(3) is dogs and their mortality, the words 'dog' and 'mortal' are immaterial with respect to the deductive validity of (1)–(3).

It is due to other words (and the 'structure' of the argument) that the argument is valid. Indeed, in principle, we could concoct indefinitely many arguments that are intuitively valid and that intuitively seem to have the same form as (1)–(3). This is why we can say of argument (8)–(10), though it is about boys and their height, and of argument (11)–(13), though it is about people who work, that they are deductively valid for whatever reason argument (1)–(3) is. What we need to figure out is how we can ascribe structure to these and parallel arguments, as we did in PL, by virtue of which their validity can be determined. To that end, we need to reconsider the class of simple statements and introduce some new categories for distinguishing members within this class.[1] We begin by introducing three new types of symbols: singular terms, property predicates, and quantifiers.

9.2   Singular Terms

There is a difference between terms like 'Aristotle', on the one hand, and 'man' and 'Italian', on the other. We will call the former *singular* terms, the latter *general* terms.

Unlike general terms, singular terms can refer to, describe, name, or designate particular objects. So, singular terms include not only proper names like 'Aristotle', but also definite descriptions, demonstratives, and pronouns. So, 'Mark Twain', 'Bill Clinton', 'Venus', 'Rutgers University', 'New Jersey', and 'Venice' are all singular terms. So are definite descriptions: that is, expressions typically formed by placing the definite article in front of a noun, qualified or unqualified.[2] 'The present king of Norway', 'the man with a martini glass in his hand', and 'the author of *Waverly*' are all definite descriptions.[3] Singular demonstrative pronouns are expressions like 'this' and 'that'. Utterances of these expressions are often accompanied by a gesture of pointing, which is called 'ostension'. Singular pronouns include 'I', 'you', 'me', 'she', 'her', 'herself', and 'it'. The contribution of such terms to the meaning of a statement depends, as is true also of demonstratives, on the context in which they are used.[4]

Any one of these expressions can be the grammatical subject of what have been traditionally called singular subject–predicate statements. The expressions in boldface below are all singular terms in the following subject–predicate statements:

Rutgers University is very large.
The man sitting next to Frank is tall.
The man in the corner with the snake is dangerous.
Frank's father is in town.
That is bad.
This is rather red.
He is in my class.
I don't like bananas.

We will use the lower-case letters 'a', 'b', 'c', 'd', . . . , 'w' to symbolize singular terms (reserving 'x', 'y', and 'z' for another duty; see chapter 12). We can subscript any singular term – for example, 'a' – to form a new singular term, for example, 'a_1'. So, the number of distinct singular terms that can appear in an argument has no arbitrary finite upper bound.

So, expressions on the right-hand side of (14)–(18) are partial symbolizations into Property Predicate Logic (PPL) of the statements on the left-hand side.

14. **Ludwig** is a dog.   l is a dog.
15. **Ludwig** is small.   l is small.

16. **Rover** is a dog.   r is a dog.
17. **The Rembrandt** is lost.   t is lost.
18. **That** is tall.   m is tall.

In (18) 'm' is selected as the symbolization of the singular term 'that' to illustrate that the choice of lower-case letters is arbitrary. Ordinarily, for convenience you might select 't' instead.

9.3 Property Predicates

In contrast to singular terms, which can refer to, describe, name, or designate particular objects, other expressions in our language are applied to, or predicated of, these objects. In (14)–(18) the expressions that are not singular terms are predicates. Predicates ascribe or attribute properties (features, characteristics, or attributes) to the object that the singular term refers to. English and the grammar of logic differ in important respects, but still harking back to what you know about English grammar may be helpful.

The subject of the statement is that thing which is spoken about. In (14)–(18) the subjects are singular. For example, Ludwig is the subject of (14), and the term 'Ludwig', which names him, is a singular term and the grammatical subject of (14).[5] Whenever an English statement has a subject, it has a predicate. In English grammar the predicate is that which says something about the subject. Sometimes the term 'predicate' is understood, in a limited sense, as applying to a verb and sometimes, in a larger sense, as applying to a verb together with its modifiers and complements. In the first sense the English predicate in (14) is the verb 'is'. In the second sense the predicate is 'is a dog', which consists of the verb 'is' plus 'a dog', its complement (which, if anything, completes the verb) plus the verb's modifiers if any. (More on verb modifiers in chapter 17.) In logical grammar the predicate is understood in the larger sense. It is the terminology that ascribes a property to the subject.

The term 'predicate' can be used as both a noun and a verb. Used as a noun, 'predicate' refers to the words that predicate. In (14), 'is a dog' is the predicate. When used as a verb, to predicate is to ascribe, attribute, or characterize. Thus, 'is a dog' predicates a property – being a dog – of Ludwig. If Ludwig is in fact a dog, then we can say that being a dog is truly predicated of him.

> **Property predicates are created by omitting a token of a singular term from a statement.**[6]

So, the expressions 'is a dog' (common noun), 'is brown' (adjective), 'runs' (verb) are standardly classified as property predicates. Alternatively, a property predicate is an expression such that grammatically joining it with a singular term issues in a statement.

Singular terms can be differentiated from predicates in other ways. Although a singular term refers to only one individual, a predicate may apply to many individuals.[7] Even a predicate that happens to apply to a single object such as 'is a Pope' is potentially true of a number of individuals. The Catholic Church might change its policy tomorrow and permit there to be more than one Pope at a time. This change would not alter the meaning of the predicate 'is a Pope'. Unlike a singular term, it's not part of the meaning of the predicate that it applies to a single individual. Even predicates like 'is the only professional philosopher to have won a national wrestling championship' or 'is the first aardvark born in a helicopter', which by definition (see chapter 16) apply to only one thing, do not necessarily apply to one thing. Even if Al is the only professional philosopher to have won a national wrestling championship, someone else might have been. There are also plenty of predicates that, although they don't apply to anything – for example, 'is a witch' – could have been true of something. That is, they have conditions of application, despite not actually applying to anything.

Not every statement admits of a unique subject–predicate logical analysis. From a logical point of view, 'Frank hit Bill' contains both property predicates 'hit Bill' and 'Frank hit', since either 'Frank' or 'Bill' may be omitted from the statement in order to form what we are calling a property predicate. You might find it intuitive, if you have any intuitions about these matters, to treat the statement 'Frank hit Bill' as also including a third predicate, 'hit', which expresses a relation between Frank and Bill. After all, 'hit' is a transitive verb, and a transitive verb requires a subject and an object; so why not say that 'hit' is a relational predicate connecting the subject and the object? This account is not so much wrong as inadvisable (at this stage in our development of logical notation). Logic requires that the same statement be analyzable in different ways, contingent upon the task in hand. For any given argument, logical connections between premises and conclusion determine an appropriate logical representation for statements in that argument. So, in

'Frank hit Bill', the predicate is 'hit Bill' if we take 'Frank' as the logical subject, and the predicate is 'Frank hit' (more colloquially, 'was hit by Frank') if we take 'Bill' as the logical subject.[8] (When we turn to Relational Predicate Logic in chapter 12, we will find good logical reasons for treating 'hit' in 'Frank hit Bill' as a relational predicate, but for now we restrict our attention to property predicates alone.)

Property predicates are symbolized by capital letters superscripted with the numeral '1': 'A^1', 'B^1', 'C^1', 'D^1', . . . , 'Z^1'. As with singular terms, we can subscript any property predicate symbol – for example, 'P^1' – to form a new property predicate symbol – for example, 'P_1^1'. The number of distinct property predicate symbols that can occur in an argument has no arbitrary finite upper bound. To complete symbolizations in PPL for (14)–(18), the predicates are symbolized using these letters. The left-hand sides of (19)–(23) are derived using the process of substitution of predicate letters for predicates, with the lexicon for predicate letters and singular terms on the right-hand side.

19.	D^1l	D^1: is a dog; l: Ludwig
20.	S^1l	S^1: is small
21.	D^1r	r: Rover
22.	L^1t	L^1: is lost; t: the Rembrandt
23.	T^1m	T^1: is tall; m: that

By writing a property predicate succeeded by a singular term, we form a grammatical statement of PPL. We will call these statements in PPL *singular subject–predicate statements.*[9]

9.4 Quantifiers

The grammar of general expressions like 'every fish' 'no tall boy' 'every house on the block', or 'some men who live in New Jersey' virtually agrees with that of singular terms. Replacing 'Ludwig' with 'No tall boy' in 'Ludwig left' should not affect the grammar. Both expressions function as the subject of the sentence. However, such general expressions are *logically* of a fundamentally different character. Each includes what we shall call a *quantifier*. Quantifiers are expressions superficially resembling adjectives. Often they appear with, and modify, simple and complex nouns: for example, 'many', 'a few', 'few', 'most', 'some', 'at least one', 'little', 'much', 'at most three', 'all', 'every', 'any', 'each', 'whatever', 'none', 'a(n)', 'not one', 'whichever', and so on.

This list contains different quantifier expressions that have different logical properties:

- 'Most women are tall' doesn't deductively imply 'All women are tall'.
- 'Some men are happy' doesn't imply 'A few men are happy'.
- 'No one will leave early' is consistent with 'Few people will leave early'.
- But 'No one will leave early' is not consistent with 'A few people will leave early'.

Despite these interesting differences, we will restrict our attention to just two types of quantifier expressions (and whatever other types of quantifier expressions can be defined in terms of these two): the universal and existential quantifier expressions. (See §A4.5 for further discussion of another type of quantifier that cannot be defined in terms of these two.)

9.4.1   Simple Existential Quantifier Statements

(24)–(27) are examples of existential quantifier statements which are equivalent in PPL.

24.   Something is a dog.
25.   At least one thing is a dog.
26.   There are dogs.
27.   There is at least one thing which is a dog.

They are called existential quantifier statements because, implicitly or explicitly, each asserts the existence (hence, is existential) of something, and each contains, implicitly or explicitly, a quantifier term which expresses some quantity.

Number	Quantifier expression	Existential expression
24	Something	
25	At least one	
26		There are
27	At least one	There is

(26) has no explicit quantifier expression like 'something', but we understand (26) to be equivalent to (27), which makes the quantity explicit in (27) implicit in (26). (24) and (25) begin with quantifier expressions and leave the existential reference implicit. But (24) and (25) are equivalent to (27), which makes explicit that (24) and (25) are asserting the existence of at least one dog. So each statement is true just in case at least one thing in the world is a dog.[10]

9.4.2   *Symbolizing Simple Existential Statements*

We said above that quantifier expressions are not singular terms. In this subsection we will look at several reasons for specifically *not* treating the existential quantifier as a singular term.

Suppose we try to symbolize 'something' in (24) as a singular term, say, 's', and then symbolize all of (24) as:

28. D^1s

In (28), 'something' is treated as a singular expression which refers to a particular thing. But it doesn't. When you tell me John is tall, I wouldn't usually ask who is tall unless I hadn't heard you. But when you say that something is tall, I might legitimately ask who this is. With the customary uses of quantifier expressions, no individual is (even purported to be) *singled out*. Quantifier expressions are not singular terms; they are general expressions.[11]

Here's another reason for notationally distinguishing the expression 'something' from singular terms: 'John is a dog' and 'John is not a dog' contradict each other. But 'Something is a dog' and 'Something is not a dog' have not even the superficial appearance of being contradictory. In order for both statements to be true, there must be at least two entities, one of which is a dog and the other of which is not – say, Fido and a rock. When contradictory predicates are added to two tokens of a type of singular term, the resulting statements are contradictory; but when added to two tokens of the same type of quantifier expression, the resulting statements may be consistent with each other.

The following passages from Lewis Caroll's *Alice in Wonderland* illustrate nicely how communication can break down when we treat quantifier expressions like singular terms:

'And I haven't seen the two Messengers either. They've both gone to the town. Just look along the road and tell me if you can see either of them.' 'I see *nobody* on the road,' said Alice. 'I only wish I had such eyes,' the King remarked in a fretful tone. 'To be able to see *Nobody*! And at that distance too! Why it's as much as I can do to see real people by this light!'

'Who did you pass on the road?' the King went on, holding out his hand to the Messenger for some hay. '*Nobody*,' said the Messenger. 'Quite right,' said the King, 'this young lady saw him too. So of course *nobody* walks slower than you.' 'I do my best,' the Messenger said in a sullen tone. 'I'm sure *nobody* walks much faster than I do!' 'He can't do that,' said the King, 'or else he'd have been here first.'[12]

'Nobody' is a quantifier expression. As a general term, it doesn't refer to just one object; it doesn't refer to anyone. The statements in which they appear as subject expressions are typically generalizations. (24)–(27) are examples of existential generalizations. The terms 'existential quantifier statement' and 'existential generalization' are interchangeable. 'Nobody walks slower than you' is also a generalization, but as you will see in the next section, it is not an existential generalization.

If it is wrong to symbolize existential quantifier expressions as singular terms, how then should we symbolize them? We introduce '∃' (backwards 'E') as the symbol to represent the existential quantifier. Letting 'D¹' represent the predicate 'is a dog', we shall symbolize (24)–(27) in PPL as (29).

29. $\exists D^1$

(29) is read: 'Something is a dog', or 'A dog exists', or 'There is at least one dog', or 'There is a dog', or even 'There are dogs'.

9.4.3   Simple Universal Quantifier Statements

Each of (30)–(34) is an example of a universal quantifier statement or, to use alternative language, a universal generalization or a universal statement.

30.   Everything is a dog.
31.   Each thing is a dog.
32.   Each and every thing is a dog.
33.   All things are dogs.
34.   Anything is a dog.

In general, to articulate simple universal quantifier statements in English, we take a universal quantifier expression and combine it with a property predicate. (30)–(34) are true just in case everything in the world is a dog.

Not surprisingly, universal quantifier expressions are not singular terms. As in §9.4.2, we will look at reasons for not treating the universal quantifier as a singular term.

There is no difference in truth conditions between (35) and (36).

35. John loves himself.
36. John loves John.

In most contexts, this feature of singular terms holds. (See, however, ch. 16 and also §A4.) General expressions do not exhibit this characteristic. If the universal quantifier were a singular term, then 'everything' should be substitutable for 'itself' without changing the truth-value of the statement. But (37) can be true while (38) false.

37. Everything loves itself.
38. Everything loves everything.

(We will discuss the relationships among quantifiers, singular terms, and pronouns further in subsequent chapters.[13])

If universal quantifiers are not singular terms, how are we to represent simple universal quantifier statements in PPL? We shall introduce the symbol '∀' (upside-down 'A') to represent the universal quantifier.[14] All of (30)–(34) are then symbolized as

39. $\forall D^1$

(39) is read: 'Everything is a dog', or 'All things are dogs', or 'Each thing is a dog', or 'Anything is a dog', or even 'Each and every thing is a dog'.

9.4.4 Negations of Existentials

Recall from Chapter 4 that the expression 'nothing' may be replaced by 'not something'. In PL, we are treating,

40. Nothing is a mouse.

as a paraphrase of,

41.   It is not the case that something is a mouse.

In PPL, 'Something is a mouse' is symbolized as,

42. $\exists M^1$ M^1: is a mouse

So the original statement, 'Nothing is a mouse', is symbolized in PPL as,

43. $\sim\!\exists M^1$

If we follow the rules for replacement from section 4.2, negations of existentials are easy to symbolize.

How should we treat a statement like 'There are no mice'? We have no rules for replacement to implement here, but it seems that it has the same meaning as 'Nothing is a mouse'. If this is so, then it too should be symbolized as,

44. $\sim\!\exists M^1$

This appears to be a successful technique for writing statements of the form of 'There are no x's'. In general, such statements should be treated as negations of existentials.

Exercise 9.1   Statements

- Symbolize (1)–(10) in PPL using the dictionary provided.

1. Susan is kind. (K^1: is kind; s: Susan)
2. Something tastes sweet. (T^1: tastes sweet)
3. Everything is good. (G^1: is good)
4. John is funny. (F^1: is funny; j: John)
5. Lucy works hard. (W^1: works hard; l: Lucy)
6. Everything smiles a lot. (S^1: smiles a lot)
7. Something is a rooster. (R^1: is a rooster)
8. Nothing is a flea. (F^1: is a flea)
9. There are no chairs. (C^1: is a chair)
10. Nothing caused the event. (C^1: caused the event)

9.5   Complex Predicates

Each of (45)–(49) contains a complex property predicate.

45.   John **is either a dog or a sheep.**
46.   John **is tall and yellow.**
47.   John **is not a dog.**
48.   John **is neither a dog nor a sheep.**
49.   John **is a dog if not a sheep.**

(45) contains the complex predicate 'is either a dog or a sheep'. This predicate is composed from the simpler property predicates 'is a dog' and 'is a sheep'. However, if we look at the symbolization for (45) (and (46)–(49)) in PPL, any appearance of predicate complexity evaporates. (50)–(54) are symbolizations in PPL for (40)–(44) respectively.

50. $D^1j \lor S^1j$	D^1: is a dog; S^1: is a sheep; j: John
51. T^1j & Y^1j	T^1: is tall; Y^1: is yellow
52. $\sim D^1j$	
53. $\sim(D^1j \lor S^1j)$	
54. $\sim S^1j \supset D^1j$	

The apparent complexity of the predicates in (45)–(49) is revealed upon symbolization in PPL to be complexity due to logical connections between statements. (45)–(49) are truth-functional compound statements. (45), for example, is a disjunction, each disjunct of which contains a simple property predicate. But how are we to symbolize (55)–(59) in PPL?

55.   Something is either a dog or a sheep.
56.   Something is tall and yellow.
57.   Something is not a dog.
58.   Something is neither a dog nor a sheep.
59.   Something is a dog if it is not a sheep.

Is (56) a logical conjunction like (46)? Is (57) a logical negation like (47)? We know from our discussion of statement connectives in chapters 3 and 4 (and §A1) that they are not. Instead, they are existential statements with honest-to-goodness complex predicates that cannot be decompounded by statement connectives.

If every statement were like those in (45)–(49), there would be no need to introduce complex property predicates into PPL. We could take predicates of these types and treat them in the manner of (50)–(54). But when quantifiers and predicates are combined, complex property predicates can become necessary.

If (56) were a conjunction, what would its conjuncts be? Presumably (60) and (61).

60.   Something is tall.
61.   Something is yellow.

But (60) and (61) together do not imply (56). From the truth of (60) and (61), we have no guarantee, as we do with (56), that there is (at least) one thing which is both tall and yellow, an additional reason why quantifier expressions are not singular terms. How then should we symbolize (55)–(59)? Since each is an existential statement, we know their symbolizations should take the form

$$\exists \underline{\hspace{2cm}}$$

where the blank is filled in with some complex predicate. In (55) my bet is that your inclination is to treat it as a disjunctive predicate: 'is either a dog *or* a sheep'. How, though, are we to symbolize disjunctive predicates in PPL? We do so by introducing compound predicates into PPL, predicates formed by applying statement connectives to predicates. So to symbolize (55) in PPL, we symbolize its predicate as

$$(D^1 \vee S^1)$$

and then complete the symbolization for (55) as

62. $\exists(D^1 \vee S^1)$

Similarly for (56)–(59).

63. $\exists(T^1 \ \& \ Y^1)$
64. $\exists \sim D^1$
65. $\exists \sim(D^1 \vee S^1)$
66. $\exists(\sim S^1 \supset D^1)$

Strictly speaking, the uses of the familiar statement connectives in (62)–(66) are ungrammatical. The reason is quite simple. We have defined, for example, '&' as a truth-functional symbol such that the truth of any statement in which it occurs as the main connective is true just in case its conjuncts are true. But '$(T^1$ & $Y^1)$' is not true just in case 'T^1' is true and 'Y^1' is true, since neither is true or false. So, for at least those uses which combine predicates with '&', we will have to redefine it. But at this stage in the development of PPL we rely on naive intuition. In the next chapter, when we take up evaluating arguments in PPL, rules for determining validity will have to explain in what sense predicates can be logically disjoined, conjoined, negated, or conditionalized.

English and PPL statements   Exercise 9.2

- Assuming 'D^1' represents 'is a dog', 'S^1' represents 'is a sheep', 'T^1' represents 'is tall', and 'Y^1' represents 'is yellow', what English statements do (1)–(8) symbolize?

1. $\forall(D^1 \vee S^1)$
2. $\forall(T^1$ & $Y^1)$
3. $\forall\sim D^1$
4. $\forall\sim(D^1 \vee S^1)$
5. $\forall(\sim S^1 \ldots D^1)$
6. $\exists S^1$
7. $\exists(D^1$ & $Y^1)$
8. $\exists(T^1 \vee S^1)$

9.6 Well-formedness in PPL

Let us now describe and systematize well-formed expressions that comprise property predicate logic.

Predicates: There are two types of predicates: simple and compound. Simple predicates are symbolized using capital letters (superscripted with '1'): A^1, B^1, C^1, ..., Z^1. Compound predicates come in a variety of kinds: conjunctive, disjunctive, conditional, and negative. Put more formally, if α, β are predicates, then so are (α ∨ β), (α & β), (α ⊃ β), ~α. As in propositional logic, simple predicates represent whatever English predicates are not compound.

Singular terms: These are lower-case letters from a to w (numerically subscripted or not). (We save x, y, and z for another purpose, which we will take up in chapter 12.)

Statements: There are two types of statements in PPL, simple and complex. Simple statements are of one kind:

> *Singular subject–predicate statements* are those that consist of a simple property predicate followed by a singular term: for example, 'D¹l'.

Complex statements come in three kinds:

> *Existential statements*: if α is a predicate, simple or complex, then ∃α is a statement.

> *Universal statements*: if α is a predicate, simple or compound, then ∀α is a statement.

> *Conjunctions, conditionals, disjunctions, negations*: If α, β are statements, complex or simple, then so are α & β, α ∨ β, α ⊃ β, ~α.

But we're not done. Every English statement must be representable within whichever logic we are considering at any given moment. Given this requirement, we must ask whether any English statements do not fall into one of the seven above categories. The answer is that there are indefinitely many such English statements. Consider, for example, (67)–(70).

67. Most things are tall.
68. A few things are happy.
69. Many things have tips.
70. Few things are blond.

(67)–(70) seem to be quantifier statements, suggesting that they might most naturally be classified as either existential or universal; but they are not either. On the one hand, symbolizing any of (67)–(70) as '∀H¹' implies that all things are tall, and so on. However, none of (67)–(70) has universal import. On the other hand, though each of (67)–(70) has existential import, no existential statement by itself implies any of (67)–(70). For example, (67) implies that more things are tall than are non-tall. The existential quantification would imply merely that at least one thing is tall. Therefore, symbolizing any of these statements as '$\exists H^1$' is wrong. Since each begins with a quantifier expression, not a singular term, symbolizing (67)–(70) using a singular expression as in 'H^1a' would also be wrong. So, following an earlier strategy from Propositional Logic, we shall symbolize (67)–(70) and any other English statements which do not belong to one of the seven types of complex statements as simple statements, using familiar capital letters (without superscripts): A, B, C, . . . , Z.

As before, treating a statement as simple does not mean that it is without logical structure. Recall that from the point of view of PL, existential, universal, and singular subject–predicate statements were represented as simple statements. The whole point of moving to PPL was to accommodate deductively valid logical structures invisible to PL. The bottom line is that, like PL, PPL is insufficient for symbolizing the logical structure of every English statement. A more elaborate logical system needs to be developed to accommodate arguments which depend for their validity on quantified statements like those in (67)–(70). However, such system elaboration would take us beyond the scope of an introductory text. (See the bibliography at the end of this chapter and §A4.5 for more on English quantifier expressions that are not definable by the universal and existential quantifiers.)

This completes the discussion and systemization of the grammar of PPL. Nothing else is a statement.

| Well-formedness | Exercise 9.3 |

- Which of (1)–(23) are grammatical PPL statements?
- What type of statement is each?
- For those that are grammatical in PPL, concoct English statements they might symbolize.

1. $\exists D^1$
2. $\forall D^1 \vee G^1$

3. $\forall(D^1 \,\&\, G^1)$
4. $D^1a \lor G^1a$
5. $D^1b \lor D^1c$
6. $\forall D^1 \supset \forall G^1$
7. $F^1a \supset \exists b$
8. $K^1n \lor \forall(G^1 \,\&\, H^1)$
9. $H \lor \exists G^1$
10. $\exists(K^1 \,\&\, H^1 \lor R^1)$
11. $\exists D^1 \supset \forall H^1$
12. $H^1b \supset K^1a$
13. $\exists(H^1 \lor K^1) \supset L^1a$
14. $\forall P^1 \supset \exists(T^1 \,\&\, L^1)$
15. $\sim L^1a$
16. $\sim\forall(H^1 \,\&\, I^1)$
17. $\sim\exists \sim H^1$
18. $\exists \sim(Y^1 \,\&\, P^1)$
19. $\forall \sim \sim O^1$
20. $\forall(P^1 \,\&\, (L^1 \supset T^1))$
21. $K^1a \lor L^1a \lor \exists(K^1 \lor L^1)$
22. $\forall(H^1 \supset P^1a)$
23. $\exists(M^1a \,\&\, L^1)$

9.7 Quantifiers Modifying General Terms

9.7.1 *Existential Quantifiers and General Terms*

In English and every other natural language, quantifier expressions like 'some' and 'every' are almost always accompanied by nouns that restrict the range of the quantifier expression.[15] Consider statements (71)–(73).

71. Some **girl** is tall.
72. Some **animal** is a dog.[16]
73. Some **rabbis** are Italians.

How should we symbolize them in PPL? In an effort to effect ease of transition from English into the notation of PPL, we will begin with an intuitive strategy (that will not be fully developed until chapter 13). Here's the intuition. (71) has a superficial resemblance to 'John is tall', which we symbolized as 'T¹j'. Since 'Some girl' functions as the subject of (71), a natural thought is to symbolize it in a similar manner. For this purpose we will temporarily introduce notational devices that are part of neither English nor the language of PPL. (See §9.6.) So, let 'T¹' represent 'is tall', but let '∃G' temporarily represent the subject 'some girl', where '∃' is the familiar existential quantifier and 'G' (not a predicate of PPL) stands for 'girl'. Then a first *approximation* towards a symbolization in PPL for (71) is (74), which is *not* an expression in PPL.

74. $T^1_{\exists G}$

How shall we proceed from (74) to a formula in PPL? We might introduce a distinct type of existential quantifier for every noun that an existential quantifier expression can modify. We might have '∃$_g$' for 'some girl', '∃$_b$' for 'some boy', and so on. One difficulty with this suggestion is that there are just too many nouns for existential quantifiers to modify. The class of nouns is open-ended. Just as 'girl' is a general term, so too is 'girl whom Bill knew' and 'girl whom Bill knew before he left for college' and 'girl whom Bill knew in his junior year before he left for college'. The number of modifiers we can add to form a new complex noun has no obvious upper limit. If we accommodated English quantifier expressions with modifying nouns by introducing a new quantifier for each new noun, we would engender indefinitely many types of existential quantifiers in PPL. We will take a simpler, more conservative route.

We first convert noun phrases like 'some girl' into an existential quantifier plus a property predicate. To this end, we introduce a procedure for symbolizing English statements of this form.

> **Procedure: If a statement has a subject–predicate form with ∃α as its subject (where α is a noun) and β as its predicate, transform the statement into ∃(α & β).**

(We will generalize this strategy in relational predicate logic in chapter 13.) The most important features of this procedure are that α is converted into a predicate, and that since β falls within the immediate scope of an existential quantifier, we connect it by an '&' to the newly introduced property predicate α.

This procedure recommends that we treat (71)–(73) as complex existential quantifier statements. This is acceptable, because intuitively (71)–(73) have the same truth conditions as (71′)–(73′) respectively.

71′.   Something is a girl and is tall.
72′.   Something is an animal and is a dog.
73′.   Something is a rabbi and is Italian.

(71′)–(73′) should be symbolized in PPL respectively as (75)–(77).

75. $\exists(G^1 \, \& \, T^1)$ G^1: is a girl; T^1: is tall
76. $\exists(A^1 \, \& \, D^1)$ A^1: is an animal; D^1: is a dog
77. $\exists(R^1 \, \& \, I^1)$ R^1: is a rabbi; I^1: is Italian

But this means that we should also symbolize (71)–(73) as (75)–(77). So, finally, following the procedure above, the correct answer to our question as to how we should symbolize (71) is as (75). We went from (71) to (74) to (75).

71.   Some **girl** is tall.
74. $T^1_{\exists G}$
75. $\exists(G^1 \, \& \, T^1)$

In other words, in (71)–(73) we treat 'girl', 'animal', and 'rabbis' as the property predicates 'is a girl', 'is an animal', and 'is a rabbi' respectively.[17]

9.7.2   *Universal Quantifiers and General Terms*

(78)–(81) are complex universal quantifier statements.

78.   All rabbis are Italians.
79.   Every man is tall.
80.   Each animal is a dog.
81.   Any boy is human.

The nouns 'rabbis', 'man', 'animal', and 'boy' are all property predicates.

How should we symbolize (78)–(81) in PPL? Once again, in order to effect ease of transition from English into the notation PPL, we will begin with an intuitive strategy (that will not be fully developed until

Chapter 13). Since, e.g., 'every man' functions as the subject of (79), let's try to symbolize it in a manner similar to 'John' in 'John is tall'. Again, we will employ a notation that is neither part of English nor the language of PPL. Letting '∀M' represent 'every man', with '∀' the familiar universal quantifier, and 'M' (not a predicate of PPL) standing for 'man'. Then a first approximation towards a symbolization in PPL of (79) is as follows:

$$T^1_{\forall M}$$

How shall we proceed from this to a formula of PPL?

By what means, for example, should these predicates be connected in PPL? Should we use predicate conjunctions as with an existential statement? (78) has a superficial resemblance to (71), so you might be tempted to think that universal and existential statements should be symbolized in similar ways. (78) would then be symbolized in PPL by (78′),

78′. $\forall(R^1 \;\&\; I^1)$

which states that everything is a rabbi and Italian. But (78) does not claim everything to be a rabbi, and it does not assert that anything is a rabbi. Rather, it asserts that anything that is a rabbi is Italian; it asserts only that *if* a thing is a rabbi, *then* it is an Italian. Similarly, (79) says that, for any thing, *if* it is a man, *then* it is tall. So the appropriate connective in (78)–(81) is the horseshoe. In general, the procedure for symbolizing statements of this form is:

> **If a statement has subject–predicate form, with ∀α as its subject (where α is a noun) and β as its predicate, transform the statement into ∀(α ⊃ β).**

So, following this procedure, the correct symbolizations for (78)–(81) in PPL are:

82. $\forall(R^1 \supset I^1)$
83. $\forall(M^1 \supset T^1)$ M^1: is a man
84. $\forall(A^1 \supset D^1)$
85. $\forall(B^1 \supset H^1)$ B^1: is a boy; H^1: is human

The procedure reveals an interesting relation between the horseshoe and the universal quantifier. As characterized, the universal quantifier ranges literally over everything there is! But in (78)–(81), the quantifier expression is restricted. Each speaks only of a particular subset of all things, 'All rabbis', 'Every man', 'Each animal', and 'Any boy'. The puzzle for us has been how to utilize the universal quantifier of PPL so as to accommodate restricted English quantifier expressions in (78)–(81). Our solution has been to exploit the horseshoe. We begin by quantifying over everything. Each of (82)–(85) begins with a universal quantifier followed by a left parenthesis with a matching right one as the last symbol in the formula. This means that each of (82)–(85) is an unrestricted universal statement. But even though there is no visible occurrence of 'if' in (78)–(81), in our symbolizations in PPL we still immediately restrict this universality by saying, 'if it is a rabbi', or 'if it is a man', or 'if it is an animal', or 'if it is a boy'. Though we use the universal quantifier, our interest is limited to men, animals, and so on. In this sense, (78)–(81) are symbolized in PPL as if they paraphrase (78′)–(81′).

78′. For any object, if it is a rabbi, then it is an Italian.
79′. For any object, if it is a man, then it is tall.
80′. For any object, if it is an animal, then it is a dog.
81′. For any object, if it is a boy, then it is a human.

Exercise 9.4   PPL statements

- For (1)–(39), indicate whether each statement is simple, singular subject–predicate, existential, universal, conjunctive, disjunctive, negative, or conditional, and symbolize using the dictionary provided.

1. Jimmy Carter was President. (P^1: was President; j: Jimmy Carter)
2. Frank's class is in geometry. (f: Frank's class; G^1: is in geometry)
3. The tallest person I know is short. (t: the tallest person I know; S^1: is short)
4. John speaks quickly. (j: John; S^1: speaks quickly)
5. Some Italians are dark. (I^1: is Italian; D^1: is dark)
6. At least one person is leaving. (P^1: is a person; L^1: is leaving)
7. Some fish swim. (F^1: is a fish; S^1: swims)
8. Every rabbi is Italian. (R^1: is a rabbi; I^1: is Italian)

9. Every rabbi is not Italian.
10. Four is a number. (f: four; N^1: is a number)
11. All feet have toes. (F^1: is a foot; T^1: has toes)
12. All that glitters is gold. (G^1: glitters; H^1: is gold)
13. Every tree does not have leaves. (This is ambiguous. T^1: is a tree; L^1: has leaves)
14. There are women in the tub. (W^1: is a woman; T^1: is in the tub)
15. No rugs are on the floors. (R^1: is a rug; F^1: is on the floor) (Recall from chapter 4 how to symbolize statements of the form: No α's are β's.)
16. Anything worth buying is worth selling. (W^1: is worth buying; S^1: is worth selling)
17. Each day is pretty. (D^1: is a day; P^1: is pretty)
18. All students are intelligent. (S^1: is a student; I^1: is intelligent)
19. Any student is intelligent.
20. Not all students are intelligent.
21. Some things are neither good nor bad. (G^1: is good; B^1: is bad)
22. Some things are either good or bad.
23. Each thing is either good or bad.
24. Everything is good only if it is not bad.
25. Everything is good if it is not bad.
26. Everything is good if and only if it is not bad.
27. Every human has legs and feet. (H^1: is human; L^1: has legs; F^1: has feet)
28. No sailors allowed. (S^1: is a sailor; A^1: is allowed)
29. There are goblins. (G^1: is a goblin)
30. Every number is either odd or even. (N^1: is a number; O^1: is odd; E^1: is even)
31. Every number is odd, and every number is even.
32. All men played, and all men left. (M^1: is a man; P^1: played; L^1: left)
33. If a cock crows, someone will die. (C^1: is a cock; R^1: crows; P^1: is a person; D^1: will die)
34. There is a Frenchman in the class. (F^1: is a Frenchman; C^1: is in the class)
35. If Joe leaves, everything will go to ruin. (j: Joe; L^1: leaves; R^1: will go to ruin)
36. Either everyone leaves, or John leaves. (P^1: is a person; L^1: leaves; j: John)
37. Some people screamed, some people died, and some didn't do either. (P^1: is a person; S^1: screamed; D^1: died)
38. Every man is tall if John is tall. (M^1: is a man; j: John; T^1: is tall)
39. Some boy is leaving if Mary leaves. (B^1: is a boy; L^1: is leaving (leaves); m: Mary)

- Explain why (40)–(47) cannot be symbolized adequately in PPL.

40. An American citizen is murdered (by someone) every minute. (A¹: is an American citizen; M¹: is murdered every minute)
41. Many men left early.
42. A few girls own trains.
43. Most boys I know are not tall.
44. Few apples are rotten.
45. Almost all the sheep are in.
46. Little time was wasted on studies.
47. Much time was wasted on boozing.

Exercise 9.5   **PPL arguments**

- Symbolize each of arguments (1)–(8) in PPL, using the dictionary included.

1. No dogs are cats. Fido is not a cat. So, Fido is a dog. (C¹: is a cat; D¹: is a dog; f: Fido)
2. All hogs and cows are mammals. All animals are mammals. Therefore, all hogs are animals. (H¹: is a hog; C¹: is a cow; M¹: is a mammal; A¹: is an animal)
3. Each priest and minister is a clergy person. No clergy person is either rude or extravagant. Some ministers are extravagant and faultless. Some priests are not faultless. Therefore, some priests are dowdy. (P¹: is a priest; M¹: is a minister; C¹: is a clergy person; R¹: is rude; E¹: is extravagant; F¹: is faultless; D¹: is dowdy)
4. No acrobats are clumsy. Therefore, if Al is a waiter, then if all waiters are clumsy, Al is not an acrobat. (A¹: is an acrobat; C¹: is clumsy; a: Al; W¹: is a waiter)
5. Some apes are chimps. All chimps are of the genus gorilla. So, some apes are of the genus gorilla. (A¹: is an ape; C¹: is a chimp; G¹: is of the genus gorilla)
6. Not all soil animals are beneficial. For example, some beetle and fly larvae are crop pests. Any crop pest is not beneficial. All beetle and fly larvae are soil animals. (S¹: is a soil animal; B¹: is beneficial; E¹: is a beetle larva; F¹: is a fly larva; C¹: is a crop pest)
7. All cats are mammals. Hence, all cats are either mammals or rodents. (C¹: is a cat; M¹: is a mammal; R¹: is a rodent)
8. All men are rational. Some animals are not men. Therefore, some animals are not rational. (M¹: is a man; R¹: is rational; A¹: is an animal)

Notes

1   A commonly held view is that the main distinction between Predicate Logic and Propositional Logic is that we do not need to look inside statements in Propositional Logic, whereas in Predicate Logic we do. This is a false distinction; we have been looking inside statements in order to determine whether they are conjunctions, disjunctions, negations or conditionals. With respect to the structure of arguments in English, the main difference between the two logics is that they focus on different logical relations among statements.

2   In ch. 16, arguments will be provided against always treating definite descriptions as singular terms.

3   Though definite descriptions typically begin with 'the', it's not stretching the notion of a definite description to include genitive noun phrases like 'Smith's murderer' and 'my father', as well as other nominalizations like 'what she did for a living' and 'where Nixon attended school' as definite descriptions.

4   Not every token of a pronoun or a demonstrative purports to refer to an object. Such tokens are not singular terms. For example, in the statement 'Every man loves **himself**', 'himself' is not functioning as a singular term; it does not purport to refer to anyone specifically. In the statement 'Every number is smaller than **that** number which is its successor', 'that number' is also not functioning as a singular term. More on these usages in chs 12–15.

5   See ch. 2, n. 1, for the two senses of 'subject': one as the subject matter, what the sentence is about; the other the grammatical notion of the noun with which the main verb must agree.

6   Property predicates are also called 'one-place predicates', 'monadic predicates', and 'predicates of degree one'.

7   Plurals like 'the dogs' will not be analyzed in this book. What's your intuition about them: singular term or predicate? See the bibliography at the end of the chapter for a reference on plurals.

8   Other examples of property predicates are 'loves Mary', 'is taller than Bill', 'loves no one'. What all these expressions have in common is that statements produced by grammatically joining some property predicate ('hit Bill', 'loves Mary', etc.) to a singular term is true just in case the predicate is true of the object designated by the singular term.

9   At this stage it may seem completely arbitrary that symbols for singular terms occur after (and not before) symbols for property predicates, as in, e.g., (19), where 'l', which stands for 'Ludwig', comes after the predicate letter 'D^{1}', reversing the order in English. Actually there are good reasons for adopting this practice, which we will discuss in chs 12, 13, and §A5.1.

10   Some readers might think that (24) and (26) are not true under the same circumstances. They believe that there need be only one dog in order for (24) to be true, but that there must be more than one dog in order for (26)

to be true. But must (26) be false if there is but one dog? Consider the context where you and I are talking about my farm. You ask me what animals I have on my farm. I say there are dogs, fish, sheep, and cows. You visit the farm and, lo and behold, you find only one dog. Did I lie when I said there are dogs on my farm? What might be going on here is another conflation of conversational etiquette with deductive inference. It may not be part of the meaning of 'There are dogs' that there be more than one dog. Still, in uttering these words in most contexts, though they do not literally say it, might convey to the hearer that there is more than one dog. So, it is misleading to use these words if you know there is only one dog.

Alternatively, what may be going on here is a failure to appreciate plural and singular as grammatical categories. For example, 'every' is singular and 'all' is plural, even though 'Every man is tall' and 'All men are tall' have exactly the same truth conditions. Once you appreciate such nuances in English, you may be less tempted to make the logical inference from 'some are' to 'more than one is'.

G. E. Moore affirmed that 'Some men are Greek' required for its truth at least two Greek men. But then 'It's false that some men are Greek' would be true if only one man is Greek. That doesn't seem right.

11   As general rather than singular expressions, quantifier terms can in some cases, as we will see below, introduce existential and universal generalizations.

12   Lewis Carroll, *Alice's Adventures in Wonderland and Through the Looking Glass* (New York: Collier Books, 1872), p. 247.

13   We could use the same argument for not treating 'something' (or just about any other general quantifier expression) as a singular term. The following pairs of statements are not synonymous:

Something loves itself.   Few things loves themselves.
Something loves something.   Few things loves few things.

14   There are some good reasons for thinking that the quantifier expressions in (30)–(34) differ in meaning, even though in PPL they will be given a uniform treatment. See bibliography at the end of the chapter.

15   Even in maximally general words like 'something' and 'everything', 'some' and 'every' are appended to the noun 'thing'.

16   (72) contains the predicate nominal 'a dog'. This expression, as it occurs here, is grammatically indistinguishable from its occurrence in

A dog is happy.

However, in PPL we will not treat the article 'a(n)' in predicate nominals as an existential quantifier. The problem is that in English a noun like 'dog' cannot be used as a predicate without an article. So, even though 'a dog' in

'Fido is a dog' and 'Fido chased a dog' are grammatically indistinguishable, the forms we assign these statements in relational predicate logic are quite different. More on this in chs 12–15.

17   Many introductory students are tempted to assign to statements like 'Some Italians are artists' the erroneous reading '$\exists(I^1 \supset A^1)$', 'Something is such that if it is Italian, then it is an artist'. This PPL formula is true if at least one thing is such that *if* it's Italian, *then* it's an artist. But this is equivalent to saying that there is at least one thing such that either it's not Italian or it is an artist. This is bound to be true, except where everything is an Italian and nothing is an artist. Obviously, this is not what was intended by the original English statement 'Some Italians are artists'.

Bibliography

Barwise, J. and Cooper, R., 'Generalized Quantifiers and Natural Language', *Linguistics and Philosophy* 4 (1981), 159–219.

Bollinger, D., 'Adjectives in English: Attribution and Predication', *Lingua* 18 (1967), 1–34.

Higginbotham, J. and May, R., 'Questions, Quantifiers, and Crossing', *Linguistic Review* 1 (1981), 41–80.

Keenan, E. and Stavi, J., 'A Semantic Characterization of Natural Language Determiners', *Linguistics and Philosophy* 9 (1986), 253–326.

Larson, R. and Segal, G., *Knowledge of Language* (Cambridge, MA: MIT Press, 1995).

Peterson, Philip, 'On the Logic of "Few", "Many", and "Most"', *Notre Dame Journal of Formal Logic* 20 (1979), 155–79.

Quine, W. V. O., *Methods of Logic*, 4th edn (Cambridge, MA: Harvard University Press, 1982), chs 18–20.

Rescher, N., 'Plurality-Quantification', *Journal of Symbolic Logic* 27/3 (1962), 373–4.

Schein, Barry, *Plurals and Events* (Cambridge, MA: MIT Press, 1993).

Seigel, E., 'Capturing the Russian Adjective', in B. Partee (ed.), *Montague Grammar* (New York: Academic Press, 1976), 293–309.

Strawson, P. F., *Introduction to Logical Theory* (London: Methuen, 1952).

Vendler, Z., *Linguistics and Philosophy* (Ithaca, NY: Cornell University Press, 1967), ch. 3.

Wiggins, D., ' "Most" and "All": Some Comments on a Familiar Program and on the Logical Form of Quantified Sentences', in M. Platts (ed.), *Reference, Truth and Reality* (London: Routledge and Kegan Paul, 1980), 318–46.

10

Evaluating Arguments in Property Predicate Logic

The truth table method for evaluating arguments in PL cannot determine the validity of arguments in PPL. Take an intuitively valid argument like (1)–(3).

1. All men are mortal.
2. Socrates is a man.
3. So, Socrates is mortal.

Letting 'M^1' represent 'is a man', 'R^1' represent 'is mortal', and 's' represent 'Socrates', the correct symbolization of this argument in PPL is

4. $\forall(M^1 \supset R^1)$, M^1s ∴ R^1s

Suppose we construct a truth table for (4). Since both premises and the conclusion are simple statements from the perspective of PL, a complete truth table for (4) is

$\forall(M^1 \supset R^1)$,	M^1s ∴	R^1s
T	T	T
F	T	T
T	F	T
F	F	T
T	T	F
F	T	F
T	F	F
F	F	F

According to this truth table, (4) is deductively invalid: it is possible for its premises to be true and its conclusion false. Witness row 5. Something has gone wrong. The problem is that the truth table method (as we have devised it) cannot discern the structure in virtue of which argument (4) is deductively valid. The truth table method is designed to determine the truth-value of a complex statement depending on the truth-values of its simpler parts. This requires that the parts of these complex statements are themselves statements, since only statements have truth-values. Although the statements in (4) have complexity, they are not composed of simpler statements. The complexity in virtue of which (4) is valid depends on the predicates, singular terms, and quantifiers of which the premises and the conclusion are composed. Since predicates, singular terms, and quantifiers are neither true nor false, we need another method for determining whether (4) (and other arguments like it) is valid.

The truth tree method, as presented so far, is also inadequate for determining whether PPL arguments are valid. A simple expansion of the truth tree method accommodates PPL arguments, however.[1] But first we need to extend the notions of scope and the main connective from §§5.2 and 5.3 to PPL.

10.1   Quantifiers and Scope

We now extend the notion of scope so that it applies to tokens of quantifiers '∃' and '∀'. Recall from §5.3 that the scope of a token of an expression is the shortest well-formed formula in which this token occurs. The grammar for PPL admits two distinct types of complex well-formed formulas: predicates and statements. So, for example, the scope of the sole token of '&' in '∃$(M^1$ & $L^1)$' is '$(M^1$ & $L^1)$', which is a predicate, not a statement; but the scope of the sole token of '∃' in this same well-formed formula is a statement, not a predicate – namely, '∃$(M^1$ & $L^1)$'.

We can also extend from §5.2 the notion of the scope of a token of an expression α being wider than the scope of a token of an expression β within some well-formed formula Φ. α has wider scope than β within Φ just in case the scope of the token of β is a proper part of the scope of the token of α within the well-formed formula Φ. So in '∃$(M^1$ & $L^1)$', '∃' has wider scope than '&'. For this reason '∃$(M^1$ & $L^1)$'

is an existential statement, not a conjunction. As in PL, this information is essential in proving the deductive validity of arguments in PPL. As we shall now see, unless we know which type of formula a given statement is (i.e., which expression has widest scope), we cannot prove that arguments in which this statement occurs are deductively valid or invalid.

Exercise 10.1   *Scope*

- For those formulas in exercise 9.3 that are well formed in PPL, which expression has primary (widest) scope?
- Where applicable, which has secondary (second-widest) scope?
- Where applicable, which has tertiary (third-widest) scope? And so on.
- Are there any formulas with more than one token connective such that neither has (wider) scope over the other?

10.2   The Truth Tree Method Extended

The truth tree method gave us a way of checking the validity of arguments in PL. Since the arguments we are now confronting have novel notations in them, we will need to change the way we write truth trees. To this end, we extend the truth tree method by adding three new rules to the original seven presented in chapter 8.[2] Our discussion of the new rules will be somewhat abstract, but once we begin to use these rules (and their accompanying strategies) in proving the validity of PPL arguments, it will be apparent which rule to use and why.

One basic intuition should be acknowledged up front, before introducing the rules. The three new quantifier rules have the collective effect of converting quantified statements in PPL into unquantified statements. Once these conversions are effected, the original seven branching and non-branching rules from chapter 8 can be applied to the analysis of familiar compound statements into simple statements and negations of simple statements.

The first rule, the Quantifier Exchange Rule, has two parts; each, in effect, licenses moving a quantifier across a negation sign.

10.2.1   *Quantifier Exchange Rule (QE)*

The non-branching Quantifier Exchange Rule (QE), applies to negated quantified statements, whether universal or existential. The rule allows conversion of negated universal quantifier statements into unnegated existential statements and of negated existential statements into unnegated universal statements.

Quantifier Exchange Rule	
$\sim\!\forall\alpha$	$\sim\!\exists\alpha$
$\exists\!\sim\!\alpha$	$\forall\!\sim\!\alpha$

From the negation of a universal statement, you can derive a statement which results from replacing the universal quantifier by an existential quantifier and transposing the tilde. If it's *not* the case that *every* triangle has a right angle, then *some* triangles (at least one) do *not* have right angles. From the negation of an existential statement, you can derive a statement which results from replacing the existential quantifier by a universal quantifier and transposing the tilde. If it is *not* the case that *some* odd number is divisible by two, then *every* odd number is *not* divisible by two.

So, if a negated universal statement is on an open branch of a truth tree, add to that branch the statement you get by replacing the negated universal quantifier with an existential quantifier followed by the negation. If a negated existential statement is on an open branch of a tree, add to that branch the statement you get by replacing the negated existential quantifier with a universal quantifier followed by the negation.

A rule of thumb: for any negated quantifier, change the quantifier ('$\exists$' to '$\forall$' and '$\forall$' to '$\exists$') and push through the '$\sim$' from the left- to the right-hand side of the quantifier.

10.2.2   *Universal Quantifier Rule (UQ)*

The intuitive idea behind the Universal Quantifier Rule is that if a universal generalization is true, *every* instance of it is true as well. So, for example, if (5) is true, so are (6)–(8), and indeed any other instance of (5).

5.   Everybody is tall.

6. Al Gore is tall.
7. Sting is tall.
8. Michael Jordan is tall.

In order to use the non-branching Universal Quantifier Rule, UQ for short, we need the notion of *instantiation* (or a substitution instance) of a quantifier statement.

> **An instantiation (or a substitution instance) of a quantifier statement is achieved by placing a token of a singular term of the same type after *every* property predicate within the scope of that quantifier.**

For example, the conditional statements (10) and (11) are instantiations of universal quantifier statement (9).

9. $\forall(P^1 \supset D^1)$
10. $P^1a \supset D^1a$
11. $P^1b \supset D^1b$

(12), however, is not an instantiation of (9), since only tokens of the *same type* of singular term can be placed on the right-hand side of each predicate within the scope of the quantifier being instantiated.

12. $P^1\mathbf{b} \supset D^1\mathbf{a}$

The UQ rule, then, is as follows:

> **Universal Quantifier Rule: For any universal quantifier statement on a branch of a tree, you can add any instantiation of it to that branch.**

So, for example, if (9) is on an open branch of a tree, UQ permits us to add lines (10) and (11) to that branch. UQ is so obviously correct that the only question left is how exactly to employ it effectively in a tree. Suppose we begin a tree with (1)–(2) below. How should we effectively employ UQ?

1. $\forall P^1$
2. $G^1a \supset D^1c$

We might start simply by adding instantiations of (1) to the tree indiscriminately; thus we might begin with (3)–(5).

3. P^1a (from 1, UQ)
4. P^1b (from 1, UQ)
5. P^1c (from 1, UQ)

But where should we stop? Since there are indefinitely many singular terms in the language of PPL ('a', 'b', 'c', ..., 'w', 'a_1', 'a_2', ..., 'a_n', 'b_1', 'b_2', ..., 'b_n', ...), UQ permits us to augment any open branch with a universal quantifier statement with indefinitely many instances of that statement. We surely don't want to be in a position of having to examine each possible instantiation, because we could never complete the tree. So what we need is some guidance as to how to apply UQ. The following strategy is intended to restrict our usage of UQ in a productive way.

> **Strategy for applying UQ: If a universal quantifier statement is on an open branch, add to that branch an instantiation for every singular term that occurs on the branch. If no singular terms occur on the branch, pick a singular term arbitrarily and instantiate to it.**

So in the tree (1)–(5) above, only steps (3) and (5) are licensed by our strategy. We should instantiate to 'a' and 'c' alone, because they are the only singular terms to occur on the tree (in (2)).

So consider the following simple argument in PPL:

$\forall(P^1 \supset D^1), P^1a \therefore D^1a$

A truth tree for it is (1)–(5).

1. $\forall(P^1 \supset D^1)$ (premise)
2. P^1a (premise)
3. $\sim D^1a$ (negation of conclusion)
√4. $P^1a \supset D^1a$ 1, UQ

5. $\sim P^1a \quad D^1a$ 4, $\supset$
        ×   ×

Following the strategy for applying UQ, on line (4) we instantiated to 'a', the sole singular term in the tree.

What about a tree that begins like (1)–(2) below?

1. $\forall P^1$
2. $\exists G^1 \supset \exists D^1$

Since no singular term occurs in (1)–(2), our strategy for employing UQ recommends that we add only step (3), where we arbitrarily instantiate to 'a'; we could have chosen 'b' or 'c' or any other singular term, but we need choose only one.

3. $P^1 a$ (from 1, UQ)

Let us turn now to our third and final rule, the Existential Quantifier Rule.

10.2.3   *Existential Quantifier Rule (EQ)*

Suppose an existential quantifier statement is true – for example, (13).

13.   Someone murdered Nicole.

Surely (13) is true if, and only if, there is someone in the world who killed Nicole. But now we must move with care. We cannot by logic alone infer (14) from (13).

14.   Therefore, Orenthal murdered her.

(13) could be true because someone other than Orenthal, who happens to be innocent, killed Nicole. Yet, on the assumption that (13) is true, and therefore, that at least one such individual exists, let's dub (or baptize) him or her 'the killer'. 'The killer' will serve as a temporary singular term to refer to whichever individual (or at least one such individual, if there is more than one) killed Nicole.

The intuitive idea behind the non-branching Existential Quantifier Rule, EQ for short, is that whenever an existential quantifier statement is true, there must be at least one individual that makes it true; more specifically:

> **Existential Quantifier Rule: If an existential quantifier statement is on an open branch of a tree, you can instantiate it to a singular term, provided that singular term occurs *nowhere else* on the branch.**

So, for example, suppose a tree begins with the existential quantifier statement (15).

15. $\exists(R^1 \& G^1)$

Then, by EQ, we can infer line (16),

16. $R^1a \& G^1a$

where 'a' can be selected because no instance of 'a' appears above line (16) in the tree.

We are encouraged to think of the inference from (15) to (16) as a dubbing or baptism ceremony. Dubbings and baptisms are more common than you might think. Suppose that a detective investigating a murder case believes that a single murderer killed Nicole, used a knife, lived in Beverly Hills, and so on. For simplicity, he dubs this murderer 'Sam'. Does this mean that when the real murderer is found and his actual name is revealed as not 'Sam', our detective should let him walk free? Absolutely not! The detective simply dubbed the murderer 'Sam' for his own investigative convenience. The name functions as a placeholder for the real murderer, whoever he or she is. This is what we did in (16). We did not know who this individual is who has both 'R^1' and 'G^1' true of it, or even whether there is only one such individual. But we can still use 'a' to baptize an individual, since if (15) is true, there must be at least one. Of course, the singular term chosen must be chosen arbitrarily, in the sense that we have no particular individual so named in mind when we choose it. The restriction in EQ guarantees such arbitrary selection.

Return to the invalid inference from (13) to (14), letting 'M^1' represent 'murdered Nicole' and 'o' represent 'Orenthal'. The following tree for this argument is ill constructed, because it violates EQ.

$\checkmark$1. $\exists M^1$ (premise)
 2. $\sim M^1o$ (negation of conclusion)
 3. M^1o 1, EQ
          $\times$

The move to (3) from (1) violates the restriction on EQ, since the singular term introduced in (3) already occurs in (2). In symbolizing argument (13)–(14), 'o' was chosen to symbolize 'Orenthal'. Thus, on step (3) in the above tree, 'o' is not an admissible selection. By choosing 'o' rather than an arbitrary letter unrepresented above in the tree, the tree renders the obviously invalid argument valid. This violation of the EQ restriction results in a truth tree which closes, giving the mistaken impression that (13)–(14) is valid when it is not. For this reason, EQ restricts the selection of singular terms, thereby blocking the entry of lines into the tree that would lead to erroneous assessments of validity. If we obey the EQ restriction instantiating to an arbitrarily selected singular term other than 'o', we end up with the following tree.

$\sqrt{1}$. $\exists M^1$ (premise)
2. $\sim M^1 o$ (negation of conclusion)
3. $M^1 a$ 1, EQ

The open branch shows the argument's invalidity.
Another invalid inference is from (17) to (18).

17.   Some Democrats do not tend bars.
18.   So, it is false that some Democrats do tend bars.

Symbolized in PPL, with 'D^1' representing 'is a Democrat' and 'T^1' representing 'tends bars', the argument is

$$\exists(D^1 \ \& \ \sim T^1) \ \therefore \ \sim\exists(D^1 \ \& \ T^1)$$

An ill-constructed tree for this argument is

$\sqrt{1}$. $\exists(D^1 \ \& \ \sim T^1)$ (premise)
$\sqrt{2}$. $\sim \sim\exists(D^1 \ \& \ T^1)$ (negation of conclusion)
$\sqrt{3}$. $\exists(D^1 \ \& \ T^1)$ (from 2, double negation)
$\sqrt{4}$. $D^1 a \ \& \ \sim T^1 a$ 1, EQ
$\sqrt{5}$. $D^1 a \ \& \ T^1 a$ 3, EQ
6. $D^1 a$ (from 5, &)
7. $T^1 a$ (from 5, &)
8. $D^1 a$ (from 4, &)
9. $\sim T^1 a$ (from 4, &)
$\times$

The derivation of line (5) violates the restriction on EQ, since the singular term used on line (5) occurs on the preceding line (4). As 'a' is already assigned a use on line (4) (to refer to whatever individual makes line (1) true), it is not randomly selected on (5). These two arguments show the necessity for the restriction on EQ. No other restriction is needed for the construction of truth trees in PPL.

10.3   Super Strategy

We now construct a more complex truth tree employing two of the quantifier rules of PPL. Consider the PPL argument

$$\forall(S^1 \supset I^1), \forall(I^1 \supset {\sim}E^1) \therefore {\sim}\exists(S^1 \,\&\, E^1)$$

(1)–(11) constitute an adequate truth tree for this argument.

1.	$\forall(S^1 \supset I^1)$	(premise)
2.	$\forall(I^1 \supset {\sim}E^1)$	(premise)
√3.	$\sim {\sim}\exists(S^1 \,\&\, E^1)$	(negation of conclusion)
√4.	$\exists(S^1 \,\&\, E^1)$	(from 3, double negation)
√5.	$S^1a \,\&\, E^1a$	4, EQ
√6.	$S^1a \supset I^1a$	1, UQ
√7.	$I^1a \supset {\sim}E^1a$	2, UQ
8.	S^1a	(from 5, &)
9.	E^1a	(from 5, &)

10. $\sim S^1a \qquad I^1a$ (from 6, $\supset$)
       ×

11. $\sim I^1a \quad \sim E^1a$ (from 7, $\supset$)
            ×   ×

Notice first the check marks to the left on lines (3)–(7), but the *absence of check marks* on lines (1) and (2). The check marks on lines (3)–(7) indicate, as is customary, that a rule has been applied to the statements on those lines. However, the absence of check marks next to (1) and (2) doesn't tell us that the statement is not capable of analysis. Both (1) and (2) are universally quantified statements, so the rule UQ applies to each. However, at any stage in the construction of a truth tree, a universally quantified statement may have UQ apply or even reapply to it. This follows because, as we noted above when we introduced UQ, universally quantified statements have indefinitely manyinstantiations. Therefore, we can never complete their analysis in a finite number of steps (though we may exhaust their utility to us by demonstrating the validity or invalidity of any given argument). For this reason,

Universally quantified statements are never checked.

Note too that the existential quantification on line (4) was instantiated by EQ before the universal quantifications by UQ on lines (1) and (2). This respects the restriction on EQ. The following procedural strategy should be followed:

Whenever possible, employ EQ before UQ.

Of course, there are other obvious strategies one ought to follow when applying the truth tree rules to a set of statements. For example, recall from chapter 8,

Apply non-branching rules before branching rules when both are applicable.

Apply QE before applying the other quantifier rules.

This latter strategy is important, since its application determines which type of quantified statements are ultimately on the truth tree.

Exercise 10.2   Truth trees

- Construct truth trees for PPL arguments (1)–(13).
- Be sure to say why the tree shows the argument to be valid, if it is valid; or invalid, if it is invalid.
- Include complete justifications.

1. $\forall(R^1 \supset (P^1 \lor \sim T^1)), \exists(\sim T^1 \& P^1) \therefore \exists(\sim R^1 \lor S^1)$
2. $\forall(P^1 \supset \sim Q^1), \forall(\sim Q^1 \supset T^1) \therefore \exists P^1 \supset \exists T^1$

3. ∃(P¹ ∨ Q¹), ∀(P¹ ⊃ S¹), ∀(Q¹ ⊃ S¹) ∴ ∃S¹
4. ∃P¹ ∨ ∃Q¹, ∀(P¹ ⊃ S¹), ∀(Q¹ ⊃ S¹) ∴ ∃S¹
5. ∃(A¹ & B¹) ∴ ∃(A¹ & ~B¹)
6. ~∃(A¹ & ~B¹) ∴ ∃(A¹ ⊃ B¹)
7. ~∀~(A¹ ⊃ B¹) ∴ ~∃(A¹ & B¹)
8. ∃C¹, ∃D¹ ∴ ∃(C¹ & D¹)
9. ∀(A¹ ⊃ B¹) ∴ ~∃(A¹ & B¹)
10. ∀(A¹ ⊃ B¹) ∴ ∃(A¹ & B¹)
11. ∃(S¹ & J¹), ∀(J¹ ⊃ L¹) ∴ ∀(S¹ ⊃ L¹)
12. M¹a & N¹a, ∃(M¹ & J¹) ∴ ∃(J¹ & N¹)
13. K¹a & B¹b, ∃(K¹ & D¹), ∀(D¹ ⊃ B¹) ∴ B¹a ∨ K¹b

10.4 PPL Logical Equivalences and Non-equivalences

Any statement of the form

∃(α & β)

where α and β are any predicates, compound or simple, is not logically equivalent to a statement of the form

∃α & ∃β

Put in terminology perhaps familiar from elementary algebra, '∃' does not distribute over '&'. Although '∃(α & β)' implies '∃α & ∃β', the converse fails. There are evil people, and there are good people, but there are no evil good people.

Any statement of the form

∃(α ∨ β)

is logically equivalent to a statement of the form

∃α ∨ ∃β

'∃' distributes over '∨'. Plainly, something is either round or red just in case something is round or something is red. It is not excluded, of course, that there be both round and red things; nor is it excluded that some round things are also red.

Any statement of the form

$$\forall (\alpha \lor \beta)$$

is not logically equivalent to a statement of the form

$$\forall \alpha \lor \forall \beta$$

'∀' does not distribute over '∨'. 'Every positive integer is odd or even' is true, but 'Every positive integer is odd or every positive integer is even' is false. (For a more extended discussion about which statements are and are not logically equivalent in PPL see §A4.2.)

Exercise 10.3   Logical equivalences and non-equivalences

- Prove the following logical equivalences and non-equivalences (1)–(5) using the truth tree method.
- Showing that two formulas φ and ψ are logically equivalent requires showing both that a truth tree on ~(φ ⊃ ψ) closes and that a truth tree on ~(ψ ⊃ φ) closes.
- Showing that they are non-equivalent requires showing that either a truth tree on ~(φ ⊃ ψ) does not close or one on ~(ψ ⊃ φ) does not close.
- Present your work in full, showing justifications for all steps.

1. ∀(α & β) is logically equivalent to ∀α & ∀β.
2. ∃(α ⊃ β) is not logically equivalent to ∃α ⊃ ∃β.
3. ∀(α ⊃ β) is not logically equivalent to ∀α ⊃ ∀β.
4. ∃~α is not logically equivalent to ~∃α.
5. ∀~α is not logically equivalent to ~∀α.

10.5   Other Logical Properties and Relations

10.5.1   *Consistency*

Recall from §8.6.1 that a set of statements is consistent just in case a completed truth tree on that set remains open.

Consistency   Exercise 10.4

- Determine whether the following sets are consistent, using the truth tree method.

1. $\{\sim\exists(C^1 \,\&\, D^1),\ \sim D^1b,\ \sim C^1b\}$
2. $\{\forall(A^1 \supset C^1),\ \sim\exists(C^1 \,\&\, (D^1 \vee E^1)),\ \exists(B^1 \,\&\, E^1 \,\&\, F^1),\ \exists(A^1 \,\&\, \sim F^1),\ \exists(A^1 \,\&\, D^1)\}$

10.5.2   Logical Equivalence

Recall from §8.6.3 that statements of forms α and β are logically equivalent just in case a completed tree for α and $\sim\beta$ and a completed tree for β and $\sim\alpha$ both close.

Logical equivalence   Exercise 10.5

- Determine whether the following pairs of statements are logically equivalent, using the truth tree method.

1. $\sim\exists(A^1 \,\&\, C^1),\ W^1a \supset (\forall(W^1 \supset C^1) \supset \sim A^1a)$
2. $\exists(P^1 \,\&\, R^1) \supset \forall(P^1 \supset R^1),\ \forall(P^1 \supset R^1) \vee \sim\exists(P^1 \,\&\, R^1)$

10.5.3   Contradiction, Logical Truth, Contingency

Recall from §8.6.2 that a statement β is a contradiction just in case a completed tree for it closes; a statement β is a logical truth just in case a completed tree for $\sim\beta$ closes; and a statement β is contingent just in case a completed tree for β and a completed tree for $\sim\beta$ both remain open.

Properties of statements   Exercise 10.6

- Determine for each of the following whether it is contingent, logically true, or logically false, using the truth tree method.

1. $\forall(D^1 \supset P^1) \supset \forall(S^1 \supset P^1)$
2. $\exists(D^1 \& W^1) \supset \forall(D^1 \supset W^1)$
3. $\exists(P^1 \& A^1) \supset \exists(P^1 \& A^1)$

Notes

1 There is a way of revising the truth table method so that it too accommodates these sorts of arguments, but this is not the way we will follow.
2 These ten rules will exhaust our set of truth tree rules all the way through ch. 15. In ch. 16 we will expand the truth tree method once again, by adding two rules.

Bibliography

Jeffrey, R. C., *Formal Logic: Its Scope and Limits*, 2nd edn (New York: McGraw-Hill, 1981).
McCawley, James D., *Everything That Linguists have Always Wanted to Know about Logic but were Ashamed to Ask*, 2nd edn (Chicago: University of Chicago Press, 1993).
Smullyan, R., *First-Order Logic* (Berlin: Springer, 1968).
Strawson, P. F., *Introduction to Logical Theory* (London: Methuen, 1952), chs 5 and 6.

11

Property Predicate Logic Refinements

Debates about correct symbolizations are often debates about meaning. We debate what statements mean or what type of contribution the component parts make to the meaning of entire statements. We begin this chapter with an example to shore up this point.

11.1 Literal Meaning

There are no explicit quantifier expressions in (1) and (2).

1. Lions are carnivorous.
2. Lions are in the building.

However, the 's' in 'lions' indicates plurality. How should we read plurality? In (1) 'Lions' would typically be taken to indicate 'All lions';[1] (2), however, seems best read as 'Some lions'. This ambiguity is eliminated in the different symbolizations that we assign to (1) and (2) in PPL. (1) is best symbolized as a universal statement:

3. $\forall(L^1 \supset C^1)$ L^1: is a lion; C^1: is carnivorous

(2) is best symbolized as an existential statement:

4. $\exists(L^1 \ \& \ B^1)$ B^1: is in the building

Most readers will intuitively agree with these symbolizations (even though it's unlikely that they have ever seen them before). Some linguists argue that we could not understand novel statements unless we learned the meanings of individual words first (along with some grammatical constructions). They think we can understand a sentence we have never encountered before only because it contains words with meanings we already know. They contend that each word in our language has a definite, identifiable, isolable meaning, and that it is in virtue of knowing this meaning that we can understand novel sentences. But (1) and (2) shows that this view isn't entirely correct. For some sentences we must attend to their meaning in the context before we can even guess their structure.[2] Context must be used to determine whether 'Lions' indicates universality or not in a sentence in which it occurs.[3] (In §A4.3 further examples are discussed.)

11.2   'Any' as an Existential

(5) and (6) are symbolized identically in PPL as (7).

5.   Anyone can join.
6.   Everyone can join.

7. $\forall(P^1 \supset J^1)$ P^1: is a person; J^1: can join

Yet pairs (8)–(9) and (10)–(11) are not synonymous.

8.   If everyone can join, then David can.
9.   If anyone can join, then David can.

10.   John didn't eat every apple.
11.   John didn't eat any apple.

(8) means that everyone's being able to join is sufficient for David's joining. But (9) means that if one person can join, then David can. (10) means that there is at least one apple that John didn't eat. (11) means there is no apple that John ate.

We will discuss first how to symbolize (8) and (9) in PPL, and then (10) and (11). The symbolizations of these statements in PPL must exhibit their differences in meaning.

(8) is symbolized in PPL as (12).

12. $\forall(P^1 \supset J^1) \supset J^1 d$ d: David

(12) is a conditional statement, with a universal antecedent and a singular subject–predicate consequent. (9), however, is symbolized into PPL as

13. $\exists(P^1 \,\&\, J^1) \supset J^1 d$

(13) is a conditional statement with an *existential* antecedent.

This treatment should strike the reader as somewhat puzzling, since we have been treating 'every' and 'any' as synonyms, or at least as both indicating universality. This is partially substantiated by the fact that (5) and (6) are synonymous. But how, then, can 'any' issue in an existential in (13)? We are, *prima facie*, inclined to believe that if two statements are synonymous, then in any context in which one occurs, the other can be substituted without a change in meaning. So, for example, (14) and (15) are synonymous; substituting (15) for (14) in (16) issues in its paraphrase (17).

14. John is a bachelor.
15. John is an unmarried man.
16. If John is a bachelor, then he is unlikely to live as long as a married man.
17. If John is an unmarried man, then he is unlikely to live as long as a married man.

This is all as it should be. But what (8)–(11) show us is that a correct understanding of an expression is not generally to be attained through slavish dependence upon a catalog of idioms. Once again, we must reflect upon context rather than invoke a standardized prescription for symbolization.[4] In the context of (9), for example, where 'any' occurs in the antecedent of a conditional, it behaves as an existential quantifier expression like 'some', and not as a universal quantifier expression like 'every'. This rendering is further borne out by the fact that (9) is synonymous with (18).

18. If **someone** can join, then David can join.

Turning to (10) and (11), (10) is symbolized best in PPL as (19).

19. $\sim\forall(A^1 \supset E^1)$ A^1: is an apple; E^1: John ate __

(10) is the negation of a universal statement; but (11) shows us that circumstances similar to 'any' occurring in the antecedent of a conditional arise when 'any' falls within the scope of a negative expression like 'not'. (11) is best symbolized as (20).

20. $\sim\exists(A^1 \ \& \ E^1)$

(20) is a logical negation of an existential statement. Here again we see 'any' behaving not like a universal expression, but rather like an existential expression. This is also borne out by the fact that (11) paraphrases not (10), but (21).

21.   It is not the case that John ate some apple.

11.3   Restrictive Relative Clauses

Quite commonly, quantifier expressions modify nouns, which in turn include relative clauses.[5] The grammatical subject of (22) is 'Every woman who is married'.

22.   Every woman who is married drives.

In the subject the quantifier expression 'Every' modifies the complex nominal 'woman who is married'. The nominal 'woman who is married' includes the relative clause 'who is married'. The class of nominals restricted by relative clause expressions is unlimited in English. We need some procedure for symbolizing such clauses in PPL. How, for example, should we symbolize (22)?

We will treat relative clauses as introducing conjunctions, but not statement conjunctions; rather *predicate* conjunctions. So we will symbolize (22) in PPL as (23).

23. $\forall((W^1 \ \& \ M^1) \supset D^1)$

                                 W^1: is a woman; M^1: is married; D^1: drives

Paraphrased, (23) reads as (24).

24. For any thing, if it is a woman *and* it is married, then it drives.

In general, statements of the form

25. α + who (whom, that, which, ...) + β ...

where α is a general term, and β is a predicate, will be symbolized as (26).

26. ... α & β ...

Following this convention, (27) and (28) are correctly symbolized in PPL by (29).

27. Every student who was lucky passed.
28. All students who were lucky passed.

29. $\forall((S^1 \ \& \ L^1) \supset P^1)$ S^1: is a student; L^1: was lucky; P^1: passed

11.4 Pronouns Revisited

11.4.1 Deixis and Anaphora

The pronouns in statements (30) and (31) are used to refer to someone.

30. She ate at home on Friday.
31. He is the president.

To indicate, without further elaboration, which person is being indicated in these statements by 'She' and 'He' respectively, a pointing gesture or a nod or some similar non-linguistic means is usually needed. Such uses of pronouns are called *deictic* ('daɪktɪk'). To symbolize these deictic uses, we need to introduce a singular term, say, 's' for 'she' in (30), and 'h' for 'he' in (31). And then their correct symbolizations would be (30') and (31').

30'. $H^1 s$ H^1: is at home on Friday
31'. $P^1 s$ P^1: is president

A pronoun can also be used in a context where such non-linguistic means are unnecessary for determining what, if anything, the pronoun is referring to, because the pronoun is intended to be linked to an antecedent expression. For these uses, so-called anaphoric uses, the reference of a pronoun is determined by the reference of an antecedent expression, where the antecedent is called the pronoun's anaphor. Reflexive pronouns are obvious anaphoric uses, as in 'Mary is quite angry with herself'. This sentence clearly means the same as 'Mary is quite angry with Mary'. For these uses, we need to do something different (than what we did for deictic uses) in symbolizing them. So, for (32), read anaphorically, we do not introduce a new singular term for 'he'. Instead, we replace it with 'John' and symbolize it as (32').

32.   John is tall and he is happy too.
32'. T^1j & H^1j T^1: is tall; H^1: is happy

What about symbolizing anaphoric uses of pronouns whose antecedents are quantifier expressions? How do we symbolize them? For example, on the assumption that 'he' is anaphoric use of a pronoun in (33), how do we correctly symbolize it?

33.   Some boy is tall, but he is not rich.

In order to symbolize (33), we must recognize that the scope of the quantifier expression 'some boy' extends until the end of the sentence. Only in this way can we guarantee that 'he' falls within its scope, which it must since 'he' is (we are assuming) an anaphoric use of a pronoun whose antecedent is 'some body'. So a correct symbolization for (33) is (33'):

33'. $\exists((B^1$ & $T^1)$ & $\sim R^1)$ B^1: is a boy; T^1: is tall; R^1: is rich

We do the same thing for 'Every boy is tall, or he is rich', on the assumption that 'he' is being used anaphorically, which would then be symbolized as:

$\forall((B^1 \supset (T^1 \vee R^1))$

11.4.2   Quantification and Anaphora

(34) is a conditional with an existential antecedent and a singular subject–predicate consequent. We symbolize it accordingly as (35).

34. If something is tall, then David is happy.
35. $\exists T^1 \supset H^1 d$ T^1: is tall; H^1: is happy; d: David

Does (36) have the same conditional form as (34)? Can we correctly symbolize (36) as (37), a conditional statement with an existential antecedent?

36. If something is tall, then it is happy.
37. $\exists T^1 \supset H^1$'it'

One problem is that (36) is ambiguous in a way that (34) is not. In (34), 'David' is a proper name referring to some unique individual David. In (36), however, 'it' is a vague pronoun. It could be a deictic pronoun referring to something that is pointed out through a gesture or some other non-verbal indicator. With some stretch of the imagination, one can envisage a reflective philosopher type at the zoo, uttering (36) while nodding toward a giraffe nibbling at leaves. In this context the reference of 'it' is that specific giraffe, and 'it' functions as a singular term, much like 'He' in (31), with (38) being a perfectly acceptable symbolization of (36) in PPL.

38. $\exists T^1 \supset H^1 i$ i: it

'i' is a singular term referring to an individual indicated by some non-linguistic cue.

Suppose, though, for some utterance of (36), that 'it' is not being used deictically, but is instead being used anaphorically. Intuitively, the quantifier is extending out to *cover* the pronoun 'it'. Revisiting terminology used earlier, we can say that the pronoun *falls within* the quantifier expression's scope. Other ways of speaking make the same point. We can say that the pronoun is not *free* of the quantifier. Falling within the quantifier's scope, the pronoun gets *captured* and *bound* within the quantifier's scope.

Given the anaphoric sense, 'it' then falls within the scope of the quantifier expression 'something'. So 'it' does *not refer*, because its antecedent 'something' is not a singular term, but a quantifier expression. Thus we see straightaway that not every anaphoric pronoun is a singular term.

As a first attempt to represent (36) in PPL, we might try to symbolize it, on this anaphoric interpretation, utilizing parentheses, as in (39).

39. $\exists(T^1 \supset H^1)$

(39), though, is not synonymous with (36). (39) is an odd statement; it says that there is something which is such that if it is tall, then it is happy. Although there might be some such reading of (36) in English, it surely is not a standard one. The standard reading of (36) in English is 'Anything which is tall is happy'. Therefore, (36) should be symbolized in PPL as (40).

40. $\forall(T^1 \supset H^1)$

In summary, we will symbolize statements of form,

If something is α, then β

where α is any predicate, and β is any statement, as conditionals with existential antecedents *unless* there is an anaphoric pronoun in its consequent bound by an existential expression like 'something' in its antecedent. In such cases we will symbolize statements of this form as universal statements with their initial universal quantifier taking wide scope over a conditional predicate.[6]

In §11.2 we learned how to symbolize statements like (41).

41. If anything is tall, then David is happy.

(41) is a conditional statement, but instead of having a universal antecedent, as it may appear, we symbolize it with an existential antecedent. In English 'if any' means 'if some', not 'if all'. Therefore, (41) is symbolized in PPL as (42).

42. $\exists T^1 \supset H^1 d$

Extending this insight to (43), we see that (43) and (36), since synonymous, should both be symbolized as (40).

36. If something is tall, then it is happy.
43. If anything is tall, then it is happy.

It follows from what we have been saying that, regardless of whether (44) *seems* to be a conditional statement with identical antecedent and consequent, it cannot be.

44. If any donkey moves, then any donkey moves.

Intuitively (44) means that if at least one donkey moves, they all do. In certain contexts, people behave very much like asses in this respect. Since (44) includes an 'if any' construction like the antecedent of (41), it should be treated accordingly. It cannot correctly be symbolized as (45).

45. P ⊃ P

Instead, (44) should be symbolized in PPL as (46).

46. ∃(D¹ & M¹) ⊃ ∀(D¹ ⊃ M¹)   D¹: is a donkey; M¹: moves

(44) means that if some donkey moves, then every donkey moves. What is unusual about (44) is that component statement tokens of the same type occurring in the same complex statement are interpreted differently.

Statements   Exercise 11.1

- Symbolize (1)–(5) in PPL using the dictionary provided.

1. If Bob can sing, then he can dance. (S¹: can sing; D¹: can dance; b: Bob)
2. Lisa is pretty, and she's also athletic. (P¹: is pretty; A¹: is athletic; l: Lisa)
3. If Wendy goes to the party, she will have fun. (G¹: goes to the party; F¹: will have fun; w: Wendy)
4. Anyone who can sing is lucky. (S¹: can sing; L¹: is lucky)
5. If anyone will be a millionaire, Laura will be a millionaire. (M¹: is a millionaire; l: Laura)
6. If something is frozen, it is cold. (F¹: is frozen; C¹: is cold)
7. If someone touches the gold, he will die. (P¹: is a person; T¹: touches the gold; D¹: dies)
8. If anyone can laugh, then everyone can laugh. (P¹: is a person; L¹: can laugh)

11.5 Only

How should we symbolize (47)?

47. Only men are fools.[7]

What type of statement is it? It seems to make a universal claim, and therefore we should treat it as a universal statement. In general a universal statement begins with a universal quantifier usually read as 'all' or 'every'. Does 'only' have the same sense? 'All men are fools' is true just in case a particular relationship of inclusion exists between the class of men and the class of fools: namely, that the class of men is included in the class of fools. But this relationship does not preclude other classes of creature – women, children, etc. – from likewise being included in the class of fools. To say that 'Only men are fools' is to say that none but men are fools, or 'All fools are men'; that is, 'Everything which is a fool is a man'. 'Only' reverses the class inclusion relationship and the order of the predicates. To generalize, statements of form (48), where α and β range over predicates, not statements, shall be symbolized as (49).

48.   Only α's are β's,
49. $\forall(\beta \supset \alpha)$

Therefore, statement (47) should be symbolized as (50).

50. $\forall(F^1 \supset M^1)$ $\qquad\qquad\qquad\qquad$ F^1: is a fool; M^1: is a man

How do we symbolize (51)?

51.   Only animals that are humans are featherless bipeds.

In (51) the relative clause 'that are humans' modifies the noun 'animals'. It appears connected to the noun, which might lead one to think that (51) should be symbolized as (52).

52. $\forall(F^1 \supset (A^1 \ \& \ H^1))$
$\qquad\qquad$ F^1: is a featherless biped; A^1: is an animal; H^1: is a human

(52) states that every featherless biped is a human animal. In certain contexts, a person uttering (51) might mean (52), which can be stated precisely in PPL. More typically by (51), people mean (53).

53.   All animals that are featherless bipeds are human.

When (51) means (53), it should be symbolized as (54).

54. $\forall((A^1 \ \& \ F^1) \supset H^1)$

What we are seeing is that statements of form (55) can give rise to ambiguity between readings (56) and (57).

55. Only β that are α are Γ.
56. ∀((β & Γ) ⊃ α)
57. ∀(Γ ⊃ (β & α))

In (51), reading (57) is preferred, but this may be solely due to background information we bring to the interpretation. Other cases – for example, (58) – suggest reading (56).

58. Only men that have a child can enter the park.

If (58) is uttered in a context where the speaker has in mind only men, and she is saying of them that only those with a child can enter the park, then the temptation would be to symbolize it as (59).

59. ∀((M¹ & E¹) ⊃ C¹)
   M¹: is a man; E¹: can enter the park; C¹: has a child

However, if the speaker uttered (58) in the context where at the entrance to the park there were lots of people – men, women, and children, perhaps even some animals – and she intended to indicate by her assertion that of all the individuals waiting to get into the park only the men with children can, we naturally would symbolize her assertion as (60).

60. ∀(E¹ ⊃ (M¹ & C¹))

These interpretations obviously differ both in meaning and in their logical properties and relations. You can use the truth tree method to show whether either logically implies the other.

11.6 Restrictive Words in English

(61) may be symbolized in PPL as (62).

61. Everything which has mass is visible.
62. ∀(M¹ ⊃ V¹)   M¹: has mass; V¹: is visible

In (61) we confine quantification over whatever has mass by adding the restrictive relative clause 'which has mass'. As we saw earlier, sometimes we restrict the intended class of objects that a quantifier ranges over by having it modify a general term as in (63)–(66).

63. **All men** are mortal.
64. **Some boys** are tall.
65. **Each fish** got caught.
66. **No child** is eligible.

Suppose we want to restrict attention to persons in order to say

67.   Each person drinks water.

In English we restrict quantification over persons normally by employing quantifier expressions like

Everybody, everyone, anyone, nobody, no one, none, somebody, someone.

(68) is best symbolized in PPL as (69).

68.   Everybody drinks water.
69. $\forall(P^1 \supset D^1)$ P^1: is a person; D^1: drinks water

Generally, in symbolizing a statement containing a person quantifier expression, the symbolization should include an appropriate personal predicate. (70)–(72) are symbolized by (73)–(75) respectively, in which the predicate for persons is made explicit, although it is merely implicit in the former.[8]

70.   Someone left.
71.   Nobody wrestles.
72.   Everyone runs.

73. $\exists(P^1 \,\&\, L^1)$ P^1: is a person; L^1: left
74. $\sim\exists(P^1 \,\&\, W^1)$ W^1: wrestles
75. $\forall(P^1 \supset R^1)$ R^1: runs

PPL statements   Exercise 11.2

- Symbolize statements (1)–(43) in PPL.
- Disambiguate, if necessary.

1. No evergreen is deciduous. (E^1: is evergreen; D^1: is deciduous)
2. All fruit trees are deciduous. (T^1: is a fruit tree)
3. Not all evergreens are pines. (P^1: is a pine)
4. Magnolias are deciduous. (M^1: is a magnolia)
5. Magnolias and pines are evergreens.
6. Someone is a wealthy philosopher. (P^1: is a person; W^1: is wealthy; H^1: is a philosopher) (Read §A4.4 before doing this problem.)
7. If no philosopher is wealthy, then either Socrates is a philosopher or he's wealthy. (s: Socrates)
8. Not all wealthy figure skaters are philosophers. (F^1: is a figure skater)
9. If any philosophers who are not wealthy are not figure skaters, then Socrates is not wealthy.
10. If Tom, who is not wealthy, is not a figure skater, then Socrates is not wealthy. (t: Tom)
11. Some men are not mortal. (M^1: is a man; R^1: is mortal)
12. Foreigners that vote must leave. (F^1: is a foreigner; V^1: votes; L^1: must leave)
13. Every large man has a large wife.
14. If someone can do this, then anyone can do this. (P^1: is a person; C^1: can do this)
15. If anybody can turn this program around, David can. (P^1: is a person; C^1: can turn this program around; d: David)
16. Dogs and sheep are permitted beyond this point. (D^1: is a dog; S^1: is a sheep; P^1: is permitted beyond this point)
17. If some doors are wooden, then all doors are wooden. (D^1: is a door; W^1: is wooden)
18. Either everything is mental or everything is physical. (M^1: is mental; P^1: is physical)
19. There are borrowers if and only if there are lenders. (B^1: is a borrower; L^1: is a lender)
20. Someone is going to get killed unless someone fixes the light. (P^1: is a person; G^1: is going to get killed; F^1: fixes the light)

21. If anyone passes, then someone will die. (P^1: is a person; A^1: passes; D^1: will die)

22. If everyone passes, then someone will die.

23. Republicans and Democrats did not have much of a choice. (R^1: is a Republican; D^1: is a Democrat; H^1: has much of a choice)

24. Every Rutgers lineman holds, but not every one gets caught. (R^1: is a Rutgers lineman; H^1: holds; G^1: gets caught)

25. All students have fathers, and all students have wings. (S^1: is a student; F^1: has a father; W^1: has a wing)

26. Conservatives have power, but Frank is not worried. (C^1: is a conservative; P^1: has power; f: Frank; W^1: is worried)

27. No conservative who runs will not win. (R^1: runs; O^1: will win)

28. There are fish who swim. (F^1: is a fish; S^1: swims)

29. There are fish who do not swim.

30. Every rabbi who is Japanese is not Italian. (R^1: is a rabbi; J^1: is Japanese; I^1: is Italian)

31. Whales are mammals. (W^1: is a whale; M^1: is a mammal)

32. A whale is in the room. (I^1: is in the room)

33. A whale is a mammal.

34. No one pleases me. (P^1: is a person; A^1: pleases me)

35. Horses that lose are left to die. (H^1: is a horse; L^1: loses; D^1: is left to die)

36. A thing is good only if it is not bad. (G^1: is good; B^1: is bad)

37. A thing is in the kitchen only if it is not on the porch. (K^1: is in the kitchen; P^1: is on the porch)

38. Only men who are tall are entitled to leave. (M^1: is a man; T^1: is tall; E^1: is entitled to leave)

39. The only people who can speak are those who have a table. (P^1: is a person; S^1: can speak; T^1: has a table)

40. Dogs are the only animals with smiles. (D^1: is a dog; A^1: is an animal; S^1: smiles)

41. Unhappy inmates escaped. (Universal or existential?)

* Symbolize (42) both in PL and in PPL. Include a dictionary for each symbolization.

42. If some officers are present, then if all officers present are captains, then some captains are present.

43. Some but not all men are honest. (M^1: is a man; H^1: is honest)

11.7 Evaluating Symbolizations of English in Logical Notation

A good practice is to symbolize an argument in PL before trying to symbolize it in PPL. If a statement is a logical conditional, conjunction, disjunction, or negation in PL, then it remains so in PPL. After symbolizing an English statement in PPL, one good way to check whether your symbolization is correct is to translate it back into English. If the two statements intuitively paraphrase each other, then you have a good indication that the original English statement has been symbolized correctly in PPL. So consider (76).

76. No man is both happy and sad.

Putting it in PL first requires us to symbolize it as a negation of a simple statement; so, assuming 'M' symbolizes 'Some man is both happy and sad', '~M' correctly symbolizes (76) in PL. Turning to PPL, suppose our dictionary is: M^1: is a man; H^1: is happy; S^1: is sad. Suppose, further, that our proposed symbolization for (76) in PPL is (77).

77. $\sim\exists(M^1 \ \& \ (H^1 \ \& \ S^1))$

Using just the dictionary and (77), we can derive the awkward, but still English, statement (78).

78. It is not the case that there is something such that it is a man and happy and sad.

Intuitively, (78) captures the meaning of the original statement (76), indicating that (77) is correct.

   Suppose, though, that the proposed symbolization for (76) in PPL were (79).

79. $\sim\forall(M^1 \supset (H^1 \ \& \ S^1))$

Using the same dictionary and (79), we can derive the English statement (80).

80. It is not the case that every man is happy and sad.

It should be clear enough to you that (80) is *not* close in meaning to the original English statement (76). (80) is compatible with many men being both happy and sad, whereas (76) asserts that *no* man is both happy and sad; so (79) incorrectly represents (76) in PPL.

Exercise 11.3   **Arguments**

- Symbolize each of (1)–(25) in PPL.
- You may need to add missing premises or a conclusion.

1. This argument you encountered in the first chapter. You are finally ready to tackle it.
   Anyone who deliberates about alternative courses of action believes he is free. Since everybody deliberates about alternative courses of action, it follows that we all believe ourselves to be free.
   (P^1: is a person; D^1: deliberates about alternative action; B^1: believes he is free)

2. No man is mortal. No tall man is immortal. So, all tall men are mortal. (M^1: is a man; R^1: is mortal; T^1: is tall)

3. Anyone who is not privileged in New York is unlucky. Some privileged people are unlucky. Since privileged people are unlucky, all New Yorkers are unlucky. (P^1: is a person; A^1: is privileged; C^1: is unlucky; W^1: is a New Yorker)

4. If anyone has the right to live, every person does. It follows that either every person has the right to live or no one does. (Note that you can symbolize this argument in PL and still discern its validity. Give two symbolizations for it, one in PL and one in PPL.) (P^1: is a person; R^1: has the right to live)

5. Anyone maimed, mauled, trampled, and dismembered is eligible. Gerry was mauled and trampled. Therefore, he is eligible. (M^1: is maimed; U^1: is mauled; T^1: is trampled; D^1: is dismembered; P^1: is a person; E^1: is eligible; g: Gerry)

6. Arnie has a navy blue shirt. Any man with a navy blue shirt is rich. It follows that Arnie is rich. (N^1: has a navy blue shirt; a: Arnie; M^1: is a man; R^1: is rich)

7. Long-armed brown monkeys do not like fish. Only monkeys who crave fish can live on the river. So no long-armed monkey can live on the river.

(L^1: is long-armed; Y^1: is brown; M^1: is a monkey; C^1: craves fish; O^1: can live on the river)

8. No perfect being is immoral. Any individual who fails to value intellectual honesty is imperfect. No moral individual who values intellectual honesty would punish agnosticism. It follows that if God is perfect, he will not punish agnosticism. (P^1: is perfect; M^1: is moral; V^1: values intellectual honesty; g: God; U^1: punishes agnosticism)

9. *Clown*: ... 'He that comforts my wife is the cherisher of my flesh and blood; he that cherishes my flesh and blood loves my flesh and blood; he that loves my flesh and blood is my friend; ergo, he that kisses [comforts] my wife is my friend' (Shakespeare, *All's Well That Ends Well*, Act 1, scene iii, lines 45–9).

10. Only citizens are voters. Not all residents are citizens. Therefore, some residents are not voters. (C^1: is a citizen; V^1: is a voter; R^1: is a resident)

11. All tenors are either overweight or tall. No overweight tenor is tall. Some tenors are tall. Therefore, some tenors are overweight. (T^1: is a tenor; O^1: is overweight; A^1: is tall)

12. If every worker is a partner, then every supporter that is a carpenter is a liberal. Liberals do not teach. It follows that some workers are not partners, since some supporters do not teach. (W^1: is a worker; N^1: is a partner; S^1: is a supporter; C^1: is a carpenter; L^1: is a Liberal; T^1: is a teacher)

13. No child is innocent. He is an urchin that is not obedient. Every innocent child is an obedient child. Hence, all children are urchins. (The second premise is a universal statement but it contains no quantifier expressions.) (C^1: is a child; I^1: is innocent; U^1: is an urchin; O^1: is obedient)

14. The only students permitted to miss the final are those who don't. Clearly, those who are not permitted to miss the final do not miss the final. Thus, no one misses the final. (P^1: is a student; M^1: is permitted to miss the final; A^1: misses the final)

15. To those who consider San Marino a city, say, like Rome, note that San Marino has its own cities and so cannot be city itself. (Missing premise.) (F^1: is San Marino; O^1: has a city; B^1: is a city)

16. For a teacher to be an administrator she must have ten years' experience and an advanced degree. Coaches do not have an advanced degree, so they are not administrators. (Missing premise: Coaches are teachers.) (A^1: is a teacher; K^1: is an administrator; S^1: has ten years' experience; C^1: has an advanced degree; P^1: is a coach)

17. If there are any geniuses, then all great composers are geniuses. If anyone is temperamental, all geniuses are temperamental. Therefore,

if anyone is a temperamental genius, then all great composers are temperamental. (C^1: is a great composer; P^1: is a person; T^1: is temperamental; G^1: is a genius)

18. All radioactive substances either have a very short life or have medical value. No uranium isotope that is radioactive has a very short life. Therefore, if all uranium isotopes are radioactive, then all uranium isotopes have medical value. (S^1: has a very short life; M^1: has medical value; U^1: is a uranium isotope; R^1: is a radioactive substance)

19. If there are any liberals, then all philosophers are liberals. If there are any humanitarians, then all liberals are humanitarians. So, if there are any humanitarians who are liberals, then all philosophers are humanitarians. (L^1: is a liberal; P^1: is a philosopher; H^1: is a humanitarian)

20. Any vegetable that isn't high in vitamin C must not be green, since every green vegetable is high in vitamin C.

21. If something is a Ford or a Chevy, it's inexpensive. It follows that Fords are good buys. After all, something isn't a good buy only if it's expensive. (F^1: is a Ford; C^1: is a Chevy; E^1: is expensive; G^1: is a good buy)

22. If something is filling, it's unhealthy. The proof is this: anything filling or fattening is sweet, but nothing sweet is healthy. (F^1: is filling; H^1: is healthy; A^1: is fattening; S^1: is sweet)

23. The only people alive didn't take the drug. Everyone who took the drug is not alive. So, if Bill took the drug, he is not alive.

24. If someone is late, he cannot enter the party. But anyone who can enter the party must have a ticket. So, it is not the case that not being late is sufficient for entering the party. (P^1: is a person; L^1: is late; E^1: can enter the party; T^1: has a ticket)

25. Someone can vote only if he is registered. Those who did not register ought to be ashamed. But not everyone who ought to be ashamed didn't register. So, it is false that voting is necessary for being ashamed.

Exercise 11.4   Arguments

- Construct truth trees for your symbolizations for the arguments in exercise 2.
- Present your work in full, showing justifications for all steps.

Notes

1 The interpretation of (1) as a *bona fide* universal is not uncontroversial. Were we to discover a vegetarian lion, it would probably not disconfirm the claim that lions are carnivorous. There is a rather large literature on so-called generic readings of statements like (1); see the bibliography at the end of this chapter.
2 How we can determine the meaning of a sentence from the context in which it occurs is an interesting question, but answering it is beyond the scope of this book.
3 An interesting question is whether it is the *linguistic* or the *non-linguistic* context which must be invoked in assigning meaning to such statements.
4 We find something analogous with 'some'. In the context of a statement like 'Someone like Kennedy would have liked Clinton', there is a distinct pull towards symbolizing 'some' as a universal.
5 Relative clauses are introduced and discussed in §A3.4, with an emphasis on so-called nonrestrictive relative clauses like

  John, **who is smart,** studies every night.

  See §A3.4 for instructions about how to symbolize nonrestrictive relative clauses.
6 The data under discussion have been known at least as far back as the ancient Stoics. In recent debates the matter goes under the name of 'donkey anaphora' owing to examples which the philosopher Peter Geach used to portray it. His examples have become standard in the literature. ('If someone owns a donkey, then he beats it.')
7 And its paraphrase 'Men alone are fools'.
8 This point extends to spatial and temporal quantifier words like 'some place', 'nowhere', 'every time', 'never', and 'always'. We return to these when we turn to Relational Predicate Logic in ch. 12.

Bibliography

Carlson, Gregory, 'On the Semantic Composition of English Generic Sentences', in G. Chierchia, B. Partee, and R. Turner (eds), *Properties, Types, and Meaning*, 2 vols (Dordrecht: Kluwer, 1989), 167–92.

Carlson, G. N. and Pelletier, F. J. (eds), *The Generic Book* (Chicago: University of Chicago Press, 1995).

Cooper, R., 'The Interpretation of Pronouns', in F. Heny, and H. Schnelle (eds), *Syntax and Semantics*, vol. 10 (New York: Academic Press, 1979), 61–92.

Evans, Gareth, 'Pronouns', *Linguistic Inquiry* 11 (1980), 337–62.

Geach, Peter, *Reference and Generality* (Ithaca, NY: Cornell University Press, 1962).

Haik, I., 'Pronouns of Laziness', in S. Berman et al. (eds), *NELS 16* (Amherst, MA: University of Massachusetts Press, 1986), 197–216.

Higginbotham, J., 'Logical Form, Binding, and Nominals', *Linguistic Inquiry* 14 (1983), 395–420.

Kadmon, N. and Landman, F., 'Any', *Linguistics and Philosophy* 16 (1993), 353–422.

Kamp, H., 'Two Theories about Adjectives', in E. Keenan (ed.), *Formal Semantics of Natural Language* (Cambridge: Cambridge University Press, 1975), 123–55.

Keenan, E. and Stavi, J., 'A Semantic Characterization of Natural Language Determiners', *Linguistics and Philosophy* 9 (1986), 253–326.

Klein, E., 'A Semantics for Positive and Comparative Adjectives', *Linguistics and Philosophy* 4 (1980), 1–45.

Krifka, M., Pelletier, F. J., Carlson, G. N., Meulen, A. ter, Chierchia, G. and Link, G., 'Genericity: An Introduction', in Carlson and Pelletier (eds), *Generic Book*, 1–124.

Linebarger, M., 'Negative Polarity and Grammatical Representation', *Linguistics and Philosophy* 10 (1987), 325–87.

Ludlow, P., 'The Logical Form of Determiners', *Journal of Philosophical Logic* 24 (1995), 47–69.

Parsons, T., 'Some Problems Concerning the Logic of Grammatical Modifiers', in D. Davidson, and G. Harman (eds), *Semantics of Natural Language*, (Dordrecht: Reidel, 1972), 127–41.

Pospesel, H., *Predicate Logic* (Englewood Cliffs, NJ: Prentice-Hall, 1976).

12

Relational Predicate Logic

This chapter is primarily intended to introduce you to the logic of relations. You will need to be patient as you move from Property Predicate Logic to the intricacies of Relational Predicate Logic.

12.1 Limits of Property Predicate Logic

Consider (1) and (2).

1. John loves Mary.
2. John is tall.

A traditional grammarian describes (1) as including a transitive verb 'loves' along with its subject 'John' and its direct object 'Mary'. In (1) the verb 'loves' is joined with its grammatical complement, the direct object 'Mary', to form the property predicate 'loves Mary'. In (2) the adjective 'tall' is the complement of the intransitive verb 'is'. 'Tall' is added to the verb 'is' to form the predicate 'is tall'. Although the predicates 'is tall' and 'loves Mary' are formed from different types of verbs and have different types of complements in traditional grammar, these differences become blurred in the logical grammar of PPL. (1) can be translated as 'L^1j' and (2) as 'T^1j'. In PPL their logical structures are identical.

Is the fact that PPL lacks the means to distinguish between transitive and intransitive predicates problematic? This question gives rise to a related one. Are there any deductively valid arguments in English which cannot be correctly translated into a deductively valid argument in PPL owing to its limited syntax?

It turns out that there are indefinitely many deductively valid arguments which cannot naturally be demonstrated in PPL but can quite naturally be demonstrated in what is called Relational Predicate Logic (RPL). The inference from (1) to (3) is obviously deductively valid. (1) cannot be true without at least one thing (i.e., John) loving at least one thing (i.e., Mary).

1.   John loves Mary.
3.   So, something loves something.

Can we demonstrate its formal deductive validity in PPL? To do so, we need to fuse the verb and the object (or verb and subject) into a property predicate as in (4) and (5).

4. L^1j L^1: loves Mary; j: John
5. $\therefore \exists S^1$ S^1: loves something

Now to the proof.

1. L^1j (premise)
2. $\sim\exists S^1$ (negation of conclusion)
3. $\forall\sim S^1$ 2, QE
4. $\sim S^1j$ 3, UQ

Since this completed truth tree remains open, the argument (4)–(5) is invalid in PPL. Although line (4) in the above tree denies something of John, and line (1) affirms something of him, what is affirmed and what is denied are different, so no contradiction results. The verb 'loves' in (1) and (3) takes different objects, 'Mary' and 'something' respectively. But these differences are masked in PPL, because PPL forms property predicates by fusing the verb and its complement. So the argument cannot go through. To demonstrate the deductive validity of (1) and (3), a more discriminating logic that distinguishes verb and object is needed. To this end, we turn to Relational Predicate Logic.

Of course, the validity of the inference from (1) to (3) has nothing to do with John or Mary, or even love for that matter. Replacing either name with any other singular term, and replacing the main verb with any other transitive verb, will still result in a deductively valid argument. So this inference is valid in virtue of its logical form (see chapter 2). We can conclude, then, that indefinitely many deductively valid inferences are not obviously or naturally susceptible to adequate treatment in PPL. Moving beyond PPL allows us to capture in a natural way the deductive validity of arguments like from (1) to (3) by virtue of their logical form.

To develop the more powerful system of Relational Predicate Logic, we begin with some conventions for symbolizing statements like (1) and (6)–(10).

12.2 Convention 1: Number

1. John loves Mary.
6. Mary does not love John.
7. John loves Mary, but she does not love him.
8. The blue car sits between the red car and the truck.
9. The truck sits between the red car and the blue car.
10. The truck moves next to the red car and the blue car.

In these statements the verbs, each of which is transitive, express a relationship between at least two entities. In (1), the relational term – the predicate expressing the relationship – is 'loves'. John is the subject of the statement, and Mary is the direct object of 'loves', a transitive verb. (1) asserts a love relationship to hold between John and Mary, who are said to be the *relata*, the entities between whom the love relationship is alleged to hold. In (1) only one relation is purported to hold between the two *relata* – the love relationship. Any relationship that holds between just two *relata* is called a two-place (a dyadic) relationship; among three *relata*, a three-place (triadic) relationship; among four *relata*, a four-place (quadratic) relationship, and so on.

As a limiting case, property predicates are treated as relations in RPL. In RPL 'is tall' in (2) is described as a 'property predicate'. In RPL it is also properly referred to as a one-place or monadic relation, since the relation is affirmed to be true of only one thing, John. Indeed, in RPL the terms 'predicate' and 'relation' are interchangeable. One can refer to monadic, dyadic, or triadic relations or predicates interchangeably.

Symbolizations for (1) and (6)–(10) in RPL must show *the number of places* or the number of entities or *relata* a relationship relates together, as well as *the order of the places* in a predicate. (See convention 2 below.) To achieve this end, we adopt the convention of moving from left to right through English statements in determining the number and order of places. In (1) the predicate is a two-place predicate with 'John' as its subject and 'Mary' as its object. Given the dictionary – L^2: loves; j: John; m: Mary – we will symbolize (1) as (11).

11. L^2jm

The superscript '2' following the relational predicate in (11) indicates that this predicate is two-place (dyadic), as opposed, for example, to the three-place (triadic) predicate 'sits between' in (8) and (9), or the four-place (quadratic) predicate 'kissed' in (12).

12.   John kissed Mary in the park at noon.

Although (8)–(10) all include a conjunction expression, only the last is a logical conjunction; the first two are not. Instead, we symbolize (8) and (9) as (13) and (14) respectively, singular statements with a three-place relational predicate 'S^3'.

13. S^3brt b: the blue car; r: the red car; t: the truck
14. S^3trb

The superscript '3' following the predicate in (13) and (14) indicates that the predicate is three-placed (triadic) because the relationship of sitting between holds among three *relata*: the blue car, the red car, and the truck.

12.3   Convention 2: Order

The order of the singular terms in (11) is 'j' first and 'm' second. This ordering follows the order of occurrence of the *relata* in (1). Moving left to right, 'John' occurs first, and 'Mary' occurs second. Similarly, for (13), the order of the singular terms tracks the order of their occurrence in the English statement (8). Moving left to right, 'the blue car' occurs first, 'the red car' second, and 'the truck' last. With these conventions we symbolize (6)–(7) and (9)–(10) as (15)–(18) respectively.

15. $\sim L^2mj$
16. L^2jm & $\sim L^2mj$
17. S^3trb S^3: __ sits between __ and __
18. M^2tr & M^2tb M^2: __ moves next to __

(18) is interesting. You might be inclined to symbolize (10) with a single triadic predicate, as in (19).

19. M^3trb M^3: __ moves next to __ and __

If you were so inclined, you would be claiming that (10) is more like (9), which is a simple statement, than like a logical conjunction.

However, treating the expression 'moves next to' in (10) as fusing the grammatical conjunction which follows it, as does 'sits between' in (9), seems unnatural. Intuitively, 'moving next to' is a dyadic relation that holds between one object and another and 'sits between' is a triadic relation between one object and the two others that it sits between. These intuitions are supported when we replace 'and' in (10) by 'or'. The statement which results is perfectly acceptable.

20.   The truck moved up next to the red car or the blue car.

But we cannot do the same in (9).

21.   *The blue car sits between the red car or the truck.[1]

These considerations suggest that 'and' in (10) indicates a logical conjunction, whereas 'and' in (9) does not.
    How might we symbolize (12)?

12.   John kissed Mary in the park at noon.

We said earlier that it has a four-place predicate. Suppose we let that predicate be 'K⁴' (' __ kissed __ in __ at __ '), then (12) is symbolized in RPL as (22).

22. K^4jmpn j: John; m: Mary; p: the park; n: noon

    Which English statements do (23) and (24) represent?

23. M^2rb & M^2rj
24. $\sim L^2jm$ & L^2mj

12.4   Convention 3: Active/Passive Voice

How should we symbolize simple relational predicate statements in the passive voice like (25) and (26)?

25. Harry **was called by** Mike.
26. Mike **was called by** Harry.

If we introduce a predicate in the passive voice like 'was called by' for (25) and (26), we will not be able to explain from a logical point of view why the inferences from (25) to (27), and from (26) to (28) are deductively valid.

27. Mike called Harry.
28. Harry called Mike.

The pairs (25) and (27) and (26) and (28) seem to paraphrase each other; but if we symbolize (25) as (29) and (26) as (30), then the fact that these pairs paraphrase each other is lost.

29. K^2hm K^2: was called by
30. K^2mh

To ensure that these paraphrases are respected, we will introduce the following convention:

Symbolize passive statements in the active voice.

So, (25) and (27) are both symbolized as (31); and (26) and (28) are both symbolized as (32).

31. C^2mh C^2: called
32. C^2hm

(See §A5.1 for further discussion of the passive voice; however, you are not recommended to read §A5.1 until you have read §13.8.)

12.5   Convention 4: Single Quantifiers

How are we to symbolize (33) and (34)?

33. John loves something.
34. Something loves John.

It will not do to symbolize (33) as (35).

35. $\exists L^2 j$

For how would we then symbolize (34)? Apparently we should symbolize it also as (35), yet they differ in meaning. You might now be wondering why we ever decided to put the quantifier out front in the first place, in chapter 9. Suppose we change that earlier notational decision and place the quantifier after the predicate, in the order in which it occurs in the English statement as we already do with singular terms. Accordingly (33) and (34) would be symbolized as (36) and (37) respectively.

36. $L^2 j \exists$
37. $L^2 \exists j$

Several problems militate against this decision. First, how are we to symbolize (38), assuming that 'it' in the consequent has as its anaphor the quantifier expression 'something' in its antecedent?

38. If John owns *something*, then John beats *it*.

We might try symbolizing (38) as a conditional, with 'John owns something' as its antecedent and 'John beats it' as its consequent (O^2: owns; B^2: beats).

39. $O^2 j \exists \supset B^2 j \text{'it'}$

But this symbolization won't do. 'It' in the consequent of (39) is not bound by '$\exists$' in the antecedent, and therefore we cannot assume that it has '$\exists$' as its anaphor, as is required by the interpretation of (38) that we are assuming.

As a remedy we might treat 'it' as a grammatical substitute (which we might call a 'pronoun of laziness') for '$\exists$' as in (40).

40. $O^2 j \exists \supset B^2 j \exists$

This symbolization won't do either. (40) differs in meaning from (38). (40) does not guarantee that the something that John beats is the something he owns.

What about (41)?

41. $\forall (O^2 j \supset B^2 j)$

Although (41) drops the existential quantifier, it has the advantage of respecting our convention from §11.4.2 for treating a statement like (42), which has a pronoun in its consequent bound by an existential anaphor in its antecedent. Recall that that convention treats such statements as universals. So in PPL (42) is symbolized as (43).

42.   If *something* is tall, then *it* is happy.
43. $\forall(T^1 \supset H^1)$ T^1: is tall; H^1: is happy

However, we cannot adequately symbolize (38) in RPL as (41). Even if we were to treat (41) as grammatical in RPL (which it isn't), it would still remain indeterminate on the basis of (41) alone which place in the two-place predicates 'O^2' and 'B^2' the universal quantifier is binding. Is the quantifier binding the first or the second position in the two two-place predicates in (41)? Consequently, (41) is ambiguous four ways. It can mean (38), but it can also mean any of (44)–(46).

44.   If something owns John, then it beats John.
45.   If something owns John, then John beats it.
46.   If John owns something, then it beats John.

Ambiguity is impermissible in our notation. How, then, should we modify the notation of RPL in order to distinguish among (38) and (44)–(46)?

Many different strategies recommend themselves. We might try building into the meaning of the predicates the place we need, as in (47), in which 'O^1' means 'John owns', and 'B^1' means 'John beats'.

47. $\forall(O^1 \supset B^1)$

Although this strategy provides a 'correct' symbolization of (38), it is a regression to PPL. Once we regress to PPL, we cannot demonstrate the validity of any argument relying on relational features of multi-place predicates. Argument (48)–(49) is intuitively valid, but we lose its validity if we return to PPL symbolizations.

48.   If someone owns something, then he beats it.
49.   Therefore, if John owns something, then he beats it.

We cannot naturally capture the validity of (48)–(49) in PPL, for the same reason we could not capture the validity of (1) and (3) in PPL.

1. John loves Mary.
3. So, something loves something.

We need a device for determining which place in a relational predicate a quantifier binds.

12.6   Variables

(50) is a pictorial representation of what we need in order to represent (38).

38. If John owns *something*, then John beats *it*.

50. $\forall(O^2j \supset B^2j\,)$

(51) represents (44).

51. $\forall(O^2\,j \supset B^2\,j)$
44. If something owns John, then it beats John.

Rather than add elaborate diagrammatic devices as in (50) and (51) to RPL (which will become even more intricate and cumbersome when we investigate statements with many quantifiers), we introduce *variables* as placeholders for *relata*.

12.6.1   Convention 5: Variables and Quantifiers

Variables are the lower-case letters ('x', 'y', and 'z') that we have been saving from the end of the Roman alphabet since chapter 9.[2] What a variable does is *fix* the place that a quantifier *binds* inside a predicate. First we attach a token of a variable to the right of a token of the quantifier; then we place a token of the same variable in each place of the predicate that we want the quantifier to bind. By placing tokens of variables in predicate places, we are also able to keep track of the number and order in those predicates.

Using variables, we symbolize (38) in any of the following (logically) equivalent ways.

52. $(\forall x)(O^2 jx \supset B^2 jx)$
53. $(\forall y)(O^2 jy \supset B^2 jy)$
54. $(\forall z)(O^2 jz \supset B^2 jz)$

Each of (52)–(54) correctly symbolizes (38). The choice of 'x', 'y', or 'z' makes no difference, since variables are merely placeholders. They are called 'variables' because what occupies the places they hold can vary, as in (52)–(54), where the same placeholder is filled variously by 'x', 'y', and 'z'. The variable tokens 'x' in (52), 'y' in (53), and 'z' in (54) link a place in the predicates 'O^2' and 'B^2' with the quantifier symbol at the front of each statement. Which of the English statements do (55) and (56) represent?

55. $(\forall x)(O^2 xj \supset B^2 jx)$
56. $(\forall z)(O^2 jz \supset B^2 zj)$

(55) means the same as (57), and (56) means the same as (58).

57. Anything that owns John he beats.
58. Anything John owns beats him.

12.6.2   *Convention 6: Variables and Property Predicates*

RPL adopts and extends the syntax of PPL. In RPL, and for the remainder of this book, variables will be used in symbolizing every statement with a quantifier, whether its predicates are property predicates (one-place), relational predicates, or both. (60) correctly symbolizes (59); (62) correctly symbolizes (61); and (64) correctly symbolizes (63).

59. If something is tall, then Bill is happy.
60. $(\exists y)T^1 y \supset H^1 b$ T^1: is tall; H^1: is happy

61. If something is tall, then it is happy.
62. $(\forall y)(T^1 y \supset H^1 y)$

63. Something is tall, something is dead, and something is both.
64. $(\exists x)T^1 x \ \& \ (\exists y)D^1 y \ \& \ (\exists z)(T^1 z \ \& \ D^1 z)$ D^1: is dead

Strictly speaking, variables are not needed in any of (60), (62), or (64). But once property predicates get mixed up with relational predicates, variables become necessary. For example, consider the ungrammatical formula (65).

65. $*(\forall z)(O^1 \supset B^2 zj)$

Nothing in the notation of (65) indicates that the universal quantifier which begins the formula is supposed to be binding the single place in 'O¹'. We might try adopting the convention that it is simply bound by that quantifier; however, we will see in the next chapter cases which show why this proposal is unacceptable.

12.6.3   General Comments about Variables

At this stage in the development of RPL, the variable type we choose in symbolizing an English statement in RPL is irrelevant. In (62) we could have used an 'x' instead of a 'y'; in (64) we could have swapped the 'x' with the 'y' or the 'y' with the 'z', or any other combination. All that matters is that we link each quantifier to the places in the predicate that the quantifier is binding (with property predicates being the degenerate case). To achieve this end, we may use an 'x', or a 'y', or a 'z', or an 'x_1', and so on. However, once we assign a variable to a quantifier token, that same variable must be used uniformly throughout the scope of that quantifier, in order to indicate which places inside a predicate the quantifier is binding.

In (59)–(64), we extended the notation of variables to PPL formulas, so that they can be incorporated in RPL and meet the standard to be specified for being well-formed statements of RPL. This strategy is important, because arguments expressed in RPL will include statements which contain property as well as relational predicates, causing us to mix property predicates with relational predicates in the same statements and arguments.

Given the dictionary j: John; H^2: hit; D^1: died, how should we symbolize (66)?

66.   If John hit something, then it died.

If the pronoun in the consequent of (66) is anaphoric, then (67) correctly symbolizes (66) in RPL.

67. $(\forall x)(H^2jx \supset D^1x)$

What about (68), using the same dictionary?

68.   John hit something, but it did not die.

If the pronoun in the second grammatical conjunct in (68) is an anaphoric pronoun, and not a deictic pronoun (see §11.4.1), then (69) correctly symbolizes it in RPL.

69. $(\exists y)(H^2jy \ \& \sim D^1y)$

We cannot correctly symbolize (68) with (70).

70. $*(\exists y)H^2jy \ \& \sim D^1y$

(70) is incorrect, because the token of variable 'y' in 'D^1y' is not bound by any quantifier. The scope of the quantifier '$(\exists y)$' in (70) extends only through 'H^2jy', and therefore does not bind the third token of the variable 'y' in (70).

> **Whenever there is a token of an unbound variable in a formula (that is, not within the scope of a quantifier aligned with that variable, as is true of the last token of 'y' in (70)), then that formula is ill formed in RPL.**

This requirement is not novel to RPL; we saw its like in PPL. In (71) the existential quantifier does not bind (does not have within its scope) the predicate 'H^1', and therefore (71) is ungrammatical in PPL, and of course in RPL as well.

71. $*\exists G^1 \supset H^1$

This convention for variables is an obvious extension of the earlier one from PPL, that every predicate in a well-formed formula must either be bound by a quantifier or have a singular term sealing its predicate place. (See §9.6.)

(72) is also a patently incorrect symbolization of (68), since (72) means the same as (73).

72. $(\exists x)H^2jx$ & $(\exists x)\sim D^1x$
73.   John hit something, and something did not die.

(72) provides no guarantee that it is the same thing which John hit and which did not die.

We find in (72) four tokens of the variable 'x', the first two within the scope of the first token of an existential quantifier, the second two within the scope of the second token of the existential quantifier. This circumstance does not, however, license us to read (72) as (74).

74.   John hit something, and **this same thing** did not die.

Anyone who interprets (72) as (74) misunderstands the role that variables play. Variables are placeholders associated with the quantifier that binds them. In (72) the first token of '$(\exists x)$' binds the 'x' in 'H^2jx', and the second token of '$(\exists x)$' binds the 'x' in '$\sim D^1x$'. That both quantifier tokens in (72) are of the same type – namely, '$(\exists x)$' – is irrelevant, just as it is irrelevant that there are two tokens of 'he' in (75).

75.   He is tall, and he too is tall.

In English we would naturally interpret the two tokens of 'he' in (75) to be referring to different individuals. Similarly, one is not forced to interpret the variables in (72) as referencing the same object. Falling within the scope of different quantifier tokens, the variables may be placeholders for different objects.

Using the dictionary B^2: beats; P^1: is a person; p: Paul, (76) is correctly symbolized as (77).

76.   Someone beats Paul.
77. $(\exists x)(P^1x$ & $B^2xp)$

The pronoun 'one' is implicit in the quantifier expression 'someone'; it surfaces in symbolization (77), as was also the case in PPL, as 'is a person'. (See §11.6.) So here too we see property predicates intermingling with relational predicates.

In §12.2, we adopted the protocol that a singular term appears in a symbolization at that place in which it appears in the original English statement, moving left to right (assuming that the statement, if in the passive voice, has been converted into the active voice). This convention extends somewhat to RPL statements with variables. When translated into RPL, a quantifier expression invariably precedes the predicate(s) it binds, as in (72) and (77). Its variable token appears at that place in the RPL symbolization where the English quantifier expression appeared in the original English statement. In (78), for example, 'Something' occurs before 'Mary', moving left to right. (79) symbolizes (78) in RPL.

78.   Something likes Mary.
79. $(\exists x)L^2xm$

The quantifier expression '$(\exists x)$' occupies the leftmost position and introduces the statement; the second token of the variable 'x' is placed to the left of the singular term 'm', tracking the positioning in (78) where the quantifier expression 'Something' is positioned left of the token of the singular term 'Mary'.

In (80), we find the reverse. (81) correctly symbolizes (80) in RPL.

80.   Mary likes something.
81. $(\exists x)L^2mx$

In (80) the quantifier expression 'something' is to the right of the singular term 'Mary', so the second token of the variable 'x' in (81) is positioned to the right of the singular term 'm'.

Exercise 12.1   **RPL statements**

- What types of statement are (1)–(5)? For example, 'R^4bdac' is a singular statement, but '$(\exists x)(F^2xa \ \& \ B^3xac)$' is an existential statement.
- Make up English statements that each might symbolize.

1. R^3abc
2. $(\exists x)F^2xa$

3. $(\forall y)(F^2ya \supset S^3yab)$
4. $(\forall x)F^2xa$ & $(\forall x)S^2xb$
5. $(\exists z)I^3azb \lor (\forall y)F^2ys$

Statements

- Symbolize (1)–(5) In RPL using the dictionary provided.

1. Everyone likes Rebecca. (P^1: is a person; L^2: likes; r: Rebecca)
2. Either John lost something, or John found something. (L^2: lost; F^2: found; j: John)
3. Joan sang to someone. (P^1: is a person; S^2: sang to; j: Joan)
4. There's a mat that Domino the cat sat on. (S^2: sits on; M^1: is a mat; d: Domino the cat)
5. Alan teaches every student on Tuesday. (T^3: __ teaches __ on __ ; S^1: is a student; a: Alan; t: Tuesday)

Arguments

- Symbolize arguments (1)–(3) in RPL using the dictionary provided.

1. Rachel has every Beanie Baby. Flip is a Beanie Baby. So, Rachel has Flip. (H^2: has; B^1: is a Beanie Baby; r: Rachel; f: Flip)
2. Nadia bought her roommate a chicken. Hence, Nadia's roommate has a chicken. (n: Nadia; r: Nadia's roommate; C^1: is a chicken; B^3: __ bought __ for __ ; H^2: has)
3. Carly kissed Erik in Boston. So, Carly kissed someone in Boston and someone kissed Erik in Boston. (K^3: __ kissed __ in __ ; P^1: is a person; c: Carly; e: Erik; b: Boston)

Notes

1 As elsewhere, the asterisk flags unacceptability or ungrammaticality.
2 In addition to 'x', 'y', and 'z', there are indefinitely many distinct variables: 'x_1', . . . , 'x_n', 'y_1', . . . , 'y_n', 'z_1', . . . , 'z_n'.

Bibliography

Bach, E., 'In Defense of Passive', *Linguistics and Philosophy* 3 (1980), 297–341.
Davison, Alice, 'Peculiar Passives', *Language* 56 (1980), 42–66.
Haik, I., 'Bound Variables that Need to be,' *Linguistics and Philosophy* 11 (1987), 503–30.
Higginbotham, J., 'Pronouns and Bound Variables', *Linguistic Inquiry* 11 (1980), 679–708.

13

Relational Predicate Logic with Nested Quantifiers

This chapter expands upon the last by introducing more complicated English statements for you to translate into RPL. At first glance these statements may seem intimidating, because their translations may be long, complicated, and contain unfamiliar elements. The purpose of this chapter is to teach you how to break down the English statements into elements that have a more familiar appearance, so that you can treat them using familiar strategies and procedures. To begin with, let's husband some of what is already familiar to you and start to make use of that knowledge and skill. Consider statements (1)–(3).

1. John loves Mary.
2. Everyone is lost.
3. Every man loves some woman.

(1) is familiar from the last chapter. It can be translated into RPL as (4).

4. L^2jm

(4) is a well-formed statement of RPL. By convention, the predicate letter 'L^2' is moved to the leftmost position, with the singular terms following in the order of their appearance in the English sentence. Intuitively, (4) can be said to have the form depicted in (5).

5. θ __ __ (with the number of dashes equal to a predicate θ's degree[1])

θ stands for any relation whatever. If θ stands for a one-place relation or predicate, then the structure of the statement in which it appears would be represented as 'θ^1 __ '; if two-place, then 'θ^2 __ __ '; if a three-place relation, then 'θ^3 __ __ __ '; if a four-place relation, then 'θ^4 __ __ __ __ '; and so on. The dashes function as placeholders for the singular terms that refer to the objects related. In the case of (4), 'loves' is a two-place relation which is asserted to hold between John and Mary, who are the individuals whose names are slotted into the placeholders.

Now consider (2). By now you can probably translate (2) automatically into PPL as (6), as any fluent user of PPL would.

6. $\forall(P^1 \supset L^1)$ P^1: is a person; L^1: is lost

(6) is very different from (4); it contains a quantifier, two predicates, and a connective, and it does not obviously share the structure of (5). But let's look more closely.

If you were looking at a statement like (2) for the very first time, trying to figure out how to symbolize it, you might think of it as akin to (1), as having a similar structure. The predicate in (2) is 'is lost', which, following the treatment for (1), you would move to the leftmost position. Since in (2) 'is lost' is a one-place predicate, (5) would take the form 'L^1 __ '. The question now becomes, what belongs in the placeholder? One answer to this question is the subject of the sentence, whatever the predicate 'is lost' is being predicated of. But the subject of (2) is very different from the subject of (1). 'Everyone' is a general term, whereas 'John' is a singular term. Yet the two terms perform the same function in their respective statements: they are about their subjects, whatever is spoken about in the English statements. The blank in 'L^1 __ ' is a placeholder for the subject, even though it happens in this case to be everyone, a class rather than an individual thing. We can represent (2), then, as (7) (which of course is not well formed in PPL).

7. $L^1_{\forall P^1}$

This intuitive procedure yields an analysis of sorts. We have broken down (2) into two parts: a predicate ('L^1') and its subject ('$\forall P^1$'). This process has the advantage of allowing us to tackle the symbolization piecemeal, translating one part at a time. After the translations of the parts are complete, we then have two remaining tasks: to figure out how the parts are to be connected, and to figure out the order in which they are to be placed.

In the case of (7), 'L¹' and '∀P¹' are already well-formed expressions of PPL. It doesn't require more work to symbolize 'is lost' or 'Everyone' correctly. So we can pass on to the remaining tasks. First we need to find out how the parts are connected. As we have seen since chapter 9, (2) is a universal statement which has a quantifier that has a conditional predicate within its scope. The parts of the conditional predicate (antecedent and consequent) are connected by the horseshoe. So the horseshoe is the connective that needs to be inserted in the symbolization.

Now we turn to the ordering of the elements of the statement. According to conventions familiar from §9.7, you are directed to 'kick out' the quantifier and put it in the leftmost position. The ordering of the subject and predicate terms follows their order in the English sentence; the connective comes between the parts it connects, and parentheses are added to show the scope of the quantifier, resulting in the PPL (6).

6. $\forall(P^1 \supset L^1)$

But *in RPL* (6) is ill formed. It has a quantifier without corresponding variables. In RPL, we would symbolize (2) not as (6), but as (8).

8. $(\forall x)(P^1x \supset L^1x)$

We are now ready to tackle (3).

13.1   Multiply General Statements

(3) is a *multiply general* statement. It contains more than one quantifier expression (unlike (2), which contains only one, and is on that account called a *singly general* statement). You have encountered multiply general statements before, and will be given a more detailed account in what follows. (9) should be a familiar sort of example of a multiply general statement.

9.   If every Franciscan is devout, then some Franciscans are saintly.

(9) contains two generalizations, one of which is a universal generalization, and the other an existential generalization; so (9) contains two

quantifier expressions. It is multiply general. However, its symbolization is unproblematic in PPL.

10. $\forall(F^1 \supset D^1) \supset \exists(F^1 \& S^1)$

F^1: is Franciscan; D^1: is devout; S^1: is saintly

(10) is a conditional statement, with the scope of its universal quantifier being its antecedent, and the scope of its existential quantifier the consequent. Neither quantifier has the other within its scope.

Returning to (3), it too is a multiply general statement, but in this case the matter is more complicated.

3.   Every man loves some woman.

In (3) 'loves' is a two-place relation. We argued in chapter 12 that it cannot be accommodated in PPL – at least, not if the goal is to accommodate all the formally valid arguments which it contributes to. In RPL its correct symbolization is (11), which will look *un*familiar at this stage in several respects.

11. $(\forall x)(M^1 x \supset (\exists y)(W^1 y \& L^2 xy))$

M^1: is a man; W^1: is a woman; L^2: loves

Note that the scope of the universal quantifier is the entire statement, including the existential quantifier, which appears after the '$\supset$'; so now we have an example of a statement that includes *nested* quantifiers: that is, quantifiers that fall within the scope (formally defined below) of other quantifiers. This chapter is primarily about such quantifiers.

How do we effect the translation from (3) to (11)? No one method is right. The real test of any method is whether it results in correct symbolizations. The procedures described below are recommended because they are systematic and lead reliably to correct translations.

Step 1:   Determine the degree of the main predicate.

From a grammatical point of view, (3) has as its subject the noun phrase 'Every man', as its object the noun phrase 'some woman', and as its main verb the transitive verb 'loves'. Symbolizing (3) in RPL requires first choosing a two-place predicate symbol to represent the main verb, in this case, 'L²'. We will temporarily symbolize the subject 'Every man' as '∀M¹' and the object 'some woman' as '∃W¹', where '∀' and '∃' are the familiar universal and existential quantifiers respectively, and 'M¹' and 'W¹' represent the general terms 'man' and 'woman' respectively.

Step 2: Fill in the non-RPL format.

As a second step toward symbolizing (3) in RPL, set up an informal representation of (3) using placeholders, as we did previously in (5).

5. θ __ __ (with the number of dashes equal to a predicate θ's degree)

Then, substituting 'L²' for θ and following the order of appearance of subject and predicate in (3), fill in the placeholders to yield the non-RPL formula (12).

12. $L^2{}_{\forall M^1, \exists W^1}$

(12) shows that (3) has three parts, which need to be disentangled, treated separately, and then reassembled in the right order.

Step 3: Symbolize the grammatical subject term.

Using the language of RPL, symbolize the element occupying the placeholder for the grammatical subject first.[2] This step results in '(∀x)M¹x'.

Step 4: Symbolize the expressions occupying the other placeholders.

Symbolize the element or elements occupying the remaining placeholders next. In the case of (12), there is only one, '∃W¹', which is symbolized as '(∃y)W¹y'.

Although introducing a new variable letter is not necessary in all cases, you are advised to do so. (It can avert problems, and it can't do any harm.)

> **Step 5:   Determine the connections among the parts: universal quantifier.**

According to conventions already presented in chapter 9, the universal quantifier '$(\forall x)$', which is part of the expression in the placeholder for the grammatical subject, gets disconnected from its associated logical predicate 'M^1'. It is 'kicked out', or discharged, and placed in the leftmost position of the statement. The logical predicate 'M^1' goes inside the scope of the universal quantifier, occupying the leftmost position to the left of the horseshoe. The expression 'some woman', which occupies the placeholder for the object in (12), goes to the right of the horseshoe. The predicate moves to the right of the horseshoe as well, linking the predicate and the object to the right of the horseshoe, yet within the scope of the universal quantifier. With these considerations in mind, we derive at this stage the unfamiliar non-RPL configuration (13).

13. $(\forall x)(M^1 x \supset L^2 x_{\exists W^1})$

(13) determines straightaway that, although not every English statement that starts with 'Every' is a universal statement, (3), like (2), plainly is.

Next we will generalize the universal quantifier procedure that took us from (12) to (13).

13.2   Universal Quantifier Procedure

> **(a)   If a formula is of the form $\theta^n \ldots_{\forall\alpha} \ldots$, where θ^n is an n-place predicate and α any nominal, and $\forall\alpha$ may be flanked by other expressions of types $\forall\beta$, $\exists\beta$, singular terms, or variables, transform the formula into a formula of the form $(\forall x_i)(\alpha x_i \supset \theta^n \ldots x_i \ldots)$**

So (a) has us convert the English general term 'man', as we did in PPL, into a predicate; and since a universal quantifier precedes it, the predicate α is connected by a '$\supset$' to the original predicate θ^n; and, lastly, the noun phrase $\forall\alpha$ is replaced by a token of some brand new variable 'x_i' of the quantifier.

To illustrate how this universal quantifier procedure works, consider (14).

14. Every obstacle stands between John and Mary.

Letting 'O¹', 'j', 'm', and 'S³' represent 'is an obstacle', 'John', 'Mary', and 'stands between', respectively, then, as a first step towards symbolizing the statement in RPL, we begin with our hybrid of English and RPL notation as (15).

15. $S^3_{\forall O^1}jm$

Looking at procedure (a) above, we see that θ^n is occupied by 'S³', and 'j' and 'm' fill in the dots to the right of '$\forall O^1$', in that order. So we can now apply procedure (a), which tells us to transform the hybrid (15) into (16).

16. $(\forall x)(O^1 x \supset S^3 xjm)$

> **Step 6: Determine the order of the parts: existential quantifier.**

Before refining (a), let us establish a procedure for the existential noun phrase, so that we have both procedures on the table for discussion together.

13.3 Existential Quantifier Procedure

> **(b)** If a formula has the form $\theta^n \ldots {}_{\exists\alpha} \ldots$, where θ^n is an *n*-place predicate and α any nominal, and where $\exists\alpha$ may be flanked by other expressions of types $\forall\beta$, $\exists\beta$, singular terms, or variables, transform the formula into a formula of the form $(\exists x_i)(\alpha x_i \,\&\, \theta^n \ldots x_i \ldots)$

The main difference between procedures (a) and (b) is that (b) conjoins via '&', whereas (a) conditionalizes via '⊃'. With (a) and (b) in hand, let's complete our transformation of (3) into RPL, picking up where we left off at (13). By next discharging the existential quantifier in (13), we finally obtain the RPL well-formed formula (11), which we had stated at the outset was the correct translation of (3).

11. $(\forall x)(M^1 x \supset (\exists y)(W^1 y \,\&\, L^2 xy))$

13.4   Double Binding Variables

(11) illustrates some important matters regarding scope and the binding of variables. (12) is a non-RPL formulation of (3), leading up to the correct symbolization of (3) as (11).

12. $L^2_{\forall M^1, \exists W^1}$
 3.   Every man loves some woman.

To render (12) a universal statement, the universal quantifier phrase in (12), the grammatical subject of (3), is discharged first. The existential quantifier phrase in (12), the grammatical object of (3), is discharged second, and it conjoins with the main verb. When the second quantifier is discharged from (12), a new variable type 'y' is introduced into the symbolization for the existential quantifier. We must do this in order to prevent two quantifiers binding the same token of a variable.

> **When symbolizing statements with nested quantifier tokens, no more than one quantifier token can bind the same variable token.**

If we did not introduce the new variable type to attach to the second quantifier in (11), we would be unable to discern which quantifier token (the universal or the existential) binds the last three variable tokens, as in the ungrammatical (17).

17. $*(\forall x)(M^1 x \supset (\exists x)(W^1 x \ \& \ L^2 xx))$

In (17) we do not know whether it is the universal or the existential quantifier that is binding the last three tokens of 'x'. The purpose of introducing variables is defeated: namely, to hold a place for the quantifier to bind.
  To repeat:

> **In order to preserve well-formedness, not every quantifier token in a statement must introduce a new variable type; however, introducing a new variable type in each instance is a good strategy. It creates no new problems, and it helps avoid some.**

Let's look at another example, in order to tighten our grip on procedures (a) and (b) and the importance of correctly binding variables. Consider statement (18).

18. Every man gave every woman some toy.

Informally speaking, the verb 'gave' describes an action involving three essential participants: a giver, a recipient, and a gift. So 'gave' is a three-place relation. Its grammatical subject is 'Every man'; its indirect object is 'every woman', and its direct object is 'some toy'. As a first step towards symbolizing (18) in RPL, 'G³' represents 'gave' and 'M¹', 'W¹', and 'T¹' represent 'is a man', 'is a woman', and 'is a toy' respectively.

19. $G^3_{\forall M^1, \forall W^1, \exists T^1}$

Applying procedures (a) (twice) and (b) in that order to (19), we obtain in sequence non-RPL formulas (20) and (21), and lastly the RPL well-formed formula (22).

20. $(\forall x)(M^1x \supset G^3x_{\forall W^1, \exists T^1})$ (from 19, by (a))
21. $(\forall x)(M^1x \supset (\forall y)(W^1y \supset G^3xy_{\exists T^1}))$ (from 20, by (a))
22. $(\forall x)(M^1x \supset (\forall y)(W^1y \supset (\exists z)(T^1z \ \& \ G^3xyz)))$ (from 21, by (b))

(18) has three English quantifier expression tokens. These are reflected in (19). (22), a correct symbolization of (18) in RPL, has three corresponding quantifier tokens. Attached to each quantifier token is a distinct variable type; universal quantifier expressions introduce '$\supset$', and existential quantifier expressions introduce '&'. (22) has three pairs of parentheses, indicating the limiting scope of a corresponding quantifier token.

This material is difficult. Logicians generally agree that statements with nested quantifiers are among the hardest to symbolize in RPL. You will need to be patient. The benefits of the system will become clear and the process of symbolization easier as you practice.

A final example should help clarify residual concerns or confusions about how to apply the universal and existential quantifier procedures (a) and (b). Consider (23).

23. Every man gave some woman every toy.

Setting (23) up for transformation into RPL, capitalizing on what we have learned thus far, we start with the non-RPL formula (24).

24. $G^3{}_{\forall M^1, \exists W^1, \forall T^1}$

First we apply the universal procedure (a) to (24), beginning with '$\forall M^1$', which occupies the first place in 'G^3' in (24). This step issues in the formula (25), which is not yet an RPL formula.

25. $(\forall x)(M^1 x \supset G^3 x_{\exists W^1, \forall T^1})$

Next we apply the existential procedure (b) to '$G^3 x_{\exists W^1, \forall T^1}$' in (25), since the next quantifier to be kicked out, moving from left to right in (22), is the existential '$\exists W^1$'. Applying (b) to (25) issues in (26), still a non-RPL formula.

26. $(\forall x)(M^1 x \supset (\exists y)(W^1 y \ \& \ G^3 xy_{\forall T^1}))$

Lastly we apply the universal procedure (a) again to '$G^3 xy_{\forall T^1}$', since (26) has one last universal quantifier expression '$\forall T^1$'. Applying (a) to (26) issues in the RPL well-formed formula (27), which is the correct symbolization of (23) in RPL.

27. $(\forall x)(M^1 x \supset (\exists y)(W^1 y \ \& \ (\forall z)(T^1 z \supset G^3 xyz)))$

Three variable types are introduced in order to make unambiguous which quantifier binds which variables. Placement of parentheses clarifies the relative scope of the quantifiers, as does their position.

13.4.1   Kicking Out

We have had a policy in effect since we began exporting quantifier expressions from non-RPL halfway representations that is worth making explicit.

When a quantifier phrase '$Q\alpha$' is exported in a context, $\theta'' \ldots {}_{Q\alpha} \ldots$, its replacement proper quantifier is to be given the *smallest possible* scope, relative to $\theta'' \ldots$ (that is, to the remaining temporary non-RPL matrix).

That is, given, for example,

$$(\forall x)(F^1x \supset R^3x, \exists_{G^1}, \exists_{H^1})$$

we go to

$$(\forall x)(F^1x \supset (\exists y)(G^1y \ \& \ R^3x,y, \exists_{H^1}))$$

and not to

$$(\exists y)(G^1y \ \& \ (\forall x)(F^1x \supset R^3x,y, \exists_{H^1}))$$

Put somewhat differently, when kicking out (or exporting) a quantifier from a non-RPL halfway house matrix – for example, $\ldots \theta'' \ldots _{Q\alpha \ldots}$ – any part of the formula already derived and not part of the matrix is irrelevant to the final product. Nothing that the procedures recommend can change the scope of any expression not already in the matrix.[3]

13.5 Systematic and Analytic Procedures

The procedures or techniques of §§13.2–13.4 for manipulating English statements into RPL, which we will continue to develop throughout the remainder of this book, feature important advantages.

The procedures are systematic: They make the process of translation into an orderly progression. An early step determines the type of statement being translated, hence essential features of its internal structure. If the first quantifier expression translated is universal, for example, then the resulting formula will be a universal statement containing a horseshoe as a connective among internal parts. This structure is fixed at the outset and is invariant throughout the process, providing a logical framework into which the translated parts are fit.

The procedures are also analytic: They break down English statements which are sometimes very complex into parts organized and assembled into an intermediary informal (or quasi-formal) language that is part English and part RPL, a kind of halfway house. One at a time, each part is symbolized and positioned in the developing translation according to the rules. A major benefit of this process is that once you have completed a part, symbolizing and placing it, that part is finished. Neither the symbolization nor the placement will alter materially as a result of translation of the remaining parts. In effect, the system allows you to whittle away at the problem. Each completed part is finished, requiring no further attention or thought. When the last part is translated, the translation is complete, and if the steps have been followed precisely, the translation should be correct in RPL.

Exercise 13.1   Statements

- Symbolize (1)–(6) in RPL. Use the dictionary G^3: __ gave __ __ ; M^1: is a man; W^1: is a woman; T^1: is a toy; L^3: __ loves __ at __ ; P^1: is a person; T^1: is a time; b: Bill; t: 10:00 p.m.; m: Mary; A^2: is an admirer of; N^1: is a pineapple.

1. Some man gave every woman every toy.
2. Some woman gave every man every toy.
3. Every man gave every man every toy.
4. Everyone loves someone sometime, but someone loves everyone always.
5. Bill loves someone at 10:00 p.m.
6. All of her admirers gave Mary a pineapple.

Exercise 13.2   Arguments

- Symbolize (1)–(3) in RPL.
- Use the dictionary provided.

1. Every bobcat can outrun every tiger. Jones is a bobcat, but he cannot outrun Ed. So, Ed is not a tiger. (m: Ed; j: Jones; B^1: is a bobcat; T^1: is a tiger; O^2: can outrun)
2. Every son has a father. Therefore, since Bill is a father, Bill has a son. (F^1: is a father; S^1: is a son; H^2: has; b: Bill)
3. Every optimist expects to be president. So, every optimist expects every optimist to be president. (O^1: is an optimist; E^2: expects to be president)

13.6   A Grammar for Well-formedness in RPL

Let us now collect and systematize the notational innovations that this text brings to Relational Predicate Logic:

Predicate letters are capital letters superscripted with any positive integer: 'A^1', . . . , 'A^n', 'B^1', . . . , 'B^m', . . . , 'Z^1', . . . , 'Z^n'. The degree of a simple predicate is the integer that superscripts it. So, for example, the degree of 'P^3' is three; the degree of 'P^9' is nine.

Terms: There are two types: singular terms and variables:
   Singular terms are the lower-case letters (subscripted or not) 'a', . . . , 'w', 'a$_1$', . . . , 'a$_n$', . . . , 'w$_1$', . . . , 'w$_n$'.
   Variables are the lower-case letters 'x', 'y', 'z', 'x$_1$', . . . , 'x$_n$', 'y$_1$', . . . , 'y$_n$', 'z$_1$', . . . , 'z$_n$'.

Statements: There are eight types:
   i.   *Singular statements* are those that consist of a simple predicate of degree n followed by n singular term tokens (for example, 'P^{3}abc', 'R^{2}aa', 'S^{1}d').
   ii–v.   *Conjunctions, conditionals, disjunctions, and negations*: If α and β are statements, then so are α & β, $\alpha \supset \beta$, $\alpha \vee \beta$, ~α.
   vi.   *Universal statements*: If α is a statement of RPL (with at least one singular term), and x$_i$ is a variable that does not occur in α, then $(\forall x_i)\alpha^*$ is a universal statement of RPL, where α^* is a formula that results from α by replacing at least one token of a singular term by x$_i$. So, for example, let α = 'P^{2}ab'. 'x$_1$' does not occur in α. So, '$(\forall x_1)$P^{2}x$_1$b' is a universal statement, with 'P^{2}x$_1$b' = α^*.
   vii.   *Existential statements*: If α is a statement of RPL (with at least one singular term), and x$_i$ is a variable that does not occur in α, then $(\exists x_i)\alpha^*$ is an existential statement of RPL, where α^* is a formula that results from α by replacing at least one token of a singular term by x$_i$. So, for example, let α = 'R^{3}acb'. 'x$_2$' does not occur in α. So, '$(\exists x_2)$R^{3}ax$_2$b' is an existential statement, with 'R^{3}ax$_2$b' = α^*.

How do we decide if (28) is a well-formed statement of RPL?

28. $(\exists x)(F^2xa$ & $R^1x)$

First note that (29) is a statement of RPL, by (i) and (ii) above.

29.   (F^2aa & R^1a)

Since there are no tokens of the variable type 'x' in (29), (30) results from (29) by replacing at least one token (in fact, two) of the singular term 'a' by 'x'.

30.   (F^2xa & R^1x)

So, by (vii), (28) is a well-formed statement of RPL. It's an existential statement.

viii.   *Simple statements* are capital letters (without superscripts) ('A', 'B', ..., 'Z', 'A_1', ..., 'A_n' ..., 'Z_1', ..., 'Z_n').

This completes our characterization of statements in RPL.

Nothing is a statement in RPL that is not established to be a statement by (i)–(viii).

Exercise 13.3   Well-formedness

- Which of (1)–(13) are well-formed statements in RPL?
- What type of statement is each?
- For those that are well formed in RPL, make up English statements they might symbolize.

1. $F^7abcdefg$
2. P & F^2aa
3. $(\forall x)F^2xy$
4. $(\forall z)F^2za \supset F^2az$
5. $(\forall x)F^1a$
6. $(\exists z)((P^1z$ & $(\forall y)F^2yz) \lor G^2za)$
7. $(\forall x)(P^2xa \supset (\exists z)(F^1z$ & $R^2xy))$
8. $F^2ab \lor (\exists x_1)G^2x_1x_1$
9. $(\forall x)(\forall y)(F^2xy \supset P^2xy)$
10. $\sim(\forall x)(B^1x \supset (\exists y)(D^1y$ & $L^2xy))$

11. $(\forall x)((\forall y)(S^1y \supset W^2xy) \supset M^1x)$
12. $(\exists x)(G^1x \,\&\, (\exists y)(B^1y \,\&\, (L^2xy \,\&\, \sim L^2yx)))$
13. $(\forall x)(G^1x \supset \sim O^1x)$

13.7 Nested Quantifiers, Variables, and Scope

We have been assuming throughout this chapter that the notion of scope introduced for PPL extends quite naturally to RPL. Now we officially extend this notion to include tokens of quantifiers nested within tokens of other quantifiers. Recall that the scope of a token of an expression is *the shortest formula in which this expression occurs.* So, for example, the scope of the sole token of '$\forall$' in (31) is all of (32).

31. $(\exists x)(M^1x \,\&\, (\forall y)(L^1y \supset R^2xy))$
32. $(\forall y)(L^1y \supset R^2xy)$

The scope of the sole token of '$\exists$' in (31) is itself.

Because the scope of '$\forall$' in (31) falls within the scope of '$\exists$' in (31), '$\exists$' has wider scope in (31) than '$\forall$'. Or, putting it the other way around, '$\forall$' has narrower scope than '$\exists$'.

Relative scope   Exercise 13.4

1. In '$(\forall x)(\exists y)F^2yx$', which quantifier has primary (widest) and which quantifier has secondary (second-widest) scope?
2. In '$\sim(\forall x)(B^1x \supset (\exists y)(D^1y \,\&\, L^2xy))$' which has wider scope, the negation or the universal quantifier?
3. In '$(\forall x)((M^1x \,\&\, (\exists x_1)S^2x_1x) \supset (\exists y)((W^1y \,\&\, (\exists y_1)S^2y_1y) \,\&\, (\exists z)((T^1z \,\&\, E^1z) \,\&\, G^3xyz)))$' there are four existential quantifier tokens and one universal quantifier token. What is the order of scope? That is, which quantifier token has the widest (or primary) scope? Which has secondary scope? Which has tertiary scope, and so on? Are there any two quantifier tokens in this formula such that neither is within the scope of the other?
4. In '$(\exists x)(T^1x \,\&\, (\forall y)(S^1y \supset (\exists z)(A^1z \,\&\, S^3yzx)))$' what is the order of scope among the three quantifier tokens?

13.8 Order and Scope Refinements

Consider the statements (33) and (34) (and the latter's grammatical variant (35)).

33. Every student studies some subject with a teacher.
34. A teacher has every student studying some subject with him.
35. There is a teacher that every student studies some subject with.

Although (33), on the one hand, and (34) and (35), on the other, have different meanings, they are logically related. The inference from (34) or (35) to (33) is deductively valid, but not vice versa. If there really is some sort of super-teacher with whom every student studies, then trivially every student studies with some teacher: namely, the super-teacher. The inference from (33) to (34) or (35), however, is not deductively valid. (33) represents the normal state of affairs and is true of every student, but (34) and (35) are exceedingly rare, perhaps true in some small understaffed school. This section discusses how to represent the logical difference between these two and similar statements in RPL.

The inference from (35) to (33) is not only deductively valid, but its validity is in virtue of its logical form (§2.1). To see that this claim is so, uniformly replace 'studies', 'student', 'subject', and 'teacher' with any other expressions that respect the grammaticality of (33) and (35). For an example, see the inference from (37) to (36).

36. Every player caught a ball with a glove.
37. There is a glove that every player caught a ball with.

We can explain the logical relations between this and other such pairs by appeal to the notion of the relative *scope* of the quantifiers in the statements. Following the procedures for translating quantified statements into RPL, we derive (38), the halfway house for (33) ('S^3' representing ' __ studies __ with __ ', 'S^1' representing 'is a student', 'A^1' representing 'is a subject', and 'T^1' representing 'is a teacher').

38. $S^3{}_{\forall S^1, \exists A^1, \exists T^1}$

Once we unpack the quantifiers in (38), we arrive at (39), the correct RPL symbolization for (33).

39. $(\forall y)(S^1 y \supset (\exists x)(A^1 x \,\&\, (\exists z)(T^1 z \,\&\, S^3 yxz)))$

In (33) the grammatical subject is 'Every student', and the main verb is 'studies'. But in (34) 'a teacher' is the grammatical subject, and the main verb is 'has'. *The choice of dictionary matters.* If certain terms in the premises and the conclusion do not overlap, we will have no obvious basis for affirming in our notation that this inference really is formally valid. One way to preserve the validity of the inference from (34) to (33) is to figure out some way to render (34) so that we retain 'studies' as its main verb (or predicate).

But if we try to represent (34) with the same dictionary we used to represent (33), including the three-place predicate 'S^3', where its first place ranges over those who study, its second over what's studied, and its third over those with whom the studying takes place, then the halfway formulation for (34) would again be (38), which, as we saw above, issues in a symbolization in RPL as (39). Something has gone wrong. If (39) were the correct symbolization of (34) in RPL, then (33) and (34) would be logically equivalent, which we know is not the case.

How, then, should we accommodate (34) in RPL? We need to come up with a solution that shows that (34) logically implies (33) but is not logically equivalent to it.

Looking at (34), one thing which obviously distinguishes it from (33) is *the order in which its English quantifier expressions occur,* moving from left to right. The first token of a quantifier expression in (33) is 'Every student', the second is 'some subject' and the last is 'a teacher', whereas (34) begins with 'A teacher', followed by 'every student' and then by 'some subject'. Perhaps the mistake in representing (34) with (38) lay in placing the quantifier expressions in it in the wrong order? Perhaps (40) would be a more faithful representation.

40. $S^3_{\exists T^1, \forall S^1, \exists A^1}$

But (40) can't be right either, since it unpacks as (41).

41. $(\exists x)(T^1 x \,\&\, (\forall z)(S^1 z \supset (\exists y)(A^1 y \,\&\, S^3 xzy)))$

(41) says something quite strange: namely, that there is a teacher who studies some student with every subject. It's grammatical, but barely intelligible. Again, what's gone wrong?

So far, the practice of having the places in a predicate track the order in which the quantifier terms binding them appear in the English statement has been unproblematic, although no formal procedure was ever established to sanction this practice. For example, 'x', 'z', and 'y' in the predicate 'S³' in (41) follow the order of appearance of their respective quantifier terms in (35). The result is an odd translation that doesn't capture the meaning of (35).

Our solution to these problems is elegant but simple. We want to follow two procedures. The first is familiar: the quantifiers in a symbolization should follow the order of appearance of the corresponding quantifier expressions in the English statement. The second procedure is new: the ordering of the places in a predicate should preserve meaning. In the case of the three-place predicate 'studies', meaning is preserved when the right relationship is preserved among its three *relata*: the thing that studies (who) coming first, the subject studied (what) coming second, and the individual studied with (whom) coming last.

Now let's return to (34) (and (35)). In (34) 'A teacher' has widest scope, 'every student' secondary scope, and 'some subject' narrow scope. We can achieve this by numbering the quantifier expressions in the order, moving from left to right, in which they are tokened in (34).

With these considerations in mind, we can adopt a procedure by which the ordering of the quantifiers in the non-RPL formulation of (34) follows the ordering of the places in the main predicate. But at the same time we also adopt as a mnemonic device a numbering procedure to remind us of the order of appearance and the scope of the quantifiers in the English expression. So the halfway formulation from English into RPL for (34) is not (38), but (42).

42. $S^3{}_{\forall S^1, \exists A^1, \exists T^1}$
           2   3   1

In symbolizing the quantifiers in (42), '$\exists T^1$' is symbolized first, '$\forall S^1$' second, and '$\exists A^1$' last, as in (43)–(45) respectively.

43. $(\exists x)(T^1 x \ \& \ S^3{}_{\forall S^1, \exists A^1}, x)$
44. $(\exists x)(T^1 x \ \& \ (\forall y)(S^1 y \supset S^3 y_{\exists A^1}, x))$
45. $(\exists x)(T^1 x \ \& \ (\forall y)(S^1 y \supset (\exists z)(A^1 z \ \& \ S^3 yzx)))$

It's essential to note that the order of the variable tokens in 'S³' in (45) corresponds exactly to the order in which the quantifier expressions in

(42) were symbolized. The order of appearance of the quantifiers parallels the order in which their English counterparts appear in (34). What has changed is the ordering of the tokens of the variables in the predicate 'S³yzx' so as to preserve its meaning.

13.8.1   The Order and Scope Procedure

(c)   English quantifier expressions should be symbolized (kicked out) in the order in which they appear in the English statement, moving from left to right.

Another example will help to consolidate all this information. (46) should be transformed first into (47), which, by applying the scope procedure (c), the universal procedure (a) (twice), and the existential procedure (b), in that order, issues in (48).

46.   Not every subject has every student studying it with some teacher.
47. $S^3{}_{\forall S^1, \sim \forall A^1, \exists T^1}$
       2   1   3
48. $\sim(\forall x)(A^1 x \supset (\forall y)(S^1 y \supset (\exists z)(T^1 z \;\&\; S^3 yxz)))$

As another example, consider (49). It should be transformed first into (50), which issues in RPL as (51).

49.   No teacher has every subject studied with him by a student.
50. $S^3{}_{\exists S^1, \forall A^1, \sim \exists T^1}$
       3   2   1
51. $\sim(\exists x)(T^1 x \;\&\; (\forall y)(A^1 y \supset (\exists z)(S^1 z \;\&\; S^3 zyx)))$

At this stage it would be advisable to read the discussion of the passive voice in §A5.1.

13.8.2   Choosing the Right Predicate

The importance of the preliminary stage in symbolizing English statements with nested quantifiers in RPL cannot be overemphasized. Just how crucial it is can be appreciated by considering the task of symbolizing an example such as (52).

52.   Some subject does not have every student studying it with some teacher.

(52) is logically equivalent to (46), but in this form it presents additional problems, because the negation is not helpfully prefixed to a quantifier phrase.

Suppose we want to deal with this, using 'S³' (abbreviating ' __ studies __ with __ ') as the main predicate. You might easily think that the outcome of your initial transformation of (52) into its halfway representation ought to be (53).

53. $\sim S^3{}_{\forall S^1, \exists A^1, \exists T^1}$
             2   1   3

Applying the various relevant procedures, you would then wind up with (54).

54. $(\exists x)(A^1x$ & $(\forall y)(S^1y \supset (\exists z)(T^1z$ & $\sim S^3yxz)))$

But (54) correctly symbolizes not (52), but instead (55).

55.   Some subject is such that for every student there is some teacher with whom she does not study it.

(55) is intelligible enough, but it is not what (52) means.

What has gone wrong is that the vital preliminary stage has not been gone through. You need first to paraphrase (52) so as to feature the English expansion of 'S³', to get something like (56).

56.   Some subject is such that not every student studies it with some teacher.

From (56) you should, if all goes well, get (57),

57. $S^3{}_{\sim \forall S^1, \exists A^1, \exists T^1}$
             2   1   3

and thence the correct symbolization (58).

58. $(\exists x)(A^1x$ & $\sim(\forall y)(S^1y \supset (\exists z)(T^1z$ & $S^3yxz)))$

Of course, this preliminary stage can't be fully mechanized, and requires you to think about what you want to treat as the main verb in a statement in the context of an argument, where it interacts with other main verbs in the other statements comprising the argument as a whole.

Statements   Exercise 13.5

- Using the dictionary provided, symbolize statements (1)–(11). (S^3: __ studies __ with __ ; S^1: is a student; A^1: is a subject; T^1: is a teacher)

1. Every teacher has some subject that some student studies with him.
2. Each subject has a student who studies it with every teacher.
3. No subject is such that every student studies it with every teacher.
4. There is a teacher such that some student studies every subject with him.
5. Someone likes everyone. (P^1: is a person; L^2: likes)
6. Someone is liked by everyone.
7. Some mailbox is such that every boy put every letter in it. (P^3: __ put __ into __ ; B^1: is a boy; L^1: is a letter; M^1: is a mailbox)
8. Some girl didn't push a boy into every puddle. (P^3: __ push __ into __ ; G^1: is a girl; P^1: is a puddle; B^1: is a boy)
9. Every dog had some student walk it in a park. (W^3: __ walked __ in __ ; D^1: is a dog; S^1: is a student; P^1: is a park)
10. Some book has a student reading it at all times. (R^3: __ read __ at __ ; B^1: is a book; T^1: is a time)
11. There's a conundrum that every professor struggled over every day. (S^3: __ struggled over __ on __ ; C^1: is a conundrum; P^1: is a professor; D^1: is a day)

Arguments   Exercise 13.6

- Symbolize arguments (1)–(4), using the dictionary provided.

1. Every living organism must perform a life function at some time. There are living organisms. Therefore, there's some life function which at some time has a living organism performing it. (P^3: __ performs __ at __ ; L^1: is a living organism; F^1: is a life function; T^1: is a time)

2. Someone is always eating some food. So, at all times, some food is being eaten by someone. (E^3: ___ eats ___ at ___ ; P^1: is a person; F^1: is a food; T^1: is a time)

3. At least one tree isn't climbed up by every cat in a garden. So, for every cat, there's a garden in which there's a tree that she climbs up. (C^3: ___ climbs up ___ in ___ ; T^1: is a tree; C^1: is a cat; G^1: is a garden)

4. Every leaf is lost by some tree every winter. There are leaves. Thus, some leaf is such that every winter some tree loses it. (L^3: ___ loses ___ in ___ ; L^1: is a leaf; W^1: is a winter; T^1: is a tree)

13.9 Summary of the Overall Procedure for Symbolizing English Statements with Nested Quantifiers into RPL

Given an English sentence (not itself a truth-functional compound of simpler sentences – in case it is, work on the component(s)) ripe for symbolization in the formal language of RPL, proceed in two main stages (prescinding, for the moment, from an important complication).

(1) Identify the main verb and decide its adicity – identify the noun phrases (which may be singular terms or, more interestingly, quantified noun phrases such as 'every boy' 'some girl', etc.) filling its argument places. Then, abbreviate any quantified noun phrases by appropriate quantifier symbols coupled with predicate letters representing the remainder of the noun phrase (e.g., replace 'every boy' by '$\forall B^1$', 'some girl' by '$\exists G^1$', and so on). Finally, write an intermediate non-RPL symbolization of the statement by putting the main verb (symbolized by a predicate letter of appropriate adicity), followed by the abbreviated quantified noun phrases, etc. which are its arguments in the order in which the expression they replace figure in the original English sentence – for example, 'Every boy loves some girl' goes over into '$L^2_{\forall B^1, \exists G^1}$'.

(2) Successively export the abbreviated quantified noun phrases, moving from left to right through the matrix, as follows. Turn

$$\ldots \theta^n \ldots \forall\alpha \ldots$$

into a universally quantified conditional,

$$\ldots (\forall x_i)(\alpha x_i \supset \theta^n \ldots x_i \ldots)$$

where 'x_i' is some variable not already used and α is a predicate, simple or complex. Turn

$$\ldots \theta^n \ldots {}_{\exists \alpha} \ldots$$

into

$$\ldots (\exists x_i)(\alpha x_i \ \& \ \theta^n \ldots x_i \ldots)$$

(same constraint on 'x_i'). Carry on until you have dealt with all the argument places. Now you're done. There are, however, at least two important complications, as follows.

The first complication is due to the fact that, typically, (1) is not quite the first stage. Typically, or at least commonly, the English sentence you want to deal with won't employ the longhand version of the n-place predicate you want to figure as the main predicate. This happens when, say, you've already symbolized 'Every boy loves some girl' using the two-place predicate letter 'L^2 __, __ ' abbreviating ' __ loves __ ', and you now want to deal with 'Some girl is loved by every boy', using the same main predicate/verb. So you must first paraphrase your English sentence, eliminating (in this case) the passive form ' __ is loved by __ ' in favor of the active ' __ loves __ ', to get (in this case) something like 'Some girl is such that every boy loves her'. Now we have something to which the stage (1) procedure can be applied.

The second complication is due to the fact that the argument places in your main predicate/verb are such that the sense of the statement that results from filling them depends on which fillers go in which places. For example, if the predicate/verb is ' __ loves __ ', then the expression that fills the first argument place should denote what (according to the original English sentence) does the loving, and that which goes in the second should denote what is loved. So, when we complete stage (1) for 'Some girl is such that every boy loves her', we should end up with '$L^2{}_{\forall B^1, \exists G^1}$', not '$L^2{}_{\exists G^1, \forall B^1}$'. As a result, the order of the temporary quantifier phrases in the matrix may no longer match the order in which they occur in the statement to which stage (1) is applied, and so may no longer match the order in which they are to be exported. To keep track, write an appropriate numeral beneath each such phrase, corresponding to its ordinal position in the initial statement, thus:

$$L^2{}_{\forall B^1, \exists G^1}$$
$$\quad 2 \quad 1$$

Now, when you come to stage (2), export phrases in the order indicated by the underscribed numerals.

This is, save for some small but important refinements that we will deal with later, in chapter 15, our basic procedure.

Notes

1   The degree of a predicate is also sometimes called the number of places of the predicate and also the predicate's adicity.

2   English grammar and logical grammar are not identical. In English grammar, the subject of (3) is 'Every man'. In logical grammar, however, 'Every man' contains the quantifier expression 'Every' and the logical predicate 'man'. To avoid confusion in certain contexts, we will use the term 'grammatical subject' or 'grammatical predicate' to refer to the English grammar subject and predicate respectively. We will use the term 'logical predicate' to refer to the predicates as generally used in the text.

3   The one possible exception to this constraint is discussed in §15.5.

Bibliography

Abusch, D., 'The Scope of Indefinites', *Natural Language Semantics* 2 (1994), 83–136.

Carden, Guy, *English Quantifiers: Logical Structure and Linguistic Variation* (New York: Academic Press, 1973).

Gil, D., 'Quantifier Scope, Linguistic Variation, and Natural Language Semantics', *Linguistics and Philosophy* 5 (1988), 421–72.

King, J., 'Are Indefinite Descriptions Ambiguous?', *Philosophical Studies* 53 (1988), 417–40.

Ludlow, Peter and Neale, Stephen, 'Indefinite Descriptions: In Defense of Russell', *Linguistics and Philosophy* 14 (1991), 171–202.

Strawson, P. F., 'Positions for Quantifiers', in M. K. Munitz and P. Unger (eds), *Semantics and Philosophy* (New York: New York University Press, 1974), 63–79.

14

Extending the Truth Tree Method to RPL

No new rules need be added to the truth tree method for PPL to extend the method to RPL; however, you will need to learn new strategies and sensitize yourself to potential pitfalls that truth trees for statements with nested quantifiers introduce. We will begin with unproblematic arguments and work our way up to the difficult cases.

14.1 RPL Arguments without Quantifiers

An argument with relational predicates without quantifiers can be tested for deductive validity using the original seven rules from PL. So consider the RPL argument:

P^2cd, $H^3abc \lor D^2cb$ ∴ $(P^2cd \ \& \ \sim H^3abc) \supset D^2bc$

(1)–(8) constitutes a truth tree for this argument.

1.	P^2cd	(premise)
√2.	$H^3abc \lor D^2cb$	(premise)
√3.	$\sim((P^2cd \ \& \ \sim H^3abc) \supset D^2bc)$	(negation of conclusion)
√4.	$P^2cd \ \& \ \sim H^3abc$	
5.	$\sim D^2bc$	3, $\sim \supset$
6.	P^2cd	
7.	$\sim H^3abc$	4, &

$$\qquad\qquad 8.\quad H^3abc \quad D^2cb \qquad\qquad 2, \lor$$
$$\qquad\qquad\qquad\times$$

This tree has no quantifiers in it, so there is no need to apply any of the three quantification rules UQ, EQ, or QE. The tree is complete and open, since the right branch is not closed. Note that 'D²cb' on line (8) does not contradict '~D²bc' on line (5). They are consistent statements.

14.2   RPL Arguments without Nested Quantifiers

Consider next an argument in RPL where the premises and the conclusion have only one quantifier apiece (i.e., where there is no multiple generality), as in

$(\exists x)F^2ax, (\forall x)(F^2ax \supset P^2cx) \therefore (\exists x)P^2cx$

(1)–(8) comprise a truth tree for this argument.

√1.	$(\exists x)F^2ax$	(premise)
2.	$(\forall x)(F^2ax \supset P^2cx)$	(premise)
√3.	$\sim(\exists x)P^2cx$	(negation of conclusion)
4.	$(\forall x)\sim P^2cx$	3, QE
5.	F^2ab	1, EQ
√6.	$F^2ab \supset P^2cb$	2, UQ
7.	$\sim P^2cb$	4, UQ
8.	$\sim F^2ab \qquad P^2cb$	6, $\supset$
	$\times \qquad \quad \times$	

Since all the branches in this tree close, the original argument is deductively valid.

There are several noteworthy points about this truth tree. First, notice that we had to extend the notion of an instantiation from §10.2.2. Consider any well-formed quantifier statement $(\exists x_i)\alpha$ or $(\forall x_i)\alpha$ of RPL, where α is a well-formed predicate of RPL, simple or complex, and x_i is an unbound variable in α. Let us define $\alpha(x_i/t)$ to be an *instantiation* of $(\exists x_i)\alpha$ or $(\forall x_i)\alpha$, obtained by uniformly substituting a singular term 't' for every x_i in α. So, on line (5) above, we find 'F²ab', which is an instantiation of '$(\exists x)F^2ax$' on line (1), 'b' replacing 'x'.

Notice also something already familiar from §10.3, that though (2) and (4) are both universal statements and therefore complex, they are *not* checked off when we applied rules to them to derive lines (6) and (7) respectively, because universal statements have no limit to the number of times UQ can be applied to them. For this reason we adopted the strategy that on a given branch we need only instantiate to the singular terms that already occur on that branch (if there are any); otherwise, branches would extend indefinitely, since there are indefinitely many singular terms.

We in fact violate this strategy in (1)–(8) above. Strictly speaking, had we followed the strategy religiously, the tree for the above argument would be significantly more complex. For example, whereas we instantiated (4) to (7) only in applying UQ, the strategy for UQ asks us to instantiate (4) to every singular term type that occurs on the tree. So we should have instantiated to 'a' and 'c' as well. The fact of the matter is that we didn't need to instantiate to these singular terms in order to close the tree. That is something I foresaw, and that is why I didn't add the other instantiations to the tree. Had I not done so, the truth tree would have been as follows:

$\sqrt{}$1. $(\exists x)F^2ax$ (premise)
2. $(\forall x)(F^2ax \supset P^2cx)$ (premise)
$\sqrt{}$3. $\sim(\exists x)P^2cx$ (negation of conclusion)
4. $(\forall x)\sim P^2cx$ 3, QE
5. F^2ab 1, EQ
$\sqrt{}$6. $F^2ab \supset P^2cb$ 2, UQ
7. $F^2aa \supset P^2ca$ 2, UQ
8. $F^2ac \supset P^2cc$ 2, UQ
9. $\sim P^2ca$ 4, UQ
10. $\sim P^2cb$ 4, UQ
11. $\sim P^2cc$ 4, UQ
               $\diagup\diagdown$
12. $\sim F^2ab$ P^2cb 6, $\supset$
       $\times$ $\times$

Truth tree (1)–(12) closes. Lines (7), (8), (9), and (11) are all irrelevant. You should have realized by now that if a truth tree closes, then adding any line to it cannot change the result. You can use your own ingenuity to reduce the steps in a tree if you can see that instantiations to a particular constant will result in closing it.

14.3   RPL Arguments with Nested Quantifiers

You are ready for the novel complications that arise when there are nested quantifiers. So consider the argument

$$(\forall x)(\exists y)F^2yx, (\forall x)(\forall y)(F^2xy \supset P^2xy) \therefore (\forall x)(\exists y)P^2yx$$

The truth tree (1)–(11) constitutes a complete and closed truth tree for this argument.

1.	$(\forall x)(\exists y)F^2yx$	(premise)
2.	$(\forall x)(\forall y)(F^2xy \supset P^2xy)$	(premise)
√3.	$\sim(\forall x)(\exists y)P^2yx$	(negation of conclusion)
√4.	$(\exists x) \sim(\exists y)P^2yx$	3, QE
√5.	$\sim(\exists y)P^2ya$	4, EQ
6.	$(\forall y) \sim P^2ya$	5, QE
√7.	$(\exists y)F^2ya$	1, UQ
8.	F^2ba	7, EQ
9.	$\sim P^2ba$	6, UQ
√10.	$F^2ba \supset P^2ba$	2, UQ (twice)
11.	$\sim F^2ba \qquad P^2ba$	10, $\supset$
	$\times \qquad\quad \times$	

On line (4) only the first quantifier '$\exists x$', gets instantiated on line (5). The second existential quantifier '$\exists y$', cannot be instantiated because there is a negation in front of it. Once quantifier exchange is applied above (on line 6), we may instantiate its universal quantifier to any singular term.

We chose to instantiate the existential quantifier on line (7) to the singular term 'b' on line (8) before we instantiate the universal quantifier '$\forall y$' on line (6). The rationale is familiar. The existential quantifier forces us to introduce a new singular term 'b' to the tree, whereas the universal quantifier does not. Eliminating all existential statements first is strategically wise. Existential statements determine how many distinct singular terms the tree needs (the universe of discourse, so to speak) for the purposes of evaluating the argument at hand.

On line (10) two universal quantifiers are instantiated simultaneously. There is nothing wrong with doing this, but you must be cautious while instantiating distinct variable types simultaneously. Suppose we find on a tree the following line:

$(\exists x)(\exists y)F^2xy$

We can liberalize the rules so that it's legitimate to instantiate both existential quantifiers, but it is illegitimate to instantiate them to the same singular term type, as in

F^2aa

The truth of '$(\exists x)(\exists y)F^2xy$' alone does not guarantee that something bears the relationship to itself, but this is exactly what 'F^2aa' asserts. Therefore, as the existential rule dictates, there must be distinct singular term types for each instantiated existential quantifier, as in

F^2ab

14.4   Choosing Singular Terms to Instantiate

Consider the following argument:

$(\forall x)(\forall y)F^2yx \therefore F^2ab \ \& \ F^2bc \ \& \ F^2ac$

Here is a truth tree for it:

1.	$(\forall x)(\forall y)F^2yx$	(premise)
√2.	$\sim(F^2ab \ \& \ F^2bc \ \& \ F^2ac)$	(negation of conclusion)
3.	F^2aa	1, UQ (twice)
4.	F^2bb	1, UQ (twice)
5.	F^2cc	1, UQ (twice)
6.	F^2cb	1, UQ (twice)
7.	F^2ba	1, UQ (twice)
8.	F^2ca	1, UQ (twice)
9.	F^2ac	1, UQ (twice)
10.	F^2bc	1, UQ (twice)
11.	F^2ab	1, UQ (twice)

12. $\sim F^2ab$ $\sim F^2bc$ $\sim F^2ac$ 2, $\sim$ &

     ×   ×   ×

If you look closely at this tree you should notice that lines (3)–(8) are superfluous. The three branches close because of lines (9)–(11) respectively. Had you looked at line (2) prior to instantiating (1), you should have seen that only (9)–(11) could be relevant. Had you seen this, you would have opted for truth tree (1)–(6) below instead.

1. $(\forall x)(\forall y)F^2yx$ (premise)
√2. $\sim(F^2ab \mathbin{\&} F^2bc \mathbin{\&} F^2ac)$ (negation of conclusion)
3. F^2ab 1, UQ (twice)
4. F^2bc 1, UQ (twice)
5. F^2ac 1, UQ (twice)

6. $\sim F^2ab$ $\sim F^2bc$ $\sim F^2ac$ 2, $\sim$ &
       ×   ×   ×

The lesson should be clear. You should instantiate a universal statement to every singular term in the tree only if you cannot see an easier way either to close the tree or to devise a counterexample to its validity.

Let's try another example. Consider the RPL argument

$(\forall x)(A^1x \supset B^2xx), \sim(\forall x)B^2xx \therefore (\exists x)A^1x$

The complete open truth tree (1)–(9) establishes its invalidity.

1. $(\forall x)(A^1x \supset B^2xx)$ (premise)
√2. $\sim(\forall x)B^2xx$ (premise)
√3. $\sim(\exists x)A^1x$ (negation of conclusion)
√4. $(\exists x)\sim B^2xx$ 2, QE
5. $(\forall x)\sim A^1x$ 3, QE
6. $\sim B^2aa$ 4, EQ
7. $\sim A^1a$ 5, UQ
√8. $A^1a \supset B^2aa$ 1, UQ

9. $\sim A^1a$ B^2aa 8, $\supset$
            ×

14.5   Infinite Truth Trees for RPL Arguments

Truth trees for PL and PPL arguments are always finite. A finite number of steps decides the question of whether an argument is deductively valid, whether a set of statements is consistent, whether two statements are logically equivalent, whether one statement logically implies another, or whether a statement is contingent, contradictory, or logically true. But in RPL not every set of statements has a complete finite truth tree. Consider the argument

$(\forall x)(\exists y)F^2yx \therefore (\exists x)(\forall y)F^2yx$

Let's try to construct a truth tree for it.

1.	$(\forall x)(\exists y)F^2yx$	(premise)
√2.	$\sim(\exists x)(\forall y)F^2yx$	(negation of conclusion)
3.	$(\forall x)(\exists y)\sim F^2yx$	2, QE (twice)
√4.	$(\exists y)F^2ya$	1, UQ
5.	F^2ba	4, EQ
√6.	$(\exists y)\sim F^2ya$	3, UQ
√7.	$(\exists y)\sim F^2yb$	3, UQ
8.	$\sim F^2ca$	6, EQ
9.	$\sim F^2db$	7, EQ

Does (1)–(9) constitute a complete open truth tree? Can we conclude that the original argument is deductively invalid given what we have so far? Strictly speaking, by applying EQ to (4) to derive (5) and EQ to (6) and (7) to derive (8) and (9) respectively, we added three new singular terms in addition to 'a' to the tree. We need to check to see whether instantiating to these new singular terms might not close the tree. So minimally we need to add lines (10)–(12) to this tree.

√10.	$(\exists y)F^2yb$	1, UQ
√11.	$(\exists y)F^2yc$	1, UQ
√12.	$(\exists y)F^2yd$	1, UQ

But now we must apply EQ again to (10)–(12) in order to derive (13)–(15) respectively.

13.	F^2eb	10, EQ
14.	F^2fc	11, EQ
15.	F^2gd	12, EQ

By now you should see a regress forming. We can neither close nor complete this tree. At each new step we introduce a novel singular term, requiring us to go back and reapply UQ in order to instantiate to this new singular term type. But each time we add a new singular term, UQ issues in a new existential statement, requiring a new instantiation via EQ to a new singular term, and so on.

The culprit here is not just the unbridled power of UQ. We already have an effective strategy in place to prevent every single universal statement from generating an infinite truth tree, like

1. $(\forall x)F^1 x$
2. $F^1 a$ 1, UQ
3. $F^1 b$ 1, UQ
4. $F^1 c$ 1, UQ
5. $F^1 d$ 1, UQ

and so on. This tree can be continued indefinitely, by adding one new singular term type after another. However, faithful adherence to our strategies would prevent this sort of infinite truth tree from developing. Recall our strategies.

14.6   Summary of Truth Tree Strategies

- Apply non-branching rules before branching rules when both are applicable.
- Apply QE whenever applicable.
- Apply EQ before applying UQ when both rules are applicable.
- When applying UQ to a universal statement, instantiate to singular terms already on the branch in which that statement occurs; if none occur, pick one to instantiate to arbitrarily.
- Apply rules to statements that lead to (some) closure before applying rules to statements that do not lead to closure.

The fourth strategy about applying the UQ rule would never allow us to devise a tree like (1)–(5) above. It tells us to stop at line (2).

When confronted with what looks like an infinitely descending truth tree, you are advised to look for a pattern of repetition or a *recursion*. A recursion is a series of steps which leads to a repetition of the same steps over and over. In (1)–(5), the application of UQ to (1) does not close the tree. Following the procedures for truth trees, you go back to (1) and instantiate again, this time to (3). But (3) fails to close the tree, so you return yet again to (1), and so on. At this point the pattern should be clear enough for you to infer that the tree won't close. (The same applies to tree (1)–(15) above.) However, this advice is only a suggestion. No technique exists for ferreting out those arguments whose trees are infinite and are therefore invalid from those that are complex but close. There is no guarantee that you will always know when you have started on an infinitely long, never closing truth tree or whether you have merely started what might be a long truth tree that will eventually close after a large number of steps. (See the relevant references in the bibliography for more on this problem.)

Truth trees   Exercise 14.1

- Construct truth trees for arguments (1)–(9).

1. ~($\forall$x)($\exists$y)P^2yx ∴ ($\exists$x)($\exists$y) ~ P^2yx
2. ($\forall$x)(F^1x ⊃ ($\forall$y)~M^2yx), F^1d ∴~M^2pd
3. ($\exists$x)($\exists$y)F^2xy, ($\forall$x)($\forall$y)(F^2xy ⊃ P^2xy) ∴ P^2ab
4. ($\forall$x)R^2xx ∴ ($\forall$x)($\forall$y)(R^2xy ⊃ R^2yx)
5. ($\forall$x)(G^2xx ∨ ($\exists$y)F^2xy), ~($\exists$z)G^2zz ∴($\exists$x)($\exists$y)F^2xy
6. ($\forall$x)($\forall$y)(F^2xy ⊃ P^2xy) ∴ ($\forall$x)($\forall$y)(F^2xy ⊃ (P^2xy & P^2yx))
7. ($\forall$x)(H^1x ⊃ A^1x) ∴ ($\forall$x)(($\exists$y)(H^2xy & T^2xy) ⊃ ($\exists$z)(A^1z & T^2xz))
8. ($\forall$x) ~ B^2xx, ~($\forall$x)(A^1x ⊃ ($\exists$y)B^2xy) ∴ ($\exists$x)(A^1x & B^2xx)
9. ($\forall$x)($\forall$y)(R^2xy ⊃ R^2yx) ∴ ($\forall$x)($\forall$y)($\forall$z)((R^2xy & R^2yz) ⊃ R^2xz)

Truth trees   Exercise 14.2

- Determine the deductive validity of arguments (1)–(3), according to your solutions to exercise 13.2, using the truth tree method.

Truth trees   Exercise 14.3

- Determine the deductive validity of (1)–(3), according to your solutions to exercise 12.3, using the truth tree method.
- Determine the deductive validity of (1)–(4), according to your solutions to exercise 13.6, using the truth tree method.

Exercise 14.4   Statement properties

- Determine whether (1)–(11) in exercise 13.5 are contingent, logical truths, or logical falsehoods, using the truth tree method.
- Recall from §10.5.3 and §8.6.2 that a statement β is a contradiction just in case a completed truth tree for it closes; a statement β is a logical truth just in case a completed truth tree for ~β closes; and a statement β is contingent just in case a completed truth tree for β and a completed truth tree for ~β both remain open.

Bibliography

Jeffrey, R. C., *Formal Logic: Its Scope and Limits*, 2nd edn (New York: McGraw-Hill, 1981).

Smullyan, R., *First-Order Logic* (Berlin: Springer, 1968).

15

Negation, Only, and Restrictive Relative Clauses

15.1 Negation

The negative particle 'not' in (1) has a different relative scope to its subject quantifier 'Some' than it has to its subject quantifier 'every' in (2). In (1), the quantifier 'Some' is said to have wide scope over the negative particle 'not', but in (2) the quantifier 'every' has narrow scope. It does not have 'not' within its scope.[1]

1. Some boy does not like some dog.
2. Not every boy likes some dog.

The symbolization strategies that this book recommends quite naturally accommodate scope distinctions. Let 'B^1' symbolize 'is a boy', 'D^1' 'is a dog', and 'L^2' ' __ likes __ '. (1) and (2) are symbolized in the hybrid English/RPL as (3) and (4) respectively.

3. $\sim L^2_{\exists B^1, \exists D^1}$
4. $L^2_{\sim \forall B^1, \exists D^1}$

Placing the tilde '$\sim$' directly before the relational predicate 'L^2' in (3) guarantees that '$\sim$' will have narrow scope in (5). The negation attaches to the relational predicate 'likes', which ends up within the scope of both existential quantifiers. But by placing '$\sim$' in the subject term place in (4), the negative particle takes wide scope in (6).

5. $(\exists x)(B^1x \ \& \ (\exists y)(D^1y \ \& \ \sim L^2xy))$
6. $\sim(\forall x)(B^1x \supset (\exists y)(D^1y \ \& \ L^2xy))$

From the perspective of RPL, there are three distinct types of negation: statement negation (what we have been calling 'logical negation'), predicate negation, and quantifier negation. These types are illustrated in (7)–(9) respectively.

7. **It's not true that** everyone likes someone.
8. Everyone **doesn't** like someone.
9. Someone likes **no** one.

(7)–(9) should be symbolized first in hybrid English/RPL (10)–(12), then finally in well-formed RPL statements (13)–(15) respectively.

10. $\sim(L^2_{\forall P^1, \exists P^1})$ P^1: is a person
11. $\sim L^2_{\forall P^1, \exists P^1}$
12. $L^2_{\exists P^1, \sim \exists P^1}$

13. $\sim(\forall x)(P^1x \supset (\exists y)(P^1y \ \& \ L^2xy))$
14. $(\forall x)(P^1x \supset (\exists y)(P^1y \ \& \ \sim L^2xy))$
15. $(\exists x)(P^1x \ \& \ \sim(\exists y)(P^1y \ \& \ L^2xy))$

In (13) the negation takes wide scope, in (14) narrow scope, and in (15) it negates the second existential formula.

Exercise 15.1   Negation

- Symbolize statements (1)–(6) in RPL.
- Use the dictionary provided above.

1. No boy likes every dog.
2. Everybody likes no dog.
3. No one is happy always. (H^2: is happy at; T^1: is a time; P^1: is a person)
4. No one is never happy
5. Some cow doesn't eat grass. (E^2: eats; C^1: is a cow; G^1: is grass)
6. Every cow eats no grass.

Exercise 15.2   Arguments

- Symbolize the arguments (1)–(4) in RPL.
- Use the dictionary provided.

1. It is false that everyone is smarter than everyone. So, no one is smarter than everyone. (S^2: is smarter than; P^1: is a person)
2. No one hates everyone all of the time. But everyone hates someone sometime. Therefore, someone hates someone never. (H^3: _____ hates __ at __ ; P^1: is a person; T^1: is a time)
3. All hydrogens have a proton, but not a neutron. All hydrogens are atoms. So, it's not true that all atoms have protons and neutrons. (C^3: __ have __ and __ ; H^1: is a hydrogen; P^1: is a proton: N^1: is a neutron; A^1: is an atom)
4. Nothing dead breathes. Everything is either dead or alive. Some people are not alive. So it's false that no one doesn't breathe. (D^1: is dead; B^1: breathes; A^1: is alive; P^1: is a person)

15.2 'Only' as a Quantifier

In §11.5 we treated 'only' as a universal quantifier in which the order of the subject nominal to which 'only' attaches and the predicate are reversed. So, for example, (16), is symbolized in PPL as (17), which means the same as (18).

16. Only dogs are rabid.
17. $\forall(R^1 \supset D^1)$ R^1: is rabid; D^1: is a dog
18. Anything rabid is a dog.

We will continue to follow this procedure in RPL, but we will need to refine it in order to accommodate nested quantification. Our strategy will be to treat 'only' as a quantifier, using the non-RPL symbol 'O' to mean 'only'. Accordingly, the first step towards symbolizing (19) in RPL is (20).

19. Only men work every shift.
20. $W^2 OM^1, \forall S^1$

In (19) 'only' is the first quantifier expression to occur, so it gets kicked out first. Remember, 'only' states a necessary condition. (16) and (18) mean that being a dog is a necessary condition for being rabid. Necessary conditions occur in the consequents of conditionals. In (17), the symbolization of (16) in PPL, the predicate 'dogs' occupies the position of the consequent in the expression '$R^1 \supset D^1$'. Similarly, in translating 'OM^1' in (20), the quantity is expressed by '$(\forall x)$' in the leftmost position of the formula, but the attached predicate 'M^1' moves to the position of a necessary condition, to the right of the horseshoe, as in (21).

21. $(\forall x)(W^2x_{\forall S^1} \supset M^1x)$

'$W^2x_{\forall S^1}$' takes up the position of the sufficient condition to the left of the horseshoe. Next, the remaining quantifier expression is symbolized in the normal way, as in (22).

22. $(\forall x)((\forall y)(S^1y \supset W^2xy) \supset M^1x)$

So, generalizing the procedure for symbolizing 'only' in PPL from §11.5, we get:

> **(d)   If a formula is of the form $\theta'' \ldots {}_{O\alpha} \ldots$, where O$\alpha$ is flanked by quantifier expressions, variables, or singular terms, transform it into a formula of the form: $(\forall x_i)(\theta'' \ldots x_i \ldots \supset \alpha x_i)$**

The same important advantages of the prior procedures accrue to (d) as well; it is both systematic and analytic in how it breaks down complex expressions and issues in completed RPL symbolizations.

In logico-English, (22) says that for anything x, if every shift is such that x works it, then x is a man. More colloquially, (22) can be read back into English as (23).

23.   Everything who works every shift is a man.

Ever since chapter 7 we have been treating 'only' as introducing a necessary condition. (19) (and (23)) says it is a necessary condition of someone working every shift that he be a man.

Exercise 15.3   Only

- Symbolize statements (1)–(6) in RPL.

1.   Only cats have fur. (H^2: __ has __ ; C^1: is a cat; F^1: is fur)
2.   Only fish can breathe under water. (B^2: can breathe under; F^1: is a fish; W^1: is water)

3. Everyone can breathe only air. (B^2: can breathe; P^1: is a person; A^1: is air)
4. Not only students study only books. (S^2: studies; S^1: is a student; B^1: is a book)
5. Some men work only shifts. (W^2: works; M^1: is a man; S^1: is a shift)
6. Only men work only shifts.

Arguments   Exercise 15.4

- Symbolize arguments (1)–(4), using the dictionary provided.

1. Only students study some subject with a teacher. So, it is false that some teacher studies a subject with a teacher. (S^1: is a student; A^1: is a subject; T^1: is a teacher; S^3: __ studies __ with __)
2. Every student studies only subjects with a teacher. Therefore, no student studies a non-subject with a teacher.
3. Only cats climb trees. Only tree climbers catch squirrels. So, only cats catch squirrels. (C^2: climbs; A^2: catches; C^1: is a cat; S^1: is a squirrel; T^1: is a tree)
4. Only trees lose only leaves. Some people lose books. Thus, not every person is a tree. (L^2: loses; T^1: is a tree; L^1: is a leaf; B^1: is a book; P^1: is a person)

15.3 Restrictive Relative Clauses

Consider the following six arguments:

24. Everyone loves a good drink.
25. So, everyone who owns a car loves a good drink.

26. Every student who studies will do well.
27. So, every student will do well.

28. Some children who never went to school will never learn.
29. So, some children will never learn.

30. Some players never get into the game.
31. So, some players who are unskilled never get into the game.

32. No university that cares about its students will permit drugs on campus.
33. So, no university will permit drugs on campus.

34. No hurricane has ever hit Aruba.
35. So, no hurricane that had a hundred-mile-an-hour winds has ever hit Aruba.

(24)–(25) is deductively valid. What's true of an unrestricted universal statement must be true of any restriction on it. However, (26)–(27) is deductively invalid. You cannot validly infer the unrestricted universal claim (27) from the restrictive (26). We see just the opposite with regards to existentials. (28)–(29) is valid, but (30)–(31) is invalid. Interestingly, the negative quantifier expression 'no' behaves like the universal quantifier, and not the existential. Like the inference from (26) to (27), the inference from (32) to (33) is invalid, and like the inference from (24) to (25), the inference from (34) to (35) is valid.

What all these arguments have in common is that their validity or invalidity is entirely formal (see §2.1). So, were we to make grammatically acceptable substitutions for the various nouns and verbs that populate these arguments, they would retain their logical properties, which raises the questions of why some arguments built up out of restrictive relative clauses are valid, and why others are invalid. To answer these questions, we let the non-RPL symbol 'M*' temporarily represent the noun phrase 'man who has a son', 'W*' temporarily represent the noun phrase 'woman who has a son', and 'T*' temporarily represent the noun phrase 'toy which is expensive'. Let 'G³' symbolize ' __ gave __ __ '. Postponing a more minute analysis for the moment, a first step toward symbolizing (36) in RPL is (37).

36. Every man who has a son gave some woman who has a son some toy which is expensive.
37. $G^3_{\forall M^*, \exists W^*, \exists T^*}$

By applying the universal procedure (a) and then the existential procedure (b) twice to (37), we derive (38).

38. $(\forall x)(M^*x \supset (\exists y)(W^*y \ \& \ (\exists z)(T^*z \ \& \ G^3xyz)))$

(38) is of course not a well-formed formula of RPL, since 'M*', 'W*', and 'T*' are not symbols of RPL. Next we introduce some new predicates.

Let 'M¹', 'W¹', and 'T¹' stand for 'is a man', 'is a woman', and 'is a toy' respectively; and let 'S²' stand for 'is the son of', and 'E¹' stand for 'is expensive'. Then, continuing our practice from §11.3 of treating restrictive relative clauses as predicate conjunctions, (38) issues in (39), which correctly symbolizes (36) in RPL.[2]

39. $(\forall x)((M^1x \mathbin{\&} (\exists x_1)S^2x_1x) \supset ((\exists y)((W^1y \mathbin{\&} (\exists y_1)S^2y_1y) \mathbin{\&} (\exists z)((T^1z \mathbin{\&} E^1z) \mathbin{\&} G^3xyz))))$

Put more simply, 'M*x' represents the RPL formula '$(M^1x \mathbin{\&} (\exists x_1)S^2x_1x)$', which means 'x is a man who has a son', given the assigned dictionary. (Similarly for 'W*y' and 'T*z'.) The general procedure behind this transformation, at this stage, is as follows.

15.3.1   The Quantificational Restrictive Relative Clause Procedure

> (e) • First introduce an abbreviated predicate to temporarily represent the complex RPL predicate consisting of a general term and its relative clause.
> • Then symbolize as though the abbreviated predicate were actually in RPL.
> • Finally, unpack the abbreviated predicate (using an adequate RPL dictionary).

General procedure (e) introduces nothing that you have not already seen in our study of PPL.

Employing the same dictionary as for (36), as a first step, represent (40) as (41).

40. Every man who has no son gave some woman who has a son every toy which is not expensive.

41. $G^3{}_{\forall M^*, \exists W^*, \forall T^*}$

Applying procedures (a), (b), and (a) in that order to (41) issues in (42).

42. $(\forall x)(M^*x \supset (\exists y)(W^*y \mathbin{\&} (\forall z)(T^*z \supset G^3xyz)))$

Next we must replace 'M*x', 'W*y', and 'T*z', which represent respectively 'x is a man who has no son', 'y is a woman who has a son', and 'z is a toy which is not expensive'. First reflect on 'M*x'. It has a restrictive relative clause. Therefore, according to procedure (e), the first step is to replace 'M*x' with (43), then replace 'W*y' with (44), and finally 'T*z' with (45).

43. $(M^1x$ & $\sim(\exists x_1)S^2x_1x)$
44. $(W^1y$ & $(\exists y_1)S^2y_1y)$
45. $(T^1z$ & $\sim E^1z)$

Directing your attention back to (42), replace asterisk predicates with their representations in RPL. The result is (46), a correct symbolization for (40).

46. $(\forall x)((M^1x$ & $\sim(\exists x_1)S^2x_1x) \supset (\exists y)((W^1y$ & $(\exists y_1)S^2y_1y)$ & $(\forall z)((T^1z$ & $\sim E^1z) \supset G^3xyz)))$

Exercise 15.5   **Statements**

- Symbolize the statements (1)–(3) in RPL, using the dictionary from above for (1)–(2) and the dictionary provided below for (3).

1. Every man who has some son gave every woman some toy.
2. Every woman who hasn't a son didn't give every man who hasn't a son no toy.
3. Only boys who eat every apple win always. (B^1: is a boy; E^2: eats; W^2: wins at; T^1: is a time; A^1: is an apple)

Exercise 15.6   **Arguments**

- Symbolize arguments (1)–(6) in RPL.
- Use the dictionary provided.

1. Anyone who can beat everyone can beat Frank. So, Frank cannot beat himself. (B^2: can beat; f: Frank; P^1: is a person)
2. A horse is an animal. So, whoever owns a horse owns an animal. (H^1: is a horse; A^1: is an animal; O^2: owns; P^1: is a person)
3. Every man who has a son gave every woman a toy that is not expensive. Therefore, every man gave some woman a toy.

4. Everyone who knows someone loves someone. But not everyone loves someone. So, not everyone knows someone. (K^2: knows; L^2: loves; P^1: is a person)

5. A man in town shaves every man in town who does not shave himself. So, some man in town shaves himself. (S^2: shaves; M^1: is a man in town)

6. Any barber who shaves a barber shaves someone who does not shave himself. But any barber who shaves himself does not shave someone who shaves every barber. So, there is a barber who shaves himself. (S^2: shaves; B^1: is a barber; P^1: is a person)

15.4   Quantifiers and Anaphora

(47) seems to be a conditional, with 'some boy likes Bill' as its antecedent and 'he likes Frank as well' as its consequent.[3]

47.   If some boy likes Bill, then he likes Frank as well.

As a first approximation towards symbolizing (47) in RPL, let's try to treat it as a conditional. Letting 'L^2' stand for 'likes', 'b' for 'Bill', 'f' for 'Frank', and 'B^1' for 'is a boy', we get (48).

48. $(L^2{}_{\exists B^1},\ b \supset L^2\ \text{'he'},\ f)$

Ordinarily, we symbolize the antecedent and the consequent of a conditional independently. For example, in the case of (49), (50) would be a good halfway house on the way to its correct symbolization in RPL as (51).

49.   If some boy likes Bill, then Bill likes Frank.
50. $L^2{}_{\exists B^1},\ b \supset L^2 bf$
51. $(\exists x)(B^1 x\ \&\ L^2 xb) \supset L^2 bf$

However, as when symbolizing in PPL, the pronoun 'he' in (48) preempts any move analogous to the one we made in getting from (49) and (50) to (51).

(52) is a non-RPL expression, which highlights this point. When presented with statements containing an anaphoric pronoun having as its anaphor a quantifier expression such as 'some boy', one can draw a

line connecting the quantifier expression to the pronoun to notate the relationship.

52. $(L^2_{\exists B^1}, b \supset L^2\text{'he'}, f)$

Converting this diagrammatic suggestion into a procedure that issues in RPL formulas gives us the following (already recommended in §11.4.2).

15.4.1   *The Existential Quantifier, Anaphoric Pronoun, and Conditional Procedure*

> **(f)**   **If there is an existential quantifier expression in the antecedent of an English conditional statement which is the anaphor of a pronoun in the consequent, convert the existential into a universal quantifier and apply the universal quantifier strategy.**

Applying this strategy to (52) issues in (53).

53. $(\forall x)(B^1x \supset (L^2xb \supset L^2xf))$

The fourth (and final) token of 'x' in (53) replaces 'he' in (52), and this token is within the scope of (bound by) the universal quantifier.

Notice that '$(L^2xb \supset L^2xf)$' occurs in (53). Although (53) is a universal, not a conditional, the complex predicate that the universal quantifier has within its scope in (53) reveals the basis for our intuition that (48) *is* a conditional, thus respecting our intuition that (47) has a conditional aspect.

The idea behind procedure (f) is simple; yet it generalizes to complex and difficult statements. Consider (54); like (47), it too appears to be a conditional statement.

47.   If some boy likes Bill, then he likes Frank as well.
54.   If **some** boy doesn't like **some** girl, then **he** doesn't kiss **her**.

Let 'he' and 'her' be anaphoric pronouns, with their anaphors being 'some boy' and 'some girl' respectively. Letting 'K^2' represent 'kisses', a first approximation for representing (54) in RPL is (55).

55. $(\sim L^2_{\exists B^1, \exists G^1} \supset \sim K^2\text{'he', 'her'})$

Proceeding from left to right in (55), discharge the first existential quantifier token, which in this case binds the first pronoun ('he') in the consequent. Applying procedure (f), this quantifier is transformed into a universal, as in (56).

56. $(\forall x)(B^1 x \supset (\sim L^2 x_{\exists G^1} \supset \sim K^2 x, \text{'her'}))$

Applying procedure (f) to (56) issues in a correct symbolization (57) of (54) in RPL.

57. $(\forall x)(B^1 x \supset (\forall y)(G^1 y \supset (\sim L^2 xy \supset \sim K^2 xy)))$

Although upon first glance (55) seemed to be a conditional, it makes a universal claim, something like 'Any boy who doesn't like a girl won't kiss her'. Yet a trace of its conditionality remains in (57), indicated by '$(\sim L^2 xy \supset \sim K^2 xy)$'.

15.4.2   *Existential Quantifiers, Anaphoric Pronouns, and Non-conditionals*

(58) and (59) have pronouns with anaphors that are existential quantifier expressions, but these quantifier expressions are not within the scope of a negation; nor are they in the antecedent of anything which even appears to be a conditional.

58.   Either some girl loves Bill, or she doesn't love herself.
59.   Some girl loves some boy, but he doesn't love her.

Though we need a variable to bind the pronoun across the disjunction and the conjunction respectively in (58) and (59), strategy (f) does not apply to (58) and (59), since their anaphoric pronouns are not in any consequent (since (58) and (59) have no element of conditionality). Correct symbolizations for (58) and (59) in RPL are (60) and (61) respectively.

60. $(\exists x)(G^1 x \ \& \ (L^2 xb \lor \sim L^2 xx))$
61. $(\exists x)(G^1 x \ \& \ (\exists y)(B^1 y \ \& \ (L^2 xy \ \& \ \sim L^2 yx)))$

In (58) 'some girl' has wider scope than 'Either . . . or . . .'. (58) is equivalent in meaning to 'Some girl either loves Bill, or she doesn't love herself'. Similarly, in (59), 'Some girl' has wider scope than 'but'. (59) is equivalent in meaning to 'Some girl loves some boy who doesn't love her', which, following our procedures for restrictive relative clauses, is symbolized in RPL as '$(\exists x)(G^1x \ \& \ (\exists y)((B^1y \ \& \ \sim L^2yx) \ \& \ L^2xy))$'. This symbolization is logically equivalent to (61). (58), instead of being a disjunction, turns out to have a 'disjunctive predicate'; (59), instead of being a conjunction, turns out to have a 'conjunctive predicate'.

Exercise 15.7   Statements

- Symbolize (1)–(10), employing the appropriate procedures.
- Use the dictionary if provided. Make your own if not.

1. If some boy loves Mary, then some girl loves her too.
2. If some boy loves Mary, then he loves Bill too.
3. If any boy loves Mary, then Bill loves him.
4. Some girl loves some boy, but she doesn't love any fish.
5. Either some boy loves Mary, or she doesn't love him.
6. If a girl who has a son loves Bill, then she loves Frank.
7. Everyone who knows anyone knows Bill.
8. Everyone who drank any water got sick. (P^1: is a person; D^2: drank; W^1: is water; S^1: got sick) (Ask yourself what 'any' signifies here.)
9. Only students who had read (some) phrenology attended (some) lectures. (S^1: is a student; R^2: read; A^2: attended; L^1: is a lecture; P^1: is (about) phrenology)
10. No student will pass unless he studies. (R^1: is a student; S^1: studies; P^1: will pass)

Exercise 15.8   Arguments

- Symbolize arguments (1)–(4).
- Use the dictionary provided.

1. If anything is missing, then some person stole it. If anything is damaged, then some person broke it. Something is either missing or damaged.

So, some person either stole something or broke something. (M¹: is missing; S²: stole; P¹: is a person; D¹: is damaged; B²: broke)

2. If a person smokes something, then he risks illness. It follows that all people who smoke 'crack' risk illness. (m: crack; R¹: risks illness; S²: smokes; P¹: is a person)

3. Every person whom Bill knows likes someone sometime. But if somebody doesn't like someone sometime, then he likes that person never. Therefore, if Bill likes someone sometime, then he likes him always. (L³: ___ likes ___ at ___ ; P¹: is a person; T¹: is a time; K²: knows; b: Bill)

4. If every dog bites every cat, then some cats bite all girls. But if any cat bites a girl, then it is killed. Therefore, if no dog bites any cat, then every girl is not killed. (B²: bites; C¹: is a cat; D¹: is a dog; G¹: is a girl; K¹: is killed)

15.5 Anaphora and Restrictive Relative Clauses

Continuing the project of transforming nested quantifier English statements in RPL, what's the halfway formulation for (62)?

62. Every man who has a son adores him.

Is it (63), where 'M*' means 'man who has a son'?

63. $A^2_{\forall M^*}$, 'him' A^2: adores

The problem is that the anaphor for 'him' is 'a son', not 'Every man who has a son'. Contrast (62) with (64).

64. Every man who has a son adores himself.

Here the anaphor for 'himself' is 'Every man who has a son'.

How do we symbolize (62) so as to avoid this ambiguity? Let's symbolize the universal quantifier first.

65. $(\forall x)(M^*x \supset A^2x, \text{'him'})$

Now let's try unpacking 'M*' as (66).

66. $(\forall x)(M^1x \ \& \ (\forall y)((S^1y \ \& \ H^2xy) \supset A^2xy))$

M^1: is a man; S^1: is a son; H^2: has

Inside this universal statement the main connective is '&', so (66) logically implies that everything is a man; (62) has no such implication.

We can solve this problem by modifying slightly the original procedure in §11.4.2 governing quantifiers binding pronouns in the consequents of conditionals. The key to understanding the refined procedure requires us to recognize that if '$(\forall y)$' has all of '$((M^1x \ \& \ (S^1y \ \& \ H^2xy)) \supset A^2xy)$' within its scope, then a correct symbolization of (62) in RPL is (67).

67. $(\forall x)(\forall y)((M^1x \ \& \ (S^1y \ \& \ H^2xy)) \supset A^2xy)$

So, the new procedure is as follows.

15.5.1   *Refined Quantifier and Anaphora Procedure*

> **(g)   When a quantifier is kicked out of a relative clause in the antecedent of a conditional in order to bind a pronoun in the consequent, give it the widest possible scope (without changing the scope of any other quantifier).**

Notice the proximity in meaning between (62) and (68). Indeed, they are intuitively logically equivalent.

62. Every man who has a son adores him.
68. If a man has a son, then he adores him.

Both the pronouns 'he' and 'him' in the consequent in (68) are anaphoric. The correct symbolization for (68) is not (69).

69. $(\forall x)(M^1x \supset (\forall y)((S^1y \supset H^2xy) \supset A^2xy))$

Read back into English, (69) states that 'any man who has *every* son adores him'. The correct symbolization for (68) is (70).

70. $(\forall x)(M^1x \supset (\forall y)(S^1y \supset (H^2xy \supset A^2xy)))$

Notice that (67) and (70) are logically equivalent. Perhaps the correct conclusion to draw from all this is that 'a man' and 'a son' are functioning as universally quantified noun phrases in (68).

Logical equivalence   **Exercise 15.9**

- Prove, using the truth tree method, that (67) is logically equivalent to (70).

Procedure (g) also easily accommodates pronouns bound by quantifiers inside restrictive relative clauses in general. The halfway formulation of (71) is (72), which issues in (73),

71. Some man who has a son loves him.
72. $L^2_{\exists M^*}$, 'him'
73. $(\exists x)(M^*x \ \& \ L^2x, \text{'him'})$

where 'M^*x' represents '$(M^1x \ \& \ H^2x_{\exists s^1})$'. Unpacking '$M^*$' routinely leaves you with a dangling unbound variable (pronoun). If you symbolize (73) in RPL, you wind up with an ill-formed formula, since the last token of 'y' in (74) is unbound. (We saw the same phenomenon in (65) above, which led us to refine our quantifier and anaphora procedure into (g).)

74. $(\exists x)((M^1x \ \& \ (\exists y)(S^1y \ \& \ H^2xy)) \ \& \ L^2xy)$

Since there is an anaphoric relationship between 'Some man who has a son' and 'him' in 'loves him', we must apply strategy (g), which issues in a correct symbolization in RPL for (71), namely, (75).

75. $(\exists x)(\exists y)((M^1x \ \& \ (S^1y \ \& \ H^2xy)) \ \& \ L^2xy)$

There is no conditional expression in (71), but the quantifier still needs to be pulled out from the restrictive relative clause so that it binds the pronoun (variable) in the rightmost conjunct.

Exercise 15.10   Statements

- Symbolize (1)–(7).
- Use the dictionary provided.

1. No one who steals a car owns it. (C^1: is a car; S^2: steals; P^1: is a person; O^2: owns)
2. Only people who own a car can register it. (This is a very difficult sentence to interpret. It's not even clear that it's grammatical.) (C^1: is a car; R^2: registers; P^1: is a person; O^2: owns)
3. If everyone wants something, then no one gets it. (That is, anything everyone wants, no one gets.) (G^2: gets; W^2: wants; P^1: is a person)
4. Every student who studies (a subject) with a teacher will not forget him. (S^1: is a student; A^1: is a subject; T^1: is a teacher; S^3: __ studies __ with __ ; F^2: forgets)
5. Every son of a son loves a son of a son of a son. (S^1: is a son; L^2: loves; O^2: of)
6. Every man who loves a woman doesn't love a man who doesn't love a woman. (M^1: is a man; W^1: is a woman; L^2: loves)
7. Sam dealt mercilessly with every critic who had unfavorably reviewed any of his books. (s: Sam; D^2: dealt mercilessly with; C^1: is a critic; R^2: favorably reviewed; B^2: is a book of)

Exercise 15.11   Arguments

- Symbolize arguments (1)–(13), using the dictionary provided.

1. Every number has some number as its successor. So, every number is the successor of some number. (N^1: is a number; G^2: is a successor of)
2. Every boy who didn't leave will catch the train. But not every boy who did leave will catch the train. So, every boy who did leave will not catch the train. (B^1: is a boy; L^1: did leave; C^2: will catch; t: the train)
3. No father who has a son adores him. But then it follows that every son is not adored by his father. (F^1: is a father; A^2: adores; H^2: has; S^1: is a son)
4. Everyone who owns a cat brushes it. Each cat that is brushed by someone is silky. Therefore, every owned cat is silky. (O^2: __ owns __ ; B^2 __ brushes __ ; P^1: is a person; C^1: is a cat; S^1: is silky)

5. Any strong base that mixes with a strong acid reacts with it. Sodium hydroxide is a strong base and hydrogen chloride is a strong acid. Thus, if sodium hydroxide mixes with hydrogen chloride, it will react with it. (M^2: __ mixes with __ ; R^2: __ reacts with __ ; A^1: is a strong acid; B^1: is a strong base; s: sodium hydroxide; h: hydrogen chloride)

6. Anyone that sits on a flea kills it. But not every flea that is killed by someone is sat on (by him). So, there's someone who sat on a flea and didn't kill it. (P^1: is a person; S^2: sits on; K^2: __ kills; F^1: is a flea)

7. No teacher has students studying every subject with him. So, there is a subject such that some teacher has no student studying it with him. (S^3: __ studies __ with __ ; S^1: is a student; A^1: is a subject; T^1: is a teacher)

8. Only teachers have students studying subjects with them. So, no student has a student studying a subject with him.

9. Whenever a cat catches a mouse, he'll eat it. Mouse eaters will not go hungry. So, no cat that catches a mouse goes hungry. (C^2: catches; C^1: is a cat; M^1: is a mouse; E^2: eats; H^1: goes hungry)

10. Only people who are loved by everyone are perfect. Everyone has someone who doesn't love him. Thus, it follows that nobody is perfect. (L^2: loves; P^1: is a person; F^1: is perfect)

11. No one is unhappy who plays with a dog. Not everyone has a dog he plays with. Thus, it's not the case that everyone who plays with a dog is not unhappy. (P^1: is a person; U^1: is unhappy; P^2: plays with; D^1: is a dog)

12. John is successful if, and only if, all his books are published. If he made typos, his books will not be published. Being accurate is necessary for not making typos. Therefore, if John is not accurate, he will not be successful. (S^1: is successful; P^1: is published; B^1: is a book by John; j: John; T^1: is a typo; M^2: made; A^1: is accurate)

13. No one who does not study for tests will do well on them. No one who doesn't do well on tests will do well in courses. So, only people who study for tests will do well in courses. (P^1: is a person; T^1: is a test; S^2: studies for; C^1: is a course; W^2: does well in)

15.6 Quantification in English

It is surprisingly easy to accommodate scope distinctions among quantifiers when you apply the recommended strategy (c) in §13.8.1. Pretty much all you need to see is in which order the quantifier expressions (not occurring in relative clauses) occur in statements, moving linearly from left to right. A number of logicians and linguists would take exception. So, for example, consider a statement like (76).

76. Everything loves something.

Often statements like (76) are said to be ambiguous between two readings, in somewhat contrived English, (77) and (78).

77. Everything is such that there is something (or other) that it loves.
78. There is some one thing which is loved by everything.

Using 'L²' to symbolize 'loves', these two alleged readings are represented in RPL as (79) and (80) respectively.

79. $(\forall x)(\exists y)L^2xy$
80. $(\exists y)(\forall x)L^2xy$

But doesn't following procedures (a) and (b) according to the order in which the English quantifier expressions occur in (76) require us to come up with (79), *not* (80)? Put somewhat differently, by virtue of endorsing certain procedures, does this book in effect bar interpreting (76) as (80)? That depends on whether we run the procedures on English sentences or on their interpretations – what we have been calling 'statements'. If statement (78) is really a possible interpretation of *sentence* (76), then we can insist on paraphrasing (78) so as to feature the two-place 'loves', so that it goes over into something like 'Something is such that everything loves it', and then acknowledging this as one possible disambiguation of (76), the other being (77).

But what about (81), which might seem even more problematic if you agree with those who cannot interpret it with 'Someone' taking wide scope over 'every minute'.

81. Someone dies every minute.

Let's introduce 'D²' for 'dies', 'P¹' for 'is a person', and 'M¹' for 'is a minute'. Moving linearly from left to right in (81), a first approximation is (82).

82. $D^2_{\exists P^1, \forall M^1}$

But applying procedures (a) and (b) to (82) in the order in which the quantifier expressions occur in (81) issues in (83).

83. $(\exists x)(P^1x \mathrel{\&} (\forall y)(M^1y \supset D^2xy))$

(83) seems at best to be a rather odd interpretation for (81). (81) does *not* seem to be saying that there is some person – say, Harry – who dies at every minute; rather, it seems to be more naturally read as saying that for every minute there is some person or other, presumably a different one for every minute, who dies, represented in RPL as (84).

84. $(\forall x)(M^1x \supset (\exists y)(P^1y \mathrel{\&} D^2yx))$

Another example is 'I draw a breath every minute', which obviously does not mean that there is some single breath which I keep on drawing. Similarly, for 'An oak grew out of every acorn'. Any sensible scheme for rendering these sentences in RPL is going to treat them with the universal quantifier having widest scope.

Is there anything to say in defense of the claim that (81) can be interpreted as (83) rather than (84)? There might be. First of all, notice that plenty of sentences begin with an existential quantifier expression followed by a universal quantifier expression, in which it is natural to read the initial existential quantifier as taking wide scope. Consider (85)–(87).

85. Some boy kissed every girl.
86. Someone ate every apple.
87. Some team wins every game.

It's natural to read (87) as proclaiming that there is an undefeated team. The other possible order of the quantifiers issues in a claim hardly worth making: namely, that every game has a winner. Does the fact that the existential has wide scope in each of (85)–(87) on their most natural readings provide any insight into what is going on when we read (81) as having the universal taking wide scope? Perhaps we are exploiting the non-linguistic fact that under normal circumstances people die only once?[4] If this were right, should logical form be sensitive to this non-linguistic information? It's been the position of this book that it should not. Many with this information about dying may feel compelled to impose reading (84) on (81). But, so we have been assuming, such information is irrelevant to the enterprise of symbolizing English statements in logic. The main defense for this position is that logical grammar should remain insensitive to lexical meaning and attend only to logical structure.[5]

Of course, most of you will find that following procedures (a)–(g) rigidly will take you too far afield from the intuitive 'logical form' of English statements. You should then refrain from employing them blindly. Even though this book adopts a certain convention – namely, following procedures (a)–(g) – it doesn't follow that you cannot apply them more selectively when your intuitions disagree with a blind commitment to them.[6]

Notes

1 Although talk of scope is loosely applied when extended beyond formal languages, this extended usage should be fairly intuitive by this stage.

2 Note that 'x' ≠ 'x₁' and 'y' ≠ 'y₁'.

3 The discussion in this section and several that follow assume that all pronouns that are anaphoric on quantified noun phrases can be treated as variables bound by those quantifiers. This assumption is controversial. See the 1977 paper by Evans listed in the bibliography below.

4 There is an important disanalogy between examples (85)–(87), on the one hand, and (81) and 'I take a breath every minute', on the other: viz., in each of the former the main verb is transitive, but in (81) and the last sentence, the main verb is intransitive. Although we are treating all the verbs here as two-place verbs, this distinction is not the same as the transitive/intransitive one. See the bibliography below for references.

5 It's not clear that (81) has two readings. Why isn't (84) a conversational inference (§3.2) from (81) and not necessarily part of its meaning? Put simply, why not stipulate that the procedures issue in the correct readings for English statements, and that their alleged counterexamples to the contrary are in fact either conversational inferences or the result of non-linguistic information a reader brings to bear on the interpretation of any given statement? There is nothing linguistically odd about saying 'A man dies every minute; it's amazing he keeps coming back to life and dying again and again, like clockwork. Perhaps it's a miracle.'

6 In §A5.2 there is a discussion of the properties of relations, which is of logical interest.

Bibliography

Atlas, J. D., *Philosophy without Ambiguity* (Oxford: Oxford University Press, 1989).

Chierchia, G. and McConnell-Ginet, S., *Meaning and Grammar*, 2nd edn (Cambridge, MA: MIT Press, 2000).

Davies, M., *Meaning, Quantification, Necessity* (London: Routledge and Kegan Paul, 1981).

Evans, G., 'Pronouns, Quantifiers and Relative Causes (I)', *Canadian Journal of Philosophy* 7 (1977), 467–536.

—— 'Pronouns', *Linguistic Inquiry* 11 (1980), 337–62.

Geach, P., *Reference and Generality* (Ithaca, NY: Cornell University Press, 1962).

Kempson, R. and Cormack, A. 'Ambiguity and Quantification', *Linguistics and Philosophy* 4 (1981), 159–309.

Larson, R. and Segal, G., *Knowledge of Meaning* (Cambridge, MA: MIT Press, 1995).

Reinhart, T. 'Syntactic Domains for Semantic Rules', in F. Guenthner and S. J. Schmidt (eds), *Formal Semantics and Pragmatics for Natural Language* (Dordrecht: D. Reidel, 1979), 107–30.

16

Relational Predicate Logic with Identity

16.1 Limits of Relational Predicate Logic

Argument (1)–(3) is intuitively valid.

1. The author of *Huckleberry Finn* is the author of *Tom Sawyer*.
2. The author of *Huckleberry Finn* was from Missouri.
3. So, the author of *Tom Sawyer* was from Missouri.

Its validity seems independent of the meaning of any 'non-logical' expression in this sense: replacing the singular term types 'the author of *Huckleberry Finn*' and 'the author of *Tom Sawyer*' in (1)–(3) with any other singular term types issues in a new valid argument. Both (4)–(6) and (7)–(9), for example, are valid.

4. Rutgers University is the State University of New Jersey.
5. Rutgers University is large.
6. So, the State University of New Jersey is large.

7. Lewis Carroll is the author of *Through the Looking Glass*.
8. Lewis Carroll liked little Alice.
9. So, the author of *Through the Looking Glass* liked little Alice.

These three arguments are all deductively valid, partly because each of the arguments has co-referring singular term types. However, any effort to symbolize these arguments in RPL will issue in deductively *invalid* RPL arguments. Let 'h' represent 'the author of *Huckleberry Finn*', 't' represent 'the author of *Tom Sawyer*', then represent 'was from Missouri' as 'M^1' and the 'is' in (1) as the relational predicate 'R^2'. With this dictionary, symbolizing (1)–(3) in RPL results in (10)–(12).

10. R^2ht
11. M^1h
12. ∴ M^1t

(10)–(12) is obviously deductively invalid in RPL.[1] In RPL, (1)–(3) has the same logical form as the obviously deductively invalid argument

Howard raced Tom.
Howard is a miler.
So, Tom is a miler.

Following the practice of previous chapters, we shall introduce new notation to facilitate demonstration of the formal deductive validity of (1)–(3), (4)–(6), and (7)–(9).

First, we introduce a predicate for *sameness*. It is convenient and suggestive to borrow from arithmetic for this purpose the two-place (binary) predicate symbol '='. The statement 'a = b' means 'a and b are the same individual', or 'a is (identical to) b'. Correspondingly, 'a ≠ b' means 'a and b are distinct', or 'a is not (identical to) b'. ('a ≠ b' may be written alternatively as '~(a = b)'.) With the identity symbol at our disposal, (1)–(3) can be rendered in this extension of RPL as (13)–(15) respectively.

13. h = t
14. M^1h
15. M^1t

(4)–(6) and (7)–(9) are treated similarly.

We will refer to this extension of RPL as *Relational Predicate Logic plus Identity* (RPL⁼).

Arguments   Exercise 16.1

- Symbolize arguments (1)–(4) in RPL⁼, using the dictionary provided.

1. The author of *Hamlet* is the author of *Lear*. The author of *Hamlet* was a genius. Hence, so was the author of *Lear*. (h: the author of *Hamlet*; l: the author of *Lear*; G^1: was a genius)

2. Mount Everest is the tallest mountain in the world. But Mount Everest is the same as Mount Chomolungma. Therefore, Mount Chomolungma is the tallest mountain in the world. (e: Mount Everest; c: Mount Chomolungma; t: the tallest mountain in the world)
3. Hydrogen chloride reacts with every base. Hydrogen chloride is the same as hydrochloric acid. So, hydrochloric acid reacts with every base. (R^2: reacts with; B^1: is a base; h: hydrogen chloride; a: hydrochloric acid)
4. Alan's cat purrs everyday. Alan's cat is Domino. Thus, Domino purrs everyday. (c: Alan's cat; d: Domino; D^1: is a day; P^2: purrs on)

16.2   Extending the Truth Tree Method to RPL⁼

To demonstrate the validity of a simple argument like (13)–(15) in RPL⁼, the truth tree method must be extended to accommodate the logical features of identity. To this end, we add two new rules, the last two rules for the truth tree method to be introduced in this book: namely, the Identity-out and the Identity-in rules.

16.2.1   *Identity-out Rule*

Paul Robeson is the most famous alumnus of Rutgers University; Paul Robeson lived for some time in Russia. What can you infer about where the most famous alumnus of Rutgers University lived for some time? Obviously, that he lived for some time in Russia. However, the current set of truth tree rules will not validate this inference, although it seems independent of the specific details of the example. In general, if a is identical to b, and if some property is ascribed to a, it follows that the same property holds of b as well. The Identity-out rule is designed specifically to capture this intuition.

If on a branch of a truth tree there is an expression of the form

$$\alpha = \beta$$

(where α and β are any singular terms), then any line on that branch may be repeated with one or more tokens of α replaced by tokens of β. More formally:

> **Identity-out (IO): For any singular terms α and β, if α = β (or β = α)²**
> **occurs on a branch of a tree, and for a formula Φ on this same**
> **branch, if α occurs in Φ, then a statement obtained by replacing α in**
> **Φ by β can be added to the branch.**

Demonstrating the validity of (13)–(15) is easy once the Identity-out rule is available. A truth tree for it is as follows:

1. $h = t$ (premise)
2. M^1h (premise)
3. $\sim M^1t$ (negation of conclusion)
4. M^1t 1, 2, IO
      ×

The validity of Identity-out is hard to deny; it captures something basic about the concept of identity. How could some object o have some predicate – say, ψ – true of it and o be identical to some object m without ψ being true of m as well? If Mary is your mother and Mary is tall, then surely your mother is tall as well. Identity-out is intended to say no more than this. (However, see §A6.4.)

16.2.2 *Identity-in Rule*

The Identity-in rule is perhaps even more obvious.

> **Identity-in (II): for any singular term α, α = α can be added on any**
> **branch in a tree.**

This rule is different from the other rules previously introduced. The earlier rules were applied to an existing line or lines in order to add a new line to the truth tree. But identity-in has no such dependency. For any singular term whatever, the rule permits adding a line to a tree without reference in the justification column to any prior line. So, for example, you can simply add the lines 'a = a', 'b = b', 'c = c', and so on, so to speak, at will. The justification for such a practice is based on the intuitive truth of the universal statement that everything is identical to itself. Can you imagine any thing that isn't? From this universal truth, it follows by UQ that for any individual thing that it is identical to itself.

You might wonder whether II is necessary or whether it is really just a sub-rule of IO, a convenience but eliminable. For suppose 'a = b' occurs on a branch. Then surely you can infer by IO on the same branch that 'a = a'. But, suppose, instead 'a ≠ a' occurs on a branch. This statement says '**a** is not identical to itself'. You might ask what is a identical to if not itself? Indeed, you might surmise that 'a ≠ a' is a self-contradiction from which anything could follow. You would be right! Everything is provable from a contradiction. For example, the argument (1)–(2) is valid.

1.   a ≠ a
2.   F¹a

But with IO alone a truth tree for this argument won't close. With IO alone the validity of (1)–(2) and an infinite array of valid arguments that infer a conclusion from the denial of self-identity cannot be established in RPL⁼. However, if we add II, we can add to any truth tree for (1) and the negation of (2) the statement 'a = a', thus producing a tree which includes (1) and its denial, hence a closed tree. The intuition that any argument with (1), or for that matter any denial of self-identity as a premise, is deductively valid provides strong justification for Identity-in as a separate rule.

But suppose your intuition is that not everything follows from a contradiction, then consider the following obviously valid argument as support for introducing II:

$(\forall x)(x = a \supset F^1x) \therefore (\exists x)F^1x$

(1)–(7) is a closed truth tree for this argument that establishes its validity.

1.	$(\forall x)(x = a \supset F^1x)$	(premise)
√2.	$\sim(\exists x)F^1x$	(negation of conclusion)
3.	$(\forall x)\sim F^1x$	2, QE
4.	$\sim F^1a$	3, UQ
√5.	$a = a \supset F^1a$	1, UQ

6.   a ≠ a   F¹a   5, ⊃
                ×

7.   a = a   II
        ×

Were we not able to add the self-identity statement 'a = a' on line (7) licensed by II, we could not establish the validity of this argument.

Truth trees   Exercise 16.2

- Construct a truth tree for the arguments you devised for exercise 16.1.

Deductive validity   Exercise 16.3

- Prove arguments (1)–(6) deductively valid using the truth tree method.

1. F^1a & $(\forall x)(F^1x \supset x = a)$, $(\exists x)(F^1x$ & $G^1x)$ $\therefore$ G^1a
2. $(\forall x)(P^1x \supset Q^1x)$, $(\forall x)(Q^1x \supset R^1x)$, P^1a & $\sim R^1b$ $\therefore$ $a \neq b$
3. $(\exists x)((P^1x$ & $(\forall y)(P^1y \supset y = x))$ & $Q^1x)$, $\sim Q^1a$ $\therefore$ $\sim P^1a$
4. $(\exists x)(\forall y)((\sim F^2xy \supset x = y)$ & $G^1x)$ $\therefore$ $(\forall x)(\sim G^1x \supset (\exists y)(y \neq x$ & $F^2yx))$
5. $(\exists x)(P^1x$ & $((\forall y)(P^1y \supset y = x)$ & $Q^1x))$, $(\exists x)$ $\sim$ $(\sim P^1x \vee \sim F^1x)$
   $\therefore$ $(\exists x)(F^1x$ & $Q^1x)$
6. $(\forall x)(F^2xa \supset (B^1x$ & $C^1x))$; F^2ba $\therefore$ $(\exists x)(B^1x$ & C^1x & $x = b)$

16.3   Sameness and Distinctness in English

16.3.1   'Only' Again

Since chapter 9, we have treated 'only' as a universal quantifier word which makes any general term it modifies a necessary condition over which the universal quantifier has wide scope. Were we to follow procedure (d) in §15.2, (16) should then be symbolized in RPL as (17).

16.   Only Everest is worth climbing.
17. $(\forall x)(W^1x \supset x$ is Everest) W^1: is worth climbing

But how should we symbolize 'is Everest'? Were we to add as a premise to (16) that 'Everest is identical to Chomolungma', we could logically infer from (16) that 'Only Chomolungma is worth climbing'. What this makes explicit is that the 'is' in (17) and of course (16) is the 'is' of identity, as in (18).

18. $(\forall x)(W^1 x \supset x = e)$ e: Everest

(18) reveals that a necessary condition for being worth climbing is *being identical to* Everest. Seeing that this is so promotes the following generalization:

> **When 'only' modifies a singular (and not a general) term, identity is implicitly invoked.**

16.3.2 *Words of Distinction: Except, But, Other (than), Besides, Else*

The words 'except', 'but', and 'besides' can all invoke distinctness. At first glance they seem grammatically to require a quantifier, as the following pair of statements suggests:

> Everything except (but, besides) the house burned to the ground.
> *John except (but, besides) Bill left.

Using 'except' to modify a proper noun produces an ungrammatical statement. So perhaps we need a treatment of terms of distinctness only insofar as they function as modifiers of quantifier expressions. But not every quantifier word seems to take the term 'except' felicitously, as in

> *Something except the house burned to the ground.

However, substituting 'besides' for 'except' results in

> Something besides the house burned to the ground.

This is perfectly acceptable.
With these considerations in mind, we introduce a convention such that (19) is symbolized as (20).

19. Everyone except (besides, but, other than) Bill left.
20. $(\forall x)((P^1 x \;\&\; x \neq b) \supset L^1 x)$ L^1: left; b: Bill; P^1: is a person

Essentially, what each of these words of distinction is adding is something like a relative clause, i.e. 'who is not Bill', So, in effect, (19) means 'Everyone who is not Bill left'.

Put more generally, if a statement includes an expression of the form

... except (besides, but, other than) α ...

for some singular term α, its symbolization into RPL$^=$ will require adding a distinctness relative clause '... $x_i \neq \alpha$ ...' for some variable 'x_i'.

So, for example, a symbolization of (21) requires adding a distinctness clause as in (22).

21. Nobody but Clinton knows.
22. $\sim(\exists x)((P^1x \ \& \ x \neq c) \ \& \ K^1x)$

P^1: is a person; K^1: knows; c: Clinton

Another expression that invokes distinctness is 'else'. (23) should be symbolized as (24).

23. John ran, and someone else hid.
24. $R^1j \ \& \ (\exists x)((P^1x \ \& \ x \neq j) \ \& \ H^1x)$ R^1: ran; H^1: hid; j: John

In (23), the individual whose hiding is being designated is not John, for the occurrence of 'else' signals the exclusion of John from whatever 'someone' quantifies over. So in (24) '$(\exists x)((P^1x \ \& \ x \neq j)$' corresponds to 'someone else'.

The word 'other' sometimes functions like 'else' and 'except'; sometimes not. For example, (25) should be symbolized as (26).

25. Every other mountain is smaller than Everest.
26. $(\forall x)((M^1x \ \& \ x \neq e) \supset S^2xe)$

M^1: is a mountain; S^2: is smaller than; e: Everest

In other contexts, however, the use of 'other' results in grammaticality, yet 'else' does not. For any common noun α, 'other' may occur in such constructions as 'someone other than α', 'every other α', and 'any other α', but 'else' may not (as in, *'every else α', *'any else α', *'someone else than α'). The word 'except' works in the first case, results in ungrammaticality in the second, and may be grammatical in the third.

The word 'else' occurs grammatically in such constructions as 'something else', 'everywhere else', 'no one else', and generally as a constituent of a quantifier phrase lacking a common noun α.

In all these constructions a domain of discourse is determined not by some general term α, but rather by the 'applications' of the quantifier word. Thus 'someone' ranges over people, 'everywhere' ranges over places, and so on.[3]

Exercise 16.4   **Statements**

- Symbolize (1)–(9) in RPL⁼, using the dictionary provided.

1. Only Alfred and his brother are able to solve the problem. (F^2: is able to solve; a: Alfred; b: the problem; B^2: is brother of)
2. Only Joe reads Greek. (j: Joe; c: Greek; G^2: reads)
3. Greensleeves jumps further than any other frog in Calaveras County. (g: Greensleeves; G^1: is a frog in Calaveras County; F^2: jumps further than)
4. Someone besides Mary stole the book. (P^1: is a person; S^2: stole; b: the book; m: Mary)
5. John loves Mary, and someone else loves Beth.
6. Someone other than John loves Mary.
7. Only John loves his mother. (j: John; L^2: loves; M^2: is mother of)
8. If any other show-off eats a raw egg, Hank and Frank will too. (S^1: is a show-off; h: Hank; f: Frank; E^1: eats a raw egg)
9. Harry attended the conference and arrived at it before everyone else who attended it except Mary. (h: Harry; c: the conference; m: Mary; F^2: attended; G^3: arrived at __ before; P^1: is a person)

16.4 Numerical Adjectives

When quantifier expressions were first discussed in chapter 9, we decided somewhat arbitrarily to investigate only those English quantifier expressions that could be defined in terms of '∃' and '∀'. With these two quantifiers we were able to represent the English 'some', 'any', 'every', 'all', 'none', 'only', and a few other expressions. Once identity is added to RPL, however, we can adequately represent indefinitely many other logically distinct quantifiers. This result makes the language of RPL more powerful, bringing it modestly closer to realizing the logical ideal of being able to translate every meaningful English sentence unambiguously and in a logically revealing way.

16.4.1 *At Least* n

In (27) 'two' is an adjective attached to 'airports', but 'two' does not modify 'airports' in the same way that 'red' modifies 'shoes' in (28). (See §A4.4.)

27. London has (at least) two airports.
28. The pump is a red shoe.

We can distribute 'shoe' and the adjective 'red' modifying it by paraphrasing (28) as (29), but we cannot use the same strategy to paraphrase (27) as (30).

29. The pump is red, and the pump is a shoe.
30. *London has at least two, and London has airports.

That (30) does not paraphrase (27) is problematic, because there seem to be indefinitely many arguments the formal deductive validity of which depends on the use of numerical adjectives. If (27) is true, then London must have at least one airport. Similarly, if (31) is true, so too must (32) be.

31. The United States has fifty states.
32. So, the United States has at least forty states.

This feature is perfectly general. Replacing 'the United States' and 'states' uniformly in (31) and (32) with any other nouns issues in a deductively valid argument.

The classroom has fifty seats.
So, the classroom has at least forty seats.

The parade has fifty floats.
So, the parade has at least forty floats.

Earlier we treated such arguments as deductively valid in virtue of logical form. This leaves us with two choices: either we augment our logical notation (as we did in moving from the language of PL to PPL, PPL to RPL, and RPL to RPL$^=$), or we introduce new symbolization techniques. Using identity, we will not need to elaborate our notation, but we will need to introduce new techniques for symbolizing numerical adjectives in the language of RPL$^=$.

Since chapter 9 we have symbolized statements containing the quantifier expression '(at least) one' with an existential quantifier. Thus, '$\exists S^1$' adequately symbolizes 'There is at least one student' in PPL. What about (33)?

33.   There are at least two students.

We cannot, for example, symbolize (33) as (34).

34. $\exists S^1$ & $\exists S^1$ S^1: is a student

One and the same object, by being a student, makes both conjuncts in (34) true, so the repetition of the quantifier does nothing to ensure that there are at least two students, whereas (33) implies that two distinct students exist. However, using the identity predicate, we correctly symbolize (33) in RPL$^=$ as (35).

35. $(\exists x)(S^1 x$ & $(\exists y)(S^1 y$ & $x \neq y))$

(35) introduces two variables, 'x' and 'y'. But given how variables function, '$(\exists x)S^1 x$' and '$(\exists y)S^1 y$' assert the same thing: 'something is a student'. But when we add that 'x is not identical with y', we are forced to interpret the two quantifiers in (35) to be ranging over at least two distinct students, which is what (33) implies.

This point can be generalized. Translating any statement with an 'at least *n*' quantifier in it, for some positive integer *n*, requires introducing *n* distinct existential quantifier tokens. Take (33'), for example:

33'.   There are at least three students.

Here the number of students has increased by one, so you need to add a third existential quantifier expression, say, '$(\exists z)S^1 z$'. Next you have to use the identity symbol to make clear that the three variable types 'x', 'y', and 'z' correspond to distinct entities. To accomplish this task, you need to add additional non-identity conjuncts, resulting in (35').

35'. $(\exists x)(S^1x \ \& \ (\exists y)(S^1y \ \& \ (\exists z)(S^1z \ \& \ x \neq y \ \& \ y \neq z \ \& \ x \neq z)))$

As the number of entities described increases, the number of non-identity conjuncts has to be increased to ensure that no two quantifiers are quantifying over the same object. So, for example, if the quantifier expression were 'at least four', the number of non-identity conjuncts needed to establish that none of the variable types correspond to the same entity would be six. An increase of one in the 'n' for (33') results in an increase of three in the number of non-identity conjuncts required.

The following recipe formalizes this procedure, providing general instructions for symbolizing indefinitely many numerically distinct quantifiers of the form 'There are at least n α', for any positive integer n in RPL$^=$.

At least n procedure: If a statement is of the form 'There are at least n α', where α is a nominal, then transform it into a formula of the form

$$(\exists x_i)(\alpha x_i \ \& \ldots \& \ (\exists x_n)(\alpha x_n \ \& \ x_i \neq x_{i+1} \ \& \ldots \& \ x_i \neq x_n \ \& \ x_{i+1}$$
$$\neq x_{i+2} \ \& \ldots \& \ x_{i+1} \neq x_n \ \& \ldots \& \ x_{n-1} \neq x_n) \ldots),$$

where 'x_i' corresponds to the first variable in an ordering of distinct variable types.

This recipe enjoins us to introduce n tokens of the existential quantifier, followed by a variable (a different variable type each time), attached to n tokens of αx_i, for each of the n variable types x_i, followed by a conjunction $x_i \neq x_j$ for each pair of distinct variable types (ending with n right parentheses matching the corresponding left parenthesis for each existential quantifier introduced).

Consider as an example (36) in which $n = 3$.

36. At least three men died.

We introduce three tokens of the existential quantifier, each attaching to a distinct variable type. We also introduce three non-identity formulas, the number sufficient to guarantee pairwise distinctness among the variable types. After conjoining these, we conjoin three predicates, one for each variable type, asserting that someone died. The symbolization finishes with three right parentheses corresponding to the three left ones introduced by the three existential quantifier tokens. The final product is (37).

37. $(\exists x)(M^1 x \mathbin{\&} (\exists y)(M^1 y \mathbin{\&} (\exists z)(M^1 z \mathbin{\&} x \neq y \mathbin{\&} x \neq z \mathbin{\&} y \neq z \mathbin{\&} D^1 x$
     $\mathbin{\&} D^1 y \mathbin{\&} D^1 z)))$ M^1: is a man; D^1: died

16.4.2   At Most n (No More than n)

'At most' statements like (38) do not make existence claims.

38.   There is at most one student.

(38) states that if there are any students, then the maximum number is one. (38) is correctly symbolized as (39).

39. $(\forall x)(S^1 x \supset (\forall y)(S^1 y \supset x = y))$ S^1: is a student

(39) is a universal because (38) does not assert that there actually are any students, but rather that no more than one exists. (38) would be true even if there were no students, as well as if there is exactly one. Suppose you are asked to watch a certain classroom. Later you are asked how many students were in that classroom. You might reply that you are not sure, but you are certain that only one person left. You are uncertain whether that person was a student or a teacher; still, you can correctly infer that there was no more than (or at most) one student in that classroom. This inference is obviously consistent with your having seen only teachers leave.

   (40) asserts that the maximum number of students, if any, is two.

40.   There are at most two students.

Suppose we try to symbolize (40) by (41).

41. $(\forall x)(S^1 x \supset (\forall y)(S^1 y \supset (\forall z)(S^1 z \supset (x = y \lor y = z))))$

(41) incorrectly symbolizes (40), since (41) asserts only that there is no more than *one* student. To see that this is so, note that (41) together with (35), the correct symbolization for 'There are at least two students', is inconsistent. The following truth tree establishes their inconsistency.

41. $(\forall x)(S^1x \supset (\forall y)(S^1y \supset (\forall z)(S^1z \supset (x = y \lor y = z))))$

√35. $(\exists x)(S^1x \,\&\, (\exists y)(S^1y \,\&\, x \neq y))$

√3. $S^1t \,\&\, (S^1d \,\&\, t \neq d)$ 35, EQ (twice)

4. S^1t

5. S^1d

6. $t \neq d$ 4–6, from 3, &

√7. $S^1t \supset (\forall y)(S^1y \supset (\forall z)(S^1z \supset (t = y \lor y = z)))$ 41, UQ

8. $\sim S^1t$ $(\forall y)(S^1y \supset (\forall z)(S^1z \supset (t = y \lor y = z)))$ 7, $\supset$

     ×

√9. $S^1d \supset (\forall z)(S^1z \supset (t = d \lor d = z))$ 8, UQ

10. $\sim S^1d$ $(\forall z)(S^1z \supset (t = d \lor d = z)))$ 9, $\supset$

         ×

√11. $S^1t \supset (t = d \lor d = t)$ 10, UQ

√12. $\sim S^1t$ $t = d \lor d = t$ 11, $\supset$

           ×

13. $t = d$ $d = t$ 12, $\lor$

            ×

14. $t \neq t$ 6,13, IO

15. $d \neq t$ 13,14, IO

                    ×

Judicious attention to instantiations of the three universal quantifiers in (41) to 'd' and 't' alone issues in the closed truth tree (1)–(15), establishing that (41) and (35) cannot both be true together. Since (35) asserts that there are at least two students, it follows that (41) is incompatible with any state of affairs in which there are two students. However, (40) is explicitly compatible with this state of affairs. In order to correctly represent (40) in RPL⁼ we need to insure that any two of the variables may be quantifying over the same object. (42) achieves exactly this end.

42. $(\forall x)(S^1x \supset (\forall y)(S^1y \supset (\forall z)(S^1z \supset (x = y \lor y = z \lor x = z))))$

As an exercise you might try first devising a truth tree to show that (35) and (42) are consistent, and then devise another to show that (41) and (42) are not logically equivalent.

The following recipe formalizes a procedure, providing general instructions for symbolizing indefinitely many numerically distinct quantifiers of the form 'There are at most n α', for any positive integer n into RPL⁼.

> **At most *n* procedure: If a statement is of the form 'There are at most *n* α',** where α **is a nominal, then transform it into a formula of the form**
>
> $$(\forall x_i)(\alpha x_i \supset \ldots \supset (\forall x_{n+1})(\alpha x_{n+1} \supset (x_i = x_{i+1} \vee \ldots \vee x_i = x_{n+1} \vee x_{i+1} = x_{i+2}$$
> $$\vee \ldots \vee x_{i+1} = x_{n+1} \vee \ldots \vee x_n = x_{n+1}) \ldots),$$
>
> **where 'x_i' corresponds to the first variable in an ordering of *n* + 1 distinct variable types.**

This recipe enjoins us to introduce $n + 1$ tokens of the universal quantifier, followed by a variable (a different variable type each time), attached to $n+1$ tokens of αx_i, for each variable type x_i, followed by a disjunction of $x_i = x_j$ for each pair of distinct variables types (ending with $n + 1$ right parentheses matching the corresponding left parenthesis for each universal quantifier introduced).

Exercise 16.5   At most n

- How would you go about representing that at most three students left (or, no more than three students left)? Use the dictionary 'S¹' for 'is a student', and 'L¹' for 'left'. Following the procedure, we must first introduce four tokens of the universal quantifier, each attaching to a distinct variable type. We must also end by disjoining six identity formulas, the number sufficient to guarantee that any two variable types may be quantifying over the same object.

Exercise 16.6   Numerical Adjectives

- Symbolize (1) and (2), using the dictionary provided.

  1. At least two people are happy. (P¹: is a person; H¹: is happy)
  2. No more than one turkey will die. (T¹: is a turkey; D¹: will die)

16.4.3 *Exactly* n

Suppose that (43) is true.

43. Exactly one student left.[4]

If exactly one student left, surely at least one student left. So, part of the meaning of 'Exactly one' is captured by the phrase 'At least one'. Part of what (43) means can be represented as '$(\exists x)(S^1x \,\&\, L^1x)$'. But if exactly one student left, then at most (no more than) one student left. So the rest of what 'Exactly one' means is captured by the phrase 'At most one' (or 'No more than one'). Thus, (43) is correctly symbolized as (44).

44. $(\exists x)((S^1x \,\&\, L^1x) \,\&\, (\forall y)((S^1y \,\&\, L^1y) \supset x = y))$

(44) asserts that at least one student left, and if any other (alleged) student left, she is identical to the first – that is, at least one student left, and at most one student left – which is exactly what (43) affirms.

Thus 'exactly one' can be broken down into 'at least one' and 'at most one'. The same principle applies to all sentences containing 'exactly n', no matter how big n is. To symbolize a sentence like (45), we decompose into an 'at least' claim, and an 'at most' claim.

45.   Exactly two people are tall.

(45) asserts that *at least* two people are tall, so its symbolization should include '$(\exists x)((P^1x \,\&\, T^1x) \,\&\, (\exists y)((P^1y \,\&\, T^1y) \,\&\, x \neq y))$. (Remember that an *at least n* sentence requires *n* existentials, and a claim that none of the existentially quantified variables are identical.) (45) also asserts that *at most* two people are tall, so we need to add that anyone who is tall *must* be one of these two people. Thus (45) is correctly symbolized as (46):

46. $(\exists x)((P^1x \,\&\, T^1x) \,\&\, (\exists y)((P^1y \,\&\, T^1y) \,\&\, x \neq y \,\&\, (\forall z)((P^1z \,\&\, T^1z)$
$\supset (z = x \lor z = y))))$

In general, a statement of the form 'there are exactly n' should be symbolized as follows:

Exactly *n* Procedure: If a statement is of the form 'There are exactly *n* α', where α is a nominal, then transform it into a formula of the form

$$(\exists x_1)(\alpha x_1 \,\&\, \ldots \,\&\, (\exists x_n)(\alpha x_n \,\&\, x_1 \neq x_2 \,\&\, \ldots \,\&\, x_1 \neq x_n \,\&\, x_2 \neq x_3 \,\&\, \ldots \,\&\,$$
$$x_{n-1} \neq x_n \,\&\, (\forall x_{n+1})(\alpha x_{n+1} \supset (x_{n+1} = x_1 \lor \ldots \lor x_{n+1} = x_n))) \ldots)$$

where 'x_i' corresponds to the first variable in an ordering of distinct variable types.

Exercise 16.7   Exactly

- Symbolize (1) and (2) in RPL$^=$, using the dictionary provided.

1. There is exactly one person, and he lives in Montana. (L^2: lives in; m: Montana; P^1: is a person)
2. Exactly one person lives in Montana.
3. Susan is loved by exactly one person (L^2: loves; s: Susan; P^1: is a person)
4. Exactly one person ate every cabbage. (E^2: eats; C^1: is a cabbage.)
5. There are exactly two frogs. (F^1: is frog)
6. Exactly two frogs hopped. (H^1: hopped)
7. Exactly three students passed. (S^1: is a student; P^1: passed)
8. There are exactly three students and they passed.
9. Exactly two boys have turtles. (B^1: is a boy; T^1: is a turtle: H^2: has)
10. Every boy has exactly two turtles.

16.4.4   Counting Pairs

The *at most n*, *at least n*, and *exactly n* procedures all call for lists of identities or non-identities, at the end of the statements. For example, 'there are at least three students' would be symbolized as

$$(\exists x)(S^1 x \ \& \ (\exists y) \ \& \ S^1 y \ \& \ (\exists z)(S^1 z \ \& \ x \neq y \ \& \ x \neq z \ \& \ y \neq z)))$$

$$(S^1: \text{is a student})$$

According to the procedure for *at least n*, we have to end the symbolization with conjunctions of the non-identities of each pair of variables. Similarly, we have to end symbolizations of *at most n* with disjunctions of the identities of each pair of variables. Keeping track of all these pairs can become tricky, especially if we have to symbolize larger numerical adjectives. If we had to symbolize, say, at least six, it would be quite hard to make sure we had remembered every single pair of variables. Fortunately, there are easy formulas that can tell us how many pairs of variables we have to account for.

At least n
Thee should be **n(n−1)/2** pairs of non-identities.

At most n
There should be **n(n+1)/2** pairs of identities.

Exactly n

There should be **n(n−1)/2** pairs of non-identities and **n** pairs of identities.

16.4.5 *Combinatorics (optional)*

We might wonder how these formulas are derived. In the branch of mathematics called combinatorics, one often asks the following question: given a set with n members, how many subsets are there of size k? The answer is given by the formula *n choose k*:

$$\textit{n choose k} = \textbf{n! / ((n−k)! k!)}$$

where n! denotes *n factorial* which equals $n(n−1)(n−2) \ldots (3)(2)(1)$.

We notice that the question of how many pairs of variables are needed is equivalent to the question of how many 2-element subsets (i.e. pairs) are there of a set of n elements (i.e. the set of variables). This answer is given by *n choose* 2, as our subsets are of size 2. According to the formula above, *n choose* 2 is

$$n! \ / \ ((n−2)! \ 2!)$$

This can be simplified if we notice that $n! = n(n−1) \ ((n−2)(n−3) \ldots (2)(1))$ $= n(n−1)(n−2)!$, and that $2! = (2)(1) = 2$

$$(n(n−1)(n−2)!) \ / \ ((n−2)! \ 2!) = n(n−1) \ / \ 2! = n(n−1) \ / \ 2$$

which is our formula for the number of pairs needed in *at least n* statements.

Why then do we need $n(n+1) \ / \ 2$ pairs in *at most n* statements? The relevant difference between *at most n* and *at least n* statements is simply that *at most n* statements have n+1 variables, (see section 16.4.2), while *at least n* statements have n variables. Thus instead of using the formula for *n choose* 2 we simply use *n+1 choose* 2.

16.5 Definite Descriptions

In chapter 9, we included definite descriptions among the class of singular terms. For purposes of evaluating many arguments, this treatment is perfectly acceptable, because if one does not look too closely, in a vast number of cases definite descriptions behave like proper names. Both expressions seem to apply to single individuals. For this reason we provisionally grouped them together in chapter 9 as singular terms. But from a logical point of view, the policy of treating definite descriptions as singular terms cannot be pursued indiscriminately. In this section we will cite several reasons for not treating definite descriptions as singular terms.[5]

Consider the simple and obviously deductively valid argument (47)–(49).

47. Venus is the morning star.
48. Venus is the evening star.
49. So, any morning star is an evening star.

(49) logically follows from (47) and (48) because Venus is one and only one planet, and it is identical with both the morning and the evening stars. Symbolizing (47)–(49) in RPL$^=$ (with m: the morning star; e: the evening star; v: Venus; M^1: is a morning star; E^1: is an evening star) issues in (50)–(52).

50. $v = m$
51. $v = e$
52. $\therefore (\forall x)(M^1x \supset E^1x)$

(50)–(52) is invalid in RPL$^=$. (Use the truth tree method to establish its invalidity.) The problem is that the deductive validity of (47)–(49) builds on the occurrences of the nominals 'morning star' and 'evening star'. Symbolizing (47)–(49) in RPL$^=$ as (50)–(52) ignores this linguistic (and logically relevant) fact. To quote a famous president, the problem depends on what 'is' is: that is, what 'is' means. In (50) and (51) the 'is' of identity is invoked; in this case 'is' means 'is identical with'. But in (52) the 'is' of predication is invoked; here 'is' means 'has the property of being . . .'. For this reason the identity symbol is used in (50)–(51), thereby requiring singular terms 'm' and 'e' to flank the identity symbol (along with 'v'), but in (52) the predicate symbols 'M^1' and 'E^1' must be used. These choices prevent us from acknowledging whatever information (50)–(52) share. We need a new symbolization technique that acknowledges the shared information.

(53) and (54) give us another reason for seeking a new symbolization technique for definite descriptions.

53. The present king of France is bald.
54. The present king of France is not bald.

Suppose (53) is false since there is no such king. If 'the present king of France' is a singular term, then the negation of (53) – that is, (54) – should be true, since (53) is false. But (54) seems false too, for the same reason: there is no such king. However, treating 'the present king of France' as a singular term requires either (55) or (56) to be true, by the definition of negation.

55. B¹t   B¹: is bald; t: the present king of France
56. ~B¹t

One way out might be to say that since there is no present king of France, (53) is neither true nor false; it is without truth-value altogether. But if (53) has no truth-value at all, then any complex statement truth-functionally built out of (53) has no truth-value either. So far, so good, since we don't want (54) to be true or false. However, if (53) and (54) are without a truth-value, so too are (57) and (58). This result follows from the truth tables for 'or' and 'and'.

57. Either the present king of France is bald, or the present king of France is not bald.
58. Both the present king of France is bald and the present king of France is not bald.

But (57) looks to be a tautology, and (58) looks to be a contradiction. Tautologies must be true, and contradictions must be false.

There is also a related problem about deductive validity. If we adopt the policy of not assigning truth-values to statements with singular terms like 'the present king of France' which lack a referent, how then do we account for the deductive validity of (59)–(61)?

59. If the round square is Bill's favorite object, then Mary lives with the married bachelor.
60. The round square is Bill's favorite object.
61. So, Mary lives with the married bachelor.

The alleged singular terms 'the round square' and 'the married bachelor' in (59)–(61) cannot refer. According to the current proposal, the statements in which these definite descriptions appear would be neither true nor false; but then, by definition, (59)–(61) are not even statements, and argument (59)–(61) is not deductively valid, because validity is a relationship that holds among statements – that is, between premises and a conclusion. This maneuver towards not assigning truth-values to certain types of statements jeopardizes the entire project of determining deductive validity by virtue of logical form. Is there an alternative solution?

One generally accepted solution is to treat the definite article used to form a definite description as a type of quantifier like 'every' or 'some'. Argument (62)–(63) is deductively valid (by virtue of form) only if, as seems reasonable, we interpret the definite description in (62) as requiring the existence of the object described.

62. The author of *Huckleberry Finn* lived in New York.
63. Therefore, something is an author of *Huckleberry Finn*.

If we adopt this treatment, we can break down the meaning of the definite description into parts with the aid of the following dictionary: h: *Huckleberry Finn* (the eponymous novel, not its protagonist); A^2: authored; N^1: lived in New York. As a first effort, we will partially symbolize (62)–(63) as (64)–(65) respectively.

64. $(\exists x)(A^2xh \ \& \ N^1x)$
65. $\therefore \ (\exists x)A^2xh$

Showing that (64)–(65) is deductively valid is trivial. However, this symbolization cannot be the whole story, for consider argument (62) and (66)–(67), which is also clearly deductively valid.

62. The author of *Huckleberry Finn* lived in New York.
66. Shakespeare did not live in New York.
67. Therefore, Shakespeare did not author *Huckleberry Finn*.

If we symbolize (62) as (64), no formal proof for this argument can be devised. Suppose *Huckleberry Finn* had been coauthored, Shakespeare having started the novel in the sixteenth century and Mark Twain having finished it in the nineteenth. (64) does not exclude this possibility. Without symbolizing the idea that there is only one author of

Huckleberry Finn – which is, by the way, clearly part of the meaning of the definite description in (62) – the argument does not succeed. To introduce this additional information, we utilize the identity predicate. Saying 'only x has a certain property' is equivalent (§16.3.1) to saying 'anything having that property is identical to x'. Hence, with 's' for 'Shakespeare', argument (62) and (66)–(67) can be symbolized as (68)–(70) respectively.

68. $(\exists x)(A^2xh \ \& \ (\forall y)(A^2yh \supset y = x) \ \& \ N^1x)$
69. $\sim N^1s$
70. $\therefore \ \sim A^2sh$

Truth tree   **Exercise 16.8**

- Construct a truth tree for argument (66)–(68), showing it valid.

In short, we may, when necessary, interpret statements containing definite descriptions of form (71)

71. The α is β

as conjoining three distinct statements:

There is at least one α;
there is at most one α; and
α is also β.

In RPL⁼ (71) is then represented as (72).

72. $(\exists x)(\alpha x \ \& \ (\forall y)(\alpha y \supset y = x) \ \& \ \beta x)$

This way of representing definite descriptions helps to explain the existence of what appear to be false and true statements about non-existent objects. As stated above, (53) appears to be false, so (73), its denial, should be true.

53.   The present king of France is bald.
73.   It is not the case that the present king of France is bald.

Instead of symbolizing (73) as (56), we can render (53) in RPL$^=$ as (74), letting 'K^1' represent 'is a present king of France'.

56.   ~B^{1}t
74. $(\exists x)(K^1x \ \& \ (\forall y)(K^1y \supset y = x) \ \& \ B^1x)$

(73) is true since it really denies the false (53); therefore, it should be symbolized in RPL$^=$ as the negation of (74): namely, as (75).

75. $\sim(\exists x)(K^1x \ \& \ (\forall y)(K^1y \supset y = x) \ \& \ B^1x)$

By negating (74), (75) denies that all three conditions that are required in order to satisfy (74) obtain: either there does not exist a present king of France, or there exists more than one, or if there is one, he's not bald. Since no present king of France exists, the first condition of (74) is not satisfied, so (75) is true and (74) false on this interpretation. Therefore, truth functionality is preserved.

Note too that (75) need not paraphrase (54), which can also be represented in RPL$^=$ as (76).

54.   The present king of France is not bald.
76. $(\exists x)(K^1x \ \& \ (\forall y)(K^1y \supset y = x) \ \& \ \sim B^1x)$

Since we are now recommending treating 'the' as a quantifier, we can speak of the scope of this quantifier with respect to, for example, a negation. In (75) the negation took wide scope, negating (74) *in toto*. But if we interpret (54) merely to be denying the baldness of the present king of France, then the negation should take small scope. (54) would be properly symbolized in RPL$^=$ as (76). The ability of this symbolization technique to disambiguate this ambiguity in English statements like (54) is another benefit of treating 'the' as a quantifier expression and not as part of a singular term.

Following the practice of chapters 12–15, we introduce a definite description quantifier procedure for symbolizing (certain) statements with definite descriptions.

16.5.1   The Definite Description Quantifier Procedure

> **(h)   If a formula is of the form Φ . . . ₜₕₑ ₐ . . . , where Φ is a predicate, and *The* α is a definite description flanked by other expressions of the types ∀β, ∃β, singular terms, or variables, transform the formula into one of the form $(\exists x_i)(\alpha x_i \ \& \ (\forall x_k)(\alpha x_k \supset x_k = x_i) \ \& \ \Phi \dots x_i \dots)$**

Let us apply procedure (h) to the symbolization of (77), a statement that contains an explicit quantifier expression.

77.   The man loves every woman.

As a first step, with dictionary M^1: is a man; W^1: is a woman; L^2: loves, we can represent (77) by the non-RPL⁼ (78) (where 'TM¹' temporarily represents 'the man').

78. $L^2{}_{TM^1, \forall W^1}$

Applying the definite description procedure (h) to the non-RPL⁼ (78) issues in (79).

79. $(\exists x)(M^1 x \ \& \ (\forall y)(M^1 y \supset y = x) \ \& \ L^2 x_{\forall W^1})$

Finally, applying the universal quantifier procedure to the non-RPL⁼ (78) issues in the RPL⁼ well-formed formula (80).

80. $(\exists x)(M^1 x \ \& \ (\forall y)(M^1 y \supset y = x) \ \& \ (\forall z)(W^1 z \supset L^2 xz))$

One important feature of the definite description procedure is that it dictates that once we treat 'the' as a quantifier expression, we must treat any statement in which 'the' occurs as making both an 'at least' and an 'at most' statement. (See §A6.2 for a discussion of other interesting features of definite descriptions that strongly suggest that we treat them as quantifier expressions and not as singular terms.)

This completes our discussion of identity in this chapter. However, many other interesting questions can be raised about the logical aspects of identity that would take us beyond the scope of this book. Some of these issues are touched on in §A6.

Exercise 16.9   Arguments

- Symbolize arguments (1)–(4) in RPL$^=$, using the dictionary provided.

1. The person who wrote *Lear* was a genius. Therefore, anyone who wrote *Lear* was a genius. (P^1: is a person; W^2: wrote; G^1: is a genius; l: *Lear*)
2. The article on the South in today's paper is well written. Nothing written by more than one person is well written. Hence, the person who wrote the article on the South in today's paper is capable of good writing. (Missing premise) (A^1: is an article on the South in today's paper; C^1: is capable of good writing; W^1: is well written; P^1: is a person; W^2: writes)
3. The morning star is Venus. The evening star is Venus. Therefore, every morning star is an evening star. (M^1: is a morning star; E^1: is an evening star; v: Venus)
4. There were exactly two judges. At least one was asleep. So no more than one judge was awake. (J^1: is a judge; A^1: was awake)

Exercise 16.10   Definite descriptions

- Symbolize statements (1)–(17) in RPL$^=$, using the dictionary provided.
- This exercise is designed to help you see how definite descriptions can interact with all the other linguistic phenomena attended to in this book.

1. The girl doesn't hate Bill. (G^1: is a girl)
2. The man hates only fish. (F^1: is fish; M^1: is a man)
3. Mary hates the girl who insults Bill. (H^2: hates; G^1: is a girl; I^2: insults; b: Bill; m: Mary)
4. Mary hates the girl who insults her.

The remaining exercises are increasingly more difficult.

5. Every boy hates the girl who insults him. (B^1: is a boy)
6. If the man hates Bill, then he hates Frank also.
7. If a woman hates the man who fired her, then she will punish him.
8. The status of a man is important to him. (S^2: is the status of; M^1: is a man; I^2: is important to)
9. Pergolesi was the most promising composer of his time. (a: Pergolesi; F^2: was more promising than; G^1: is a composer; H^2: was a contemporary with)

10. The product of distinct positive integers is less than their sum if and only if one of them is equal to its square. (A^3: the product of __ and __ ; B^3: the sum of __ and __ ; C^2: the square of; F^1: is a positive integer; G^2: is less than)

11. Each bird's owner fed it. (In §9.2 we noted that definite descriptions, though they typically begin with 'the', also include genitive noun phrases like 'Each bird's owner' or 'your cousin'.) (O^2: owns; F^2: feeds; B^1: is a bird)

12. Only the man that hates Frank hates Bill. (H^2: hates; M^1: is a man; b: Bill; f: Frank)

13. The only man that hates Frank hates Bill.

14. The man that hates Frank hates Bill.

15. Exactly two men left. (M^1: is a man; L^1: left)

16. The two men left.

17. The boy who was fooling her kissed the girl who loved him.

Arguments   Exercise 16.11

• Symbolize arguments (1)–(3) in RPL$^=$, using the dictionary provided.

1. The person who is from Sayreville left. Everyone who is from either Sayreville or Woodbridge bought a car. So, the person who is from Sayreville bought a car. (There is an obvious missing premise.) (P^1: is a person; S^1: is from Sayreville; L^1: left; W^1: is from Woodbridge; B^2: bought, C^1: is a car)

2. The father of the father of Annette flies. Anyone who has a father who flies fears loss. So, the father of Annette fears loss. (F^2: is a father of; a: Annette; P^1: is a person; L^1: fears loss; V^1: flies)

3. Nothing is taller than itself. Ewing is taller than Jordan. So, Ewing is not identical to Jordan. (j: Jordan; e: Ewing; T^2: is taller than)

Limits of RPL$^=$ Exercise 16.12

Consider the plural 'some' as in the 'Some critics admire only each other'. Try to symbolize this sentence in RPL$^=$, letting A^2: admires; C^1: is a critic.

Exercise 16.13   Arguments

- Symbolize in RPL$^=$, using the dictionary provided.

1. The only man who loves Lucy left. So, exactly one man left. (L^2: loves; L^1: left; M^1: is a man; l: Lucy)
2. No more than two people are eligible. Nadia is eligible, and so is Laura. Therefore, Mike is not eligible. (E^1: is eligible; P^1: is a person; n: Nadia; l: Laura; m: Mike)
3. Anna has at least two husbands. Craig is her husband and Ken is her husband. Thus, if Craig and Ken are the same person, Anna has another husband. (H^2: has; H^1: is a husband; c: Craig; k: Ken)

Notes

1   Treating 'is the author of *Tom Sawyer*' as a property predicate in (1) in effect obliterates logical relations among (1)–(3) by failing to recognize that the grammatical predicate in (1) and the subject in (3) share logically relevant information.

2   We need to use IO in a form that permits substitution of either term in the identity premise for the other, not just the second term for the first, thus the parenthetical extension.

3   Another use of 'other' which, though similar to its use in (25), cannot be assimilated to it, is the quantifier 'each other' (and 'one another'), as in

> Harry and Mary kissed each other.
> Harry, Mary, and John know one another.

These sorts of constructions seem, at least *prima facie*, to be conjunctions, as in

> Harry kissed Mary, and Mary kissed Harry.
> Harry knew Mary, and Mary knew Harry, and John knew Harry, and Harry knew John, and Mary knew John, and John knew Mary.

4   Is 'Exactly one student left' synonymous with 'One student left'? If so, then they should be symbolized identically. However, any appearance of synonymy might be due more to a conversational inference than to meaning.

Normally, we would not say 'One student left' if we knew that two or more left. The meanings of these two sentences come apart when they are embedded in a more complex context. For example, as in

If two students left then one student left.
If two students left then exactly one student left.

The former is obviously true, the second is not.

5   In this section the theory for symbolizing definite descriptions (which is one among others) is due to Bertrand Russell, the important early-twentieth-century philosopher and logician. Our discussion ignores some special and interesting issues that arise with plural descriptions, such as 'The boys'.

Bibliography

Frege, G., *The Foundations of Arithmetic* (1884), trans. J. L. Austin (Oxford: Basil Blackwell).

Heim, I., *The Semantics of Definite and Indefinite Noun Phrases* (New York: Garland, 1989).

Linsky, Bernard, 'The Logical Form of Descriptions', *Dialogue* 31 (1992), 677–83.

Mates, Benson, 'Descriptions and Reference', *Foundations of Language* 10 (1973), 409–18.

Neale, Stephen, *Descriptions* (Cambridge, MA: MIT Press, 1990).

Russell, Bertrand, 'On Denoting', *Mind* 14 (1905), 479–93.

Van Fraassen, B. C., 'Singular Terms, Truth-Value Gaps, and Free Logic', *Journal of Philosophy* 63 (1966), 481–95.

17

Verbs and their Modifiers

In this chapter we will examine various inferential data that can be accommodated quite easily simply by introducing new conventions for symbolizing English verbs and their adverbial modifiers in RPL⁼. Neither new symbols nor new truth tree rules are needed. However, the conclusions of this chapter are less widely known or accepted than those of earlier chapters.

17.1   Prepositional Phrases

How should we symbolize (1) in RPL?

1.   The dog bit the man **in the park**.

Following the conventions introduced earlier (§12.3), it would be natural to symbolize (1) as (2), using the three-place predicate 'B³' for 'bit', and singular terms 'd', 'm', and 'p' for 'the dog', 'the man', and 'the park' respectively (ignoring the treatment of definite descriptions in chapter 16).

2.   B³dmp

But how, then, should (3) be symbolized?

3.   The dog bit the man.

(3) also looks like a simple statement with a transitive verb 'bit', in which case (3) ought to be symbolized in RPL as (4), using the two-place predicate 'B²'.

4. B^2dm

(4), though, fails to explain why (3) deductively follows from (1). The inference from (2) to (4) is *in*valid in RPL; no truth tree for the argument will close. Yet the inference from (1) to (3) seems to hold in virtue of logical form. Other inferences obtained by uniformly substituting other transitive verbs, prepositions, and singular terms in (1) and (3) are also deductively valid; for example:

> Mary kissed Bill on the cheek.
> Mary kissed Bill.

> Frank drove his car in the dark.
> Frank drove his car.

> The policeman hit the innocent bystander with a stick.
> The policeman hit the innocent bystander.

Employing standard symbolization conventions, we wind up with distinct simple relational predicates which disagree in their number of places. We shall refer to the number of places of a predicate as its *adicity*. Once we let 'B²' and 'B³' represent 'bit' and 'bit . . . in', we are unable to extract important logically relevant features – for example, that each is about biting. The occurrences of the letter 'B' in both relational predicates are irrelevant, no less an orthographic accident than the occurrences of the first three letters 'cat' in the word 'cattle'.

Some logicians have sought to rectify this problem by recommending a different symbolization convention: namely, symbolizing (3) not as (4) in RPL, but as (5).

5. $(\exists x)B^3dmx$

The convention behind this suggested symbolization treats (3) as if it were an abbreviation or were elliptical for the English statement (6).

6. The dog bit the man in something (or somewhere).

(5) has an advantage over (4) inasmuch as it is formally implied by (2). (Every adequate truth tree for argument (2) and (5) closes.) However, the convention behind symbolizing (3) as (5) in effect posits an extra

place in the predicate for each prepositional phrase modifier which a transitive verb can grammatically take. This strategy poses a number of difficulties.

First, the convention assumes that the number and identity of modifiers for any given predicate can be exactly specified prior to symbolization. For this strategy to work, we must know for every transitive verb just how many prepositional phrases can grammaticality modify it.[1] Since there need be no obvious upper bound to this number, we may be unable to decide the number of places of the predicate used in symbolizing the verb. For example, should we infer, based on the grammaticality of (7), that the verb in (3) has six places, and thus that (3) should be symbolized not as (5) but as (8)?

7. The dog bit the man *in* the park *after* midnight *on* Wednesday *under* his arm.
8. $(\exists x)(\exists y)(\exists z)(\exists x_1)B^6dmxyzx_1$

    B^6: __ bit __ in __ after __ on __ under __

But why stop here? The prepositional phrase 'over the hip' can be attached to (7) without compromising its grammaticality. Does this mean that whatever predicate we use to symbolize (3) should have seven places? And so on.

If English permits us to add such modifiers indefinitely without sacrificing grammaticality, then we cannot capture the logical inferences among English statements by employing this convention, because we would have to preface each relational predicate admitting of prepositional phrase modification with indefinitely many quantifiers (which, of course, we cannot do). So, if English has no upper bound on the number of modifying prepositional phrases we can add, the convention fails. Fortunately, there is another convention available to us.

17.2   The Event Approach

Suppose instead of symbolizing (3) as either (4) or (5) or even as (8), we opt for (9),

3. The dog bit the man.
9. $(\exists x)B^3xdm$

where (9) means (10).

10.   There is an event which was a biting by the dog of the man.

This convention requires increasing the adicity of a verb in symbolizing it in RPL; but, unlike the last convention, this one limits the increase to one. So, in symbolizing a transitive verb in RPL, we opt for not a two-place relational predicate but a three-place relational predicate. The extra place is reserved for quantification over events (or states): namely, whatever sort of event (or state) the verb evokes.

   In short, every transitive verb is symbolized in RPL as a three-place verb, with one place reserved for the event (or state) the verb is about: for example, a hitting, a biting, a running, a kissing, and so on.

   Next we introduce a convention for translating prepositional phrase modification into RPL. We will do so by treating prepositions as relational predicates expressing a relation between the event introduced by the verb and the grammatical object of the proposition. So, for example, (1) will be symbolized in RPL as (11),

1.   The dog bit the man in the park.
11. $(\exists x)(B^3xdm \;\&\; I^2xp)$

where 'I^2xp' expresses the in-relation between the event introduced by 'bit' and the park. (11) asserts that there is an event that was a biting by the dog of the man *and* that it (the event) occurred in the park.

   According to the event approach, the transitive verb 'bit' is symbolized in RPL not as a two-place but as a three-place predicate, say, 'B^3', which means 'x was a biting by y of z'. Prepositions are symbolized as two-place predicates; for example, 'in' in (1) is symbolized in (11) as a two-place predicate, 'I^2', which means 'x is (or occurs) in y'. The prepositions 'after', 'on', and 'under' in (7) are also symbolized as two-place predicates: for example, 'A^2' ('x is after y'), 'O^2', ('x is on y'), and 'U^2' ('x is under y'). Using the event approach, the completed symbolization for (7) in RPL is (12).

7.   The dog bit the man *in* the park *after* midnight *on* Wednesday *under* his arm.
12. $(\exists x)(B^3xdm \;\&\; I^2xp \;\&\; A^2xt \;\&\; O^2xw \;\&\; U^2xa)$
                          t: midnight; w: Wednesday; a: the man's arm

These conventions have much to recommend them; they account nicely for the option of dropping prepositional phrases in English while preserving truth. (7) logically implies (3) and (1), for example, because predicate conjuncts can be dropped while preserving truth. If any statement of the form '$\exists(\alpha \ \& \ \beta)$' is true, then obviously so is '$\exists\alpha$'. Conversely, these conventions account for the option of adding prepositional phrases indefinitely in English while preserving grammaticality. If '$\exists(\alpha \ \& \ \beta)$' is well formed, then so is '$\exists(\alpha \ \& \ \beta \ \& \ \chi)$' and so is '$\exists(\alpha \ \& \ \beta \ \& \ \chi \ \& \ \delta)$' and so on indefinitely.

The event approach, in addition to correctly capturing the logical inferences from (7) to (3) and (1), also correctly blocks reversing the argument. From 'The dog bit the man in the park' and 'The dog bit the man after midnight' it does not follow that 'The dog bit the man in the park after midnight'. The event approach, by introducing an existential quantifier, offers a simple explanation of why: it is for the same reason that from '$(\exists x)B^1x$' and '$(\exists y)P^1y$' we cannot infer '$(\exists x)(B^1x \ \& \ P^1x)$'.[2]

17.3   Indirect Support of the Event Approach

The main advantage of the event approach is that it preserves the deductive validity of indefinitely many logical inferences that the earlier two conventions we explored failed to capture. But at what cost? According to the event approach, (i) transitive verbs must be symbolized as three-place predicates, (ii) prepositions are predicates, and (iii) seemingly simple statements like (3) turn out to be existential statements.

3.   The dog bit the man.

The above claims are surprising, possibly counterintuitive. Is there any further reason to endorse any of them?

17.3.1   *Fixing Referents and Binding Anaphoric Pronouns*

(13) is a perfectly natural English statement.

13.   John buttered his toast, and he did *it* after midnight.

What binds the anaphoric pronoun 'it' in the second clause, and what is its referent? The word 'it' appears to have no anaphor to refer back to or to be bound by. Neither 'John', 'his toast', nor 'midnight' can be anaphors for 'it'. What, then, do we take 'it' to be about in (13)? The answer is obvious: buttering. In English the expression 'buttering' is a gerund, a term that functions as both a noun and a verb, a nominal describing an action or an event. On the event approach, statements like (13) quantify over events. This treatment gives the pronoun 'it' in (13) an anaphor. The anaphor of 'it' is the event variable occupying the first place in the three-place predicate ' __ was a buttering by __ of __ '. (13) is symbolized in RPL as (14).

14. $(\exists x)(B^3 xjt \ \& \ A^2 xm)$

B^3: was a buttering by __ of; A^2: occurs after; m: midnight; j: John; t: his toast

(14) affirms both that there was a buttering by John of his toast, and that it (the buttering) occurred after midnight. The existential quantifier is what binds the anaphoric 'it'.

17.3.2   *Quantification over Events*

According to the event approach, indefinitely many, seemingly simple English statements are in fact existential quantifier statements. But treating a statement like (3) as an existential statement incurs a cost. In chapter 13, we noted that the possibility of nested quantification introduces the possibility of relative quantifier scope. The difference in meaning between (15) and (16) is contingent upon the differing relative scopes of their existential and universal quantifiers.

15. $(\exists x)(M^1 x \ \& \ (\forall y)(W^1 y \supset L^2 xy))$ M^1: is a man;
                                                                        W^1: is a woman; L^2: loves

16. $(\forall y)(W^1 y \supset (\exists x)(M^1 x \ \& \ L^2 xy))$

(15) is true just in case at least one particular man loves every single woman. (16) can be true even if for every woman there is a different man who loves her. By shifting the relative scope of the quantifiers, we change meaning. Whenever different sorts of quantifiers occur in the same statement, the prospect of relative scope exists.

The event approach introduces an existential quantifier into every statement with a transitive verb. So, if a transitive verb takes a universal quantifier expression as its subject, nested quantification and possible ambiguity results. For example, consider (17).

17.   Every woman moved the piano.

The event approach allows two readings. Suppose 'W^1', 'p', and 'M^3', represent 'is a woman', 'the piano', and ' __ is a moving by __ of __ ' respectively. According to the event approach, (17) should be representable in RPL by both (18) and (19).

18. $(\forall y)(W^1 y \supset (\exists x)M^3 xyp)$
19. $(\exists x)((\forall y)(W^1 y \supset M^3 xyp))$

(18) and (19) are not logically equivalent. The chief difference between them is that in (18) the universal quantifier has wide scope over the existential quantifier, whereas in (19) it has narrow scope with respect to the existential quantifier.

The distinct renderings of (17) in RPL would be problematic if (17) were unambiguous in English. Instead of performing one of its main functions, which is to disambiguate English, RPL would be creating ambiguities which English does not support. But a careful reading of (17) shows that it too is ambiguous; it can naturally be read in two ways, and (18) and (19) correspond to these distinct readings. The English statement (17) could mean that each woman participated in some movement or other of the piano, perhaps (but also perhaps not) a different movement for each woman, corresponding to (18); or it could mean that they all participated in a group effort, corresponding to (19). So the ambiguity is over whether there was a single event or potentially many.[3] That the event approach mirrors the ambiguity of statements like (17) provides additional independent support for it.

17.3.3   *Conversational Inferences and Events*

According to this approach, (20) should be symbolized as (21).

20.   John hit Bill.
21. $(\exists x)H^3 xjb$

(21) does not say that there is only one hitting of Bill by John. An existential quantifier requires only that there be at least one such event.

There may be more. You might think, though, that part of the meaning of (20) is that one and only one event can make it true. If you have this intuition, you are most likely mistaking the conversational inference that if someone asserts (20), she conveys, perhaps unintentionally, that there is but one hitting of Bill by John.

But this inference is not part of the meaning of (20), since it can be *canceled*. There is nothing incoherent about asserting that John hit Bill, while denying that he did it just once. He could have hit him over and over again. Because the event approach averts such a commitment, it coincides in another regard with our linguistic intuitions.

17.3.4 Prepositions as Conjoined Predicates

Another aspect of the event approach that you might find peculiar is that it treats prepositions as if they were predicates conjoined to the main verb and bound by an existential quantifier. Recall that according to the event approach the four prepositional phrases in (7) are, from a logical point of view, the last four conjoined predicates in (12).

7.   The dog bit the man *in* the park *after* midnight *on* Wednesday *under* his arm.

12. $(\exists x)(B^3xdm \ \& \ I^2xp \ \& \ A^2xt \ \& \ O^2xw \ \& \ U^2xa)$

Treating prepositional phrases as predicate conjunctions in logical notation enables us to explain their optionality. We can exercise the option of dropping one or more prepositional phrases from a statement like (7) and derive a statement which deductively follows from it. The truth of the conclusion follows from the premise because, according to the event approach, each prepositional phrase is logically conjoined to the main verb, and the truth of a conjunction requires the truth of its conjuncts.

But treating prepositions as behaving logically like predicates is a radical idea. Can anything else be said in favor of this treatment besides its contributing to the preservation of deductively valid arguments that would further validate the event approach?

If prepositions are predicates conjoined to main verbs, we ought to find relative scope ambiguities due to their being treated as conjuncts. Recall from chapter 4 that an English statement like (22) is ambiguous. It could be represented by either (23) or (24) in PL.

22.   It is not true that Bill left and Mary stayed.

23.   ~B & M   B: Bill left; M: Mary stayed
24.   ~(B & M)

We get reading (24) if the negation in (22) takes wide scope over the entire statement; and we get reading (23) if the negation takes small scope over just the left conjunct. Conjuncts are the sort of thing we can negate; but what would it mean to negate a prepositional phrase such as 'in the park'? Consider (25).

25.   It is not true that John kissed Mary in the park after midnight.

(25) looks to be a simple negation, denying (26).

26.   John kissed Mary in the park after midnight.

But take a closer look! Consider (27)–(29).

27.   It is not true that John kissed Mary in the park after midnight; he bit her.
28.   It is not true that John kissed Mary in the park after midnight; he kissed her in the kitchen.
29.   It is not true that John kissed Mary in the park after midnight; he kissed her at noon.

The intelligibility of each of (27)–(29) indicates that in (25) at least one of three things can be negated. Based on the event approach, each of these readings corresponds to a statement which denies either the first, second, or third predicate conjunct. The disambiguating comment at the end of each of (27)–(29) clarifies which predicate is being denied. (30)–(32) correspond to these three readings respectively.

30. $(\exists x)(\sim\!K^3 xjm \ \& \ I^2 xp \ \& \ A^2 xt)$
31. $(\exists x)(K^3 xjm \ \& \ \sim\!I^2 xp \ \& \ A^2 xt)$
32. $(\exists x)(K^3 xjm \ \& \ I^2 xp \ \& \ \sim\!A^2 xt)$
         K^3: was a kissing by __ of __ ; I^2: occurred in;
         A^2: occurred after; j: John; m: Mary; p: the park; t: midnight

The event approach has the virtue of predicting readings that reflect ambiguities in English.

17.3.5 Methodological Reflections

Let's pause here to reflect on the nature of the arguments we have been pursuing in defense of the event approach. We have not been arguing deductively for it, and we are not claiming that it is the only approach that can accommodate all the data examined. Throughout this book our *modus operandi* has been to seek a convention or notation that best accommodates whatever problem we are confronting, at least so far as we can determine.

We have been charting English statements with ambiguities which the event approach allows us to construe and exhibit. No other approach put forward to date performs this task as well. So, tentatively, we adopt the event approach as the best available option. Other conventions may accommodate some of the data equally well. But unless a recommended convention accounts for all the data and does so in as elegant and simple fashion as the event approach, the event approach will remain preferable.

Another advantage of the event approach is that it is conservative. It does not require adding any notation to RPL, unlike the motivations that forced the transitions from PL to PPL, from PPL to RPL, and from RPL to RPL$^=$. The event approach requires adjustments in standard symbolization conventions, but not supplementation of the notational apparatus.

Arguments   Exercise 17.1

- Symbolize in RPL$^=$, using the dictionary provided.

1. Carly talked in her room at 3:00 am. So, someone was talking at 3:00 am.
   (T^2: is a talking by; I^2: occurs in; A^2: occurs at; c: Carly; t: 3:00 am; r: Carly's room)
2. Alex killed John last week. Thus, someone killed someone last week.
   (K^3: ___ is a killing by ___ of ___ ; A^2: occurs at; a: Alex; j: John; w: last week)

17.4   Adverbial Modification

The inference from (33) to (34) is intuitively deductively valid.

33.   Frank drove quickly.
34.   So, Frank drove.

Aside from some interesting counterexamples that we will take up below, this type of inference is quite general. Accordingly, we shall assume that the inference from (33) to (34) is deductively valid in virtue of logical form. (See chapter 2.) If we replace 'Frank' by any other singular term, 'drove' by any other appropriate verb, and 'quickly' by (just about) any adverb, the new inference is deductively valid. How do we account for its validity in RPL?

One tradition recommends treating (33) as having the same logical form as (35).

35.   Fido is a brown dog.

Following this suggestion, the inference from (33) to (34), when symbolized as (36)–(37), is formally valid.

36. D^1f & Q^1f D^1: drove; Q^1: was quick; f: Frank
37. $\therefore D^1f$

Something is right about this account. When we say Frank drove quickly, we are saying that Frank drove, and that he was quick (or, at least, that he did something quickly). Unfortunately, the convention behind this symbolization saddles us with unhappy results. Suppose Frank talked slowly while driving. Then (38) is true.

38.   Frank talked, and also Frank drove quickly.

Symbolized in PPL, (38) is (39), which in turn logically implies (40).

39. T^1f & $(D^1f$ & $Q^1f)$ T^1: talked
40. T^1f & Q^1f

But this strategy would have us treating the inference from (38) to (41) as deductively valid, and it isn't.

41.   Frank talked quickly.

So, adverbial modifications of the type exhibited in (33) apparently should not be symbolized as logical conjunctions. Some other convention is called for. This result is not surprising. In (33) we are being told something about the type of driving Frank did, a quick driving.

33.   Frank drove quickly.

But any symbolization technique that severs ties between the adverb and the verb it modifies obliterates logical connections between the two, which explains why we ended up with unwanted inferences.

The event approach might be able to assist us in accommodating adverbs in our logic. When prepositional phrases modify verbs, they function as adverbs. However, unlike prepositions, simple adverbs could perhaps be treated as one-place rather than two-place predicates. On this approach (33) could be symbolized in RPL as (42).

42. $(\exists x)(D^2xf \ \& \ Q^1x)$ D^2: was a driving by; Q^1: was quick

(42) issues in the desired conclusion (43), the symbolization of (44) in RPL.

43. $(\exists x)D^2xf$
44.   Frank drove (or there was an event of Frank's driving).

Symbolizing (33) as (42) has the advantage of not validating the faulty inference from (38) to (41).

38.   Frank talked, and also Frank drove quickly.
41.   Frank talked quickly.

(38) and (41) are symbolized by (45) and (46) respectively.

45. $(\exists x)T^2xf \ \& \ (\exists y)(D^2yf \ \& \ Q^1y)$
46. $(\exists x)(T^2xf \ \& \ Q^1x)$

(45) tells us that Frank performed at least one talking, and at least one quick driving, but it does not say that the talking and the driving were the same, so we cannot infer that he did anything that was a quick

talking. Not only does the inference fail, but it seems to fail for exactly the right reason. The property of being quick is being ascribed to Frank's driving, which is a distinct event from his talking. Quick drives are not quick talks, certainly not by virtue of logical form alone.

Exercise 17.2   **Arguments**

- Symbolize arguments (1)–(3) into RPL⁼, using the dictionary provided.

1. Maria sang beautifully and acted brilliantly. So, Maria sang and acted. (S^2: is a singing by; A^2: is an acting by; B^1: is beautiful; R^1: is brilliant; m: Maria)
2. Rachel played happily and worked quietly. So, it's not the case that Rachel played quietly. (P^2: is a playing by; W^2: is a working by; H^1: is happy; Q^1: is quiet; r: Rachel)
3. Someone exercises every day. Alan exercises only on Saturday and Wednesday. Therefore, there is someone who exercises that is not Alan. (P^1: is a person; E^2: is an exercising by; O^2: occurs on; a: Alan; D^1: is a day; s: Saturday; w: Wednesday)

17.5   Problems with the Event Approach

Thus far we have spent all this chapter motivating and defending the event approach. What problems, if any, face it? The event approach yields unwanted inferences if applied generally. For example, if we symbolize (47) in the manner suggested by the event approach, it logically implies (48).

47.   Orenthal allegedly killed his wife.
48.   Orenthal killed his wife.

(47) is symbolized as (49) and (48) as (50).

49. $(\exists x)(K^3xow \ \& \ A^1x)$

50. $(\exists x)K^3xow$ K^3: __ was a killing by __ of __ ;
                                    A^1: was alleged; o: Orenthal; w: his wife

Would that establishing another's guilt were so easy!

The event approach appears to work for some modifiers like 'quietly' but not for others like 'allegedly' or 'possibly'.[4] However, if you look closely at the so-called problem modifiers for the event approach, there is a non-*ad hoc* way of distinguishing them from those adverbs which the event approach accommodates.

For problem modifiers we can move from (47) to (51), and from (52) to (53) without changing meaning.

47.   Orenthal allegedly killed his wife.
51.   **It is alleged that** Orenthal killed his wife.

52.   The President possibly lied to the people.
53.   **It is possible that** the President lied to the people.

Expressions like 'allegedly' and 'possibly' don't really seem to be adverbs. Are they modifiers at all? They do not answer any of the traditional adjectival or adverbial questions. Maybe, instead, they are disguised nouns: That __ is a possibility, That __ is an allegation. If this interpretation is right, properly understood, they are predicative nominatives. However this story goes, what's clear is that being transformable along the lines of (51) and (53) distinguishes these so-called problem modifiers from regular adverbs like 'quickly' and 'happily', and so on. You cannot transform (33) into (54) without changing meaning or risking ungrammaticality.

33.   Frank drove quickly.
54.   *It was quick that Frank drove.

There may, then, be a way of distinguishing adverbs that the event approach can accommodate from those it cannot. This point does not end the issue. We still need to see how to accommodate this new class of adverbs or 'ad-sentences', but at least we have separated two distinct logical classes of expressions, one for which the event account works, and one for which it does not. That's progress!

Exercise 17.3   Symbolizing arguments

- Symbolize, using the conventions recommended by the event approach, arguments (1) and (2) in RPL$^=$.
- Construct truth trees on your solutions to determined the validity of (1) and (2).
- Use the dictionary provided.

1. John walked into the bathroom at midnight. So, John walked. (W^2: is a walking by; b: the bathroom; m: midnight; j: John; I^2: occurred in; A^2: happened at)
2. If John is running, then Bill is sleeping in the dark. John is running. So, Bill is sleeping. (j: John; b: Bill; d: the dark; R^2: is a running by; S^2: is a sleeping by; I^2: occurred in)

Exercise 17.4   Arguments

- Arguments (1)–(4) are intuitively valid, yet they are not simple instantiations of the argument form

$$\alpha \supset \beta$$
$$\alpha$$
$$\therefore \beta$$

- Symbolize them in such a way that their validity is made transparent by your symbolization, using the dictionary provided.

1. Whenever there is a fight, someone gets hurt. John is fighting Bill. So, someone is getting hurt. (F^3: ___ is a fighting by ___ of ___ ; j: John; b: Bill; P^1: is a person; G^1: gets hurt)
2. If there's a fight, we will stop the game. Bill is fighting John. So, we will stop the game. (w: we; S^1: stop the game)
3. Whenever someone talks rapidly, someone else misunderstands him. So, if Lisa talks rapidly, someone will misunderstand her. (T^2: is a talking by; M^3: ___ is a misunderstanding by ___ of ___ ; R^1: is rapid; P^1: is a person; l: Lisa)
4. If there is a big argument, someone will cry. If there is a little argument, someone will laugh heartily. So, if Jerry argues with Alison, then either someone will cry or someone will laugh. (A^3: ___ is an arguing by ___ with ___; B^1 is big; L^1: is little; H^1: is hearty; C^2: is a crying by; L^2: is a laughing by)

Notes

1 This is not exactly right, since although no finite upper bound (at least no sane one) can be set on the number and kind of argument places which might be needed, if we are to have an n-place version of, e.g., 'bit', good for all eventualities, in any given argument, a small and definite bound exists. So, strictly speaking, this strategy is not necessarily unworkable for the project of representing arguments in RPL as far as adicity goes.

2 The event approach originates with Donald Davidson in the 1960s, and was first developed by Terry Parsons in 1990. See bibliography below.

3 Because (19) logically implies (18), (19) cannot correspond to a reading that does not imply the reading that (18) is supposed to correspond to. So we cannot read (18) as 'Every single woman moved the piano *by herself*', since (19) is read as 'All the women participated in a group effort by which no single woman moved the piano by herself'.

4 Some authors have suggested that these types of problem show that the event approach is inadequate, and that we ought to adopt a radically different system for representing these so-called event statements. See §A7.5 for further discussion of an alternative approach.

Bibliography

Davidson, Donald, 'The Logical Form of Action Sentences', in *The Logic of Decision and Action* (Pittsburgh: University of Pittsburgh Press, 1967), 81–96.

Davies, Martin, 'Acts and Scenes', in *New Enquiries into Meaning and Truth* (New York: St Martin's Press, 1991), 41–81.

Higginbotham, J., 'The Logic of Perceptual Reports', *Journal of Philosophy* 80 (1983), 100–27.

Lappin, S. (ed.), *The Handbook of Contemporary Semantic Theory* (Oxford: Blackwell Publishers, 1996).

Lepore, Ernest, 'The Semantics of Action, Event and Singular Causal Sentences', in E. Lepore and B. McLaughlin (eds), *Actions and Events: The Philosophy of Donald Davidson* (Oxford: Basil Blackwell, 1985), 151–61.

Lewis, David, 'Adverbs of Quantification', in E. Keenan (ed.), *Formal Semantics of Natural Language* (Cambridge: Cambridge University Press, 1975), 3–15.

Parsons, Terry, *Events in the Semantics of English: A Study of Subatomic Semantics* (Cambridge, MA: MIT Press, 1990).

Schein, Barry, *Plurals and Events* (Cambridge, MA: MIT Press, 1993).

Taylor, Barry, *Modes of Occurrence* (Oxford: Basil Blackwell, 1985).

Thomason, Richmond and Stalnaker, Robert, 'A Semantic Theory of Adverbs', *Linguistic Inquiry* 4 (1973), 195–220.

Van Bentham, J. and ter Meulen, A. (eds), *Handbook of Logic and Language* (Cambridge, MA: MIT Press, 1996).

Appendix

In the brief sections that follow, I touch upon subjects of interest that go beyond anything normally discussed in a first logic course. Don't expect anything like a thorough examination. Each section could easily be expanded into a scholarly monograph, and in some cases it has been.

A1 Conjunction

In §3.6 we tried to see how far we could go with a purely grammatical characterization of logical conjunction: any statement is a logical conjunction if either it grammatically conjoins two statements with 'and', 'but', or an equivalent expression, or if it grammatically conjoins two phrases or clauses with one of these words. ('An equivalent expression' here is a fudge; to legitimize this suggestion, we would need to replace it with an exhaustive list of the eligible conjoining expressions.) This way of identifying logical conjunctions is simpler than the characterization in §3.1, because it requires us merely to examine a statement to ascertain whether it is a logical conjunction; we need not even understand the statement. However, as noted in §3.6, many logicians criticize this simpler account. Some of their criticisms are bad, some good. What may not be obvious is that each criticism is in effect positing a distinct meaning for the word 'and'. To the extent that you find any one of these criticisms convincing, you are agreeing that 'and' is ambiguous, inasmuch as the word makes a different sort of contribution to the meaning of statements in which it is not an indicator of logical conjunction from those in which it is.

A1.1   *Phrasal Conjunction*

We noted in §3.6 that some authors argue that not every phrasal conjunction can be expanded or decompounded into a statement conjunction.

1.   Romeo and Juliet are lovers.

(1) is not a logical conjunction, so one argument goes, because the truth of (2) and (3) follows from the truth of (1), but the truth of (1) does not follow from the truth of (2) and (3).

2.   Romeo is a lover.
3.   Juliet is a lover.

From (2) and (3) it does not follow that Romeo and Juliet love each other. The main idea behind this criticism is that the parts which (1) divides into do not 'add up' to the whole. The contents of (2) and (3) combined do not yield the content of (1). If this argument were sound, it would establish that 'and' is ambiguous in English.

What is wrong with this argument? (1) is ambiguous, but not due to the word 'and'. From the truth of (1) alone, it does not follow that Romeo and Juliet love each other. On one interpretation, (1) simply means that Romeo is a lover and that Juliet is a lover, in much the same way that (4) means the same as (5) and (6) together.

4.   Romeo and Juliet are (both) truck drivers.

5.   Romeo is a truck driver.
6.   Juliet is a truck driver.

On this interpretation (1) is a familiar example of logical conjunction. However, let's suppose we understand (1) to be saying (7).

7.   Romeo and Juliet love each other.

Then the criticism seems more persuasive only if we suppose that the sole way of analyzing (1) into parts is by (2) and (3). What is wrong with analyzing (1) into (8) and (9)?

8.   Romeo loves Juliet.
9.   Juliet loves Romeo.

(8) and (9) together capture the meaning of (7), which is a second interpretation of (1). What's more, if (8) and (9) are true, (1) (in the sense of (7)) is true as well.

The argument against treating (1) as a logical conjunction mistakenly assumes that there is but one way to analyze (1) into parts. Whether reading (1) as the conjunction of (2) and (3) or as the conjunction of (8) and (9), it comes out as a logical conjunction.

A1.2   *Distributive and Collective Readings*

We noted in §3.6 that many writers contend that (1) is ambiguous; so is (2).

1.   Tom and William moved the piano.
2.   Tom and William arrived.

On one reading, both (1) and (2) are alleged to mean that Tom and William did something together, but on another reading the statements are alleged to mean that they did something separately. If (1) means the same as (3), then (1) is not a logical conjunction.

3.   Tom and William moved the piano together.

From the truth of (3), the truth of (4) and (5) may follow, but from the truth of (4) and (5), the truth of (3) does not follow.

4.   Tom moved the piano.
5.   William moved the piano.

Therefore, (1) is not a logical conjunction on interpretation (3). What about the second reading? Suppose (1) paraphrases (any of) (6)–(8).

6.   Tom and William moved the piano separately.
7.   Tom and William each moved the piano.
8.   Both Tom and William moved the piano alone.

Is (1) then a logical conjunction? Can we in general say that if a phrasal conjunction takes the reading with 'each', 'separately', or 'alone', then it is a logical conjunction? It seems not. From the truth of any of (6)–(8), the truth of (9) and (10) follows; but (6)–(8) cannot correctly interpret (1), since from the truth of (9) and (10), the truth of (1) does not follow.

9. Tom moved the piano alone.
10. William moved the piano alone.

(1) is compatible with the truth of (11) and (12).

11. Tom moved the piano with William.
12. William moved the piano with Tom.

What follows is that no one of (6)–(8) is a logical conjunction. So both (3) and (6)–(8) are not adequate interpretations of (1). Is there a competent interpretation of it?

Perhaps (1) is a logical conjunction simply because its meaning is independent of both the joint and the independent readings? Let's test this suggestion against further examples, as in (13)–(20).

13. John and Mary left the party together.
14. Shakespeare and Marlowe wrote plays together.

15. John left with Mary.
16. Shakespeare wrote with Marlowe.

17. Both John and Mary left.
18. Both Shakespeare and Marlowe wrote plays.

19. John and Mary each left.
20. Shakespeare and Marlowe each wrote plays.

In some cases we cannot decompound, because we have a group action which fuses the subject. Any attempt to separate the individuals involved in the group action will obliterate the fact that the group acts as a single unit in performing the action in question. On the other hand, with individual efforts, as in (6), we fall short of logical conjunction, because any attempt to separate the individuals involved will obliterate the fact that the individuals acted separately. What follows (though not obviously) is that statements like (1) are not ambiguous between a collective and a distributive reading. They are neutral, and because they are, they can be treated as logical conjunctions, where both they and their conjuncts retain this neutrality. Put bluntly, statements like (1) differ in meaning from statements like (3) and (6)–(8).

Some authors think that a statement like (1) cannot imply that John moved the piano. They believe that if we say that John moved the piano, we imply that he moved it by himself. But acting independently is clearly no part of the meaning of (1) and is, at best, a conversational inference (§3.2). (21) is perfectly intelligible.

21.   Even though Tom moved the piano, he could never have done it by himself. William had to help him.

Similarly, there is a tendency to think that (22) deductively implies that Tom and William each did something (separately), but their acting separately is clearly no part of the meaning of (22).

22.   Tom moved the piano, and William moved the piano.

Separate action is, at best, a conversational inference, since (23) is perfectly intelligible.

23.   Tom moved the piano and William moved the piano, but they really needed each other's help.

With all that said, there may remain an equivocation in the above discussion of the distributive and collective readings of (1) on the meaning of the predicate 'move the piano' and interaction with tense and aspect.

Some speakers accept the inference from (1) to (4) and (5) if 'move the piano' is understood as 'help move the piano'. Compare 'Tom and William ate the apple', which does not entail that Tom ate the apple and William ate the apple. So although it is true that (9) and (10) do not entail (1) on any interpretation, this is true when (1) is taken to report a single event such that the piano is moved but once, an effect of the simple past. By contrast, consider 'Tom has moved the piano alone' and 'William has moved the piano alone'. These two statements do entail that Tom and William have moved the piano. Speaker judgments are even more straightforward and unclouded with examples such as 'Tom and William weigh 220 lb', with two distinct readings, only one of which is reducible to logical conjunction. Needless to say, there is much more that can be said about this topic, but this would take us way beyond the scope and intended sophistication of this book.

A1.3   *Subject Modifiers*

As subject modifiers, phrasal conjunctions frequently cannot be treated as logical conjunctions. We cannot divide the modifier 'red and blue' in (1), since from (1) the truth of (2) and (3) does not deductively follow, and vice versa.

1.   The red and blue flag is on the pole.

2.   The red flag is on the pole.
3.   The blue flag is on the pole.

On the basis of (1), we have no reason to believe that either a red flag or a blue flag exists. Similarly, on the basis of (2) and (3) together, we have no reason to believe that a red and blue flag exists. Sometimes, however, conjoined subject modifiers can indicate logical conjunction. (4) is ambiguous in two (but not three) ways.

4.   The red and blue flags are on the pole.

On one reading, (4) means that at least two flags are on the pole, both of which are red and blue. On its other reading, (4) means that at least one red flag is on the pole and that there is at least one blue flag on the pole. On this second reading, of course, (4) can be treated as the conjunction of (5) and (6).

5.   The red flags are on the pole.
6.   The blue flags are on the pole.[1]

A1.4   *'And' as a Conditional*

Although each statement in (1)–(4) consists of two statements grammatically conjoined by 'and', each is a conditional statement according to a reading that stresses 'I'll' ('we'll'). See chapter 7 for a discussion of conditionals.

1.   John takes the exam, and I'll take the exam.
2.   You give me the bombs, and I'll win the war.
3.   You insult me once more, and I'll punch you in the nose.
4.   You touch her there, and we'll impeach you.

When the focal stress is on 'we'll', (4), for example, means that if you touch her there, then we'll impeach you. Note that there is no deductively valid inference to 'we'll impeach you' from (4), contrary to what is the case with a genuine conjunction. As the conditional readings of (1)–(4) indicate, deploying a purely grammatical test for identifying logical conjunctions is ill advised.

A1.5   *Prepositional Phrases*

In some statements containing prepositional phrases, the prepositions take compound objects. Some of these statements are logical conjunctions; others are not.

1. John lives **between** Fourth and Fifth streets.
2. John lives **at** the corner of Fifth and Main.

3. I walked **by** the store and the river.
4. Mary knows Frank **from** school and church.

(3) and (4) are logical conjunctions. Surely, if I walked by the store and I walked by the river, then it's true that I walked by the store and the river, and conversely. Similarly, for (4). But (1) and (2) are not logical conjunctions, because they do not admit of the same sort of analysis. Try breaking up (1) into (5) and (6).

5. *John lives between Fourth.
6. *John lives at the corner of Fifth.

These component parts are not grammatical. (Asterisk (*) throughout signifies ungrammaticality or unacceptability.) So the word 'and' is making a different sort of contribution to overall meaning in (1) and (2) than in (3) and (4). (See chapter 17 for further discussion of these sorts of cases.)

A1.6   *Symmetric Predicates*

Certain transitive verbs and adjectives in English can be turned into intransitive verbs by conjoining the object of the transitive verb with the subject by 'and'.

1. John debated Bill.
2. John is similar to Bill.
3. John met Bill.
4. John married Mary.

5. John and Bill debated.
6. John and Bill are similar.
7. John and Bill met.
8. John and Mary married.

Are (5)–(8) logical conjunctions? If so, the sense in which they are logical conjunctions seems trivial, due to the redundancy in (9)–(12).

9. John debated Bill, and Bill debated John.
10. John is similar to Bill, and Bill is similar to John.
11. John met Bill, and Bill met John.
12. John married Mary, and Mary married John.

The predicates in (5)–(8) are said to be *symmetric*: from the fact that an object a bears some symmetrical relationship to an object b, we can infer in virtue of the meaning of the predicate alone that b bears this same relationship to a. If John debated Bill, it follows that Bill debated John; so the second clause in (9)–(12) adds nothing to the first. (More on symmetry in §A5.2.1.) These sorts of example require us to refine our test for logical conjunction, to which we turn directly.

A1.7 Logical Conjunction Refined

If (9)–(12) in §A1.6 are logical conjunctions, then what prevents us from treating any statement as a logical conjunction? For example, returning to collective statements, which we argued in §A1.2 were not logical conjunctions, what prevents an analysis of (1) as (2)?

1. John and Bill moved the piano together.
2. John moved the piano with Bill, and Bill moved the piano with John.

(1) paraphrases (2), and from (3) and (4) the truth of (1) follows, and vice versa.

3. John moved the piano with Bill.
4. Bill moved the piano with John.

(2) is a logical conjunction. But wouldn't treating (3) and (4) as analyzed parts of (1) trivialize the notion of analysis and, worse, the notion of logical conjunction? The problem seems to be that each part paraphrases the whole in meaning. From either (3) or (4), the truth of (1) follows. Once this type of analysis is permitted, what prevents treating any statement whatsoever as a logical conjunction?

> Any sentence α can be analyzed as a conjunction inasmuch as it can be analyzed into parts (α and α). From the truth of α, the truth of (α and α) follows, and from the truth of (α and α), the truth of α follows.

We have a decision to make. Suppose we accept this analysis and treat every statement as a logical conjunction. This practice may seem harmless enough, except that the notion of a logical conjunction loses (some of) its value in identifying argument forms. Any argument can be treated as containing logical conjunctions. An alternative is to reject this analysis and decree that

> Given a statement α, analyzed into components β and χ, α is a logical conjunction only if the following conditions obtain:

> i.   From the truth of α, the truth of β and the truth of χ follow.
> ii. From the truth of β and the truth of χ, the truth of α follows.
> iii. From the truth of β alone, the truth of α does *not* follow.
> iv. From the truth of χ alone, the truth of α does *not* follow.

Conditions (iii) and (iv) eliminate trivial cases.

Are (i)–(iv) enough? One problem is that they prevent sentences of the form 'α & α' from being analyzed as 'α & α'. That said, it would seem we should just learn to live with a notion of logical conjunction that allows any argument to be treated as containing logical conjunctions. This concession alone will not transform any intuitively invalid arguments into valid ones, or vice versa.

A1.8 Both

Although the word 'both' often indicates logical conjunction, as in (1), sometimes it does not, as in (2) and (3).

1. Both Frank and Bill died.

2. Both (of the) boys died.
3. Both women expect to win.

If you think otherwise, try to find self-standing conjuncts for (2) and (3) such that from the truth of them, the truth of (2) and (3) follows. Note too that not every statement of form (4) can be converted into a statement of form (5).

4. α and β are χ.
5. Both α and β are χ.

(6) is grammatical; (7) is not.

6. Tom and Bill met at noon.
7. *Both Tom and Bill met at noon.

A1.9   *Conversational Inferences and Deductive Validity*[2]

A1.9.1   COMMUTATIVITY AND CONJUNCTION
The order of conjuncts in a logical conjunction is immaterial to its truth or falsity. The following truth table verifies that the inference from a statement of form

α & β

to a statement of form

β & α

is deductively valid.

α β	α & β	β & α
T T	T	T
F T	F	F
T F	F	F
F F	F	F

Rejecting this result is the same as denying that logical conjunction is *commutative*. Some authors find the idea that English conjunctions are logically commutative so unintuitive that they reject the entire truth table method as a method for determining deductive validity. Behind their indictment of the truth table method is the not unintuitive claim that (1) and (2) don't say the same thing.

1.   Mary got married, and Mary got pregnant.
2.   Mary got pregnant, and Mary got married.

If someone were to assert (2), you might be inclined to deductively infer (3), but no such inference seems to follow from (1).

3.   Mary got pregnant, and then she got married.

If you agree with these intuitions, you are in effect claiming that 'and' in (2) has a *temporal* meaning of 'and then' or 'before'.
    Some have even been inclined to posit a third 'reading' of 'and' as (4).

4.   The President shouted, and his aide-de-camp jumped.

Were someone to assert (4), he would typically be taken to mean that the President's shouting contributed to the aide-de-camp's jumping. We might call this a *causal* reading of 'and'.
    What are we to make of these different meanings of 'and'? Surely someone who asserts (2) would typically be taken to mean that Mary got pregnant before she got married. Similarly, if someone asserts (4), he will typically be taken to mean that the President's shouting contributed to his aide-de-camp jumping. But should we thereby conclude that 'and' in statements like (2) and (4) does not mean '&', and that 'and' is at least ambiguous between a truth-functional and a temporal or a causal reading? Multiplying meanings in this manner is suspect, and the reasoning that leads some to do it is faulty.
    There are good reasons to think that 'and' in English is not ambiguous. With clearly ambiguous words like 'bank' and 'light', the ambiguity (or homonymy) is peculiar to English; these expressions are typically translated into other languages by two or more expressions. The two common senses of 'light' (light in weight and light in color) are realized

by *leggero* and *chiaro* in Italian. But no language seems to encode the alleged distinct meanings for 'and' in distinct words. Apparently we are dealing not with an arbitrary linguistic matter, but with some general non-linguistic fact.

If we use the so-called cancelation test, we can establish that this is so: we can assert (2) while consistently denying and thereby canceling (3); so getting pregnant first cannot be part of the meaning of (2). Therefore, the skeptic's reasoning does not succeed against the truth table method. It is based on conflating deductively valid inferences with conversational inferences. The latter are cancelable, whereas the former are not.

The tendency to think that (2) implies a temporal sequence can be explained by the fact that each conjunct describes an event rather than a state (see ch. 17) and by the presumption that speakers observe a maxim of perspicuity enjoining orderly executions. People ordinarily take a speaker to be presenting events in the order in which (the speaker believes) they occurred unless otherwise indicated. But nothing in the meaning of the words themselves warrants the interpretation that the events occurred in the order in which they are tacitly presented. The cancelation test shows that sequential ordering is not part of the meaning. The inference from (2) to (3) is not deductively valid, even though an audience, in normal circumstances, will interpret (2) as if the speaker had actually uttered (3). When uttering (2), a speaker at most conversationally (rather than deductively) implies that Mary got pregnant before she got married. (The same point extends to the so-called causal reading of 'and'.)

A1.9.2 Relevance and conjunction

Some logicians argue that when two statements are grammatically conjoined into a single statement, the component statements must share a common subject matter in order for the complex statement to be a logical conjunction. So consider (1)–(3) and (4)–(6).

1. John is happy.
2. Frank is happy.
3. John and Frank are happy.

4. John went to the store.
5. John went home.
6. John went to the store and home.

Components (1) and (2) of (3) share a predicate and therefore a common subject matter with each other. Similarly, components (4) and (5) of (6) share a grammatical subject and therefore a common subject matter. But the characterization of a logical conjunction in chapter 3 doesn't require its component statements to share any subject matter whatsoever. Any two statements can be logically conjoined regardless of their subject matter. For example, consider the unrelated statements (7) and (8).

7. Grass is green.
8. 2 + 2 = 4.

(7) grammatically conjoined with (8) issues in (9), which, according to the current characterization, is a logical conjunction.

9. Grass is green and 2 + 2 = 4.

Skeptics would argue that (9) is not a logical conjunction because its conjuncts (7) and (8) do not share a common subject matter. Shall we revise our characterization of a logical conjunction so as to require a common subject matter?

Once again, we are being asked to adjudicate a debate about the meaning of the word 'and'. Conjuncts (7) and (8) may seem unrelated. If someone were to assert (9), he might seem peculiar or silly. But maybe we, his audience, miss the relevant connection, which need not be articulated in (9) itself. Whether any two statements have something in common need not be part of their shared linguistic meaning, but may instead be part of the information an audience and a speaker bring to the statements. (9) might be a perfectly coherent and acceptable reply to the question 'What are your two favorite facts?' What connects (7) and (8) in this case, then, is not linguistic meaning, but the speaker who does so in order to express his two favorite facts.

The skeptic apparently conflates a deductively valid inference with a conversational inference. (9), on its face, seems to be violating the maxim of conversation that requires relevance. But whether two statements are connected need not be determined only by shared expressed subject matter. Shared information that the participants in a conversation bring to their conversation can also establish a connection among statements.

A2   Negation and Disjunction

The lesson of the last section of chapter 4 is that it is false that every statement which contains a 'not' or a negative particle like 'in-', as in 'ineligible', is a logical negation.

A2.1   Quantifiers and Negation

(1) and (2) are not logical negations.

1.   Some dogs are not fuzzy.
2.   Several men are ineligible.

Suppose we analyze (1) as (3).

3.   It is not the case that some dogs are fuzzy.

(3) is the denial of (4).

4.   Some dogs are fuzzy.

But (1) is not the denial of (4). It does not deny that some dogs are fuzzy. Both (1) and (4) can be true together. However, (3) and (4) cannot both be true together, since (3) is the denial of (4). A similar argument can be constructed for (2). In general, English quantifier expressions (e.g., expressions like 'some', 'all', 'every', 'many', 'most', and 'few') have priority ('wide scope') over negative expressions.[3] When we attempt to analyze a statement with a quantifier expression that has wide scope over a negative expression (as in (1) and (2)), we change the meaning of that statement if we treat it as a negation. To treat the statement as a negation, the negative particle must have wide scope over the quantifier. Another example may help.

In (5) the quantifier expression 'Many' has wide scope over the negative particle 'didn't'.

5.   Many arrows didn't hit the target.

If we treat (5) as a negation, we might try to interpret it as (6).

6.   It is not the case that many arrows hit the target.

In (6) the negative particle 'It is not the case that' has wide scope over the quantifier 'many'. But by changing the scope, we alter the meaning of (5). (5) and (6) are not synonymous, since (6) denies (7), and (5) does not.

7.   Many arrows hit the target.

(5) and (7) are not even contraries; since they can both be true, (5) is not the negation of (7). Similarly, with (8) and (9).

8.   Several men didn't pay.
9.   No man did not vote.

In general, a statement in which a quantifier expression has wide scope over a negative particle is not a negation. However, cases do exist in which it is. But usually this circumstance arises only when a statement is ambiguous between two readings, one of which is a negation and one of which is not. By placing focal stress on the quantifier words in (10) and (11), we force their interpretations as negations (12) and (13) respectively.[4]

10.   All teachers are not leaving.
11.   Every teacher is not leaving.

12.   It is not the case that all teachers are leaving.
13.   It is not the case that every teacher is leaving.

A2.2   *Modalities and Negation*

Certain modal auxiliaries (e.g., 'must', 'should', 'would', 'might') appear to take 'wide scope' over negative particles. Thus, though each of (1)–(3) contains a 'not', none is a logical negation.

1.   Smith ought not to steal.
2.   Smith might not win.
3.   John must not eat.

We might incorrectly analyze (1)–(3) as (4)–(6) respectively.

4. It is not the case that Smith ought to steal.
5. It is not the case that Smith might win.
6. It is not the case that John must eat.

(4)–(6) negate (7)–(9) respectively.

7. Smith ought to steal.
8. Smith might win.
9. John must eat.

(8) is true if, and only if, (5) is false. But (8) is not true if, and only if, (2) is true. (2) and (8) can both be true. So (2) cannot be the negation of (8). Similar arguments can be devised for the other examples. What we see here is analogous to what arose when we mixed quantifiers and negative particles.

> In English, when certain modal expressions (e.g., 'should', 'ought', 'might', 'must') have wide scope over negative particles, we cannot extract the negative particle and change its scope without changing the meaning of the statement.

There are exceptions, however. (10) and (11) negate (12) and (13) respectively.

10. Sam could not win.
11. Sam can't win.

12. Sam could win.
13. Sam can win.

Other modal auxiliaries like 'shall' and 'will' are likewise exceptional.

A2.3 Conversational Inferences

When a speaker asserts 'Either John left, or he's still inside', she conveys that she doesn't know whether John left or whether John is still inside, because if she did know which was the case, she would have been in a position to say either 'John left' or 'John is still inside', as may be the case, and so she could have said something more informative than her disjunctive claim with less linguistic effort. Since she asserted the disjunction, we take her ordinarily not to have been in a position to assert either disjunct, and thus we take her as not knowing which of the two is true.

A3   Conditionals

A3.1   *Explication of the Material Conditional Truth Table*

In §7.3, we just assumed without argument that English conditional statements have truth-values *even when* their antecedents are false or their consequents true. We also assumed without argument that the truth-values of the antecedent and consequent all by themselves suffice to determine the truth-value of an English conditional, and that the conditional is true just in case its antecedent is false or its consequent true. This means that a major assumption of this book is that English conditionals are what we shall call *material conditionals*.

Many people regard 'if' as not being truth-functional in its use, and find the claim that 'if, then' statements can be symbolized by the truth table for '⊃' bewildering. The same sort of puzzlement, however, does not arise about the relationship between 'or' and '∨', and 'and' and '&'. We turn now to take up the pros and cons of so representing 'if, then' statements in PL.

The assumption that English conditionals are material conditionals is implicitly restricted to indicative conditionals. If you go back and look at all our examples, you will find that every conditional statement we symbolized is in indicative mood. This selection of examples was deliberate because the above two assumptions are demonstrably false for conditional statements in subjunctive mood.

Subjunctive conditionals take various forms, including (1) and (2).

1. If α were the case, then β would be the case.
2. If α had been the case, then β would have been the case.

Whatever the suitable analysis of a subjunctive conditional, we can be sure it cannot be a material conditional. Statements of forms (1) and (2) can be true or false whether α or β is true or false. Subjunctive conditionals (3)–(8) conveniently show that nothing follows about the truth of a subjunctive conditional from the falsity of its antecedent or the truth of its consequent.

3. If the United States had 51 states, then there would be 102 sena-
   tors. (Antecedent false, consequent false, conditional true)
4. If the moon were made of green cheese, then the sun would be
   made of ice cream. (Antecedent false, consequent false, conditional
   false)
5. If the Yankees had played in New York, then communism would
   fall in eastern Europe. (Antecedent true, consequent true, conditional false)
6. If the Yankees were in New York, then New York would have a
   professional baseball team. (Antecedent true, consequent true, conditional true)
7. If the Yankees were in Buffalo, then New York State would have a
   professional baseball team. (Antecedent false, consequent true, conditional true)
8. If the Red Sox were in Buffalo, then New York State would have
   two professional baseball teams. (Antecedent false, consequent true,
   conditional false)

However we decide ultimately to treat subjunctive conditionals, it
should be different from how we decide to treat indicative conditionals.
Note that the following two sentences disagree in truth-value.

If Oswald didn't kill Kennedy, someone else did.
If Oswald hadn't killed Kennedy, someone else would have.

The former is obviously true, and the latter is not.
But are English indicative conditionals material conditionals? No one
denies that an English indicative conditional *can* be true, even though its
antecedent is false. Every instance of (9) is true, whether α is true or
false.

9. If α, then α.

Similarly, consider an instance of (10), where β is false.

10. If α & β, then α.

Under this condition the antecedent α & β is false. The consequent α
may or may not be true, depending on whether α is true or false. But
every instance of (10) is true, regardless.

What these sorts of examples show is that there are cases where the antecedent is false, the consequent either true or false, yet the conditional is *intuitively* true.

11. If there is a Republican president in 2020, then there is a Republican president in 2020.
12. If there is a Republican president in 2020 and a Democratic Congress, then there is a Republican president in 2020.

(11) and (12) are obviously true, even though no one has a clue about whether their antecedents or their consequents are true or false. So anyone who claims that indicative conditionals are not material conditionals, and therefore that they are not true whenever they have false antecedents and/or true consequents, needs to defend his claim.

A3.1.1   PARADOX OF IMPLICATION

Here's another argument based on deductive inferences that someone might offer in defense of the claim that English indicative conditionals are not material conditionals: If indicative conditionals are material conditionals, then the truth of (1) and (2) deductively follows solely from the falsity of the antecedent in (1) and the truth of the consequent in (2).

1. If the moon is made of cheese, then the city of Pisa is in Italy.
2. If the US is not a country, then the US is a country.

Indeed, if indicative conditionals are material conditionals, then for every statement α and β, every argument of form (3)–(4) or (5)–(6) is deductively valid.

3. It is not the case that α.
4. Therefore, if α, then β.

5. β.
6. Therefore, if α, then β.

From the negation of an arbitrary statement α, an indicative conditional which has α as its antecedent and any other statement β as its consequent follows deductively.

Similarly, from the truth of any arbitrary statement β, it follows deductively, for any other statement α, if α, then β. But it doesn't seem that the truth-values of the components alone determine the truth-values of (1) and (2). On the contrary, (1) and (2) probably seem false to you. So how can indicative conditionals be material conditionals?

A3.1.2 CONDITIONALS AND CONVERSATIONAL INFERENCES

A logician who holds that indicative conditionals are not material conditionals because of the intuitive invalidity of the inference from a false antecedent or a true consequent to a true conditional might be mistaking a conversational inference for a deductively valid inference. A speaker's choice of an 'if, then' statement normally conveys that he has non-truth-functional grounds for accepting this conditional statement. A listener hearing someone assert a conditional statement might think as follows: if the speaker's grounds for holding an 'if, then' statement were simply either his belief that its consequent is true or its antecedent false, why should he use so cumbersome and evasive a form of words as 'if, then' to express this information? His utterance would normally be misleading, or at best less informative than it ought to have been, given generally understood rules of conversation. So the speaker's choice of a conditional expression seems to warrant the inference that his assertion is based on a presumed connection between antecedent and consequent unrelated to the beliefs he has about the truth or falsity of the antecedent or consequent. His reasons for asserting that if α, then β would presumably be non-truth-functional. So we need not conclude on the basis of the so-called paradox of implication that indicative conditionals are not material conditionals.

Even if this line of defense explained the counterintuitiveness of many arguments employing indicative conditionals, it alone does not succeed in showing that English indicative conditionals are material conditionals. The argument presented seems best understood in a context in which we already assume that English indicative conditionals are material and we are trying to diagnose certain counterintuitive cases so that they do not undermine this commitment. But why commit oneself in the first place?

Those who insist on a stronger connection between antecedent and consequent than truth functionality are arguing that 'if, then' statements are more like 'because' statements than they are like, say, conjunctions or negations. The truth-values of two statements α and β alone is certainly insufficient to determine the truth of a statement of the form α because β (as noted in §3.1).

So who wins this debate about the relationship between English indicative conditionals and material conditionals? Unfortunately, pursuing the debate here would take us far beyond the scope of this book and far from our present aims. Both sides of the debate have advanced sophisticated and complicated arguments for treating versus not treating English indicative conditionals as material conditionals. Another complication is that a change in the status of the material conditional forces changes in the treatment of other connectives in PL and other languages. Often an improvement in one element of a system issues in problems with other elements. Accounts as to how best to replace the material conditional in order to arrive at a correct account for indicative conditionals vary.

We will not beg any questions here about which account is correct. However, some reasons for treating indicative conditionals as material conditionals at least within the scope of this book (even if they should turn out not to be) are worth noting in passing.

If we use the material conditional to represent in PL a deductively valid English argument having indicative conditionals as its premises, the argument will also be deductively valid in English even if the English indicative conditionals are symbolized using some other form of conditional. The reason is obvious. The material conditional is the *weakest* form of conditional; it is false in one and only one case, when the antecedent is true and the consequent is false. English indicative conditionals are not material conditionals only if they are false under further truth conditions.

If we symbolize true English conditional premises of a valid English argument as material conditionals, then, even if they are in fact not material conditionals, the validity of the argument is preserved. A valid argument based on using the material conditional to represent indicative conditional premises remains valid on stronger representations of the indicative conditional.

Similarly, if an argument with a material conditional in its conclusion is invalid, it will be invalid for stronger conditionals. So, we take no risks for these types of arguments in assuming that English indicative conditionals are material conditionals.

Of course, there are numerous other cases about which we will remain silent. A worthwhile project is to determine exactly under what circumstances treating indicative conditionals as material conditionals does or does not matter. Even if the English indicative conditional is not a material conditional, when is treating it as such detrimental to determining deductive validity? These considerations are offered without commitment to a view as to whether English indicative conditionals are indeed material conditionals.

A3.1.3 PARADOX OF IMPLICATION REVISITED

Suppose someone asserts (1).

1. Eating chocolate is neither necessary nor sufficient for doing well in logic.

What she has said is true. Yet if 'C' represents 'You eat chocolate' and 'D' 'You do well in logic', then, following the recommended conventions, the correct symbolization of (1) in PL is (2), a negation of a disjunction of two conditionals.

2. $\sim((D \supset C) \vee (C \supset D))$

However, any truth table for (2) is self-contradictory. This should be obvious, since the denial of the left disjunct is true only if 'D' is true and 'C' is false, but the denial of the right disjunct is true only if 'C' is true and 'D' is false. Therefore, since (2) denies both disjuncts, in order for it to be true, 'D' and 'C' must be both true and false, which is impossible. Yet (1) seems harmlessly true. This consequence results from adopting a (standard) convention for symbolizing necessary and sufficient conditions in PL. How bad is this consequence?

What follows is that, given any two statements α and β, either $\alpha \supset \beta$ or $\beta \supset \alpha$ is true. This means that for any two arbitrary statements α and β, either α is a necessary or a sufficient condition for β. Based on the meaning of '$\supset$', if α is true, then $\beta \supset \alpha$ is true; but if α is false, then $\alpha \supset \beta$ is true. For any two arbitrary statements α and β, either α is a necessary or a sufficient condition for β. Since two statements α and β can be such that α is neither necessary nor sufficient for β, it may be either that '$\supset$' does not faithfully represent the English conditional, or that necessary and sufficient conditions are incorrectly represented in PL by the prevailing convention.

A3.2 *'If's and 'Then's without Conditionality*

One might infer from what we have said so far that every statement with an 'if' in it presents a condition (an antecedent) and therefore a logical conditional. But in (1) 'if' is an alternative form of 'whether', as is shown by the fact that the 'if' clause may be followed by 'or not'. In (2), no conditionality is involved.

1. I wonder if John will arrive today.
2. I remember the past as if it were yesterday.

The same remarks extend to the claim that 'then' introduces a consequent.

3.   John then went to the movies.

In (3) 'then' is an adverb. Can you think of an example in which a non-adverbial 'then' introduces the main clause of a complex statement, but is not introducing a consequent?

A3.3   *Generalized Conditionals*

Although (1) looks like a logical conditional, it isn't.

1.   If anything is a unicorn, it has a horn.

Rather, (1) should be viewed, to borrow Quine's eloquent phrasing, as affirming a bundle of individual conditionals: If a is a unicorn, then a has a horn; if b is a unicorn, then b has a horn; and so on. In short:

2.   No matter what α is, if α is a unicorn, then α has a horn.

Each individual conditional in the bundle of conditionals which (2) affirms can quite satisfactorily be interpreted as a logical conditional. But (2) itself is not a conditional. (This generalized conditional is treated thoroughly in ch. 11.)

A3.4   *Relative Clauses*

What kind of logical contribution do relative clauses make to English statements? (1) and (2) contain what are called *non-restrictive relative (appositive) clauses,* by contrast with (3)–(5), which contain what are called *restrictive relative clauses.*

1.   John, **whom I like**, is tall.
2.   Amy came late, **which bothered Arena**.

3.   The boys **whom I like** are tall.
4.   Everyone **whom I like** went to the movies.
5.   Any intern **who votes for Bill** is stupid.

Some distinguishing characteristics of non-restrictive relative clauses and of restrictive relative clauses are as follows. First, restrictive clauses are not tied to proper names.

(6) is ungrammatical.

6. *John whom I like is tall.

The clause 'whom I like' should be set off by commas. One might try to use a proper name as an adjective, in which case (6) could be grammatical, as in '(The) John whom I like is tall, but (the) John whom I hate is short'.

Second, non-restrictive relative clauses can modify whole sentences.

7. He said that he would resign, which I thought wise.

How should statements with non-restrictive relative clauses like (1) be symbolized? If (1) is true, then (8) and (9) must be true as well.

1. John, whom I like, is tall.

8. John is tall.
9. I like John.

From the truth of (8) and (9), the truth of (1) follows. Non-restrictive relative clauses seem to satisfy the conditions for logical conjunctions. When we make an assertion containing a non-restrictive relative clause, we make perhaps two assertions. Restrictive relative clauses lack this characteristic. From the truth of (4), the truth of (10) and (11) do not follow.

4. Everyone whom I like went to the movies.

10. Everyone went to the movies.
11. I like everyone.

The restrictive relative clause in (4) plays a different role from the non-restrictive relative clause in (1). In (4) the relative clause is a part of the subject, further defining it. The clause in (1) does not play this role. (How to accommodate restrictive relative clauses in logical notation is discussed in chapter 11.)

Note too that conjoined phrases inside restrictive relative clauses do not indicate logical conjunctions either. (12) cannot be analyzed successfully as (13) and (14).

12. The boy who is tall and happy left.

13. The boy who is tall left.
14. The boy who is happy left.

(13) and (14) might make reference to different boys, whereas (12) makes reference to one and only one boy. (These cases are like the subject modifier examples discussed in §A1.3.)

What about the suggestion that non-restrictive relative clauses are best symbolized as logical conjunctions? Although the suggestion seems adequate enough for simple examples like (1) and (2), it won't generalize to more complex examples. (15)–(17), for example, cannot be adequately symbolized as (18)–(20) respectively (with 'L' representing 'I like John', 'T' representing 'John is tall', and 'H' representing 'Frank is happy').

15. It is not the case that John, whom I like, is tall.
16. If John, whom I like, is tall, then Frank is happy.
17. Either John, whom I like, is tall, or Frank is happy.

18. ~(L & T)
19. (L & T) ⊃ H
20. (L & T) ∨ H

(18)–(20) are compatible with my not liking John, whereas (15)–(17) are not. It follows that non-restrictive relative clauses cannot always be symbolized as logical conjunctions. But how, then, should they be symbolized?

An adequate convention for symbolizing any statement with a non-restrictive relative clause is to discharge the non-restrictive relative clause and conjoin it with the remaining statement part. So, though (1) should be symbolized as a logical conjunction, as in (21),

21. L & T

(15)–(17) should be symbolized as (22)–(24) respectively.

22. L & ~T
23. L & (T ⊃ H)
24. L & (T ∨ H)

A moment's reflection should convince you that these are correct symbolizations for the corresponding English statements (15)–(17). The important point is that this convention does not treat non-restrictive relative clauses as logical conjunctions. A non-restrictive relative clause can be pulled out of the rest of the statement without sacrificing the meaning of the main clause. So, pull out the non-restrictive clause; make it one conjunct, and then symbolize the main clause as the second conjunct.

A4   Property Predicate Logic

A4.1   *Only*

(1) and (2) cannot be treated as conjunctions in any obvious way.

1.   Only Clinton and Dole had a chance to win.
2.   Clinton and Dole alone had a chance to win.

(1) and (2) are clearly not synonymous with (3) and (4) respectively.

3.   Only Clinton had a chance to win, and only Dole had a chance to win.
4.   Clinton alone had a chance to win, and Dole alone had a chance to win.

(3) and (4) are internally inconsistent, but both (1) and (2) are perfectly intelligible; both may even be true. I argued in chapter 16 that (1) and (2) harbor hidden quantifiers, and that these quantifiers prevent treating (1) and (2) as logical conjunctions.

A4.2   *Conversational Inferences*

A4.2.1   EXISTENTIAL IMPORT
The solution to problem (10) in exercise 2 in chapter 10 may surprise you. If you constructed a correct truth tree for it, you may have concluded that this PPL argument is deductively invalid. But, since it is, then, according to the truth tree method, arguments like (1) and (2) are invalid because they share the form of argument (10).

1.   Every man is tall.
2.   So, some man is tall.

Intuitively, (1)–(2) seems valid. But the truth tree method evaluates any correct symbolization of (1)–(2) in PPL as deductively invalid. We can turn this inference into a valid inference by adding premise (3).

3.   There are some men.

A truth tree for this amended argument shows that the argument is deductively valid.

1.	$\forall(M^1 \supset T^1)$	(premise)
√2.	$\sim\exists(M^1 \,\&\, T^1)$	(negation of conclusion)
√3.	$\exists M^1$	(added premise)
4.	$\forall \sim(M^1 \,\&\, T^1)$	2, QE
√5.	M^1a	3, EQ
√6.	$M^1a \supset T^1a$	1, UQ
√7.	$\sim(M^1a \,\&\, T^1a)$	4, UQ

8. $\sim M^1a \quad \sim T^1a$ 7, $\sim$ &
    ×

9. $\sim M^1a \quad \sim T^1a$ 6, $\supset$
      ×   ×

Is it reasonable to add (3) to the argument? That depends. You might think that (3) is implicit in (1), in which case, stating (3) only makes explicit what is already implicit. However, many logicians do not regard (1) (and, in general, statements of the form 'All α's are β's') as having *existential import*. If they are right, the inference from (1) to (2) is invalid, and we would be wrong to add (3) gratuitously in order to render the argument valid.

But what about the intuition that the argument is valid? We can account for this intuition by, once again, distinguishing conversational inferences from deductively valid inferences. Do we think every inference of form (4)–(5) is deductively valid?

4.   All α's are β's.
5.   So, some α's are β's.

Consider inferences (6)–(7) and (8)–(9).

6.   All unicorns have wings.
7.   So, some unicorns have wings.

8.   All witches have supernatural powers.
9.   So, some witches have supernatural powers.

Are these inferences valid? Their conclusions are obviously false, if by 'some' in (7) and in (9) we mean '∃'. '∃' means that there exists in the world some thing. But no witches and unicorns exist. What about the premises, however? Here's an argument that their premises (6) and (8) are *not* false. In order for (6) to be false, there would have to be a unicorn which lacks wings. But since no unicorns exist, no unicorns exist which lack wings. Should we therefore conclude that (6) is true?

As an alternative, we might conclude that 'some' in English does not always mean the same as '∃'. We might also conclude that statements of form (4) sometimes do not have existential import, and that inferences from statements of form (4) to statements of form (5) are not deductively valid. Those who think that (6)–(7) and (8)–(9) are valid do so because they mistakenly presume that the existence of some α's is part of the meaning of statements of form (4). To see that this presumption is false, we need only apply the cancelation test: is there a contradiction in asserting either (10) or (11)?

10. All unicorns have wings, but there aren't actually any unicorns.
11. All witches have supernatural powers, but there aren't actually any witches.

Since both (10) and (11) are perfectly coherent (in fact, true), we can see that the existentially quantified statements (7) and (9) do not presuppose that there are any unicorns and witches. In general, statements of form (4) do not imply the existence of things being α. However, in many contexts, a listener is perfectly rational in concluding that the speaker thinks there are some α's unless he says something to defeat this belief.

A4.2.2 QUANTIFIERS

Students of logic often render the existential quantifier not just as 'at least one', but rather as 'some but not all'. However, this rendering is incorrect. The following PPL argument is invalid.

$$\exists F^1$$
$$\therefore \sim\forall F^1$$

The manner in which 'some' and 'not all' interact provides another case of conversational inference. If someone asserts (1), he is presumed to have beliefs about how all professors are. He is presumed to believe that not every professor is lazy; and on that assumption, by (1) the speaker intends to convey (2), and it would be odd to hear him later assert (3).

1. Some professors are lazy.

2. Not all professors are lazy.
3. All professors are lazy.

If he believed (3), we would expect him to assert the broader generalization before (1).

Despite these conversational considerations, the inference from (1) to (2) is cancelable; witness that (4) is perfectly coherent.

4. Some professors are lazy, perhaps all.

That (4) is perfectly intelligible and consistent constitutes strong evidence against the claim that (1) deductively implies (2).

A4.3 More on Literal Meaning

We are ordinarily inclined to understand the grammatical article 'a(n)' to mean 'one', or at least to be indicating singularity. But in some contexts 'a(n)' also indicates universality. (1) is best symbolized in PPL by (2).

1. A lion is in the building.
2. $\exists (L^1 \,\&\, B^1)$ L^1: is a lion; B^1: is in the building

But (3) is best symbolized in PPL by (4).

3. A lion is carnivorous.
4. $\forall (L^1 \supset C^1)$ C^1: is carnivorous

One might think that the difference between (1) and (3) is that in (3) we ascribe the general property of being a carnivore to lions, whereas in (1) we ascribe to lions no general property of being in the building. But what cues us as to when we are being presented with a general property and when we are not? Perhaps the prepositional phrase signals that (1) must have the existential reading (2).

However, consider (5)–(8).

5. A lion in the pen is a carnivore.
6. A lion in that genus is a carnivore.

7. A lion is fat.
8. A pig is fat.

(5) should be treated existentially, even though the 'general property' of being a carnivore is being attributed to a lion (in the pen). (6) is universal; so we cannot account for the existential character of (5) by appeal to the prepositional phrase.

Is (7) an existential statement? Is (8) a universal one? Surely whatever answer we give will have something to do with our knowledge of pigs and lions, and not any linguistic knowledge we have about the words in these statements. It is not easy to see how we could devise a principled way of discerning universal from existential statements by appeal to meaning and grammar alone. Frequently, non-linguistic knowledge assists us in fixing on an interpretation of a statement.

Even the definite article 'the', which we have assumed so far to indicate unique singularity, sometimes indicates universality. Definite descriptions like 'the United States' and 'the woman I love' seem singular, but in (9) the definite description 'The lion' indicates not singularity, but universality.

9. The lion is carnivorous.

We might try to read (9) as (10).

10. The class of lions is carnivorous.

With this reading, we might try to symbolize (9) as follows.

11. C^1t t: the class of lions

But (10) is false, whereas (9) is true. It is not the *class* of lions that is carnivorous; rather, it is the individual mammals making up this class. (9) makes no reference to a class. We will treat 'The lion' in (9) as not referring to anything. It acts as a quantifier ranging over individual members of the class of lions, and therefore (9) is best symbolized in PPL by (4).

4. $\forall(L^1 \supset C^1)$

(12), however, is best symbolized in PPL by (13), a straightforward simple subject–predicate statement.

12.   The lion is in the building.
13.   B^{1}t

Here 'The lion' indicates singularity.

  Along the same lines, consider the word 'or', which we noted in §6.5 could sometimes indicate logical conjunction. (14) is ambiguous. It could mean (16), but its most natural reading is the one where it paraphrases (15) and (17).

14.   Rainy days **or** Mondays always get me down.
15.   Rainy days always get me down **and** Mondays always get me down.
16.   Rainy days always get me down **or** Mondays always get me down.
17.   Rainy days **and** Mondays always get me down.

Similarly, (18) and (19) are synonymous.

18.   Vegetables **and** fruits are good for you.
19.   Vegetables **or** fruits are good for you.

The importance of reflecting upon context, rather than looking to any mere dictionary, is apparent in every example above.

A4.4   *Adjectival Modification and Predication*

A point stressed in chapter 11 and elsewhere in the book is that one distinctive trait of English (one not obviously shared by the signal systems of lower animals) is its productivity of combinations. We learn modes of composition as well as words, and are thus prepared to produce, and to respond to, tokens of complex expression types never before encountered. One productive mode of composition in natural language is the (adjective + noun) form in (1)–(4).

1.   Mary is a carnivorous mammal.
2.   Mary is a red shoe.
3.   Mary is a white table.
4.   Mary is a black rabbit.

Each of (1)–(4) has the grammatical form

5.   Noun is a(n) (adjective + noun)

We are able to understand the predicates in (1)–(4) partly because we know what their component words mean and partly because we know how to combine these meanings in order to understand the complexes. These particular examples of (adjective + noun) constructions are called *intersective*, because we understand these constructions to be true of just those things that, for example, are both red and shoes, as in (2). So, in symbolizing such constructions, we treat them as conjunctive. We treat both the adjective and the general noun which it grammatically modifies as predicative of the subject. Thus, for example, we symbolize (1) in PPL as

6. C^1m & M^1m m: Mary; C^1: is carnivorous; M^1: is a mammal

We adopt this approach because from (1) we can deductively infer (7) and (8), and from (7) and (8) together we can deductively infer (1).

7. Mary is carnivorous.
8. Mary is a mammal.

Similarly, for (2)–(4); they are symbolized in PPL as (9)–(11).

9. R^1m & S^1m R^1: is red; S^1: is a shoe
10. W^1m & T^1m W^1: is white; T^1: is a table
11. B^1m & R^1m B^1: is black; R^1: is a rabbit

However, not all (adjective + noun) constructions have the import of simple predication. Consider a so-called attributive adjective like 'large'. (12) does not imply (13), but it does imply (14).

12. John is a large flea.

13. John is large.
14. John is a flea.

A widespread view about attributive adjectives is that they express relations between objects and some comparison class. What counts as large in evaluating (12) depends on standards for being a flea. On this interpretation, (12) is true just in case John is large *for a flea*. The 'large for a flea' construction is not one we can adequately represent in PPL.

Now consider a different sort of adjectival modification. At least on one reading, (15) does not imply (16), whereas it does imply (17).

15. John is a gay activist.
16. John is gay.
17. John is an activist.

John could be a defender of gay rights without himself being gay. Constructions like (12) and (15) are called *subsective*.

There are also constructions in English with the grammatical form of (5), yet unlike (1)–(4) and (12) and (15), we should not infer (18), but may infer (19).

18. Noun is a noun.
19. Noun is adjective.

For example, (20) does not imply (21), but does imply (22).[5]

20. That painting is a counterfeit Vermeer.
21. That painting is a Vermeer.
22. That painting is a counterfeit.

Lastly, there are non-predicative examples – for example, (23)–(27) – that seem to have the same grammatical form as (5), yet we can infer neither (28) nor (29) from them.

23. John is a false friend.
24. John is an alleged murderer.
25. John is a reputed millionaire.
26. John is an ostensible ally.
27. John is a possible president.

28. Noun is an adjective.
29. Noun is a noun.

From (26), for example, we cannot infer either (30) or (31).

30. John is ostensible.
31. John is an ally.

Understanding statements containing expressions like 'perfect jerk', 'gay activist', 'false friend' involves understanding that the words 'perfect', 'gay', and 'false' do not modify the subjects in these statements. In addition, since conjunctive modification of the subject can break down in any of three ways, we might expect that the symbolizations in these three types of cases will exhibit different forms. Yet, within PPL we seem forced to treat these complex predicates as simple unanalyzed predicates. Therefore, under our current conventional guidelines for representing English in PPL, (12), (20), and (23) are symbolized as (32), (33), and (34) respectively.

12. John is a large flea.
20. That painting is a counterfeit Vermeer.
23. John is a false friend.

32. F^1j F^1: is a large flea; j: John
33. V^1b V^1: is a counterfeit Vermeer; b: that painting
34. A^1j A^1: is a false friend; j: John

But this treatment is unsatisfactory, since it does not bring out the distinctive contribution of adjectives like 'false', 'gay', and 'perfect' to the predicative nominatives in the statements; so it blocks deductively valid inferences. But this is the best we can do with present techniques for symbolizing

5. Noun is a(n) (adjective + noun)

constructions in PPL.[6] In order to uncover the kind of (non-predicative) modification involved in these 'deviant' examples, we would need to introduce either a new notation or new symbolization techniques for transforming English into PPL.[7]

A4.5 A Non-standard Quantifier – Most

The words 'all' and 'some' are of course not the only quantifiers to occur in English. Another prominent quantifier mentioned in §9.4 is 'most'. It's provable that this quantifier cannot be defined in PPL. It differs from 'some'. If 'Some fish swim' is true, then 'Something swims' is also true, but if 'Most fish swim' is true, it does not follow that 'Most things swim'. In this regard, 'most' is like 'every'. But 'most' differs from 'every' in other regards. If 'Every fish swims' is true, it follows that 'Every big fish swims'. But if 'Most fish swim' is true, it doesn't follow that 'Most big fish swim' is true. Still, we might try representing 'most' in an extension of PPL. So, consider (1).

1.   Most women are single.

Suppose we introduce the quantifier 'M' for 'most'. Can we identify the structure found in (1) by either (2) or (3)?

2. $(M)(W^1 \supset S^1)$ W^1: is a woman; S^1: is single
3. $(M)(W^1 \mathbin{\&} S^1)$

(3) cannot be correct; one can hold that most women are single without holding that most things are such that they are both women and single. What about (2)? Suppose that the domain of discourse consists mostly of things that are not women, but that, of the women, most are single. Then (1) and (4) will both be true if (2) correctly represents (1).

4.   Most women are not single.

(1) will be true since, when we examine all the women, we discover that most of them are single. (4) is true because when we examine the entire domain, we discover that most of the members are not women, which falsifies the antecedent of the complex conditional predicate 'if it's a woman, then it is not single', thereby making the predicate true of most things automatically, and therefore making (4) true. This is the central problem with translating 'most'. In order to make any statement of the form 'Most α are β' true, it is sufficient that most of the things in the domain not be α, surely an unintuitive result.

    In this book, we simply remain silent about, and pass over, the question of how best to accommodate the quantifiers 'most' and indefinitely many like quantifiers in logic. For further discussion see the bibliography at the end of chapter 11.

A5   Relational Predicate Logic

A5.1   *Passive Voice: Another Argument for Variables*

Our reason for introducing variables in §12.6 was based on a need for a notational device for tying quantifiers to positions in RPL predicates, as in

$(\forall x)(H^2jx \supset K^2jx)$

In this formula the first token of 'x' attaches to the universal quantifier, whereas the second and third tokens of 'x' are both in the second position of the two predicates 'H²' and 'K²', indicating that the universal quantifier binds these two places.

We now consider a different type of argument for introducing variables. How should statements like (1)–(4), where more than one quantifier binds the same relational predicate, be symbolized in RPL?

1. Something loves everything.
2. Something loves something.
3. Everything loves everything.
4. Everything loves something.

We might try one of the following three strategies, each representing a return to pre-variable notation.

	Strategy 1	Strategy 2	Strategy 3	
1'.	$\exists\forall L^2$	$L^2\exists\forall$	$\exists L^2\forall$	L^2: loves
2'.	$\exists\exists L^2$	$L^2\exists\exists$	$\exists L^2\exists$	
3'.	$\forall\forall L^2$	$L^2\forall\forall$	$\forall L^2\forall$	
4'.	$\forall\exists L^2$	$L^2\forall\exists$	$\forall L^2\exists$	

But then, how should (5)–(8) be symbolized, assuming the adequacy of any one of these three strategies?

5. Everything is loved by something.
6. Something is loved by something.
7. Everything is loved by everything.
8. Something is loved by everything.

First we might try converting (5)–(8) into the active voice, following the convention of §12.4, and then symbolize in RPL from the active voice (i.e., (1)–(4)) accordingly. (7) is the passive voice of (3), and therefore it is symbolized as any one of (3'). (6) is the passive voice of (2), and therefore is symbolized as any one of (2'). So far, so good; but what about (5) and (8)? These are the passive voice of active (1) and (4) respectively. Are (5) and (8) therefore to be symbolized as (1') and (4') respectively? Following convention §12.4 about passivization, this is the conclusion we must draw; but is it right? Contrary to what that convention claims about all active/passive pairs, (5) and (8) do *not* mean the same as (1) and (4) respectively.

(5) says that everything is loved by something, which means that, for anything in the universe of discourse, there is something which loves it. It may be a different thing for each individual, but there is always at least one such thing. (1), on the other hand, seems stronger. It says that there is at least one thing which loves everything; it is the same thing which loves every thing. Imagine a universe of discourse with three individuals: a, b, c. Suppose a loves b, b loves c, and c loves a. In this universe of discourse, (5) is true because for every individual, there is an individual which loves it. However, (1) is false. Neither a, nor b, nor c loves every individual. Thus, (1) and (5) cannot have the same meaning since they do not even have the same truth conditions. It follows that they cannot be symbolized identically in RPL. A similar argument can be constructed to show that (4) and (8) are not synonymous.

If pairs (1) and (5) and (4) and (8) should not be symbolized identically, how then should (5) and (8) be symbolized? We might just amend the dictionary so that 'L^2' symbolizes 'loves' and '$L*^2$' symbolizes 'is loved by'. (5) and (8) would then be symbolized as (5′) and (8′) respectively.

5′. $\forall\exists L*^2$ $L*^2\forall\exists$ $\forall L*^2\exists$
8′. $\exists\forall L*^2$ $L*^2\exists\forall$ $\exists L*^2\forall$

This suggestion is flawed, however; it obliterates intuitively formally deductively valid arguments. The argument with (1) as premise and (5) as conclusion is deductively valid. ((5) does not imply (1), however.) Obviously, if some one thing loves everything, then everything has something or other which loves it: namely, this one thing which loves everything. Also, (8) implies (4), but (4) does not imply (8). If one thing is loved by everything, then clearly everything loves something: namely, this one thing loved by everything. The problem with the suggestion under consideration for symbolizing (5) and (8) is that if we opt for it, then we cannot show in RPL that these two arguments are in fact formally deductively valid in (our adulterated) RPL.

$\exists\forall L^2$ $\exists\forall L*^2$
$\therefore \forall\exists L*^2$ $\therefore\forall\exists L^2$

Since the premises and conclusions in these hybrid arguments have distinct relational predicates, they are deductively invalid. To appreciate that the arguments from (1) to (5) and from (8) to (4) are valid, we must recognize that they share the predicate 'loves'. We must devise a symbolization which affirms this. Variables provide just the needed ingredient.

Symbolizing (1)–(4) using variables issues in (9)–(12) respectively.

9. $(\exists x)(\forall y)L^2xy$
10. $(\exists x)(\exists y)L^2xy$
11. $(\forall x)(\forall y)L^2xy$
12. $(\forall x)(\exists y)L^2xy$

Quantifiers precede the predicate and bind in the correct order and number the variables which succeed the predicate. Both quantifiers and variables appear in the order they appear in English. In (1) 'Something' appears first, and 'everything' appears second. In its corresponding symbolization (9), the existential appears first, the universal appears second; the variable 'x' appears first, and the variable 'y' appears second.

(10) says that there is something x and something y such that x loves y. And so on for the rest.

How, then, do we employ variables for symbolizing passive voice constructions with double-nested quantifiers in general? The following procedure provides an adequate quide.

A5.1.1   PASSIVE VOICE FOR NESTED QUANTIFIER PROCEDURE

If an English statement is in the passive voice with nested quantifiers, symbolize the quantifiers in the order in which they appear in the statement, but switch the variable tokens which the quantifiers bind to the order they would have if the statement were in the active voice.

Following this procedure does not mean that we first switch – for example, (5) to (1) – to the active voice and then symbolize. This won't work, because (5) and (1) need not be true under the same circumstances, and therefore they are not logically equivalent. (5) and (1) must be symbolized differently. Following procedure §A5.1.1 correctly, (5) should be symbolized as (13).

5.   Everything is loved by something.

13. $(\forall x)(\exists y)\ L^2yx$

In (13), the quantifiers appear in the order in which they appear in the passive voice (5), but the variables appear in the order in which they would appear in the active voice (1). (13) captures exactly what (5) says. Thus, variables are needed for another type of statement in English – passive voice statements with nested quantifiers. How, then, should we symbolize (6)–(8)?

A5.2   *Properties of Relations*

Relations have properties. Some have particular logical interest. This section concentrates on properties of dyadic – that is, two-place – relations.

A5.2.1   SYMMETRY, ASYMMETRY, NON-SYMMETRY
Some dyadic relations are symmetric.

> A relation R is symmetric just in case if any individual a bears R to an individual b, then b bears R to a.

The phrase 'is a cousin of' expresses a symmetric relation. If Anna is a cousin of Belle, then Belle must be a cousin of Anna. Other symmetric relations include both being a coauthor with and touching (at least outside Washington DC). RPL admits symbolizations which attribute symmetry. (1) should be symbolized as (2).

1. 'is a cousin of' expresses a symmetrical relation.
2. $(\forall x)(\forall y)(C^2xy \supset C^2yx)$ C^2: is a cousin of

Some relations are asymmetric.

> A relation R is asymmetric just in case if an individual a bears R to an individual b, then b does not bear R to a.

The expression 'weighs more than' expresses an asymmetric relation. If Scout weighs more than Tiger, then Tiger does not weigh more than Scout. Other asymmetric relation predicates are 'is a child of' and 'is north of'. (3) is symbolized by (4).

3. 'weighs more than' expresses an asymmetric relation.
4. $(\forall x)(\forall y)(W^2xy \supset {\sim}W^2yx)$ W^2: weighs more than

A relation which is neither symmetric nor asymmetric is non-symmetric. (5) may be symbolized by (6).

   5. 'loves' expresses a non-symmetric relation.
   6. $\sim(\forall x)(\forall y)(L^2xy \supset L^2xy)$ & $\sim(\forall x)(\forall y)(L^2xy \supset \sim L^2yx)$ L^2: loves

A5.2.2 TRANSITIVITY, INTRANSITIVITY, NON-TRANSITIVITY

A relation R is transitive just in case if an individual a bears R to an individual b and b bears R to an individual c, then a bears R to c.

The phrase 'is greater than' expresses a transitive relation; if five is greater than three and three is greater than one, then five must be greater than one. Other transitive relational predicates are 'is an ancestor of' and 'moves faster than'. (7) symbolizes (8).

   7. 'is greater than' expresses a transitive relation.
   8. $(\forall x)(\forall y)(\forall z)((G^2xy$ & $G^2yz) \supset G^2xz)$ G^2: is greater than

A relation R is intransitive just in case if an individual a bears R to an individual b, and b bears R to an individual c, then a fails to bear R to c.

The expression 'is a father of' is intransitive; if Art is the father of Brad, and Brad the father of Clark, then Art cannot be Clark's father.[8] Other examples are 'is two inches taller than' and 'is the immediate successor of'. (9) may be symbolized by (10).

   9. 'is a father of' expresses an intransitive relation.
  10. $(\forall x)(\forall y)(\forall z)((F^2xy$ & $F^2yz) \supset \sim F^2xz)$ F^2: is a father of

A relation which is neither transitive nor intransitive is non-transitive. Sample non-transitive relational predicates are 'admires', 'is ten feet from', and 'fears'. (11) may be symbolized by (12).

  11. 'admires' expresses a non-transitive relation.
  12. $\sim(\forall x)(\forall y)(\forall z)((A^2xy$ & $A^2yz) \supset A^2xz)$ &
       $\sim(\forall x)(\forall y)(\forall z)((A^2xy$ & $A^2yz) \supset \sim A^2xz)$ A^2: admires

A5.2.3 Total reflexivity, reflexivity, irreflexivity, and non-reflexivity

A relation R is totally reflexive if and only if every individual bears R to itself.

The phrase 'is identical with' is totally reflexive, since every individual is identical with itself. In RPL (13) symbolizes (14).

13. Identity is a totally reflexive relation.
14. $(\forall x)I^2xx$ I^2: is identical to

Examples of total reflexivity are uncommon and trivial. *Plain* reflexivity is different and more common.

A relation R is reflexive if and only if any individual that enters into the relation R bears R to itself.

Logical entailment is a reflexive relation, but not a totally reflexive relation. If we think of our universe of discourse as containing statements and physical objects, for example, then not everything entails itself. The city of Boston does not entail itself (since cities are not statements). So, logical entailment is not totally reflexive.[9] (15) is symbolized by (16).

15. Logical entailment is a reflexive relation.
16. $(\forall x)((\exists y)(E^2xy \lor E^2yx) \supset E^2xx)$ E^2: logically entails

Every totally reflexive relation is a reflexive relation. (Prove this, using the truth tree method.)

A relation R is irreflexive if and only if every individual does not bear R to itself.

The phrase, 'is a mother of' expresses an irreflexive relation; no woman is her own mother. Similarly, 'stands next to' is irreflexive. (18) symbolizes (17).

17. 'is a mother of' expresses an irreflexive relation.
18. $(\forall x)\sim M^2xx$ M^2: is a mother of

A relation which is neither reflexive nor irreflexive is non-reflexive. Thus 'kills' and 'respects' express non-reflexive relations. Some who kill others do not kill themselves, and some do. (19) is symbolized by (20).

19. 'kills' expresses a non-reflexive relation.
20. $\sim(\forall x)((\exists y)(K^2 xy \lor K^2 yx) \supset K^2 xx)$ & $\sim(\forall x)\sim K^2 xx$ K^2: kills

Every dyadic relation has at least one (and usually just one) property from the 'symmetry' group, at least one from the 'transitivity' group, and at least one from the 'reflexivity' group. Being older than, for example, is asymmetrical, transitive, and irreflexive.

Properties of relations   Exercise A.1

- Symbolize (1)–(3).

1. 'is two inches taller than' expresses an asymmetrical relation.
2. 'is two inches taller than' expresses an intransitive relation.
3. 'is two inches taller than' expresses an irreflexive relation.

Arguments   Exercise A.2

- Symbolize arguments (1)–(4) in RPL.
- Use the dictionary provided.

1. Jocasta was a parent of Oedipus. Jocasta and Oedipus were parents of Polyneices. Thus, it is false that 'is a parent of' expresses an intransitive relation. (j: Jocasta; o: Oedipus; p: Polyneices; P^2: is parent of)
2. Every descendant of Adam possesses original sin. Mary is a descendant of Adam. And 'descends' expresses a transitive relation. Thus, if Jesus is a descendant of Mary, then Jesus possessed original sin. (D^2: is a descendant of; a: Adam; m: Mary; j: Jesus; O^1: possesses original sin)
3. Everybody doesn't like something, but nobody doesn't like Sara Lee. So, it is false that 'likes' expresses a symmetric relationship. (P^1: is a person; L^2: likes; s: Sara Lee)
4. Someone is the brother of someone. But no one is his own brother. This shows that 'is a brother of' does not express a transitive relation.

(Missing premise: 'is a brother of' expresses a symmetric relation) (P^1: is a person; B^2: is brother of)

Exercise A.3   **Truth trees**

• Construct truth trees for (1) and (2).

1. 'R^2' is transitive; it is also symmetric. So, it is reflexive.
2. 'R^2' is asymmetric. So, it is not symmetric.

A6   Relational Predicate Logic with Identity

A6.1   *'Only' and Existential Import*

As stated previously (§11.5), when 'only' modifies a general term as in (1),

1. Only women are enrolled at Douglass College.

we symbolize such statements as universals, as in (2).

2. $(\forall x)(E^1x \supset W^1x)$
   E^1: is enrolled at Douglass College; W^1: is a woman

Yet (1) seems to have existential import. It seems to assert that some women are enrolled at Douglass College; (3), which seems contradictory, supports this intuition.

3. Only women are enrolled at Douglass College, but yet no women are enrolled there.

If (3) is self-contradictory, we would have to go back and reevaluate our convention from §11.5. There is indeed another reason to do so; we have been assuming that (4) should be symbolized as (5).

4. Only Everest is worth climbing.
5. $(\forall x)(W^1x \supset x = e)$ W^1: is worth climbing; e: Everest

(5) does not imply that Everest is worth climbing, yet (4) seems to have this implication. Perhaps we should modify our convention for symbolizing a statement like (4), so that it is correctly symbolized in RPL⁼ as (6).

6. $(\forall x)(W^1x \supset x = e)$ & W^1e

The worry we are confronting here is not exactly novel for us. We worried about these sorts of considerations when we asked about the existential import of universal claims in general (in §A4.2.1). When we introduced the universal quantifier in PPL, we noted that statements of the form

7. $\forall(\alpha \supset \beta)$

do not imply statements of the form

8. $\exists(\alpha \ \& \ \beta)$

What we are seeing with 'only', I suspect, is the same phenomenon; except that it seems more vivid with statements involving identity, like (5).

A6.2   Descriptions and Anaphora

Consider a different type of argument, which favors replacing a singular term treatment of definite descriptions with a quantifier treatment. Were we to try to symbolize (1) in RPL, treating 'the owner that feeds it' as a singular term, we would get (2).

1.   Every dog loves the owner that feeds it.
2. $(\forall x)(D^1x \supset L^2xt)$ D^1: is a dog; L^2: loves;
                                                            t: the owner that feeds it

The problem is obvious. If 'the owner that feeds it' is a singular term in (1), then it lacks internal structure. But we have no way to capture in RPL the fact that the 'it' in (1) has 'every dog' as its anaphor.

   Statements like (1) remind us that very often we can quantify into a definite description. We cannot quantify into a singular term. What can the expression 'the owner that feeds it' refer to? However, if we treat 'the' in (1) as a quantifier, recovering the correct symbolization for (1) becomes trivial. We merely note that the general term 'owner' inside this description is being modified by a restrictive relative clause. Therefore, in symbolizing (1) in RPL⁼, we invoke not only the definite description quantifier procedure, but also the universal quantifier procedure and the restrictive relative clause procedure from chapters 12–15.

So with the dictionary L^2: loves; O^2: owns; F^2: feeds; D^1: is a dog, we get (3) as a first step towards an RPL⁼ symbolization of (1).

3. $L^2_{\forall D^1, TheO^*}$

The asterisk should be familiar; it indicates that there is a restrictive relative clause modifying 'O^1'. Applying the universal quantifier procedure first issues in (4).

4. $(\forall x)(D^1x \supset L^2x_{TheO^*})$

Next apply the definite description quantifier procedure to '$L^2x_{TheO^*}$' to derive (5).

5. $(\forall x)(D^1x \supset (\exists y)(O^*y \ \& \ (\forall z)(O^*z \supset z = y) \ \& \ L^2xy))$

Next unpack the relative clause. 'O^*y' means 'y is an owner that feeds it'. Using the dictionary we get '$(O^2y, "it" \ \& \ F^2y, "it")$', leaving the question, 'who is "it"?' The answer is obvious: 'x', issuing, finally, in (6).

6. $(\forall x)(D^1x \supset (\exists y)((O^2yx \ \& \ F^2yx) \ \& \ (\forall z)((O^2zx \ \& \ F^2zx) \supset z = y) \ \& \ L^2xy))$

A6.3   *Existence*

Many true statements contain non-referring singular terms. How are we to symbolize statements like (1) and (2) in RPL⁼?

1.   Dracula doesn't exist.
2.   There is no Sherlock Holmes.

Suppose we try (3) for (1).

3. $\sim(\exists x) \ x = d$

(3) cannot be right, because it is a logical contradiction; yet (1) seems only contingently, not logically, false. Any truth tree for (3) closes. (Even

if you think (1) is not true, you don't think so on account of logic!) The reason why (3) is a logical contradiction is simple: in RPL⁼, every singular term requires a referent in its universe of discourse. In philosophical parlance, there are no *empty* names in RPL⁼. Therefore, every statement like (4) is not only true, but logically true.

4. (∃x) x = s

Many logicians criticize this feature of RPL⁼. Letting 'g' represent 'God', here's a simple proof that God exists!

√1. ~(∃x)x = g   (negation of conclusion)
  2. g = g   II
  3. (∀x)x ≠ g   1, QE
  4. g ≠ g   3, UQ
         ×

Obviously something has gone wrong. Proving God's existence can't be that easy. Equally obviously true, English statements like (1) cannot be represented in RPL⁼ by (3), on the pain of inconsistency. Many attempts have been made to deal with these problems in the history of logic: for example, forfeiting the assumption that every name must have a referent in its universe of discourse, treating 'exists' as a predicate different in meaning from '∃', or treating proper names as disguised definite descriptions. All these suggestions are interesting, and none of them should be dismissed out of hand. In this book we will leave these problems unsettled, however.

Argument   Exercise A.4

- Symbolize the following argument into RPL⁼.
- Make up your own dictionary.

1. The perfect being has all positive perfections. Existence is a perfection. So, the perfect being has existence.

A6.4   *Intensionality*

Argument (1)–(3) is invalid.

1. Andrea intended to go to Bressanone.
2. Bressanone is identical to Brixen.
3. Therefore, Andrea intended to go to Brixen.

But why is it invalid? Three cases involving identity need to be considered, one of which is trivial and another false. So, consider the following three identity statements (4)–(6).

4. Brixen is identical to Brixen.
5. Brixen is identical to Bolzano.
6. Brixen is identical to Bressanone.

(4) is trivially true; (5) is false; but (6) is neither trivially true nor trivially false. It is informative – that is, non-trivial – because it joins distinct names. At the same time, it happens to be true; its two name types are true of the same city in the Dolomites. But it is not the names that are affirmed to be identical. They are not identical. Rather, it is the Italian city which they name.

   Informative identity statements are the ones in which the named objects are the same, yet the names differ. No linguistic investigation of the names in a statement of identity will suffice, ordinarily, to determine whether an identity holds or fails. The identities (7)–(9) all depend for their substantiation upon inquiry into extra-linguistic matters of fact.

7. Hesperus = Phosphorus.
8. Mark Twain = Samuel Clemens.
9. $E = mc^2$

A6.5   *Properties of the Identity Relationship*

In §A5.2 we noted that relations have properties of logical interest. The relevant properties for identity are that it is reflexive, symmetric, and transitive.

Reflexivity: $(\forall x)x = x$
Symmetry: $(\forall x)(\forall y)(x = y \supset y = x)$
Transitivity: $(\forall x)(\forall y)(\forall z)((x = y \ \& \ y = z) \supset x = z)$

Interestingly, these three properties alone do not uniquely determine the identity relation. Many relationships have all three properties. Name some. So what distinguishes identity from other reflexive, symmetric, and transitive relations? And can these properties be stated (or 'captured') within the confines of RPL⁼? These are important and difficult questions, but not ones that we will settle here.

A6.6   *Definite Descriptions and Conversational Inferences*

The theory of definite descriptions in §16.5, though undoubtedly one of the major achievements of philosophical logic, has not been without its critics. Some philosophers believe that the theory does not do justice to ordinary usage. Recall that according to this theory, descriptions quantify and do not refer. Throughout this book, right up to chapter 16, treating descriptions as singular terms did not create any problems. How was that possible? If definite descriptions are not singular terms, then why were we so successful in so many cases in treating them as such? Perhaps we should conclude that there are two types of descriptions in English: singular terms and quantifier expressions.

Suppose two people in line at a supermarket see a very young-looking woman behind the cash register. One says to the other, 'The cashier looks awfully young to be working'. How are we to make sense of this statement if it so happens that the speaker is not referring to the young woman standing behind the cash register? Indeed, should it turn out that this young woman is only the daughter of the cashier, who just stepped outside for a moment, wouldn't we still take the speaker to be referring to this young woman, and not to the 'real' cashier? But how is this possible on the account of definite descriptions endorsed in chapter 16?

We already have at our disposal the means to distinguish referring and non-referring uses of definite descriptions without positing two types of definite descriptions in English. In particular, we have the very useful distinction between a deductively valid inference and a conversational inference. This distinction encourages us to separate what a speaker actually states from what she conversationally implies. In the context in which 'The cashier looks awfully young to be working' was uttered, the speaker intended to convey information about some particular individual – regardless of whether she was in fact the cashier or not. What was actually stated was that the cashier looks too young to be working, but since the young woman is not in fact the cashier, the statement uttered is false. Still, the desired information can be successfully conveyed.

A6.7   The Superlative

Consider argument (1)–(2).

1.   No one was better at quarterback than Joe Montana.
2.   So, Montana was a better quarterback than anyone.

Can we define 'best' in terms of 'better than' alone? Does the word 'best' connote uniqueness, or is this merely a conversational inference (see §3.2)? It is true that when one asks who the best runner in the country is, one expects a single answer naming one individual, but can't we say two best?

Consider the following definition of equivalence.

3. $(\forall x)(x$ is equivalent to y just in case $(\sim B^2xy \ \& \ \sim B^2yx))$
$$B^2: \text{ was better at quarterback than}$$

When one says that Montana was the best quarterback in football, is one saying anything more than that there was no one better than Montana and no one equivalent to Montana (in quarterback prowess)? That is, should we symbolize (1) as (4)?

4. $(\forall x)((P^1x \supset \sim B^2xm) \ \& \ \sim(\sim B^2xm \ \& \ \sim B^2mx))$
$$P^1: \text{ is a person; m: Joe Montana}$$

Is (4) a correct symbolization? How you answer the question about the relationship between the comparative and the superlative will be determined by your linguistic intuitions. Do you think that if someone says that Joe Montana is best quarterback, this implies that there is no quarterback as good as he is? Or do you think that there can be three best quarterbacks? And if there can be three best quarterbacks, does this imply that there is no best quarterback? Utilize your knowledge of conversational inferences in thinking this through. But on the assumption that you think 'the best' means the best and that no one is better, you must go with the RPL$^=$ (5).

5. $(\forall x)((P^1x \ \& \ x \neq m) \supset B^2mx)$

(5) makes it clear that Montana is the best.

A6.8 Identity and Predicative Adjectives

Note that (1) is equivalent to (2):

1. $(\exists x)(M^1x \mathbin{\&} j = x)$ $\qquad\qquad$ M^1: is a man; j: John
2. John is a man.

But it's not obvious that (1) is the best representation of the structure of (2). (1) treats the 'is' in (2) as the 'is' of identity, but this cannot be right. If it were, then we ought to be able to use it as the 'is' of identity in more complex constructions, but this doesn't seem to come out right:

3. *He is a man and John.

If the 'is in (2) were just the 'is' of identity, then we would expect that it would be okay in (3), which would mean the same as (4):

4. $(\exists x)(M^1x \mathbin{\&} h = x) \mathbin{\&} h = j$

Contrast the case of (2) and (3) with the following sentences.

> He kicked Jane.
> He kicked a man.
> He kicked a man and Jane.

So, as tempting as it might seem to treat (2) as harboring an identity, we will not do so.

A7 Verbs and their Modifiers

In the subsections that follow we will look at additional data that support the event approach.

A7.1 Infinitives and Gerunds

Notice that in English, infinitives are sometimes noun phrases, as in (1).

1. To run is better than to walk.

In (1), 'to run' is the subject. Similarly, gerunds can be noun phrases, as in (2).

2. Running is better than walking.

'Running' is the subject of (2). How might we symbolize (1) and (2) in RPL? We might try symbolizing them as universals, as in (3).

3. $(\forall x)(R^1x \supset (\forall y)(W^1y \supset B^2xy))$

The central question here is what the quantifiers range over. Do they range over people? If so, then assuming we interpret 'R^1' as 'is a runner' and 'W^1' as 'is a walker' and 'B^2' as 'is better than', then (3) would be most naturally interpreted in English as (4).

4. Every runner is better than every walker.

This clearly is not what (1) and (2) mean. For one thing, (1) and (2) do not exclude the possibility that someone can be both a runner and a walker, yet running might still be better than walking. However, (4) rules this out, since no one can be better than himself. To see that this is forced on us by the current convention for symbolization, consider the invalid argument (5)–(8).

5. Running is better than walking.
6. John is a runner.
7. Bill is a walker.
8. Therefore, John is better than Bill.

Although obviously invalid, this argument would be deemed deductively valid by the proposed symbolization convention. To see that this is so, consider argument (9)–(12).

9. $(\forall x)(R^1x \supset (\forall y)(W^1y \supset B^2xy))$
10. R^1j
11. W^1b
12. $\therefore B^2jb$

This argument is valid in RPL. (Construct a truth tree for it to convince yourself.) Therefore, we need another symbolization convention.

Here's another example that argues against the current symbolization convention. Consider the intuitively valid argument (13)–(16).

13. Loving is better than fighting.
14. John loves Mary.
15. John fights (argues) with Mary.
16. So, John's loving Mary is better than John's fighting (arguing) with Mary.

How should we symbolize (13)–(16) in RPL? The convention used for symbolizing (5)–(8) will not even get us off the ground. If 'a' picks out John's loving Mary, 'b' picks out John's fighting Mary; then we get (17)–(20).

17. $(\forall x)(L^1 x \supset (\forall y)(F^1 y \supset B^2 xy))$ L^1: is a loving; F^1: is a fighting
18. $L^2 jm$ L^2: loves; j: John; m: Mary
19. $F^2 jm$ F^2: fights
20. $\therefore B^2 ab$ B^2: is better than

(17)–(20) is invalid. Yet, again, (13)–(16) seems intuitively valid. What is nice about the event approach is that it recommends an easy and illuminating way to solve all these problems simultaneously. We symbolize (5)–(8) as (21)–(24).

21. $(\forall x)((\exists y)R^2 xy \supset (\forall z)((\exists y_1)W^2 zy_1 \supset B^2 xz)))$
          R^2: is a running by; W^2: is a walking by
22. $(\exists x)R^2 xj$
23. $(\exists x)W^2 xf$
24. $\therefore B^2 jf$

(21)–(24) is deductively invalid, and it is invalid for the right reason. Just because running is better than walking and John is a runner and Frank is a walker, nothing follows about John's being better than Frank. The first question one should ask is 'Better at what'? What follows is that John's runnings are better than Frank's walkings.

Notice that (5) states that events of running are better than events of walking. This naturally leads to (13)–(16). It should be symbolized as (25)–(28).

25. $(\forall x)((\exists y)(\exists z)L^3xyz \supset (\forall x_1)((\exists y_1)(\exists z_1)F^3x_1y_1z_1 \supset B^2xx_1))$
26. $(\exists x)L^3xjm$ L^3: __ is a loving by __ of __
27. $(\exists x)F^3xjm$ F^3: __ is a fighting by __ of __
28. $\therefore (\exists x)(L^3xjm \& (\exists y)(F^3yjm \& B^2xy))$

A7.2   Reference to Events

(1) and (2) unabashedly make reference to events and ascribe some property to them. With the event approach we can symbolize (1) and (2) as (3) and (4) in RPL$^=$.

1.   The sinking of the Titanic was a nasty event.
2.   The shooting was bloody.

3. $(\exists x)((S^2xt \& (\forall y)(S^2yt \supset x = y)) \& N^1x)$
                               S^2: is a sinking of; N^1: was nasty; t: Titanic
4. $(\exists x)((S^1x \& (\forall y)(S^1y \supset y = x) \& B^1x)$
                               S^1: was a shooting; B^1: was bloody

What we see in both these cases is that we can use identity to specify the unique events that were nasty and bloody respectively. With this convention, many intuitively valid arguments can be shown to be deductively valid in virtue of logical form.

Exercise A.5   Arguments and truth trees

- Symbolize and determine the validity of (1) and (2), using the truth tree method for RPL$^=$.

1.   The sinking of the Titanic was nasty. Therefore, something sank. (S^2: is the sinking of; t: Titanic; N^1: was nasty)
2.   John kissed Mary in the bathroom. Therefore, something happened in the bathroom. (j: John; m: Mary; b: the bathroom; K^3: __ was a kissing of __ by __ ; I^2: occurred in)

A7.3   The Logic of Perceptual Verbs

How should we symbolize (1)–(3) in RPL⁼?

1. Frank saw *Bill stab Jim.*
2. Terry watched *Mary jump into the lake.*
3. Perry heard *someone fall.*

In each of (1)–(3) the italicized clause is neither tensed nor infinitival in form; such constructions are sometimes called 'naked infinitives'.
   (1), for example, is not synonymous with (4).

4. Frank saw that Bill stabbed Jim.

(1) and (4) do not logically imply each other. The context after 'saw' in (4) is intensional (see §A6.4), whereas the context after 'saw' in (1) is not. (1) and (5) logically imply (6); but from (4) and (5), (7) does not logically follow.

5. Bill is Harry's best friend.
6. Frank saw Harry's best friend stab Jim.
7. Frank saw that Harry's best friend stabbed Jim.

As a first effort, try to represent (1) as the conjunction (8).

8. Frank saw Bill, and Bill stabbed Jim (at that time).

This cannot be right. If it were, then (10) should paraphrase (9), but it does not.

9. Frank heard Mary shoot Bill.
10. Frank heard Mary, and Mary shot Bill (then).

Frank might hear Mary shooting Bill without hearing Mary. She may have remained silent throughout the event. And Frank might hear Mary (because she is screaming while shooting Bill without hearing the shooting; maybe Mary screams really loudly).

The event approach extends to this type of sentence. On the event approach, what Frank saw was an event: namely, Bill's stabbing of Jim. (1) would be symbolized as (11) in RPL.

11. $(\exists x)(S^3 xbj \ \& \ (\exists y)P^3 yfx)$ S^3: ___ was a stabbing by ___ of ___ ;
                                                               P^3: ___ was a seeing by ___ of ___

Exercise A.6   Statements

- Symbolize statements (2) and (3) above in RPL⁼, according to the event approach, using your own dictionary.

A7.4   *Adjectival Modification Revisited*

We know from §A4.4 that problems exist with the customary treatment of adjectival modification as well. Suppose (1) is symbolized as the logical conjunction (2).

1.   Joe is a small elephant.
2. $E^1 j \ \& \ S^1 j$ E^1: is an elephant; s: is small; j: Joe

Presumably (3) is also true, naturally symbolized as (4).

3.   Joe is also a mammal.
4. $M^1 j$ M^1: is a mammal

But (2) and (4) together logically imply (5), the proposed symbolization of (6).

5. $M^1 j \ \& \ S^1 j$
6.   Joe is a small mammal.

This is intuitively incorrect. Again, we could reinterpret the symbolization so that it says at most that Joe is a mammal and Joe is small. But a small what?

This is not the only type of problem that arises with our current conventions for symbolization; certain special classes of modifiers allow other faulty inferences. For example, if we symbolize (7) as (8), we would license the inference to (9), by symbolization (10).

7. This is a fake diamond.
8. $(D^1t \& F^1t)$ F^1: is a fake; D^1: is a diamond; t: this

9. This is a diamond.
10. D^1t

A7.5   An Alternative Approach

In §17.5, we discussed some apparent problems that arise with the event approach. Confronted with these problems, some philosophical logicians have recommended alternative proposals for representing adverbial modification in logical notation. On one of these alternative proposals, we treat adverbs in our notation as modifying verbs. In notation, (1) would be symbolized as (2),

1. Frank runs slowly.
2. $[S]R^1f$ R^1: runs; f: Frank

where '[S]' attaches directly to the normal predicate 'R^1' to form the complex predicate 'runs slowly'.

This is a radical departure from the event approach, because it requires us to move to a notation very different from RPL. Advantages are supposed to be that it can accommodate the problem modifiers – for example, 'allegedly', as in (3).

3. Herman allegedly stole the cow.

(3) does not deductively imply (4).

4. Herman stole the cow.

According to this alternative proposal, simply put, we add rules that sanction some detachments: such as a rule which allows moving from (2) to (5), but no rule that would license a logical inference from, say, (6), a proposed symbolization for (3), to (7), a proposed symbolization for (4).

5. R^1f

6. $[A]S^2hc$ S^2: stole; h: Herman; c: the cow
7. S^2hc

It is beyond the scope of this book to offer detailed discussion, criticism, or development of this alternative approach. However, it is worth mentioning briefly a drawback it has.

It is that this alternative approach requires a new inference rule for each possible predicate modifier, telling which ones can detach and which ones cannot. This, on the face of it, seems *ad hoc*. It is not clear what the gain is in explanatory force. It would seem that the new approach simply describes the problem in a new vocabulary rather than solves it.

Notes

1   An interesting fact about English is that there is no reading of (4) such that red, blue, and red and blue flags are on the pole.
2   The following two subsections should not be read until after you have read ch. 5.
3   Ch. 10 contains a detailed discussion, including characterizations, of 'scope' extended to quantifiers.
4   Whether there are in fact two meanings here for the same statement, or whether we have used stress to create a conversational inference, are interesting questions which we address in ch. 15.
5   At least one writer argues that a decoy duck or a fake gun must be a duck and a gun respectively; otherwise, how are we to explain the intelligibility of questions like 'Is that duck a decoy or real?' 'Is that gun a fake or real?'
6   The non-predicative forms of modification pose another, more serious problem for the project of representing formally deductively valid arguments in logical notation. We want to symbolize (1) as (6). By so doing we commit ourselves to (1) being a logical conjunction and also to the inference from (1) to (8) being not only deductively valid, but *formally* deductively valid. However, if the inference from (1) to (8) is formally deductively valid, it follows that replacing non-logical expressions in (1) preserves formal deductive validity. We have plenty of evidence that this isn't so: simply replace 'carnivorous' in (1) by 'fake' or 'alleged'. So, unless we can devise a non-question-begging way of distinguishing adjectives like 'carnivorous' from adjectives like 'fake' and 'alleged', then either we must abandon the idea that the inference from (1) to (8) is formally deductively valid or, far worse, we must discard the idea that we can draw a substantive distinction between inferences that are valid

from those that are not by virtue of logical form. In this book we evade, unabashedly, this concern and treat statements like (1) as logical conjunctions (whatever that means).

7   The following two statements are not synonymous:

The United States has 50 states.
The United States has 50 and the United States has states.

In ch. 16 we augment our notation in order to depict this type of modification in logic.

8   The predicate 'is father of' may designate a biological or a legal relationship; the properties of these two relations differ. In this example we have in mind the biological relation.

9   Of course, if the universe of discourse is restricted to statements, then 'logical entailment' is totally reflexive.

Answers for Selected Exercises

Chapter 1

Exercise 1.1

1. Premise 1: If we are going to avoid a nuclear war in the next few years, we will have to adopt strong punitive measures now.
   Premise 2: But if we adopt such measures, many nations will be very unhappy.
   Conclusion: We are going to avoid a nuclear war in the next few years only if many nations are going to be unhappy.

2. Premise 1: The state will increase its financial support of our university only if the priorities of the legislature shift in favor of higher education.
   Premise 2: But if such a shift were to occur, the people who benefit from other state projects would complain bitterly.
   Premise 3: If the state does not increase the financial support for the university, tuition will have to be raised.
   Conclusion: Tuition will be raised.
   Missing premise 4: If the people who benefit from other state projects complain bitterly, then the state will not increase the financial support for the university.

3. Premise 1: If a man is to play some role in society, that role must be determined by nature or by society.
   Premise 2: However, if his role is determined by nature, that role will be the role of the selfish hunter on the make.

Conclusion: Either society determines a role for man, or man will play the role of selfish hunter always on the make.

4. Premise 1: If it is true that 30 out of every 50 college coeds have sexual intercourse outside marriage, then it is very important to have birth control information available from the Student Health Service.

Premise 2: It is very important to have birth control information available from the Student Health Service.

Conclusion: We know that 30 out of every 50 college coeds have sexual intercourse outside marriage.

Exercise 1.2

(1) is valid; (2) is invalid (there is no reason he can't do both; the first premise doesn't say he'll do both at the same time); (3) is invalid; (4) is valid; (5) is valid; (6) is invalid; (7) is valid; (8) is valid.

Exercise 1.3

Box 1: Every man has a head. Socrates is a man. So, Socrates has a head.

Box 2: Every man has a head. Socrates has a head. So, Socrates is a man.

Box 3: Every man has a tail. Everything with a tail has a head. So, every man has a head.

Box 4: Every man has a tail. Every man has a head. So, everything with a tail has a head.

Box 5: Impossible by definition of 'deductive validity'.

Box 6: Everyone in the National Basketball Association is over four feet tall. Your instructor is over four feet tall. Therefore, your instructor is in the National Basketball Association.

Box 7: All fish have wings. Everything with a wing has an arm. Therefore, all fish have arms.

Box 8: Ronald Reagan was Vice-President. Therefore, Donald Duck was President.

Exercise 1.4

1. Missing conclusion: Either the key is in my pocket, or we are locked out.
2. Missing premise: If Jerry publishes those photos, I lose my job.

Chapter 2

Exercise 2.1

1. 'Archie Leech' is a name of Cary Grant.
2. 'Italo Svevo' is a pseudonym of Ettore Schmitz.
3. Even if 'x' is the twenty-fourth letter of the alphabet, some writers have said 'x is the unknown'.
4. 'Oswerk' is not a word in English.

Exercise 2.2

1. True
2. False
3. False
4. True

Exercise 2.3

1. Ten tokens and ten types. No type occurs more than once.
2. Two (and not three, because although the first three letters of 'their' are 'the', it is not the case that the word 'the' is a part of the word 'their'.
3. Three.

Exercise 2.4

1. If O, then it is not the case that A. A. So, it is not the case that O. (O: Lee Harvey Oswald assassinated John F. Kennedy; A: Lee Harvey Oswald acted alone)
2. Either N or R. It is not the case that N. So, R. (N: Nixon was impeached; R: Nixon resigned the presidency of the United States)
3. S and H. Neither A nor V. So, it follows that it is not the case that E. (S: Spiro Agnew was Vice-President under Richard Nixon; H: Hubert H. Humphrey was Vice-President under Lyndon Baines Johnson; A: Spiro Agnew was (ever) President; V: Hubert Humphrey was (ever) President; E: Every Vice-President becomes President)

Chapter 3

Exercise 3.1

1. This sentence is ambiguous, one reading corresponding to what we get if 'he' refers back to Hercules, the other reading corresponding to what we get if he refers to someone completely different. Both readings are logical conjunctions, and we get two symbolizations for (1) corresponding to its two meanings: A & Q, A & H (A: Hercules will arrive tomorrow; Q: Hercules is quite strong; H: He is quite strong)

2. This statement is a logical conjunction: J & B (J: John ate meat; B: Bill ate fish)

3. This statement is a logical conjunction with three conjuncts: J & P & L (J: Michael Jordan is first in scoring; P: The Pistons are first in defense; L: The Lakers are first in offense)

4. This statement is a logical conjunction: F & G (F: A 55 mile per hour speed limit saves lives. G: Getting drunk drivers off the road could save even more lives (than a 55 mile per hour speed limit))

5. This statement is a logical conjunction: N & H (N: He aims for the naked truth; H: He hits the nation's jugular)

6. This statement is a logical conjunction: S & B (S: Simon is very happily married; B: Bill is miserably married)

7. This statement is a logical conjunction: A & J (A: John judged him to be awkward; J: John judged him to be acceptable. Note that in the conjuncts we must read 'him' as referring to the same person, so the sentence is unambiguous)

8. This statement is a logical conjunction: J & B (J: John likes to tease his own wife; B: Bill likes to tease his own wife)

9. This statement is a logical conjunction: O & H (O: He saw an old house; H: He saw an orange house. Note that, much as in (7), in the conjuncts we must read 'he' as referring to the same person, so this sentence is not ambiguous)

10. This statement is a logical conjunction: B & S (B: Mary is beautiful; S: Mary is strong)

11. This sentence is not a statement, and therefore not a logical conjunction.

12. This statement is a logical conjunction: N & B (N: Nick trimmed the garden; B: Bill weeded the garden)

13. This statement is a logical conjunction: J & O (J: John liked it; O: Others panned it)

14. This statement is a logical conjunction: P & A (P: Pro-forces were at work; A: Anti-forces were at work)
15. This statement is a logical conjunction with three conjuncts: G & A & T (G: Some are born great; A: Some achieve greatness; T: Some have greatness thrust upon them)
16. This statement is a logical conjunction: S & D (S: Fred Astaire sang; D: Fred Astaire danced)

Exercise 3.2

1. W & T (W: Danny went into a lengthy psychological analysis of Willy Loman's delusions; T: Danny talked about how crucial it was to be able to distinguish between reality and fantasy)
2. Simple statement.
3. Ambiguous; on its first reading it is a conjunction, J & M (J: Jan is married; M: Mary is married); on its second reading, it is not a conjunction, but a simple statement, J.
4. N (N: No barber gives any customer both a shave and a haircut)
5. Ambiguous; same as (3).
6. Simple statement.
7. Ambiguous; on its first reading it is a conjunction, J & B (J: John is a brother; B: Bill is a brother). On its second reading, it is not clear that it is not also a logical conjunction, A & C (A: John is brother to Bill; C: Bill is brother to John). The problem here is whether 'John' and 'Bill' must be names of men. If you think not (as I do), then on both readings (7) is a conjunction, since it doesn't follow that if John is Bill's brother, then Bill is John's brother, since Bill or John (but not both) might be a woman.
8. Ambiguous; on its first reading it is a conjunction, M & W (M: A man married yesterday; W: A woman married yesterday). On its second reading, it could also be a logical conjunction. This will depend upon your attitudes to marriage. If you think that a man may marry only a woman, and vice versa, then it is not a logical conjunction. But if you think that it's an open question, then it is a logical conjunction.
9. Ambiguous; J & B (J: John got in on one ticket; B: Bill got in on one ticket). However, if you think there is a single ticket on which both got in, then the statement is simple.
10. Simple statement.
11. Ambiguous; same as (3).

12. Ambiguous; R & B (R: Red flags are on the pole; B: Blue flags are on the pole) On the second reading, it is a simple statement.
13. This one is tricky. We examine it in chapter 16 when we take up identity. I would guess that most English speakers interpret this sentence to mean that you can come to the party and that no one else can come to the party, in which case it would be a logical conjunction, with a negation as its second conjunction.
14. Same as (13).
15. Same as (13).
16. Simple statement.
17. Simple statement. You might wonder how I could believe the conjunction without believing each of the conjuncts. Granted it would be irrational of me to do so, but not illogical. I might be psychologically incapable of separating the two subjects, Bill and Mary, in order to believe that Bill will be there.
18. Logical conjunction, four conjuncts. J & M & D & B (J: John sang; M: Mary sang; D: John danced; B: Mary danced)
19. Logical conjunction.
20. Logical conjunction, four conjuncts.
21. B & J (B: He saw Bill; J: He didn't see John)
22. Simple statement, idiom.
23. Simple statement.
24. Simple statement.
25. Simple statement.
26. Simple statement.
27. Again, ambiguous; same as (3).
28. Simple statement.
29. Simple statement.
30. Simple statement.

Chapter 4

Exercise 4.1

3. J & M (J: John stayed home all day; M: Mary stayed home all day)
4. ~J & ~S (J: John could solve the problem; S: Some of his friends could solve the problem). (Note that 'could' takes wide scope over 'not' in the left conjunct; that is, 'could not' does not mean the same thing as 'It is not the case . . . could'.)

5. ~J & ~M
6. ~B (B: He has (ever) been on time)
7. ~S (S: He saw (some)one he knows)
8. ~B
9. ~S (S: Someone read the book)
10. ~R (R: The book was read by (some)one)
11. ~S (S: Some of his students understand)
12. ~J (J: It is possible that Jack (ever) slept here) ('impossible' means the same as 'not possible')
13. ~C (C: He does go to church at the university)
14. ~I & ~N (I: This struck me as intelligible; N: I need to know further details)
15. ~A (A: I was aware at the time)
16. ~ ~S (S: My story is known)
17. ~P & R (P: Paranoid people are rare; R: Paranoid people are more dangerous than useful)
18. ~F (F: This is all Frank offers)

Exercise 4.2

1. K & J & N, ~(K & M) ∴ ~(N & M) (K: Kennedy was president; J: Johnson was president; N: Nixon was president; M: Mondale was president)
2. N ∴ ~ ~N (N: Notre Dame is beatable)
3. D & ~T ∴ ~T (D: I will do logic; T: I will take tests)

Exercise 4.3

1. Simple statement.
2. Negation: ~J (J: is likely that Jack ever slept here)
3. Simple statement.
4. Simple statement. From the fact that someone is not happy, it doesn't follow that he is unhappy about something.
5. My ear tells me that this is a negation. It's not the case that he saw something of interest in it.
6. Same as (1).
7. Ambiguous; on one reading, it is a negation: 'It's not the case that I will force you to marry someone'; on the other reading, it is a simple statement: 'I won't let you marry anyone'.
8. Single negation: ~E (E: Someone has nothing to eat)

9. Negation. It is not that often he doesn't really understand. You cannot pull out the second negation without changing the meaning; 'often' has wide scope over 'doesn't'.

10. Simple statement. Just because half the country doesn't like Clinton, it doesn't follow that it is false that half the country likes him. Maybe half *do* and half *don't*.

11. Negation (but not a double negation).

12. Negation.

13. Negation.

14. Negation.

15. Simple statement.

16. Negation.

17. Negation.

18. Simple statement.

19. Simple statement.

20. Simple statement. ('Many of the boys left' doesn't contradict 20)

21. Negation.

22. Negation.

23. Simple statement.

24. Negation.

25. Negation.

26. Simple statement.

27. Ambiguous. It is not the case that (John beats his wife because he loves her); because he loves her, it is not the case that John beats his wife.

28. Simple statement. We cannot remove the negation since 'I think John will arrive until Tuesday' is ungrammatical.

29. Simple statement.

30, 31. By my ear, (31) is more naturally read as a negation of a conjunction, but (30) is more naturally read as a conjunction of two negations – though much depends on context. Here is a context which makes the conjunctive reading salient for (31): Who went to the party? Only Fred and Mary. John and Bill didn't go.

Chapter 5

Exercise 5.1

1. This statement is well formed; it is a logical conjunction.

2. This statement is also well formed; it is also a logical conjunction.

3. This is not a well-formed statement.
4. This is not a well-formed statement.

Exercise 5.2

1. The scope of the second token of '&' is the entire formula.
2. The scope of the first token of '~' is the first conjunct '~P'.
3. The scope of the third token of '&' is the second conjunct '(R & ~S)'.

Exercise 5.3

1. Yes.
2. Yes.
3. Neither has wider scope than the other.
4. Yes, the first token of '&' has '~' within its scope.

Exercise 5.4

1. The second token of '&'.
2. The first token of '~'.
3. The sole token of '~'.
4. The first token of '&'.

Exercise 5.5

1. I S   ~(I & S),   S ∴ ~I

    T T   F   T   F
    F T   T   T   T
    T F   T   F   F
    F F   T   F   T

    This argument is valid. The only row in which the two premises are true, the conclusion is true as well (row 2).

2. N   ∴   ~ ~N

    T   T F
    F   F T

Valid. The first row is the only row with the premise true and the conclusion is true as well.

3.   D T   D & ~T   ∴   ~T

T T   F   F
F T   F   F
T F   T   T
F F   F   T

Valid. The third row is the only row with the premise true and the conclusion is true as well.

Chapter 6

Exercise 6.1

1. Not a statement; it's not true or false. It's either a command or an exhortation.
2. M ∨ F (M: John eats meat; F: Henry eats fish)
3. ~L & ~D (L: I demand liberty; D: I demand death)
4. ~(C ∨ T) (C: Coffee comes with the meal; T: Tea comes with the meal)
5. A ∨ S ∨ I (A: I'll be with Abby tonight; S: I'll be with Sharon tonight; I: I'll be with Igor tonight)
6. Ambiguous: ~(F ∨ E), ~F ∨ ~E (F: I had a good time in France; E: I had a good time in England)
7. ~(F ∨ L) (F: It has been the first experience to reinforce my belief; L: It has been the last experience to reinforce my belief)

Exercise 6.2

1. P ∨ R, ~R ∴ P (P: I will become a professor; R: I will become a rich man)
2. ~(S ∨ O) ∴ ~S (S: Shane is an officer; O: Omar is an officer)
3. ~(U ∨ J) ∴ ~(U & C) (U: The US was in the 1980 Olympics; J: Japan was in the 1980 Olympics; C: Canada was in the 1980 Olympics)
4. (F ∨ B) & ~M, ~F ∴ B (F: Frank is on the hill; B: Bill is on the hill; M: Mary is on the hill) (The English premise is ambiguous, though this interpretation is natural.)

Exercise 6.3

1. PR P ∨ R ~R ∴ P

TT	T	F		T
FT	T	F		F
TF	T	T		T
FF	F	T		F

This argument is valid, since in the only row (row 3) in which both premises are true, the conclusion is true as well.

2. SO ~(S ∨ 0) ∴ ~S

TT	F		F
FT	F		T
TF	F		F
FF	T		T

This argument is valid. The last row is the only row (row 4) in which the premise is true and the conclusion is true as well.

3. UJ C ~(U ∨ J) ∴ ~(U & C)

TT T	F		F
FT T	F		T
TF T	F		F
FF T	T		T
TT F	F		T
FT F	F		T
TF F	F		T
FF F	T		T

This argument is valid. The only rows (rows 4 and 8) in which the premise is true, the conclusion is true as well.

4. F B M (F ∨ B) & ~M ~F ∴ B

T T T	T	F	F	F		T
F T T	T	F	F	T		T

T F T	T	F F	F		F
F F T	F	F F	T		F
T T F	T	T T	F		T
F T F	T	T T	T		T
T F F	T	T T	F		F
F F F	F	F T	T		F

This argument is valid. The only row (row 6) in which both premises are true, the conclusion is true as well.

Chapter 7

Exercise 7.1

1. B ⊃ L
2. R ⊃ J
3. L ⊃ F
4. O ⊃ W
5. B ⊃ F
6. B ⊃ J

Exercise 7.2

1. J ⊃ R
2. R ⊃ A
3. ~H ⊃ L
4. L ⊃ T
5. ~P ⊃ S
6. ~~C ⊃ G

Exercise 7.3

1. (R ⊃ W) & (W ⊃ R)
2. S ∴ ~T
3. D ⊃ (C ⊃ E)
4. (O ⊃ C) & (C ⊃ O)
5. (O ⊃ C) & (C ⊃ O)

Exercise 7.4

1. Simple statement
2. Disjunction
3. Conjunction
4. Ungrammatical
5. Disjunction
6. Ungrammatical
7. Conditional
8. Disjunction
9. Conditional
10. Conjunction
11. Negation
12. Ungrammatical

Exercise 7.5

1. P ⊃ H (P: You pay for it; H: You can have it)
2. H ⊃ P (H: He does the exercise; P: He will pass the course)
3. B ⊃ M (B: You feed the birds; M: You will feed more birds)
4. C & O (C: The first two paragraphs are clear; O: The first two paragraphs are concise)
5. H ⊃ R (H: You stay healthy; R: You eat right)
6. A & M (A: He aimed at the target; M: He (still) missed the target)
7. D ⊃ S (D: You do that; S: I am your slave)
8. Ambiguous: B & W (B: Mary has black cats; W: Mary has white cats) Or just a simple statement (M: Mary has black and white cats)
9. S ∴ D (S: I started early; D: I will be done early) ('since' indicates premise and conclusion)
10. Q Simple statement
11. D Simple statement
12. ~T (T: Tax forms are as complicated as they once were)
13. (G & F) ⊃ (D & H) (G: Graff defeats Seles; F: Fernandez defaults; D: Graff goes to the finals; H: Hingis goes to the finals)
14. B ⊃ (P & ~S) (B: Bacon and eggs will be served for breakfast ('and' idiomatic); P: They run out of pancakes; S: They serve sweet rolls)
15. (F ⊃ E) & ((F & E) ⊃ M) (F: There is freedom; E: There is equality; M: All men are happy)
16. H & C (H: You had cake; C: I had cherries)

17. ~T & (A ⊃ ~E) (T: I can tell you (any)more; A: I am accepted (now); E: It can be enjoyable for me to reflect that some calculation tipped the scale)

18. N ⊃ (F ⊃ ~S) (N: New York City is in the USA; F: France is north of India; S: South Bend is somewhere)

19. E & (W ⊃ H) (E: John went east; W: John went west; H: John would be here now)

20. R ⊃ G (R: You get rich; G: You get into law school)

21. G ⊃ R

22. (R ⊃ G) & (G ⊃ R)

23. (G ⊃ R) & (R ⊃ G)

24. ((R & B) ⊃ G) & (G ⊃ (R & B)) (B: You stay bored)

25. (R ⊃ G) & (G ⊃ B)

26. H ⊃ G (H: You work hard; G: You will graduate)

27. G ⊃ H

28. H ⊃ G

29. (H ⊃ G) & (G ⊃ H)

30. S ⊃ (C ⊃ R) (S: You have a specific question; C: He calls; R: We will relay it to him)

31. W ⊃ (H & O) (W: The windows are open; H: We get hot air; O: We get outside noise)

32. (S & L) ⊃ C (S: South Vietnam goes (Communist); L: Laos goes (Communist); C: Cambodia goes (Communist))

33. M & (B ⊃ L) (M: Mary visited the team; B: Bill is there; L: Mary leaves)

34. Y ⊃ (M ⊃ R) (Y: The Yankees win the pennant; M: The Yankees play Montreal; R: I root for the Montreal)

35. M & (B ∨ J) (M: Mary left; B: Bill left; J: Julie stayed)

36. (D & R & ~H) ⊃ C (D: The news is delayed; R: You receive the main selection; H: You had ten days to notify us; C: You may return (the main selection) for credit at our expense)

37. (U & I) ⊃ (A & C) (U: Man may usefully cooperate; I: Man improves the life of the community; A: There must be freedom to assess views which seem to have validity; C: There must be freedom to compare views which seem to have validity)

38. Not a statement, an imperative.

39. Again, not a statement.

40. (G ⊃ J) & (~G ⊃ ~B) (G: You obey God's laws; J: Being a Jew is worth something; B: You are better off than a heathen)

41. (D ⊃ A) & (~D ⊃ A) (D: You do; A: You are damned)

42. (P & W & E) ⊃ (D & ~S) (P: It can be proved that dreams possess a value of their own as psychological acts; W: Wishes are the motive for (dreams') construction; E: Experiences of the preceding day provide the immediate material for (dreams') content; D: Any theory of dreams which neglects so important a procedure of research and accordingly represents dreams as a useless and puzzling reaction to somatic stimuli stands condemned; S: There is a necessity for specific criticism.) (Notice that 'D' is not a conjunction because of the restrictive relative clause.)

Exercise 7.6

1.   P ⊃ R, R ⊃ ~S, A ⊃ S ∴ P ⊃ ~A
2.   M, L ⊃ ~M, M ⊃ U, U ⊃ ~L ∴ ~L
3.   W ⊃ U, ~U ∴ ~W
4.   V ⊃ (B ⊃ T), V, B, ~W ⊃ ~T, ~C ⊃ ~W ∴ C
5.   ((H & T) ⊃ ~I) & I, P, (T ⊃ P) & (P ⊃ T) ∴ ~H
6.   I ⊃ ((H ⊃ L) & (~H ⊃ ~G)), ~(L ∨ ~G) ∴ ~I
7.   B ⊃ ((E ⊃ G) & (~E ⊃ ~L)), ~B ⊃ ((E ⊃ L) & (~E ⊃ ~G))
     ∴ (B ⊃ (G ∨ ~L)) & (~B ⊃ (L ∨ ~G))
8.   (D ⊃ (~S ⊃ ~W)) & (D ⊃ ~S) ∴ D ⊃ ~W
9.   D ⊃ ~G, (~G ⊃ ~A) & (~A ⊃ ~K), K ⊃ B ∴ B ⊃ ~D
10. ~ ~M ⊃ G, (~P ⊃ M) & (R ⊃ ~G) ∴ R ⊃ ~M
11. H, E, (H & E) ⊃ ~I ∴ ~I
12. ~(C & P), ~C ⊃ A, ~A ∴ ~P
13. ~C ⊃ ~H, (~~E ⊃ C) & (C ⊃ ~~E), ~E ∴ ~H
14. (T & J) ⊃ R, ~R ∴ ~T & ~J
15. P ⊃ ~(C ∨ S), ~ ~C & ~ ~S ∴ ~P
16. G ⊃ E, E ⊃ C, ~C ∴ ~G
17. (L ⊃ W) & (P ⊃ A), E ∴ ~(L & P) Missing premise: (W & A) ⊃ ~E
18. R ⊃ S, ~R ⊃ ~H, H ⊃ ~S ∴ ~H
19. ~D ⊃ R, ~D ∴ R
20. (F & B) ⊃ (~M ⊃ J), ~J ⊃ ~B ∴ (J ⊃ M) & (M ⊃ J)
21. T ⊃ (D ⊃ S), B & ~D, T ⊃ ~F ∴ (B & F) ⊃ (D & T)
22. B ⊃ T, W ⊃ B ∴ W ⊃ T
23. ((C & T) ⊃ B) & ~B ∴ (T ⊃ C) & (C ⊃ T)
24. G ⊃ T, ~T ∴ ~G
25. ~T ⊃ ~(W ∨ R), T ⊃ ~(W ∨ R) ∴ ~(W ∨ R)
26. ~E ⊃ ~M, M ∴ E

Exercise 7.7

2. S M J   ((S ⊃ M) & (M ⊃ S)) & ((~ J ⊃ ~S) & ~ J)


```
T T T     T   T   T     F  F  T F    F F
F T T     T   F   F     F  F  T T    F F
T F T     F   F   T     F  F  T F    F F
F F T     T   T   T     F  F  T T    F F
T T F     T   T   T     F  T  F F    F T
F T F     T   F   F     F  T  T T    T T
T F F     F   F   T     F  T  F F    F T
F F F     T   T   T     T  T  T T    T T
                             *
```

The "*" here indicates the main connective.

Exercise 7.8

1. E F   E ⊃ F   ∴   ~F ⊃ ~E

```
T T    T          F T  F
F T    T          F T  T
T F    F          T F  F
F F    T          T T  T
```

This argument is valid because in the three rows (1, 2, and 4) in which the premise is true, the conclusion is true as well.

2. D B C   D ⊃ (B & C)   ∴   B ⊃ (C ⊃ D)

```
T T T    T    T           T    T
F T T    T    T           F    F
T F T    F    F           T    T
F F T    T    F           T    F
T T F    F    F           T    T
F T F    T    F           T    T
T F F    F    F           T    T
F F F    T    F           T    T
```

This argument is invalid because the second row has a true premise and a false conclusion.

6. P Q R (P ⊃ Q) ⊃ R   ∴ P ⊃ (Q ⊃ R)

T T T	T	T	T	T
F T T	T	T	T	T
T F T	F	T	T	T
F F T	T	T	T	T
T T F	T	F	F	F
F T F	T	F	T	F
T F F	F	T	T	T
F F F	T	F	T	T

This argument is valid since every row (1, 2, 3, 4, and 7) in which the conditional premise is true, the conditional conclusion is true as well.

Exercise 7.9

1. P Q P ∨ ~Q

T T	T	F
F T	F	F
T F	T	T
F F	T	T

This statement is contingent, since there is at least one row (1, 3, and 4) in which it is true and another (2) in which it is false.

2. P Q (P & Q) & (~P & Q)

T T	T	F	F	F
F T	F	F	T	T
T F	F	F	F	F
F F	F	F	T	F

This statement is contradictory, since it is false in every row (that is, it cannot be true).

3. P Q (P ⊃ Q) & (~ P ⊃ Q)

T T	T	T	F	T
F T	T	T	T	T
T F	F	F	F	T
F F	T	F	T	F

This statement is contingent, since there is at least one row in which it is true and one in which it is false.

4. P Q   P & (P ⊃ (~P & Q))

    T T   F   F F F
    F T   F   T T T
    T F   F   F F F
    F F   F   T T F

This statement is contradictory; there is no row in which it is true.

5. P Q   P & (Q ⊃ P)

    T T   T   T
    F T   F   F
    T F   T   T
    F F   F   T

This statement is contingent, since there is at least one row in which it is true and one in which it is false.

6. D Q   (P & Q) ⊃ (P ∨ Q)

    T T   T   T   T
    F T   F   T   T
    T F   F   T   T
    F F   F   T   F

This statement is a tautology, since it is true in every row.

7. P Q R   (P ∨ Q) ∨ (~ P ∨ R)

    T T T   T   T   T
    F T T   T   T   T
    T F T   T   T   T
    F F T   F   T   T
    T T F   T   T   F
    F T F   T   T   T
    T F F   T   T   F
    F F F   F   T   T

This statement is a tautology, since it is true in every row.

Exercise 7.10

1.   P Q R   (P & Q) ∨ ~ R, R ⊃ (~ Q ⊃ P)

T T T		T		T F		T	F	T
F T T		F		F F		T	F	T
T F T		F		F F		T	T	T
F F T		F		F F		F	T	F
T T F		T		T T		T	F	T
F T F		F		T T		T	F	T
T F F		F		T T		T	T	T
F F F		F		T T		T	T	F

These two statements are consistent since both are true in at least one row.

2.   P R T   P ⊃ (R ∨ ~T), ~P ⊃ (~R ∨ T), R & ~T

T T T		T		T F	F	T	F	T		F F
F T T		T		T F	T	T	F	T		F F
T F T		F		F F	F	T	T	T		F F
F F T		T		F F	T	T	T	T		F F
T T F		T		T T	F	T	F	F		T T
F T F		T		T T	T	F	F	F		T T
T F F		T		T T	F	T	T	T		F T
F F F		T		T T	T	T	T	T		F T

These three statements are consistent, since there is at least one row in which they are all true (namely, row 5).

Exercise 7.11

1.   A B C   (A ⊃ B) ⊃ (A ⊃ C), A ⊃ (B ⊃ C)

T T T		T	T	T		T	T
F T T		T	T	T		T	T
T F T		F	T	T		T	T
F F T		T	T	T		T	T
T T F		T	F	F		F	F
F T F		T	T	T		T	F
T F F		F	T	F		T	T
F F F		T	T	T		T	T

These two statements are logically equivalent, since they have identical truth tables (under the main connectives).

Chapter 8

Exercise 8.1

Truth tree for problem (18) from exercise 7.6:

√1. R ⊃ S   (premise)
√2. ~R ⊃ ~H   (premise)
√3. H ⊃ ~S   (premise)
4.   ~ ~H   (negation of conclusion)

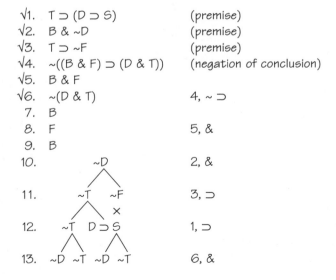

5.   ~H   ~S   3, ⊃
       ×

6.   ~R   S   1, ⊃

7.   ~ ~R   ~H   2, ⊃
      ×   ×

The truth tree closes, so the original argument is deductively valid.

Truth tree for problem (21) from exercise 7.6:

√1. T ⊃ (D ⊃ S)   (premise)
√2. B & ~D   (premise)
√3. T ⊃ ~F   (premise)
√4. ~((B & F) ⊃ (D & T))   (negation of conclusion)
√5. B & F
√6. ~(D & T)   4, ~ ⊃
7.   B
8.   F   5, &
9.   B
10.   ~D   2, &

11.   ~T   ~F   3, ⊃
                ×
12.   ~T   D ⊃ S   1, ⊃

13. ~D ~T ~D ~T   6, &

The leftmost branch is both complete and open; so the original argument is deductively invalid.

Truth tree for problem (25) from exercise 7.6:

√1.   ~T ⊃ ~(W v R)   (premise)
√2.   T ⊃ ~(W v R)   (premise)
√3.   W v R   (negation of conclusion)

4.   ~T   ~(W v R)   2, ⊃
                  ×
5.   T   ~(W v R)   1, ⊃
     ×   ×

Lines (3) and the right branch on (4) contradict each other, and that is sufficient to close this branch. Since all the branches in this tree close, the original argument is deductively valid.

Exercise 8.2

Problem 3

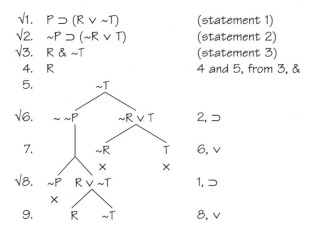

√1.   P ⊃ (R v ~T)   (statement 1)
√2.   ~P ⊃ (~R v T)   (statement 2)
√3.   R & ~T   (statement 3)
4.   R   4 and 5, from 3, &
5.   ~T

√6.   ~ ~P   ~R v T   2, ⊃

7.   ~R   T   6, v
              ×   ×
√8.   ~P   R v ~T   1, ⊃
     ×
9.   R   ~T   8, v

There are two open completed branches. So, (1)–(3) are consistent.

Exercise 8.3

Problem 2

√1. (P ⊃ Q) & (~P ⊃ (Q & (S ∨ G)))   (statement)
√2. (P ⊃ Q)
√3.   ~P ⊃ (Q & (S ∨ G))   1, &

4.   ~P   Q   2, ⊃

5. P   Q & (S ∨ G)   P   Q & (S ∨ G)   3, ⊃ (twice)
    ×

The third branch from the left is open and complete (there is nothing else to add from above on the same branch), so (1) can be true. It is therefore not a contradiction, but we need to devise another tree to see whether it is a logical truth or a contingent statement.

√1. ~((P ⊃ Q) & (~P ⊃ (Q & (S ∨ G))))   (negation of statement)

√2.   ~(P ⊃ Q)   ~(~P ⊃ (Q & (S ∨ G)))   1, ~ &
3.   P
4.   ~Q   2, (left branch), ~ ⊃

The leftmost branch is complete and open, so on the basis of these two trees we can infer that the original statement is contingent. A tree on it and its negation remain open.

Problem 3

√1. (P ∨ (G & ~D)) & (P ⊃ (~P & (S ∨ ~Q)))   (statement)
√2. P ∨ (G & ~D)
√3.   (P ⊃ (~P & (S ∨ ~Q)))   1, &

4.   P   G & ~D   2, ∨

5. ~P   ~P & (S ∨ ~Q)   ~P   ~P & (S ∨ ~Q)   3, ⊃
    ×

The third branch from the left is open and complete, so statement (1) can be true. It is therefore not a contradiction, but we need to devise another tree to determine whether it is a logical truth or a contingent statement.

√1. ~((P ∨ (G & ~D)) & (P ⊃ (~P & (S ∨ ~Q))))   (negation of statement)

√2. ~(P ∨ (G & ~D))   ~(P ⊃ (~P & (S ∨ ~Q)))   1, ~ &

3.   ~P

4.   ~(G & ~D)   2 (left), ~ ∨

5.   ~G   D   4 (left), ~ &

The two left branches are open and complete, so the original statement is contingent, since its tree and the tree on its negation both remain open.

Exercise 8.4

Problem 2

√1. D ⊃ (B & C)   (statement 1)
√2. ~(B ⊃ (C ⊃ D))   (negation of statement 2)
3.   B   3 and 4, from 2 ~ ⊃
√4. ~(C ⊃ D)
5.   C   5 and 6, from 4 ~ ⊃
6.   ~D

7.   ~D   (B & C)   1, ⊃
8.   B   8 and 9, from 7, &
9.   C

All branches are open, so (1) does not deductively imply unnegated (2).

Exercise 8.5

Problem 2

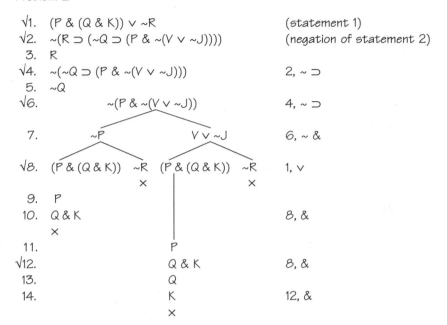

√1.	(P & (Q & K)) ∨ ~R	(statement 1)
√2.	~(R ⊃ (~Q ⊃ (P & ~(V ∨ ~J))))	(negation of statement 2)
3.	R	
√4.	~(~Q ⊃ (P & ~(V ∨ ~J)))	2, ~ ⊃
5.	~Q	
√6.	~(P & ~(V ∨ ~J))	4, ~ ⊃

7.	~P V ∨ ~J	6, ~ &
√8.	(P & (Q & K)) ~R (P & (Q & K)) ~R	1, ∨
	× ×	
9.	P	
10.	Q & K	8, &
	×	
11.	P	
√12.	Q & K	8, &
13.	Q	
14.	K	12, &
	×	

All branches close, so the first statement logically implies the second. Now we need to determine whether the second logically implies the first.

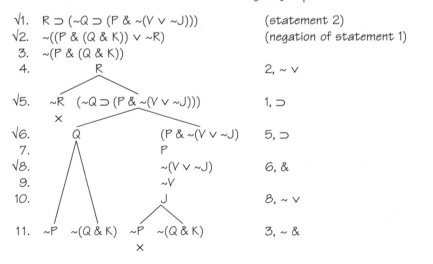

√1.	R ⊃ (~Q ⊃ (P & ~(V ∨ ~J)))	(statement 2)
√2.	~((P & (Q & K)) ∨ ~R)	(negation of statement 1)
3.	~(P & (Q & K))	
4.	R	2, ~ ∨

√5.	~R (~Q ⊃ (P & ~(V ∨ ~J)))	1, ⊃
	×	
√6.	Q (P & ~(V ∨ ~J))	5, ⊃
7.	P	
√8.	~(V ∨ ~J)	6, &
9.	~V	
10.	J	8, ~ ∨
11.	~P ~(Q & K) ~P ~(Q & K)	3, ~ &
	×	

The leftmost branch is complete and open, so the second statement does not logically imply the first, and therefore the two statements are not logically equivalent.

Chapter 9

Exercise 9.1

1. K^1s
2. $\exists T^1$
3. $\forall G^1$
4. F^1j
5. W^1l
6. $\forall S^1$
7. $\exists R^1$
8. $\sim\exists F^1$
9. $\sim\exists C^1$
10. $\sim\exists C^1$

Exercise 9.2

1. Everything is either a dog or a sheep.
2. Everything is tall and yellow.
3. Everything is not a dog.
4. Everything is neither a dog nor a sheep.
5. Everything that is not a sheep is a dog.
6. Something is a sheep.
7. Something is a yellow dog.
8. Something is either tall, or a sheep.

Exercise 9.3

1. Existential. Something is a dog.
2. Ungrammatical. Unbound property predicate.
3. Universal. Everything is dead and good.
4. Disjunction. Al is dead or good.
5. Disjunction. Bill or Carl is dead.

6. Conditional. If everything is dead, then everything is good.
7. Ungrammatical. An existential quantifier binding a singular term.
8. Disjunction. Nick is a knight, or everything is good and heavy.
9. Disjunction. Many helicopters landed safely, or something got hit.
10. Ungrammatical. There are no groupers.
11. Conditional. If something is dead, then everything is hot.
12. Conditional. If Bill is hot, then Al is keen.
13. Conditional. If something is either hot or keen, then Alice is lucky.
14. Conditional. If everything is a plant, then something is tall and light.
15. Negation. Al is not light.
16. Negation. Not everything is hot and itchy.
17. Negation. Nothing is not hot.
18. Existential. Something is not both yellow and pale.
19. Universal. Everything is not impossible.
20. Universal. Everything is purple and, if lucky, then tall.
21. Disjunction. Al is a knight or a lake, or something is a knight or a lake.
22. Ungrammatical. Quantifier ranging over a singular term.
23. Ungrammatical. Quantifier ranging over a singular term.

Even though, strictly speaking — at least as we have so far characterized well-formedness in PPL — (22) and (23) are ungrammatical, for purposes of proof we relax this restriction on grammaticality when we take up 'nested quantifiers' in chapter 13. (We need to tinker with the characterization of a predicate and with the notion of a quantifier statement.)

Exercise 9.4

1. Singular subject–predicate statement, $P^1 j$
2. Singular subject–predicate statement, $G^1 f$
3. Singular subject–predicate statement, $S^1 t$
4. Singular subject–predicate statement, $S^1 j$
5. Existential $\exists (I^1 \ \& \ D^1)$
6. Existential $\exists (P^1 \ \& \ L^1)$
7. Existential $\exists (F^1 \ \& \ S^1)$
8. Universal $\forall (R^1 \supset I^1)$
9. Universal $\forall (R^1 \supset {\sim} I^1)$
10. Singular subject–predicate statement, $N^1 f$
11. Universal $\forall (F^1 \supset T^1)$
12. Universal $\forall (G^1 \supset H^1)$
13. Universal $\forall (T^1 \supset {\sim} L^1)$, or ${\sim}\forall (T^1 \supset L^1)$

14. Existential ∃(W¹ & T¹)
15. Negation of existential ~∃(R¹ & F¹)
16. Universal ∀(W¹ ⊃ S¹)
17. Universal ∀(D¹ ⊃ P¹)
18. Universal ∀(S¹ ⊃ I¹)
19. Universal ∀(S¹ ⊃ I¹)
20. Negation of universal ~∀(S¹ ⊃ I¹)
21. Existential ∃~(G¹ ∨ B¹)
22. Existential ∃(G¹ ∨ B¹)
23. Universal ∀(G¹ ∨ B¹)
24. Universal ∀(G¹ ⊃ ~B¹)
25. Universal ∀(~B¹ ⊃ G¹)
26. Universal ∀((~B¹ ⊃ G¹) & (G¹ ⊃ ~B¹))
27. Universal ∀(H¹ ⊃ (L¹ & F¹))
28. Negation of existential ~∃(S¹ & A¹)
29. ∃G¹
30. ∀(N¹ ⊃ (O¹ ∨ E¹))
31. ∀(N¹ ⊃ O¹) & ∀(N¹ ⊃ E¹)
32. ∀(M¹ ⊃ P¹) & ∀(M¹ ⊃ L¹)
33. Conditional ∃(C¹ & R¹) ⊃ ∃(P¹ & D¹)
34. Existential ∃(F¹ & C¹)
35. L¹j ⊃ ∀R¹
36. ∀(P¹ ⊃ L¹) ∨ L¹j
37. ∃(P¹ & S¹) & ∃(P¹ & D¹) & ∃(P¹ & ~(S¹ ∨ D¹))
38. Conditional T¹j ⊃ ∀(M¹ ⊃ T¹)
39. Conditional L¹m ⊃ ∃(B¹ & L¹)
40. Simple statement. We cannot really understand how to symbolize this sentence until we turn to relational predicate logic.
41–7.   All these are simple statements that we would symbolize with capital letters, for example, A, B, C, . . ., without superscripts.

Exercise 9.5

1. ~∃(D¹ & C¹), ~C¹f ∴ D¹f
2. ∀(H¹ ⊃ M¹) & ∀(C¹ ⊃ M¹), ∀(A¹ ⊃ M¹) ∴ ∀(H¹ ⊃ A¹)
3. ∀(P¹ ⊃ C¹) & ∀(M¹ ⊃ C¹), ~∃(C¹ & (R¹ ∨ E¹)), ∃(M¹ & (E¹ & F¹)), ∃(P¹ & ~F¹) ∴ ∃(P¹ & D¹)
4. ~∃(A¹ & C¹) ∴ W¹a ⊃ (∀(W¹ ⊃ C¹) ⊃ ~A¹a)
5. ∃(A¹ & C¹), ∀(C¹ ⊃ G¹) ∴ ∃(A¹ & G¹)

6. $\exists(E^1 \ \& \ C^1) \ \& \ \exists(F^1 \ \& \ C^1), \ \forall(C^1 \supset \sim B^1), \ \forall(E^1 \supset S^1) \ \& \ \forall(F^1 \supset S^1)$
     $\therefore \ \sim\forall(S^1 \supset B^1)$
7. $\forall(C^1 \supset M^1) \ \therefore \ \forall(C^1 \supset (M^1 \vee R^1))$
8. $\forall(M^1 \supset R^1), \ \exists(A^1 \ \& \ \sim M^1) \ \therefore \ \exists(A^1 \ \& \ \sim R^1)$

Chapter 10

Exercise 10.1

1.   Since there is only one 'connective', the sole token of the existential quantifier, it has wide scope.
3.   There are two tokens of connectives in this formula, the universal and the conjunction. The universal has wide scope over the conjunction.
4.   Only one connective, the '∨', so it has wide scope.
5.   Only one connective, the '∨', so it has wide scope.
6.   The horseshoe has widest scope over both tokens of the universal quantifier.
8.   The sole token of '∨' has wide scope over both the sole token of the universal and the sole token of '&'. The universal quantifier has wide scope over the sole token of the ampersand.
9.   The '∨' has wide scope over the existential.
11.   The horseshoe has wide scope over both the universal and the existential quantifiers. Neither quantifier has scope over the other.
12.   The horseshoe is the only connective, so it has wide scope.
13.   The sole token of the horseshoe has wide scope over both the sole token of the existential and the sole token of the '∨'. The existential has wide scope over the '∨'.
14.   The horseshoe has wide scope over the other three connectives, the universal, the existential, and the ampersand. The existential has wide scope over the ampersand. Neither the universal nor the existential has wide scope over the other.
15.   The negation is the sole connective, so it has wide scope.
16.   The negation has wide scope over the universal and the ampersand. The universal has wide scope over the ampersand.
17.   The first token of the negation has wide scope over the sole token of the existential and the second token of the negation. The existential has wide scope over the second token of the negation.

Exercise 10.2

Problem 1

1.	∀(R¹ ⊃ (P¹ ∨ ~T¹)	(premise)
√2.	∃(~T¹ & P¹)	(premise)
√3.	~∃(~R¹ ∨ S¹)	(negation of conclusion)
4.	∀~(~R¹ ∨ S¹)	3, QE
√5.	~T¹a & P¹a	2, EQ
√6.	~(~R¹a ∨ S¹a)	4, UQ
√7.	R¹a ⊃ (P¹a ∨ ~T¹a)	1, UQ
8.	R¹a	
9.	~S¹a	8, 9 from 6, ~ ∨
10.	~T¹a	
11.	P¹a	10, 11 from 5, &
		7, ⊃

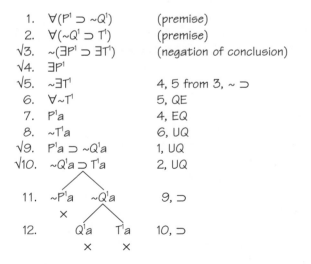

√12.	~R¹a (P¹a ∨ ~T¹a)	
	×	13, from 12, ∨
13.	P¹a ~T¹a	

Argument invalid: open branch.

Problem 2

1.	∀(P¹ ⊃ ~Q¹)	(premise)
2.	∀(~Q¹ ⊃ T¹)	(premise)
√3.	~(∃P¹ ⊃ ∃T¹)	(negation of conclusion)
√4.	∃P¹	
√5.	~∃T¹	4, 5 from 3, ~ ⊃
6.	∀~T¹	5, QE
7.	P¹a	4, EQ
8.	~T¹a	6, UQ
√9.	P¹a ⊃ ~Q¹a	1, UQ
√10.	~Q¹a ⊃ T¹a	2, UQ
11.	~P¹a ~Q¹a	9, ⊃
	×	
12.	Q¹a T¹a	10, ⊃
	× ×	

Argument valid: all branches close.

Problem 3

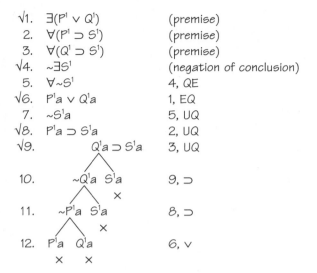

√1. ∃(P¹ ∨ Q¹)   (premise)
 2. ∀(P¹ ⊃ S¹)   (premise)
 3. ∀(Q¹ ⊃ S¹)   (premise)
√4. ~∃S¹   (negation of conclusion)
 5. ∀~S¹   4, QE
√6. P¹a ∨ Q¹a   1, EQ
 7. ~S¹a   5, UQ
√8. P¹a ⊃ S¹a   2, UQ
√9.   Q¹a ⊃ S¹a   3, UQ

10.   ~Q¹a   S¹a   9, ⊃
                      ×

11.   ~P¹a   S¹a   8, ⊃
                    ×

12. P¹a   Q¹a   6, ∨
      ×   ×

Argument valid: all branches close.

Problem 4

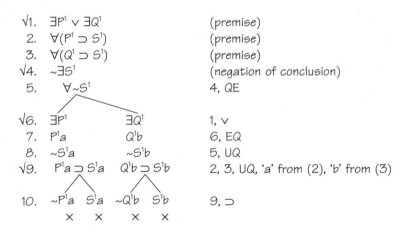

√1. ∃P¹ ∨ ∃Q¹   (premise)
 2. ∀(P¹ ⊃ S¹)   (premise)
 3. ∀(Q¹ ⊃ S¹)   (premise)
√4. ~∃S¹   (negation of conclusion)
 5.   ∀~S¹   4, QE

√6. ∃P¹   ∃Q¹   1, ∨
 7. P¹a   Q¹b   6, EQ
 8. ~S¹a   ~S¹b   5, UQ
√9. P¹a ⊃ S¹a   Q¹b ⊃ S¹b   2, 3, UQ, 'a' from (2), 'b' from (3)

10. ~P¹a S¹a ~Q¹b S¹b   9, ⊃
      ×   ×   ×   ×

Argument valid: all branches close.

A few comments are in order. On the two branches on line (6) are two existentials such that we can use the same letter. This would liberalize our EQ rule, but it is defensible, since, when the tree splits, the branches are *independent.* Also, notice how the UQ instantiations were chosen so that the shortest tree is realized. No rules guided us. I saw which (type of) instantiations provide the shortest closure. If I did not see that the tree was going to close, I would have repeated every instantiation on every open branch. Fortunately, this was not the case.

Problem 5

$\sqrt{}$1. $\exists(A^1 \,\&\, B^1)$ (premise)
$\sqrt{}$2. $\sim\!\exists(A^1 \,\&\, \sim\!B^1)$ (negation of conclusion)
   3. $\forall\sim(A^1 \,\&\, \sim\!B^1)$ 2, QE
$\sqrt{}$4. $A^1a \,\&\, B^1a$ 1, EQ
$\sqrt{}$5. $\sim(A^1a \,\&\, \sim\!B^1a)$ 3, UQ
   6. A^1a
   7. B^1a 6, 7 from 4, &

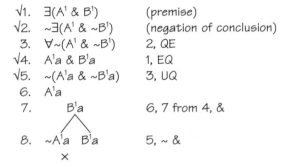

   8. $\sim\!A^1a$ B^1a 5, $\sim$ &
           $\times$

Argument invalid: open branch.

Problem 6

$\sqrt{}$1. $\sim\!\exists(A^1 \,\&\, \sim\!B^1)$ (premise)
$\sqrt{}$2. $\sim\!\exists(A^1 \supset B^1)$ (negation of conclusion)
   3. $\forall\sim(A^1 \,\&\, \sim\!B^1)$ 1, QE
   4. $\forall\sim(A^1 \supset B^1)$ 2, QE
$\sqrt{}$5. $\sim(A^1a \,\&\, \sim\!B^1a)$ 3, UQ
$\sqrt{}$6. $\sim(A^1a \supset B^1a)$ 4, UQ
   7. A^1a
   8. $\sim\!B^1a$ 6, $\sim \supset$

   9. $\sim\!A^1a$ B^1a 5, $\sim$ & (DN)
           $\times$ $\times$

Argument valid: all branches close.

Problem 7

$\sqrt{}$1. $\sim\!\forall\sim(A^1 \supset B^1)$ (premise)
$\sqrt{}$2. $\exists(A^1 \,\&\, B^1)$ (negation of conclusion)

√3. ∃~~($A^1 \supset B^1$)   1, QE
√4. A^1a & B^1a 2, EQ
√5. $A^1b \supset B^1b$ 3, EQ
6. A^1a
7. B^1a 6, 7 from 4, &

8. ~A^1b B^1b

Argument invalid: open branches.

Problem 8

√1. ∃C^1 (premise)
√2. ∃D^1 (premise)
√3. ~∃(C^1 & D^1)   (negation of conclusion)
4. ∀~(C^1 & D^1)   3, QE
5. C^1a 1, EQ
6. D^1b 2, EQ
√7. ~(C^1a & D^1a)   4, UQ
√8.   ~(C^1b & D^1b)   4, UQ

9. ~C^1a ~D^1a 8, ~ &
    ×
10.   ~C^1b ~D^1b 9, ~ &
                ×

Argument invalid: open branch.

Problem 9

1. ∀($A^1 \supset B^1$)   (premise)
√2. ~~∃(A^1 & B^1)   (negation of conclusion)
√3. ∃(A^1 & B^1)   2, ~~
√4. A^1a & B^1a 3, EQ
√5. $A^1a \supset B^1a$ 1, UQ
6. A^1a 6, 7 from 4, &
7. B^1a

8. ~A^1a B^1a 5, ⊃
    ×

Argument invalid: open branch.

Problem 10

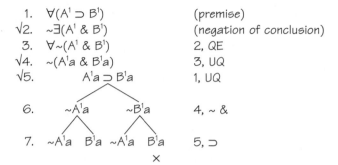

<pre>
  1.   ∀(A¹ ⊃ B¹)   (premise)
 √2.   ~∃(A¹ & B¹)   (negation of conclusion)
  3.   ∀~(A¹ & B¹)   2, QE
 √4.   ~(A¹a & B¹a)   3, UQ
 √5.   A¹a ⊃ B¹a   1, UQ

  6.   ~A¹a   ~B¹a   4, ~ &

  7.   ~A¹a B¹a ~A¹a B¹a   5, ⊃
                  ×
</pre>

Argument invalid: open branches.

Problem 11

<pre>
 √1.   ∃(S¹ & J¹)   (premise)
  2.   ∀(J¹ ⊃ L¹)   (premise)
 √3.   ~∀(S¹ ⊃ L¹)   (negation of conclusion)
 √4.   ∃~(S¹ ⊃ L¹)   3, QE
 √5.   ~(S¹a ⊃ L¹a)   4, EQ
 √6.   S¹b & J¹b   1, EQ
 √7.   J¹a ⊃ L¹a   2, UQ
 √8.   J¹b ⊃ L¹b   2, UQ
  9.   S¹b   9, 10 from 6, &
 10.   J¹b
 11.   S¹a   11, 12 from 5, ~⊃
 12.   ~L¹a

 13.   ~J¹a   L¹a   7, ⊃
                 ×
 14.   ~J¹b   L¹b
         ×
</pre>

Argument invalid: open branch.

Problem 12

<pre>
 √1.   M¹a & N¹a   (premise)
 √2.   ∃(M¹ & J¹)   (premise)
</pre>

√3. ~∃(J¹ & N¹)   (negation of conclusion)
4. ∀~(J¹ & N¹)   3, QE
√5. M¹b & J¹b   2, EQ
√6. ~(J¹a & N¹a)   4, UQ
√7. ~(J¹b & N¹b)   4, UQ
8. M¹a   8, 9 from 1, &
9. N¹a
10. M¹b   10, 11 from 5, &
11.   J¹b

12.   ~Ja   ~N¹a   6, ~ &
                    ×
13. ~J¹b ~N¹b   7, ~ &
     ×

Argument invalid: open branch.

Problem 13

1. K¹a & B¹b   (premise)
2. ∃(K¹ & D¹)   (premise)
3. ∀(D¹ ⊃ B¹)   (premise)
4. ~(B¹a ∨ K¹b)   (negation of conclusion)
5. K¹c & D¹c   2, EQ
6. D¹a ⊃ B¹a   3, UQ
7. D¹b ⊃ B¹b   3, UQ
8. D¹c ⊃ B¹c   3, UQ
9. K¹a   9, 10 from 1, &
10. B¹b
11. K¹c   11, 12 from 5, &
12. D¹c
13. ~B¹a   13, 14 from 4, ~∨
14.   ~K¹b

15.   ~D¹a   B¹a   6, ⊃
                    ×
16. ~D¹c   B¹c   8, ⊃
     ×
17.   ~D¹b   B¹b   7, ⊃

Argument invalid: open branches.

Exercise 10.4

Problem 1

√1. ~∃(C¹ & D¹)
 2. ~D¹b
 3. ~C¹b
 4. ∀~(C¹ & D¹)   1, QE
√5. ~(C¹b & D¹b)   4, UQ

 6.   ~C¹b   ~D¹b   5, ~ &

Both branches remain open, so statements (1)–(3) are consistent.

Exercise 10.6

Problem 1

 1. ~(∀(D¹ ⊃ P¹) ⊃∀(S¹ ⊃ P¹))   (negation of (1))
 2. ∀(D¹ ⊃ P¹)
√3. ~∀(S¹ ⊃ P¹)   2, 3 by ~ ⊃, 1
√4. ∃~(S¹ ⊃ P¹)   3, QE
√5. ~(S¹a ⊃ P¹a)   4, EQ
 6. S¹a
 7. ~P¹a   6, 7 by ~ ⊃, 5
√8. D¹a ⊃ P¹a   2, UQ

 9.   ~D¹a   P¹a   8, ⊃
          ✗

√1.   ∀(D¹ ⊃ P¹) ⊃ ∀(S¹ ⊃ P¹)

√2. ~∀(D¹ ⊃ P¹)   ∀(S¹ ⊃ P¹)   1, ⊃
√3.   S¹a ⊃ P¹a   2, UQ

 4.   ~S¹a   P¹a   3, ⊃

Since both trees (one on statement (1) and one on its negation) remain open, (1) is contingent.

Chapter 11

Exercise 11.1

1. $S^i b \supset D^i b$
2. $P^i l \,\&\, A^i l$
3. $G^i w \supset F^i w$
4. $\forall((P^i \,\&\, S^i) \supset L^i)$
5. $\exists(P^i \,\&\, M^i) \supset M^i l$
6. $\forall(F^i \supset C^i)$
7. $\forall((P^i \,\&\, T^i) \supset D^i)$
8. $\exists(P^i \,\&\, L^i) \supset \forall(P^i \supset L^i)$

Exercise 11.2

1. $\sim\exists(E^i \,\&\, D^i)$
2. $\forall(T^i \supset D^i)$
3. $\sim\forall(E^i \supset P^i)$
4. $\forall(M^i \supset D^i)$
5. Conjunction of two universals.
6. Ambiguous: $\exists(P^i \,\&\, W^i \,\&\, H^i)$ or $\exists(P^i \,\&\, R^i)$ (R^i: is a wealthy philosopher) The issue here is whether this sentence is claiming the person is wealthy or just wealthy for a philosopher.
7. $\sim\exists(H^i \,\&\, W^i) \supset (H^i s \vee W^i s)$
8. Same problem as with (6), depending on whether someone's being a wealthy figure skater entails that he is wealthy: $\sim\forall(S^i \supset H^i)$ or $\sim\forall((W^i \,\&\, F^i) \supset H^i)$. ($S^i$: is a wealthy skater)
9. $\exists(H^i \,\&\, \sim W^i \,\&\, \sim F^i) \supset \sim W^i s$
10. $\sim W^i t \,\&\, (\sim F^i t \supset \sim W^i s)$
11. $\exists(M^i \,\&\, \sim R^i)$
12. $\forall((F^i \,\&\, V^i) \supset L^i)$
13. Depending on whether you think being a large husband entails being large, etc., you might come up with different answers. One possible answer is: $\forall(M^i \supset W^i)$ (M^i: is a large man, W^i: has a large wife)
14. $\exists(P^i \,\&\, C^i) \supset \forall(P^i \supset C^i)$
15. $\exists(P^i \,\&\, C^i) \supset C^i d$
16. $\forall(D^i \supset P^i) \,\&\, \forall(S^i \supset P^i)$
17. $\exists(D^i \,\&\, W^i) \supset \forall(D^i \supset W^i)$
18. $\forall M^i \vee \forall P^i$

19. $(\exists L^1 \supset \exists B^1)$ & $(\exists B^1 \supset \exists L^1)$
20. $\sim\exists(P^1 \ \& \ F^1) \supset \exists(P^1 \ \& \ G^1)$
21. $\exists(P^1 \ \& \ A^1) \supset \exists(P^1 \ \& \ D^1)$
22. $\forall(P^1 \supset A^1) \supset \exists(P^1 \ \& \ D^1)$
23. $\forall(R^1 \supset \sim H^1)$ & $\forall(D^1 \supset \sim H^1)$
24. $\forall(R^1 \supset H^1)$ & $\sim\forall(R^1 \supset G^1)$
25. $\forall(S^1 \supset F^1)$ & $\forall(S^1 \supset W^1)$
26. $\forall(C^1 \supset P^1)$ & $\sim W^1 f$
27. $\sim\exists((C^1 \ \& \ R^1) \ \& \ \sim O^1)$
28. $\exists(F^1 \ \& \ S^1)$
29. $\exists(F^1 \ \& \ \sim S^1)$
30. $\forall((R^1 \ \& \ J^1) \supset \sim I^1)$
32. $\exists(W^1 \ \& \ I^1)$
33. $\forall(W^1 \supset M^1)$ Useful for you to think about this one. 'A whale' indicates plurality here.
34. $\sim\exists(P^1 \ \& \ A^1)$
35. $\forall((H^1 \ \& \ L^1) \supset D^1)$
36. $\forall(G^1 \supset \sim B^1)$
37. $\forall(K^1 \supset \sim P^1)$
38. $\forall((M^1 \ \& \ E^1) \supset T^1)$ or $\forall(E^1 \supset (M^1 \ \& \ T^1))$
39. $\forall((P^1 \ \& \ S^1) \supset T^1)$
40. $\forall((A^1 \ \& \ S^1) \supset D^1)$
41. This sentence is ambiguous; it could be either an existential or a universal.
42. Propositional Logic: $O \supset (C \supset D)$ (O: Some officers are present; C: All officers present are captains; D: Some captains are present)
    Property Predicate Logic: $\exists(O^1 \ \& \ P^1) \supset (\forall((O^1 \ \& \ P^1) \supset C^1) \supset \exists(C^1 \ \& \ P^1))$
43. $\exists(M^1 \ \& \ H^1)$ & $\sim\forall(M^1 \supset H^1)$ This example shows the merits of always trying first to symbolize an English statement in PL before trying to symbolize it in PPL. If a statement is a logical conjunction in PL, it is a logical conjunction in PPL as well (and indeed in every logic we will study; the only sort of statement that can change its status as we move from logic to logic is a simple statement).

Exercise 11.3

1. $\forall((P^1 \ \& \ D^1) \supset B^1), \ \forall(P^1 \supset D^1) \ \therefore \ \forall(P^1 \supset B^1)$
2. $\sim\exists(M^1 \ \& \ R^1), \ \sim\exists(M^1 \ \& \ T^1 \ \& \ \sim R^1) \ \therefore \ \forall((M^1 \ \& \ T^1) \supset R^1)$
3. $\forall((P^1 \ \& \ \sim A^1 \ \& \ W^1) \supset C^1), \ \exists((A^1 \ \& \ P^1) \ \& \ C^1), \ \forall((A^1 \ \& \ P^1) \supset C^1) \ \therefore \ \forall(W^1 \supset C^1)$

4. $\exists(P^1 \& R^1) \supset \forall(P^1 \supset R^1) \therefore \forall(P^1 \supset R^1) \vee \sim\exists(P^1 \& R^1)$
5. $\forall((M^1 \& U^1 \& T^1 \& D^1) \supset E^1), U^1g \& T^1g \therefore E^1g$
6. $N^1a, \forall((M^1 \& N^1) \supset R^1) \therefore R^1a$ (Missing premise: M^1a)
7. $\forall((L^1 \& Y^1 \& M^1) \supset \sim C^1), \forall(O^1 \supset (M^1 \& C^1))$ (or $\forall((M^1 \& O^1) \supset C^1)$
     $\therefore \sim\exists (L^1 \& M^1 \& O^1)$
8. $\sim\exists(P^1 \& \sim M^1), \forall(\sim V^1 \supset \sim P^1), \sim\exists (M^1 \& V^1 \& U^1) \therefore P^1g \supset \sim U^1g$
9. $\forall(C^1 \supset B^1), \forall(B^1 \supset L^1), \forall(L^1 \supset F^1) \therefore \forall(C^1 \supset F^1)$
10. $\forall(V^1 \supset C^1), \sim\forall(R^1 \supset C^1) \therefore \exists(R^1 \& \sim V^1)$
11. $\forall(T^1 \supset (O^1 \vee A^1)), \sim\exists(O^1 \& T^1 \& A^1), \exists(T^1 \& A^1) \therefore \exists(T^1 \& O^1)$
12. $\forall(W^1 \supset N^1) \supset \forall((S^1 \& C^1) \supset L^1), \forall(L^1 \supset \sim T^1), \exists(S^1 \& \sim T^1) \therefore \exists(W^1 \& \sim N^1)$
13. $\sim\exists(C^1 \& I^1), \forall(\sim O^1 \supset U^1)$ (or $\forall((C^1 \& \sim O^1) \supset U^1)), \forall((I^1 \& C^1) \supset (O^1 \& C^1))$
     $\therefore \forall(C^1 \supset U^1)$
14. $\forall((P^1 \& \sim A^1) \supset M^1), \forall((P^1 \& \sim M^1) \supset \sim A^1) \therefore \sim\exists(P^1 \& A^1)$
15. $\forall(F^1 \supset O^1), \therefore \forall(F^1 \supset \sim B^1)$ (Missing premise: $\sim\exists(O^1 \& B^1)$)
16. $\forall(A^1 \supset ((K^1 \supset (S^1 \& C^1)) \& ((S^1 \& C^1) \supset K^1))), \forall(P^1 \supset \sim C^1), (\forall(P^1 \supset A^1))$
     $\therefore \forall(P^1 \supset \sim K^1)$ Comment: We use the 'if and only if' ('biconditional') in symbolizing the first premise because when we define a notion we must give both necessary and sufficient conditions.
17. $\exists G^1 \supset \forall(C^1 \supset G^1), \exists(P^1 \& T^1) \supset \forall(G^1 \supset T^1)$
     $\therefore \exists(P^1 \& T^1 \& G^1) \supset \forall(C^1 \supset T^1)$
18. $\forall(R^1 \supset (S^1 \vee M^1)), \sim\exists(U^1 \& R^1 \& S^1) \therefore \forall(U^1 \supset R^1) \supset \forall(U^1 \supset M^1)$
19. $\exists L^1 \supset \forall(P^1 \supset L^1), \exists H^1 \supset \forall(L^1 \supset H^1) \therefore \exists(H^1 \& L^1) \supset \forall(P^1 \supset H^1)$
20. $\forall((G^1 \& V^1) \supset H^1) \therefore \forall((V^1 \& \sim H^1) \supset \sim G^1)$
21. $\forall((F^1 \vee C^1) \supset \sim E^1), \sim\forall(G^1 \supset E^1) \therefore \forall(F^1 \supset G^1)$ (The second premise here is quite interesting; notice that it is a negation.)
22. $\forall((F^1 \vee A^1) \supset S^1) \& \sim\exists(S^1 \& H^1) \therefore \forall(F^1 \supset \sim H^1)$
23. $\forall((P^1 \& T^1) \supset \sim A^1), \forall((P^1 \& \sim T^1) \supset A^1) \therefore T^1b \supset \sim A^1b$
24. $\forall((P^1 \& L^1) \supset \sim E^1), \forall((P^1 \& E^1) \supset T^1) \therefore \sim\forall(\sim L^1 \supset E^1)$
25. $\forall(P^1 \supset (C^1 \supset R^1)), \forall((P^1 \& \sim R^1) \supset O^1), \sim\forall((P^1 \& O^1) \supset \sim R^1) \therefore \sim\forall(A^1 \supset V^1)$

Chapter 12

Exercise 12.1

1. Singular statement
2. Existential statement
3. Universal statement
4. Logical conjunction
5. Logical disjunction

Exercise 12.2

1. $(\forall x)(P^1x \supset L^2xr)$
2. $(\exists x)(L^2jx) \vee (\exists y)(F^2jy)$
3. $(\exists x)(P^1x \,\&\, S^2jx)$
4. $(\exists x)(M^1x \,\&\, S^2dx)$
5. $(\forall x)(S^1x \supset T^3axt)$

Exercise 12.3

1. $(\forall x)(B^1x \supset H^2rx), B^1f \;\therefore\; H^2rf$
2. $(\exists x)(C^1x \,\&\, B^3nxr) \;\therefore\; (\exists x)(C^1x \,\&\, H^2rx)$
3. $K^3ceb \;\therefore\; (\exists x)(P^1x \,\&\, K^3cxb) \,\&\, (\exists y)(P^1y \,\&\, K^3yeb)$

Chapter 13

Exercise 13.1

1. $(\exists x)(M^1x \,\&\, (\forall y)(W^1y \supset (\forall z)(T^1z \supset G^3xyz)))$
2. $(\exists x)(W^1x \,\&\, (\forall y)(M^1y \supset (\forall z)(T^1z \supset G^3xyz)))$
3. $(\forall x)(M^1x \supset (\forall y)(M^1y \supset (\forall z)(T^1z \supset G^3xyz)))$
4. $(\forall x)(P^1x \supset (\exists y)(P^1y \,\&\, (\exists z)(T^1z \,\&\, L^3xyz))) \,\&\, (\exists x_1)(P^1x_1 \,\&\, (\forall y_1)(P^1y_1 \supset (\forall z_1)(T^1z_1 \supset L^3x_1y_1z_1)))$
5. $(\exists x)(P^1x \,\&\, L^3bxt)$
6. $(\forall x)(A^2xm \supset (\exists y)(N^1y \,\&\, G^3xmy))$

Exercise 13.2

1. $(\forall x)(B^1x \supset (\forall y)(T^1y \supset O^2xy)), B^1j \,\&\, {\sim}O^2jm \;\therefore\; {\sim}T^1m$
2. $H^2_{\forall S^1 \exists F^1} = (\forall x)(S^1x \supset (\exists y)(F^1y \,\&\, H^2xy)), F^1b \;\therefore\; H^2b_{\exists S^1} = (\exists x)(S^1x \,\&\, H^2bx)$
3. $(\forall x)(O^1x \supset E^2xx) \;\therefore\; (\forall x)(O^1x \supset (\forall y)(O^1y \supset E^2xy))$

Exercise 13.3

1. Grammatical. Simple.
2. Grammatical. Conjunction.
3. Ungrammatical. Unbound variable.

4. Ungrammatical. Unbound variable.
5. Ungrammatical. No variable bound by quantifier.
6. Grammatical. Existential.
7. Ungrammatical. The token of variable 'y' is not bound by any quantifiers.
8. Grammatical. Disjunction.
9. Grammatical. Universal.
10. Grammatical. Negation.
11. Grammatical. Universal.
12. Grammatical. Existential.
13. Grammatical. Universal.

Exercise 13.4

1. The universal quantifier has primary scope; the existential has secondary scope.
2. The negation has wider scope.
3. This statement is a universal, and so its sole universal quantifier token has wide scope over the four existential quantifier tokens within. The universal quantifier ranges over a complex conditional formula. In the antecedent of this formula there is an existential quantifier that is neither within the scope of, nor does it have wide scope over, the three existential quantifier tokens in the consequent of that conditional formula. In the consequent there are three existential quantifiers, and the order of scope is the linear order of appearance: the first has wider scope than the other two, and the third wider scope than the second.
4. The first existential with variable 'x' has widest (primary) scope. The second quantifier, the universal, has secondary scope, and the third quantifier, the existential with variable 'z', has narrowest scope.

Exercise 13.5

1. $(\forall x)(T^1x \supset (\exists y)(A^1y \ \& \ (\exists z)(S^1z \ \& \ S^3zyx)))$
2. $(\forall x)(A^1x \supset (\exists y)(S^1y \ \& \ (\forall z)(T^1z \supset S^3yxz)))$
3. $\sim(\exists x)(A^1x \ \& \ (\forall y)(S^1y \supset (\forall z)(T^1z \supset S^3yxz)))$
4. $(\exists x)(T^1x \ \& \ (\exists y)(S^1y \ \& \ (\forall z)(A^1z \supset S^3yzx)))$
5. $(\exists x)(P^1x \ \& \ (\forall y)(P^1y \supset L^2xy))$
6. $(\exists x)(P^1x \ \& \ (\forall y)(P^1y \supset L^2yx))$
7. $(\exists x)(M^1x \ \& \ (\forall y)(B^1y \supset (\forall z)(L^1z \supset P^3yzx)))$
8. $(\exists x)(G^1x \ \& \ \sim(\exists y)(B^1y \ \& \ (\forall z)(P^1z \supset P^3xyz)))$

9. $(\forall x)(D^1x \supset (\exists y)(S^1y \And (\exists z)(P^1z \And W^3yxz)))$
10. $(\exists x)(B^1x \And (\exists y)(S^1y \And (\forall z)(T^1z \supset R^3yxz)))$
11. $(\exists x)(C^1x \And (\forall y)(P^1y \supset (\forall z)(D^1z \supset S^3yxz)))$

Exercise 13.6

1. $(\forall x)(L^1x \supset (\exists y)(F^1y \And (\exists z)(T^1z \And P^3xyz)))$, $(\exists x)(L^1x)$
    $\therefore (\exists x)(F^1x \And (\exists y)(T^1y \And (\exists z)(L^1z \And P^3zxy)))$
2. $(\exists x)(P^1x \And (\forall y)(T^1y \supset (\exists z)(F^1z \And E^3xzy)))$
    $\therefore (\forall x)(T^1x \supset (\exists y)(F^1y \supset (\exists z)(P^1z \And E^3zyx)))$
3. $(\exists x)(T^1x \And (\forall y)(C^1y \supset (\exists z)(G^1z \And \sim C^3yxz)))$ (This sentence is ambiguous; if you think the sentence can be true if one or two cats climb the tree, as long as not all cats do so, then you might be inclined to symbolize it as follows: $(\exists x)(T^1x \And \sim(\forall y)(C^1y \supset (\exists z)(G^1z \And C^3yxz)))$ $\therefore (\forall x)(C^1x \supset (\exists y)(G^1y \And (\exists z)(T^1z \And C^3xzy)))$
4. $(\forall x)(L^1x \supset (\exists y)(T^1y \And (\forall z)(W^1z \supset L^3yxz)))$, $(\exists x)L^1x \therefore (\exists x)(L^1x \And (\forall y)(W^1y \supset (\exists z)(T^1z \And L^3zxy)))$

Chapter 14

Exercise 14.1

Problem 1

$\sqrt{}$1. $\sim(\forall x)(\exists y)P^2yx$ (premise)
$\sqrt{}$2. $\sim(\exists x)(\exists y)\sim P^2yx$ (negation of conclusion)
3. $(\forall x)(\forall y)P^2yx$ 2, QE (twice, and DN)
$\sqrt{}$4. $(\exists x)(\forall y)\sim P^2yx$ 1, QE (twice)
5. $(\forall y)\sim P^2ya$ 4, EQ
6. P^2aa 3, UQ (twice)
7. $\sim P^2aa$ 5, UQ
          $\times$

Tree closes, so the argument is valid.

Problem 2

1. $(\forall x)(F^1x \supset (\forall y)\sim M^2yx)$ (premise)
2. F^1d (premise)

3. M²pd   (negation of conclusion)
√4. F¹d ⊃ (∀y)~M²yd   1, UQ

5. ~F¹d   (∀y)~M²yd   4, ⊃
        ×

6.   ~M²pd   5, UQ
                    ×

All branches close, so the argument is valid.

Problem 3

√1. (∃x)(∃y)F²xy   (premise)
 2. (∀x)(∀y)(F²xy ⊃ P²xy)   (premise)
 3. ~P²ab   (negation of conclusion)
 4. F²cd   1, EQ (twice)
√5. F²cd ⊃ P²cd
√6. F²ab ⊃ P²ab   5, 6 by UQ, 2

7. ~F²cd   P²cd   5, ⊃
        ×

8.   ~F²ab   P²ab   6, ⊃
                ×

Open branch, so the argument is invalid.

Problem 4

1. (∀x)R²xx   (premise)
√2. ~(∀x)(∀y)(R²xy ⊃ R²yx)   (negation of conclusion)
√3. (∃x)(∃y)~(R²xy ⊃ R²yx)   2, QE (twice)
√4. ~(R²ab ⊃ R²ba)   3, EQ (twice)
5. R²aa
6. R²bb   5, 6 by UQ, 1
7. R²ab
8. ~R²ba   7, 8 by ~ ⊃, 4

Open branch, so the argument is invalid.

Problem 5

1.	$(\forall x)(G^2xx \vee (\exists y)F^2xy)$	(premise)
√2.	$\sim(\exists z)G^2zz$	(premise)
√3.	$\sim(\exists x)(\exists y)F^2xy$	(negation of conclusion)
4.	$(\forall x)(\forall y)\sim F^2xy$	3, QE (twice)
5.	$(\forall z)\sim G^2zz$	2, QE
√6.	$G^2aa \vee (\exists y)F^2ay$	1, UQ
7.	$\sim G^2aa$	5, UQ

$$\overbrace{\qquad\qquad}$$

√8.	$G^2aa \quad (\exists y)F^2ay$	6, v
	×	
9.	F^2ab	8, EQ
10.	$(\forall y)\sim F^2ay$	4, UQ
11.	$\sim F^2ab$	10, UQ
	×	

All branches close, so the argument is valid.

Problem 6

1.	$(\forall x)(\forall y)(F^2xy \supset P^2xy)$	(premise)
√2.	$\sim(\forall x)(\forall y)(F^2xy \supset (P^2xy \& P^2yx))$	(negation of conclusion)
√3.	$(\exists x)(\exists y)\sim(F^2xy \supset (P^2xy \& P^2yx))$	2, QE (twice)
√4.	$\sim(F^2ab \supset (P^2ab \& P^2ba))$	3, EQ (twice)
5.	F^2ab	
√6.	$\sim(P^2ab \& P^2ba)$	5, 6 by $\sim \supset$, 4
√7.	$F^2ab \supset P^2ab$	
√8.	$F^2ba \supset P^2ba$	7, 8 by UQ, 1

9.	$\sim F^2ab \quad P^2ab$	7, $\supset$
	×	
10.	$\sim P^2ab \quad \sim P^2ba$	6, $\sim \&$
	×	
11.	$\sim F^2ba \quad P^2ba$	8, $\supset$
	×	

Open branch, so the argument is invalid.

Problem 7

1.	$(\forall x)(H^1x \supset A^1x)$	(premise)
√2.	$\sim(\forall x)((\exists y)(H^2xy \ \& \ T^2xy) \supset (\exists z)(A^1z \ \& \ T^2xz))$	(negation of conclusion)
√3.	$(\exists x)\sim((\exists y)(H^2xy \ \& \ T^2xy) \supset (\exists z)(A^1z \ \& \ T^2xz))$	2, QE
√4.	$\sim((\exists y)(H^2ay \ \& \ T^2ay) \supset (\exists z)(A^1z \ \& \ T^2az))$	3, EQ
√5.	$(\exists y)(H^2ay \ \& \ T^2ay)$	
√6.	$\sim(\exists z)(A^1z \ \& \ T^2az)$	5, 6 by $\sim \supset$, 4
√7.	$H^2ab \ \& \ T^2ab$	5, EQ
8.	H^2ab	
9.	T^2ab	8, 9 by &, 7
√10.	$(\forall z)\sim(A^1z \ \& \ T^2az)$	6, QE
√11.	$\sim(A^1b \ \& \ T^2ab)$	10, UQ
√12.	$H^1b \supset A^1b$	1, UQ

```
                  /\
13.        ~A¹b      ~T²ab              11, ~ &
          /\           ×
14.  ~H¹b   A¹b                         12, ⊃
          ×
```

Open branch, so the argument is invalid.

Problem 8

1.	$(\forall x)\sim B^2xx$	(premise)
√2.	$\sim(\forall x)(A^1x \supset (\exists y)B^2xy)$	(premise)
√3.	$\sim(\exists x)(A^1x \ \& \ B^2xx)$	(negation of conclusion)
√4.	$(\exists x)\sim(A^1x \supset (\exists y)B^2xy)$	2, QE
5.	$(\forall x)\sim(A^1x \ \& \ B^2xx)$	3, QE
√6.	$\sim(A^1a \supset (\exists y)B^2ay)$	4, EQ
7.	A^1a	
√8.	$\sim(\exists y)B^2ay$	7, 8 by $\sim \supset$, 6
9.	$(\forall y)\sim B^2ay$	8, QE
10.	$\sim B^2aa$	9, UQ
√11.	$\sim(A^1a \ \& \ B^2aa)$	5, UQ

```
              /\
12.    ~A¹a      ~B²aa              11, ~ &
        ×
```

Open branch, so the argument is invalid.

Problem 9

1.	$(\forall x)(\forall y)(R^2xy \supset R^2yx)$	(premise)
√2.	$\sim(\forall x)(\forall y)(\forall z)((R^2xy \ \& \ R^2yz) \supset R^2xz)$	(negation of conclusion)
√3.	$(\exists x)(\exists y)(\exists z)\sim((R^2xy \ \& \ R^2yz) \supset R^2xz)$	2, QE (thrice)
√4.	$\sim((R^2ab \ \& \ R^2bc) \supset R^2ac)$	3, EQ (thrice)
√5.	$R^2ab \ \& \ R^2bc$	
6.	$\sim R^2ac$	5, 6 by $\sim \supset$, 4
7.	R^2ab	
8.	R^2bc	7, 8 by &, 5
√9.	$R^2ab \supset R^2ba$	
√10.	$R^2ca \supset R^2ac$	
√11.	$R^2bc \supset R^2cb$	9, 10, 11 by UQ, 1 (twice)

$$
\begin{array}{c}
\overset{\displaystyle\diagup\quad\diagdown}{}\\
12.\quad \sim R^2ab \qquad R^2ba \qquad\qquad 9, \supset\\
\times \qquad \overset{\displaystyle\diagup\quad\diagdown}{}\\
13.\qquad \sim R^2ca \quad R^2ac \qquad\qquad 10, \supset\\
\overset{\displaystyle\diagup\quad\diagdown}{}\qquad \times\\
14.\quad \sim R^2bc \quad R^2cb \qquad\qquad 11, \supset\\
\times
\end{array}
$$

Open branch, so the argument is invalid.

Chapter 15

Exercise 15.1

1. $L^2_{\sim\exists B^1,\forall D^1} = \sim(\exists x)(B^1x \ \& \ (\forall y)(D^1y \supset L^2xy))$
2. $L^2_{\forall P^1,\sim\exists D^1} = (\forall x)(P^1x \supset \sim(\exists y)(D^1y \ \& \ L^2xy))$
3. $\sim(\exists x)(P^1x \ \& \ (\forall y)(T^1y \supset H^2xy))$
4. $\sim(\exists x)(P^1x \ \& \ \sim(\exists y)(T^1y \ \& \ H^2xy))$
5. $(\exists x)(C^1x \ \& \ \sim(\exists y)(G^1y \ \& \ E^2xy))$
6. $(\forall x)(C^1x \supset \sim(\exists y)(G^1y \ \& \ E^2xy))$

Exercise 15.2

1. $\sim(S^2_{\forall P^1,\forall P^1}) = \sim(\forall x)(P^1x \supset (\forall y)(P^1y \supset S^2xy))$
   $\therefore S^2_{\sim\exists P^1,\forall P^1} = \sim(\exists x)(P^1x \ \& \ (\forall y)(P^1y \supset S^2xy))$

2. $H^3_{\sim\exists P^1,\forall P^1,\forall T^1} = \sim(\exists x)(P^1x \,\&\, (\forall y)(P^1y \supset (\forall z)(T^1z \supset H^3xyz)))$,
    $H^3_{\forall P^1,\exists P^1,\exists T^1} = (\forall x)(P^1x \supset (\exists y)(P^1y \,\&\, (\exists z)(T^1z \,\&\, H^3xyz)))$
    $\therefore\ H^3_{\exists P^1,\exists P^1,\sim\exists T^1} = (\exists x)(P^1x \,\&\, (\exists y)(P^1y \,\&\, \sim(\exists z)(T^1z \,\&\, H^3xyz)))$
3. $(\forall x)(H^1x \supset (\exists y)(P^1y \,\&\, \sim(\exists z)(N^1z \,\&\, C^3xyz)))$, $(\forall x)(H^1x \supset A^1x)$
    $\therefore\ \sim(\forall x)(A^1x \supset (\exists y)(P^1y \,\&\, (\exists z)(P^1z \,\&\, C^3xyz)))$
4. $\sim(\exists x)(D^1x \,\&\, B^1x)$, $(\forall x)(D^1x \vee A^1x)$, $(\exists x)(P^1x \,\&\, \sim A^1x)$
    $\therefore\ \sim(\sim(\exists x)(P^1x \,\&\, \sim B^1x))$

Exercise 15.3

1. $(\forall x)((\exists y)(F^1y \,\&\, H^2xy) \supset C^1x)$
2. $(\forall x)((\exists y)(W^1y \,\&\, B^2xy) \supset F^1x)$
3. $(\forall x)(P^1x \supset (\forall y)(B^2xy \supset A^1y))$
4. $\sim(\forall x)((\forall y)(S^2xy \supset B^1y) \supset S^1x)$
5. $W^2_{\exists M^1,\emptyset S^1} = (\exists x)(M^1x \,\&\, (\forall y)(W^2xy \supset S^1y))$
6. $W^2_{\emptyset M^1,\emptyset S^1} = (\forall x)(W^2x_{\emptyset S^1} \supset M^1x) = (\forall x)((\forall y)(W^2xy \supset S^1y) \supset M^1x)$

Exercise 15.4

1. $S^3_{\emptyset S^1,\exists A^1,\exists T^1} = (\forall x)(S^3x_{\exists A^1,\exists T^1} \supset S^1x) = (\forall x)((\exists y)(A^1y \,\&\, S^3xy_{\exists T^1}) \supset S^1x)$
    $= (\forall x)((\exists y)(A^1y \,\&\, (\exists z)(T^1z \,\&\, S^3xyz)) \supset S^1x)$
    $\therefore\ \sim(S^3_{\exists T^1,\exists A^1,\exists T^1}) = \sim(\exists x)(T^1x \,\&\, (\exists y)(A^1y \,\&\, (\exists z)(T^1z \,\&\, S^3xyz)))$
2. $S^3_{\forall S^1,\emptyset A^1,\exists T^1} = (\forall x)(S^1x \supset S^3x_{\emptyset A^1,\exists T^1}) = (\forall x)(S^1x \supset (\forall y)(S^3xy_{\exists T^1} \supset A^1y))$
    $= (\forall x)(S^1x \supset (\forall y)((\exists z)(T^1z \,\&\, S^3xyz) \supset A^1y))$
    $\therefore\ S^3_{\sim\exists S^1,\exists\sim A^1,\exists T^1} = \sim(\exists x)(S^1x \,\&\, (\exists y)(\sim A^1y \,\&\, (\exists z)(T^1z \,\&\, S^3xyz)))$
3. $(\forall x)((\exists y)(T^1y \,\&\, C^2xy) \supset C^1x)$, $(\forall x)((\exists y)(S^1y \,\&\, A^2xy) \supset (\exists z)(T^1z \,\&\, C^2xz))$
    $\therefore\ (\forall x)((\exists y)(S^1y \,\&\, A^2xy) \supset C^1x)$
4. $(\forall x)((\forall y)(L^2xy \supset L^1y) \supset T^1x)$, $(\exists x)(P^1x \,\&\, (\exists y)(B^1y \,\&\, L^2xy))$
    $\therefore\ \sim(\forall x)(P^1x \supset T^1x)$

Exercise 15.5

1. $G^3_{\forall M^*,\forall W^1,\exists T^1} = (\forall x)(M^*x \supset (\forall y)(W^1y \supset (\exists z)(T^1z \,\&\, G^3xyz)))$
    $= (\forall x)((M^1x \,\&\, (\exists x_1)S^2x_1x) \supset (\forall y)(W^1y \supset (\exists z)(T^1z \,\&\, G^3xyz)))$
2. $\sim G^3_{\forall W^*,\forall M^*,\sim\exists T^1} = (\forall x)(W^*x \supset (\forall y)(M^*y \supset \sim(\exists z)(T^1z \,\&\, \sim G^3xyz)))$
    $= (\forall x)((W^1x \,\&\, \sim(\exists x_1)S^2x_1x) \supset (\forall y)((M^1y \,\&\, \sim(\exists y_1)S^2y_1y) \supset \sim(\exists z)(T^1z \,\&\, \sim G^3xyz)))$
3. $W^2_{\emptyset B^*,\forall T^1} = (\forall x)(W^2x_{\forall T^1} \supset B^*x) = (\forall x)((\forall y)(T^1y \supset W^2xy) \supset B^*x)$
    $= (\forall x)((\forall y)(T^1y \supset W^2xy) \supset (B^1x \,\&\, (\forall z)(A^1z \supset E^2xz)))$

Exercise 15.6

1. $(\forall x)((P^1x \mathbin{\&} (\forall y)(P^1y \supset B^2xy)) \supset B^2xf) \therefore \sim B^2ff$
2. $(\forall x)(H^1x \supset A^1x) \therefore (\forall x)((P^1x \mathbin{\&} (\exists z)(H^1z \mathbin{\&} O^2xz)) \supset (\exists y)(A^1y \mathbin{\&} O^2xy))$
3. $(\forall x)((M^1x \mathbin{\&} (\exists x_1)S^2x_1x) \supset (\forall y)(W^1y \supset (\exists z)(T^1z \mathbin{\&} \sim E^1z \mathbin{\&} G^3xyz)))$
   $\therefore (\forall x)(M^1x \supset (\exists y)(W^1y \mathbin{\&} (\exists z)(T^1z \mathbin{\&} G^3xyz)))$
4. $(\forall x)((P^1x \mathbin{\&} (\exists z)(P^1z \mathbin{\&} K^2xz)) \supset (\exists y)(P^1y \mathbin{\&} L^2xy)),$
   $\sim(\forall x)(P^1x \supset (\exists y)(P^1y \mathbin{\&} L^2xy)) \therefore \sim(\forall x)(P^1x \supset (\exists y)(P^1y \mathbin{\&} K^2xy))$
5. $(\exists x)(M^1x \mathbin{\&} (\forall y)((M^1y \mathbin{\&} \sim S^2yy) \supset S^2xy) \therefore (\exists x)(M^1x \mathbin{\&} S^2xx)$
6. $(\forall x)((B^1x \mathbin{\&} (\exists z)(B^1z \mathbin{\&} S^2xz)) \supset (\exists y)((P^1y \mathbin{\&} \sim S^2yy) \mathbin{\&} S^2xy)),$
   $(\forall x)((B^1x \mathbin{\&} S^2xx) \supset (\exists y)((P^1y \mathbin{\&} (\forall z)(B^1z \supset S^2yz)) \mathbin{\&} \sim S^2xy))$
   $\therefore (\exists x)(B^1x \mathbin{\&} S^2xx)$

Exercise 15.7

1. $(\exists x)(B^1x \mathbin{\&} L^2xm) \supset (\exists y)(G^1y \mathbin{\&} L^2ym)$
2. $(\forall x)((B^1x \mathbin{\&} L^2xm) \supset L^2xb)$
3. $(\forall x)(B^1x \supset (L^2xm \supset L^2bx))$
4. $(\exists x)(G^1x \mathbin{\&} ((\exists y)(B^1y \mathbin{\&} L^2xy) \mathbin{\&} (\forall z)(F^1z \supset \sim L^2xz)))$
5. $(\exists x)(B^1x \mathbin{\&} (L^2xm \lor \sim L^2mx))$
6. $(\forall x)((G^1x \mathbin{\&} (\exists x_1)S^2x_1x) \supset (L^2xb \supset L^2xf))$
7. This statement should be a universal. First approximation: $K^2_{\forall P^*, b}$ This
   issues in $(\forall x)(P^*x \supset K^2xb)$
   'P^*x' is shorthand for '$(P^1x \mathbin{\&} K^2x_{anyP^1})$'. Notice that 'any' here in the
   antecedent of a conditional (predicate) must be symbolized as an
   existential, issuing in:
   $(\forall x)((P^1x \mathbin{\&} (\exists y)(P^1y \mathbin{\&} K^2xy)) \supset K^2xb)$
8. $(\forall x)((P^1x \mathbin{\&} (\exists y)(W^1y \mathbin{\&} D^2xy)) \supset S^1x)$ (('any' here means 'some'.
   Why?)
9. $(\forall x)((\exists y)(L^1y \mathbin{\&} A^2xy) \supset (S^1x \mathbin{\&} (\exists x_1)(P^1x_1 \mathbin{\&} R^2xx_1)))$
10. $\sim(\exists x)(R^1x \mathbin{\&} (\sim S^1x \supset P^1x))$

Exercise 15.8

1. $(\forall x)(M^1x \supset (\exists y)(P^1y \mathbin{\&} S^2yx)), (\forall x)(D^1x \supset (\exists y)(P^1y \mathbin{\&} B^2yx)),$
   $(\exists x)(M^1x \lor D^1x) \therefore (\exists x)(P^1x \mathbin{\&} ((\exists y) S^2xy \lor (\exists z) B^2xz))$
2. $(\forall x)(P^1x \supset ((\exists y)S^2xy \supset R^1x)) \therefore (\forall x)((P^1x \mathbin{\&} S^2xm) \supset R^1x)$

3. $(\forall x)((P^1x \,\&\, K^2bx) \supset (\exists y)(P^1y \,\&\, (\exists z)(T^1z \,\&\, L^3xyz)))$,
   $(\forall x)(P^1x \supset (\forall y)(P^1y \supset (\exists z)((T^1z \,\&\, {\sim}L^3xyz) \supset {\sim}(\exists z_1)(T^1z_1 \,\&\, L^3xyz_1))))$
   $\therefore (\forall x)(P^1x \supset (\exists y)((P^1y \,\&\, L^3bxy) \supset (\forall z)(T^1z \supset L^3bxz)))$

4. $(\forall x)(D^1x \supset (\forall y)(C^1y \supset B^2xy)) \supset (\exists x_1)(C^1x_1 \,\&\, (\forall z)(G^1z \supset B^2x_1z))$,
   $(\forall x)(C^1x \supset ((\exists y)(G^1y \,\&\, B^2xy) \supset K^1x))$
   $\therefore {\sim}(\exists x)(D^1x \,\&\, (\exists y)(C^1y \,\&\, B^2xy)) \supset (\forall x)(G^1x \supset {\sim}K^1x)$

Exercise 15.9

Proof that (70) logically implies (67):

70.	$(\forall x)((M^1x \supset (\forall y)(S^1y \supset (H^2xy \supset A^2xy)))$	(premise)
√67.	${\sim}(\forall x)(\forall y)((M^1x \,\&\, (S^1y \,\&\, H^2xy)) \supset A^2xy)$	(negation of conclusion)
√3.	$(\exists x)(\exists y){\sim}((M^1x \,\&\, (S^1y \,\&\, H^2xy)) \supset A^2xy)$	67, QE (twice)
√4.	${\sim}((M^1a \,\&\, (S^1b \,\&\, H^2ab)) \supset A^2ab)$	3, EQ (twice)
√5.	$M^1a \supset (\forall y)(S^1y \supset (H^2ay \supset A^2ay))$	70, UQ
√6.	$M^1a \,\&\, S^1b \,\&\, H^2ab$	
7.	${\sim}A^2ab$	4, ${\sim}\supset$
8.	M^1a	
9.	S^1b	
10.	H^2ab	6, &

11. ${\sim}M^1a$ $(\forall y)(S^1y \supset (H^2ay \supset A^2ay))$ 5, $\supset$
√12.   × $S^1b \supset (H^2ab \supset A^2ab)$ 11, UQ

√13. ${\sim}S^1b$ $H^2ab \supset A^2ab$ 12, $\supset$
             ×

14. ${\sim}H^2ab$ A^2ab 13, $\supset$
               ×   ×

Statement (70) logically implies (67), since all branches close. Show now that (67) logically implies (70).

Exercise 15.10

1. ${\sim}(\exists x)(\exists y)((P^1x \,\&\, ((C^1y \,\&\, S^2xy) \,\&\, O^2xy))$
2. *$(\forall x)(\exists y)((C^1y \,\&\, R^2xy) \supset (P^1x \,\&\, O^2xy))$
3. $(\forall x)(\forall z)((P^1x \,\&\, W^2xz) \supset {\sim}(\exists y)(P^1y \,\&\, G^2yz))$
4. $(\forall x)(\forall z)((S^1x \,\&\, ((\exists y)(A^1y \,\&\, T^1z \,\&\, S^3xyz))) \supset {\sim}F^2xz)$

5. $L^2_{\forall S^*,\exists S^+}$

    $(\forall x)(S^*x \supset (\exists y)(S^+y \, \& \, L^2xy))$

    $S^*x = (S^1x \, \& \, O^2x,_{\exists S^1})$

    $S^+y = (S^1y \, \& \, O^2y,_{\exists S^\#})$

    '#' and '+' play the same role here as '*': that is, to indicate a relativization we will unpack later as we complete the symbolizations.

    $(\forall x)((S^1x \, \& \, O^2x,_{\exists S^1}) \supset (\exists y)((S^1y \, \& \, O^2y,_{\exists S^\#}) \, \& \, L^2xy))$

    $(\forall x)((S^1x \, \& \, (\exists z)((S^1z \, \& \, O^2xz)) \supset (\exists y)((S^1y \, \& \, (\exists x_1)(S^\#x_1 \, \& \, O^2yx_1)) \, \& \, L^2xy))$

    $S^\#x_1 = (S^1x_1 \, \& \, O^2x_{1,\exists S^1})$

    $(\forall x)((S^1x \, \& \, (\exists z)(S^1z \, \& \, O^2xz)) \supset (\exists y)((S^1y \, \& \, (\exists x_1)((S^1x_1 \, \& \, O^2x_{1,\exists S^1}) \, \& \, O^2yx_1)) \, \& \, L^2xy))$

    $(\forall x)((S^1x \, \& \, (\exists z)(S^1z \, \& \, O^2xz)) \supset (\exists y)((S^1y \, \& \, (\exists x_1)((S^1x_1 \, \& \, (\exists y_1)(S^1y_1 \, \& \, O^2x_1y_1)) \, \& \, O^2yx_1) \, \& \, L^2xy))$

6. $\sim L^2_{\forall M^*,\exists M^+}$

    $(\forall x)(M^*x \supset (\exists y)(M^+y \, \& \, \sim L^2xy))$

    $M^*x = (M^1x \, \& \, L^2x_{\exists W^1})$

    $M^+y = (M^1y \, \& \, \sim L^2y_{\exists W^1})$

    $(\forall x)((M^1x \, \& \, L^2x_{\exists W^1}) \supset (\exists y)((M^1y \, \& \, \sim L^2y_{\exists W^1}) \, \& \, \sim L^2xy))$

    $(\forall x)((M^1x \, \& \, (\exists z)(W^1z \, \& \, L^2xz)) \supset (\exists y)((M^1y \, \& \, (\exists z_1)(W^1z_1 \, \& \, \sim L^2yz_1)) \, \& \, \sim L^2xy))$

    or

    $(\forall x)((M^1x \, \& \, (\exists z)(W^1z \, \& \, L^2xz)) \supset (\forall y)((M^1y \, \& \, (\exists z_1)(W^1z_1 \, \& \, \sim L^2yz_1)) \supset \sim L^2xy))$

Exercise 15.11

1. $(\forall x)(N^1x \supset (\exists y)(N^1y \, \& \, G^2yx)) \, \therefore \, (\forall x)(N^1x \supset (\exists y)(N^1y \, \& \, G^2xy))$

2. $(\forall x)((B^1x \, \& \, \sim L^1x) \supset C^2xt), \sim (\forall x)((B^1x \, \& \, L^1x) \supset C^2xt)$

    $\therefore \, (\forall x)((B^1x \, \& \, L^1x) \supset \sim C^2xt)$

3. $\sim(\exists x)(F^1x \, \& \, (\exists y)((S^1y \, \& \, H^2xy) \, \& \, A^2xy))$ The conclusion is ambiguous: it might mean that it's not true that every son is adored by his father, giving the negation wide scope, as in

    $\therefore \, \sim(\forall x)(S^1x \supset (\exists y)(F^1y \, \& \, H^2yx \, \& \, A^2yx))$

    Or it might mean that every son is such that his father does not adore him, giving the universal quantifier wide scope, as in

    $\therefore \, (\forall x)(S^1x \supset (\exists y)(F^1y \, \& \, H^2yx \, \& \, \sim A^2yx))$

4. $(\forall x)(\forall y)((P^1x \, \& \, C^1y \, \& \, O^2xy) \supset B^2xy), (\forall x)((C^1x \, \& \, (\exists y)(P^1y \, \& \, B^2yx)) \supset S^1x)$

    $\therefore \, (\forall x)((C^1x \, \& \, (\exists y)(P^1y \, \& \, B^2yx)) \supset S^1x)$

5. $(\forall x)(\forall y)((B^1x \& A^1y \& M^2xy) \supset R^2xy)$, $B^1s \& A^1h \therefore M^2sh \supset R^2sh$

6. $(\forall x)(\forall y)((P^1x \& F^1y \& S^2xy) \supset K^2xy)$, $\sim(\forall x)(\forall y)((F^1x \& (P^1y \& K^2yx) \supset S^2yx)$
   $\therefore (\exists x)(P^1x \& (\exists y)(F^1y \& S^2xy \& \sim K^2xy))$

7. $\sim(\exists x)(T^1x \& (\exists y)(S^1y \& (\forall z)(A^1z \supset S^3yzx)))$,
   $\therefore (\exists x)(A^1x \& (\exists y)(T^1y \& \sim(\exists z)(S^1z \& S^3zxy)))$

8. $(\forall x)((\exists y)(S^1y \& (\exists z)(A^1z \& S^3yzx)) \supset T^1x)$
   $\therefore \sim(\exists x)(S^1x \& (\exists y)(S^1y \& (\exists z(A^1z \& S^3yzx)))$

9. $(\forall x)(\forall y)((C^1x \& M^1y \& C^2xy) \supset E^2xy)$, $(\forall x)((\exists y)(M^1y \& E^2xy) \supset \sim H^1x)$
   $\therefore \sim(\exists x)(C^1x \& (\exists y)(M^1y \& C^2xy) \& H^1x)$

10. $(\forall x)((P^1x \& F^1x) \supset (\forall y)(P^1y \supset L^2yx))$, $(\forall x)(P^1x \supset (\exists y)(P^1y \& \sim L^2yx)$
    $\therefore \sim(\exists x)(P^1x \& F^1x)$

11. $\sim(\exists x)(P^1x \& (\exists y)(D^1y \& P^2xy) \& U^1x)$, $\sim(\forall x)(P^1x \supset (\exists y)(D^1y \& P^2xy))$
    $\therefore \sim(\forall x)((P^1x \& (\exists y)(D^1y \& P^2xy)) \supset \sim U^1x)$

12. $(S^1j \supset (\forall x)(B^1x \supset P^1x)) \& ((\forall y)(B^1y \supset P^1y) \supset S^1j)$, $(\exists x)(T^1x \& M^2jx) \supset$
    $(\forall y)(B^1y \supset \sim P^1y)$, $(\forall x)(\sim(\exists y)(T^1y \& M^2xy) \supset A^1x) \therefore \sim A^1j \supset \sim S^1j$

13. $\sim(\exists x)(P^1x \& (\exists y)(T^1y \& \sim S^2xy \& W^2xy))$, $\sim(\exists x)(P^1x \& (\forall y)(T^1y \supset \sim W^2xy) \&$
    $(\exists z)(C^1z \& W^2xz))$
    $\therefore (\forall x)((P^1x \& (\forall y)(C^1y \supset W^2xy)) \supset (\forall z)(T^1z \supset S^2xz))$ (This is a very
    difficult exercise, and it may be possible to get readings of the sentence
    that correspond to different symbolizations)

Chapter 16

Exercise 16.1

1. $h = l$, $G^1h \therefore G^1l$
2. $e = t$, $e = c \therefore c = t$
3. $(\forall x)(B^1x \supset R^2hx)$, $h = a \therefore (\forall x)(B^1x \supset R^2ax)$
4. $(\forall x)(D^1x \supset P^2cx)$, $c = d \therefore (\forall x)(D^1x \supset P^2dx)$

Exercise 16.2

Problem 1

1. $h = l$ (premise)
2. G^1h (premise)
3. $\sim G^1l$ (negation of conclusion)
4. G^1l 1, 2, 10
      ✕

Tree closes, so the argument is valid.

Problem 2

1. $e = t$ (premise)
2. $e = c$ (premise)
3. $c \neq t$ (negation of conclusion)
4. $e \neq t$ 2, 3, 10
    ×

Tree closes, so the argument is valid.

Exercise 16.3

Problem 1

√1. $F^1a \ \& \ (\forall x)(F^1x \supset x = a)$ (premise)
√2. $(\exists x)(F^1x \ \& \ G^1x)$ (premise)
3. $\sim G^1a$ (negation of conclusion)
4. F^1a
5. $(\forall x)(F^1x \supset x = a)$ 4, 5 by &, 1
√6. $F^1b \ \& \ G^1b$ 2, EQ
7. F^1b
8. G^1b 7, 8 by &, 6
√9. $F^1b \supset b = a$ 5, UQ

10. $\sim F^1b$ $b = a$ 9, $\supset$
    ×

11. $\sim G^1b$ 3, 10, 10
        ×

All branches close, so the argument is valid.

Problem 2

1. $(\forall x)(P^1x \supset Q^1x)$ (premise)
2. $(\forall x)(Q^1x \supset R^1x)$ (premise)
√3. $P^1a \ \& \ \sim R^1b$ (premise)
4. $a = b$ (negation of conclusion)
5. P^1a

6.   ~R¹b   5, 6 by &, 3
7.   P¹b   4, 5, 10
√8. P¹b ⊃ Q¹b   1, UQ
√9. Q¹b ⊃ R¹b   2, UQ

```
              /\
10.  ~P¹b        Q¹b         8, ⊃
      ×        /\
11.         ~Q¹b   R¹b       9, ⊃
            ×     ×
```

All branches close, so the argument is valid.

Problem 3

√1. (∃x)((P¹x & (∀y)(P¹y ⊃ y = x)) & Q¹x)   (premise)
2.   ~Q¹a   (premise)
3.   P¹a   (negation of conclusion)
√4. (P¹b & (∀y)(P¹y ⊃ y = b)) & Q¹b   1, EQ
5.   P¹b
6.   (∀y)(P¹y ⊃ y = b)
7.   Q¹b   5, 6, 7 by &, 4
√8. P¹a ⊃ a = b   6, UQ

```
            /\
9.   ~P¹a     a = b          8, ⊃
      ×       |
10.         ~Q¹b            2, 9, 10
             ×
```

All branches close, so the argument is valid.

Problem 4

√1. (∃x)(∀y)((~F²xy ⊃ x = y) & G¹x)   (premise)
√2. ~(∀x)(~G¹x ⊃ (∃y)(y ≠ x & F²yx))   (negation of conclusion)
√3. (∃x)~(~G¹x ⊃ (∃y)(y ≠ x & F²yx))   2, QE
√4. ~(~G¹a ⊃ (∃y)(y ≠ a & F²ya))   3, EQ
5.   ~G¹a
√6. ~(∃y)(y ≠ a & F²ya)   5, 6 by ~ ⊃, 4
7.   (∀y)~(y ≠ a & F²ya)   6, QE

8. $(\forall y)((\sim F^2by \supset b = y) \ \& \ G^1b)$ 1, EQ

√9. $\sim(b \neq a \ \& \ F^2ba)$ 7, UQ

√10. $(\sim F^2ba \supset b = a) \ \& \ G^1b$ 8, UQ

√11. $\sim F^2ba \supset b = a$

12. G^1b 11, 12 by &, 10

13. F^2ba $b = a$ 11, $\supset$

14. G^1a 12, 13, IO

                    ×

15. $b = a$ $\sim F^2ba$ 9, $\sim$ &

16. $\sim G^1b$ ×   5, 15, IO

      ×

All branches close, so the argument is valid.

Problem 5

√1. $(\exists x)(P^1x \ \& \ ((\forall y)(P^1y \supset y = x) \ \& \ Q^1x))$ (premise)

√2. $(\exists x)\sim(\sim P^1x \lor \sim F^1x)$ (premise)

√3. $\sim(\exists x)(F^1x \ \& \ Q^1x)$ (negation of conclusion)

4. $(\forall x)\sim(F^1x \ \& \ Q^1x)$ 3, QE

√5. $P^1a \ \& \ ((\forall y)(P^1y \supset y = a) \ \& \ Q^1a)$ 1, EQ

6. P^1a

7. $(\forall y)(P^1y \supset y = a)$

8. Q^1a 6, 7, 8 by &, 5

√9. $\sim(\sim P^1b \lor \sim F^1b)$ 2, EQ

10. P^1b

11. F^1b 10, 11 by $\sim$ $\lor$, 9

√12. $P^1b \supset b = a$ 7, UQ

13. $\sim P^1b$ $b = a$ 12, $\supset$

      × |

√14. $\sim(F^1b \ \& \ Q^1b)$ 4, UQ

15. $\sim F^1b$ $\sim Q^1b$ 14, $\sim$ &

         × |

16. Q^1b 8, 13, IO

          ×

All branches close, so the argument is valid.

Problem 6

1.	$(\forall x)(F^2xa \supset (B^1x \ \& \ C^1x))$	(premise)
2.	F^2ba	(premise)
√3.	$\sim(\exists x)\,(B^1x \ \& \ (C^1x \ \& \ x = b))$	(negation of conclusion)
4.	$(\forall x) \sim (B^1x \ \& \ (C^1x \ \& \ x = b))$	3, QE
√5.	$F^2ba \supset (B^1b \ \& \ C^1b)$	1, UQ
√6.	$\sim(B^1b \ \& \ (C^1b \ \& \ b=b))$	4, UQ

```
 √7.        ~F²ba      B¹b & C¹b              5, ⊃
              ×

  8.                      B¹b                 8, 9 from 7, &
  9.                      C¹b

 √10.          ~B¹b  ~(C¹b & b=b)             6, ~ &
                ×

 11.                  ~C¹b    b≠b            10, ~ &
 12.                   ×      b=b             11
                              ×
```

All branches close, so argument is valid.

Exercise 16.4

1. $(\forall x)(F^2xb \supset (x = a \vee B^2xa))$
2. $(\forall x)(G^2xc \supset x = j)$
3. $(\forall x)((G^1x \ \& \ x \neq g) \supset F^2gx)$
4. $(\exists x)(P^1x \ \& \ x \neq m \ \& \ S^2xb)$
5. $L^2jm \ \& \ (\exists x)(P^1x \ \& \ x \neq j \ \& \ L^2xb)$
6. $(\exists x)(P^1x \ \& \ x \neq j \ \& \ L^2xm)$
7. This statement is ambiguous; try to represent both readings in RPL$^=$. Here's one: $(\forall x)(\exists y)(M^2yx \ \& \ L^2xy) \supset x = j)$
8. Hank and Frank are not possible values of the quantifier 'any' due to the presence of 'other'. $(\exists x)((S^1x \ \& \ x \neq h \ \& \ x \neq f) \ \& \ E^1x) \supset (E^1h \ \& \ E^1f)$
9. Notice that (4) does not say that Mary arrived at the conference before Harry; only that he did not arrive before her. That's compatible with both arriving at the same time; and therefore a correct symbolization for (4) in RPL$^=$ must be non-committal about who arrived first.
   $F^2hc \ \& \ (\forall x)((P^1x \ \& \ x \neq h \ \& \ F^2xc \ \& \ x \neq m) \supset G^3hcx)$

Exercise 16.6

1. $(\exists x)((P^1x \,\&\, H^2x) \,\&\, (\exists y)((P^1y \,\&\, H^1y) \,\&\, x \neq y)$
2. $(\forall x)((T^1x \,\&\, D^1x) \supset (\forall y)((T^1y \,\&\, D^1y) \supset x = y))$

Exercise 16.7

1. $(\exists x)(P^1x \,\&\, (\forall y)(P^1y \supset x = y) \,\&\, L^2xm)$
2. $(\exists x)((P^1x \,\&\, L^2xm) \,\&\, (\forall y)((P^1y \,\&\, L^2ym) \supset x = y))$
3. $(\exists x)((P^1x \,\&\, L^2x\varTheta) \,\&\, (\forall y)((P^1y \,\&\, L^2y\varTheta) \supset x = y))$
4. $(\exists x)((P^1x \,\&\, (\forall y)(C^1y \supset E^2xy)) \,\&\, (\forall z)((P^1x \,\&\, (\forall x_1)(C^1x_1 \supset E^2zx_1)) \supset x = z))$
5. $(\exists x)(F^1x \,\&\, (\exists y)(F^1y \,\&\, x \neq y \,\&\, (\forall z)(F^1z \supset (z = x \vee z = y)))$
6. $(\exists x)((F^1x \,\&\, H^1x) \,\&\, (\exists y)((F^1y \,\&\, H^1y) \,\&\, x \neq y \,\&\, (\forall z)((F^1z \,\&\, H^1z) \supset (z = x \vee z = y))))$
7. $(\exists x)((S^1x \,\&\, P^1x) \,\&\, (\exists y)((S^1y \,\&\, P^1y) \,\&\, (\exists z)((S^1z \,\&\, P^1z) \,\&\, x \neq y \,\&\, y \neq z \,\&\, x \neq z \,\&\, (\forall x_1)((S^1x_1 \,\&\, P^1x_1) \supset (x_1 = x \vee x_1 = y \vee x_1 = z))))$
8. $(\exists x)(S^1x \,\&\, (\exists y)(S^1y \,\&\, (\exists z)(S^1z \,\&\, x \neq y \,\&\, y \neq z \,\&\, x \neq z \,\&\, (\forall x_1)(S^1x_1 \supset (x_1 = x \vee x_1 = y \vee x_1 = z) \,\&\, P^1x \,\&\, P^1y \,\&\, P^1z)))$
9. $(\exists x)((B^1x \,\&\, (\exists x_1)(T^1x_1 \,\&\, H^2xx_1)) \,\&\, (\exists y)((B^1y \,\&\, (\exists y_1)(T^1y_1 \,\&\, H^2yy_1)) \,\&\, x \neq y \,\&\, (\forall z)((B^1z \,\&\, (\exists z_1)(T^1z_1 \,\&\, H^2zz_1)) \supset (z = x \vee z = y))))$
10. $(\forall x)(B^1x \supset (\exists y)((T^1y \,\&\, H^2xy) \,\&\, (\exists z)((T^1z \,\&\, H^2xz) \,\&\, y \neq z \,\&\, (\forall x_1)((T^1x_1 \,\&\, H^2xx_1) \supset (x_1 = y \vee x_1 = z)))))$

Exercise 16.9

1. $(\exists x)((P^1x \,\&\, W^2xl) \,\&\, (\forall y)((P^1y \,\&\, W^2yl) \supset x = y) \,\&\, G^1x)$
   $\therefore (\forall x)((P^1x \,\&\, W^2xl) \supset G^1x)$
2. $(\exists x)(A^1x \,\&\, (\forall y)(A^1y \supset x = y) \,\&\, W^1x)$,
   $\sim(\exists x)(\exists y)(P^1y \,\&\, W^2yx \,\&\, (\exists z)(P^1z \,\&\, W^2zx \,\&\, y \neq z)) \,\&\, W^1x)$
   $\therefore$ $(\exists x)((P^1x \,\&\, (\exists y)(A^1y \,\&\, (\forall z)(A^1z \supset y = z) \,\&\, W^2xy) \,\&\, (\forall x_1)((P^1x_1 \,\&\, (\exists y_1)(A^1y_1 \,\&\, (\forall z_1)(A^1z_1 \supset y_1 = z_1) \,\&\, W^2x_1y_1)) \supset x = x_1) \,\&\, C^1x)$
3. $(\exists x)(M^1x \,\&\, (\forall y)(M^1y \supset x = y) \,\&\, x = v)$, $(\exists x)(E^1x \,\&\, (\forall y)(E^1y \supset x = y) \,\&\, x = v)$
   $\therefore (\forall y)(M^1y \supset E^1y)$
4. $(\exists x)(J^1x \,\&\, (\exists y)(J^1y \,\&\, x \neq y \,\&\, (\forall z)(J^1z \supset (z = x \vee z = y))))$, $(\exists x)(J^1x \,\&\, \sim A^1x)$
   $\therefore (\forall x)((J^1x \,\&\, A^1x) \supset (\forall y)((J^1y \,\&\, A^1y) \supset x = y))$

Exercise 16.10

1. $(\exists x)((G^1x \,\&\, I^2xb) \,\&\, (\forall y)((G^1y \,\&\, I^2yb) \supset x = y) \,\&\, H^2mx)$
2. $(\exists x)(G^1x \,\&\, (\forall y)(G^1y \supset x = y) \,\&\, {\sim}H^2xb)$
3. $(\exists x)(M^1x \,\&\, (\forall y)(M^1y \supset x = y) \,\&\, (\forall z)(H^2xz \supset F^1z))$
4. $H^2m_{TheG^*}$
    $(\exists x)(G^*x \,\&\, (\forall y)(G^*y \supset x = y) \,\&\, H^2mx)$
    $G^*x = (G^1x \,\&\, I^2xm)$
    $(\exists x)((G^1x \,\&\, I^2xm) \,\&\, (\forall y)((G^1y \,\&\, I^2ym) \supset x = y) \,\&\, H^2mx))$
5. $H^2_{\forall B^1, TheG^*}$
    $(\forall x)(B^1x \supset (\exists y)(G^*y \,\&\, (\forall z)(G^*z \supset z = y) \,\&\, H^2xy))$
    $G^*y = (G^1y \,\&\, I^2yx)$
    $(\forall x)(B^1x \supset (\exists y)((G^1y \,\&\, I^2yx) \,\&\, (\forall z)((G^1z \,\&\, I^2zx) \supset z = y) \,\&\, H^2xy))$

13–14. Is there a difference in meaning between (13) and (14)? And, in general, is there a difference in meaning between statements of forms:

   The α is β.
   The only α is β.

It would seem that these two forms are logically equivalent in RPL⁼. But there does seem to be something different about (13) and (14). It may be conversational. It may be that normally when someone asserts (13), it's natural to understand the quantifier 'the' to include everything – that is, as an unrestricted domain of discourse; but with (14) we would normally understand the quantifier 'the' to range over some restricted domain, determined by the context in which (14) is asserted. However, notice the difference in meaning between 'John is not the man I saw last night' and 'John is not the only man I saw last night'.

15–16. What's the difference in meaning between (15) and (16)? What does this difference tell us about the difference in meaning between 'exactly' and 'the'?

17. Look back at §15.3 and §A6.2 before trying (17).

Exercise 16.11

1. $(\exists x)((P^1x \,\&\, S^1x) \,\&\, (\forall y)((P^1y \,\&\, S^1y) \supset x = y) \,\&\, L^1x),$
    $(\forall x)((P^1x \,\&\, (S^1x \vee W^1x)) \supset (\exists y)(C^1y \,\&\, B^2xy))$
    $\therefore (\exists x)((P^1x \,\&\, S^1x) \,\&\, (\forall y)((P^1y \,\&\, S^1y) \supset x = y) \,\&\, (\exists y)(C^1y \,\&\, B^2xy))$
3. ${\sim}(\exists x)T^2xx, \; T^2ej \;\therefore\; e \neq j$

Exercise 16.13

1. $(\exists x)((M^1x \& L^2xl) \& (\forall y)((M^1y \& L^2yl) \supset x = y) \& L^1x) \therefore (\exists x)((M^1x \& L^1x) \& (\forall y)((M^1y \& L^1y) \supset x = y)$
2. $(\forall x)((P^1x \& E^1x) \supset (\forall y)((P^1y \& E^1y) \supset (\forall z)((P^1z \& E^1z) \supset (x = y \lor x = z \lor y = z)))), E^1n \& E^1l \therefore {\sim}E^1m$
3. $(\exists x)((H^1x \& H^2ax) \& (\exists y)((H^1y \& H^2ay) \& x \neq y)), (H^1c \& H^2ac) \& (H^1k \& H^2ak) \therefore c = k \supset (\exists x) (H^1x \& H^2ax \& x \neq c \& x \neq k)$

Chapter 17

Exercise 17.1

1. $(\exists x)(T^2xc \& I^2xr \& A^2xt) \therefore (\exists x)(\exists y)(P^1y \& T^2xy \& A^2xt)$
2. $(\exists x)(K^3xaj \& A^2xw) \therefore (\exists x)(\exists y)(\exists z)(P^1y \& P^1z \& K^3xyz \& A^2xw)$

Exercise 17.2

1. $(\exists x)(S^2xm \& B^1x) \& (\exists y)(A^2ym \& R^1y) \therefore (\exists x)S^2xm \& (\exists y)A^2ym$
2. $(\exists x)(P^2xr \& H^1x) \& (\exists y)(W^2yr \& Q^1y) \therefore {\sim}(\exists x)(P^2xr \& Q^1x)$
3. $(\exists x)(P^1x \& (\exists y)(E^2yx \& (\forall z)(D^1z \supset O^2yz))), (\forall x)(E^2xa \supset (O^2xs \lor O^2xw)) \therefore (\exists x)(P^1x \& (\exists y)(E^2yx) \& x \neq a)$

Exercise 17.3

1. $(\exists x)(W^2xj \& I^2xb \& A^2xm) \therefore (\exists x)W^2xj$
2. $(\exists x)R^2xj \supset (\exists y)(S^2yb \& I^2yd), (\exists x)R^2xj \therefore (\exists x)S^2xb$

Exercise 17.4

1. $(\exists z)(\exists x)(\exists y)F^3zxy \supset (\exists x_1)(P^1x_1 \& G^1x_1), (\exists z)F^3zjb \therefore (\exists x)(P^1x \& G^1x)$
2. $(\exists z)(\exists x)(\exists y)F^3zxy \supset S^1w, (\exists z)F^3zbj \therefore S^1w$
3. $(\forall x)((P^1x \& (\exists y)(T^2yx \& R^1y)) \supset (\exists z)(P^1z \& (\exists x_1) M^3x_1zx)) \therefore (\exists x)(T^2xl \& R^1x) \supset (\exists y)(P^1y \& (Ez) M^3zyl)$
4. $(\exists x)(\exists y)(\exists z)(A^3xyz \& B^1x) \supset (\exists x_1)(P^1x_1 \& (\exists y_1) C^2y_1x_1), (\exists x)(\exists y)(\exists z)(A^3xyz) \& L^1x) \supset (\exists x_1)(P^1x_1 \& (\exists y_1)(L^2y_1x_1 \& H^1y_1)) \therefore (\exists x)(A^3xja) \supset ((\exists y)(P^1y \& (\exists z) C^2zy) \lor (\exists x_1)(P^1x_1 \& (\exists y_1) L^2y_1x_1))$

Appendix

Exercise A.1

1. $(\forall x)(\forall y)(T^2xy \supset {\sim}T^2yx)$ (T^2: is two inches taller than)
2. $(\forall x)(\forall y)(\forall z)((T^2xy \;\&\; T^2yz) \supset {\sim}T^2xz)$
3. $(\forall x){\sim}T^2xx$

Exercise A.2

1. P^2jo, $P^2jp \;\&\; P^2op$ $\therefore$ ${\sim}(\forall x)(\forall y)(\forall z)((P^2xy \;\&\; P^2yz) \supset {\sim}P^2xz)$
2. $(\forall x)(D^2xa \supset O^1x)$, D^2ma, $(\forall x)(\forall y)(\forall z)((D^2xy \;\&\; D^2yz) \supset D^2xz)$
    $\therefore$ $D^2jm \supset O^1j$
3. $(\forall x)(P^1x \supset (\exists y){\sim}L^2xy) \;\&\; {\sim}(\exists z)(P^1z \;\&\; {\sim}L^2zs)$ $\therefore$ ${\sim}(\forall x)(\forall y)(L^2xy \supset L^2yx)$
4. $(\exists x)(P^1x \;\&\; (\exists y)(P^1y \;\&\; B^2xy))$, ${\sim}(\exists x)(P^1x \;\&\; B^2xx)$, $(\forall x)(\forall y)(B^2xy \supset B^2yx)$
    (missing premise) $\therefore$ ${\sim}(\forall x)(\forall y)(\forall z)((B^2xy \;\&\; B^2yz) \supset B^2xz)$

Exercise A.5

1. $(\exists x)(S^2xt \;\&\; (\forall y)(S^2yt \supset x = y) \;\&\; N^1x)$ $\therefore$ $(\exists x)(\exists x)S^2xy$
2. $(\exists x)(K^3xjm \;\&\; I^2xb)$ $\therefore$ $(\exists x)I^2xb$

Exercise A.6

2. $(\exists x)(J^2xm \;\&\; I^2xl \;\&\; S^2jx)$ (J^2: is a jumping by; I^2: occurred in; l: the lake; S^2: saw; j: Terry; m: Mary)
3. $(\exists x)(\exists y)(P^1x \;\&\; F^2yx \;\&\; H^2py)$ (F^2: is falling by; P^1: is a person; p: Perry; H^2: heard)

Logical Symbols

Symbol	Name	Meaning
=	identity	equals
&	ampersand	conjunction
~	tilde	negation
∴	conclusion marker	therefore
∨	wedge	disjunction
⊃	horseshoe	material conditional
∃	backwards 'E'	existential quantifier
∀	upside down 'A'	universal quantifier
≠	non-identity	not equals
A, B, C, . . .	statement letters	
A^n, B^n, C^n, . . . ($n = 1, 2, . . .$)	predicate letters	
x, y, z, . . . x_n, y_n, z_n ($n = 1, 2, . . .$)	variables	
⊢	half-turnstyle	derivability
(,)	parentheses	groupers
{, }	braces	sets

Index